ISLAND BIOLOGY
ILLUSTRATED BY THE LAND BIRDS
OF JAMAICA

STUDIES IN ECOLOGY

GENERAL EDITORS

D. J. ANDERSON B Sc Ph D
Department of Botany
University of New South Wales
Sydney

P. GREIG-SMITH M A Sc D
School of Plant Biology
University College of North Wales
Bangor

FRANK A. PITELKA Ph D
Department of Zoology
University of California, Berkeley

STUDIES IN ECOLOGY · VOLUME 3

ISLAND BIOLOGY

ILLUSTRATED BY THE LAND BIRDS OF JAMAICA

DAVID LACK FRS

UNIVERSITY OF CALIFORNIA PRESS

BERKELEY AND LOS ANGELES 1976

UNIVERSITY OF CALIFORNIA PRESS
Berkeley and Los Angeles, California

ISBN 0-520-03007-9
Library of Congress Catalog Card Number: 75–7194

© 1976 Blackwell Scientific Publications

Printed in Great Britain

CONTENTS

v

271464

PART II
ECOLOGY AND SYSTEMATICS OF
JAMAICAN LAND BIRDS

Introduction 231

Pigeons and Doves Columbidae   233

APPENDICES

PREFACE

Chapter 1 is not as I would have written it given more time, and the reader should know why. It represents a crystallisation of my views as I would have set them out in December 1969, when I gave a lecture on the numbers of bird species on remote islands to the British Trust for Ornithology (Lack 1969). At that time, under the influence of the MacArthur/Wilson (1963, 1967) *Theory of Island Biogeography*, it was widely held that the small numbers of species of land animals on remote islands were due to the fact that such animals reach them from outside only rarely and by chance, and their numbers are balanced by the species which disappear through random extinction, especially on small islands. I became extremely dissatisfied with this view, and thought out on my own a different view, that the general ecological poverty on remote islands favours the evolution of fewer species of land birds with broader ecological niches, which exclude in competition a greater number of specialised species, and form a stable community from which potential newcomers from outside are continually being excluded. This view aroused opposition at the time.

I did not think out the matter further when, a few months later, I spent a sabbatical year in Jamaica, nor during the next few months after my return, when I analysed the field data, examined skins and completed a draft of Part II of this book. At this point I heard that Robert MacArthur had a terminal cancer, and I did not think it right to bother him by writing about my theory, especially when I supposed that he himself held the alternative view noted in the first paragraph. Then in June 1972, I found that I likewise had a terminal cancer, and decided to spend what time I had left to write a draft of Part 1 of this book, which I completed by December. I sent ·this for criticism to various Oxford workers and then, in February 1973, sent the draft of Chapter 1 to Ernst Mayr and Jared Diamond. I would have sent it also to Robert MacArthur, but by then he had died.

Mayr's main criticism was that while he himself accepts my view on the importance of ecological poverty, I had swung too much in the opposite direction in ignoring the important effects of isolation. This I fully accept. Diamond's main criticism was that MacArthur himself held what I had supposed to be my new view, as shown especially in his last book (MacArthur 1972, pp. 247–251), and that in particular, he had advocated the idea of integrated communities of small numbers of species with broad niches on remote islands which could exclude newcomers. In short, my view was not new at all, I had merely come round to MacArthur's by a different route. I am delighted to find this, as it strengthens the likelihood of the view being true. Anyway, readers will appreciate that those in the valley of the shadow of death, as both MacArthur and I then were, do not care about priorities.

At this point, I would normally have rewritten Chapter 1 completely incorporating Mayr's and Diamond's criticisms to produce a unified statement, but by then my mental powers were too weak to make a good job of it. I have therefore retained the draft of December 1972, apart from omitting the words 'my new or seemingly new' view when referring to the theory based on ecological poverty. I should add, however, that many workers still appear to regard as extremely important the rarity of colonisation of remote islands by land organisms, and the influence of chance as set out in the first paragraph of this preface. Nor have I anywhere found that MacArthur himself related the effects of isolation with those of ecological poverty. Nor have I myself been able to relate them, and while I now accept the considerable influence of isolation on island biology, I am extremely puzzled to know how it exerts its effects. I should add that Part 2 of this book was not appreciably affected by my illness, and while one of my aims has been to provide a theoretical background, the other has been to provide a new set of facts in which those concerned with island biogeography may quarry. I could not agree more when Mayr, himself an advocate of the 'close view', wrote that at the present time there are too many theories and too few facts being published in this field.

EDITOR'S NOTE

This Preface, virtually unaltered as Dr Lack wrote it, was sent by Dr C.M. Perrins to Professor Ernst Mayr and Dr Jared Diamond, but only after Dr Lack's death on 12 March 1973. Their comments shed extra light on Dr Lack's conception of the MacArthur/Wilson views, especially on those in Dr MacArthur's book *Geographical Ecology* (1972), which are so important for the argument running through the whole of this book. Further evidence that the rate of change of avifaunas on islands is less fast than some authors have suggested is given by Linch and Johnson (*Condor* 1974, 76:370–384).

On 28 March 1973 Professor Mayr wrote

'... I do not like very much David's reference to the new theory as MacArthur's. When he came to it, it was not MacArthur's theory because he had no idea MacArthur had similar concepts.'

On 25 March 1973 Dr Diamond wrote

'... Dr Lack's view ... is that (a) ecological poverty on remote islands favors communities of few species with broad niches; (b) such communities are stable and resist invasion by competition. MacArthur did not consider (a) to be a major reason for low species numbers on remote islands ... Essentially, MacArthur and Lack disagree on how small remote islands come to have few species, but they agree that these communities of few species competitively resist invasion.'

ACKNOWLEDGEMENTS

David Lack was unable to complete this book as he would have liked before he died. He had written Part II by June 1972 when he first became ill. Realising then that he had probably only a few months to live, he concentrated on producing a draft of Part I. After he had sent it out for criticism, he managed to rewrite most of the chapters, but would have given the whole book another thorough revision if he had had time. Early in 1973, knowing he would be unable to finish the book to his own satisfaction, he asked Dr James Monk, who had already seen the early draft, if he would edit and see the book through the press. Dr Monk agreed to do this for him, and has very kindly spent much time and trouble on its completion, enabling the book to appear in its present form.

Kay Kepler has greatly contributed to the book by her line drawings of the Jamaican birds. David Lack saw the drawings, and was very pleased with them and grateful to her.

The following people read and criticised the manuscript: Dr A.W. Diamond, Drs C.B. and A.K. Kepler, P. and E. Lack, Dr D.A.H. Morse and Dr C.M. Perrins. Parts of the book were seen by others, particularly the Preface and Chapter 1 by Dr Jared Diamond and Professor Ernst Mayr, and Part II by Dr Roger Smith.

We acknowledge our gratitude to the Royal Society and the University of the West Indies for granting a visiting professorship to David Lack to work for a year in Jamaica; and to the Natural Environment Research Council for a grant enabling Dr A.W. Diamond to work as research assistant. Tony Diamond, assisted by his wife, Mrs E. Diamond, was responsible for the trapping and helped with the field observations. Peter Lack worked throughout the year as field assistant, with Andrew Lack helping in his school holidays.

Much valuable help was given by Professor I. Goodbody and his staff of the Zoology Department, University of the West Indies at Mona, particularly by Dr T. Turner, Dr J. Woodley and Mr B. Turner.

We had generous assistance from the Botany Department, especially from Dr C.D. Adams, whose book on the Jamaican plants has been used for all botanical names, and from Professor A.D. Skelding. Mrs M. Allwood very kindly identified the flowers and fruits we brought in nearly every day. Assistance was also given by the Institute of Jamaica. Local knowledge was freely given by Dr R. Smith, Mr R. Sutton and members of the Gosse Bird Club, particularly Miss L. Salmon. Robert Sutton also helped with some of the observations, and he and his family enabled us to stay at Mandeville to see those parts of the island which were otherwise difficult to reach early in the morning.

Dr James Bond's book, *Birds of the West Indies*, was invaluable both in the field and later, as also were his many helpful letters.

Comparison of bird skins was made possible and greatly helped by Dr D.W. Snow and Mr D. Goodwin at the Bird Room of the British Museum of Natural History. Mr C.W. Benson also assisted us at the Zoology Museum of Cambridge University. The Edward Grey Institute librarian, Miss D. Vincent, helped me to check the references, but any that are missing are my fault.

We were in Jamaica from 12 October 1970 to 14 July 1971.

Brief visits were made to other islands besides Jamaica by David Lack, sometimes accompanied by others, and we acknowledge with gratitude the many people who made these visits a success.

Barbados, 1–3 February: Dr and Mrs Doran, Dr Lewis, Mr and Mrs Whitaker;

Trinidad, 3–12 February, and with the Lack family, 23–27 July: Professor J.S. Kenny, Dr. A. Lill, Dr P.R. Bacon, Dr M. Buchanan, Mr D. Stradling, Mr R. ffrench;

St Lucia, with Dr A.W. Diamond, 9–13 March: Mr Stanley John, Mrs Charles;

St Vincent, with Dr A.W. Diamond, 13–17 March, and with the Lack family, 15–13 July: Dr Earle Kirby;

Grenada, with Dr A.W. Diamond, 17–21 March, and with Andrew Lack, 1–9 August;

Grand Cayman, with Peter Lack, 17–20 May: Mr I. Thompson;

Puerto Rico, with Peter Lack, 29–31 May: Drs C.B. and A.K. Kepler;

Dominica, with Peter Lack, 31 May–4 June, and with E. Lack, 2–16 June, 1972;

Tobago, with Andrew Lack, 27 July–1 August.

I would like to thank Blackwell Scientific Publications for their ready and helpful co-operation at all stages.

David Lack died before he was able to write his acknowledgements, so anyone who has been overlooked will, I hope, forgive the omission and realise that their contributions to the work, and those of everyone else, were much appreciated by him and all of us who so much enjoyed our stay in Jamaica.

Elizabeth Lack

FOREWORD

I have been priviliged to help see this book through the press for David Lack. Despite his illness, he was able to leave a complete text and set of maps which have been readily assembled for publication. The actual editing necessary has, almost throughout, been slight and the text as David Lack wrote it has been left almost unmolested.

A great deal of the work, the detailed meticulous checking, the entire compilation of the references and of the index has been done by Elizabeth Lack. She has also had assistance from Peter Lack and other members of the family; the combined knowledge and experience of the Jamaican avifauna of the two former in particular has been of essential value. David Lack was a devoted family man and he would have been delighted that final publication of this book had depended so much on a family effort. Editorial errors and shortcomings must be laid at my door, but I am glad to be able here to acknowledge my sincere thanks to Elizabeth in a sad but rewarding task.

J.F.M.

PART I

CHAPTER 1 · A THEORY OF ISLAND AVIFAUNAS*

Oceanic islands, those that have never been connected with the mainland, have far fewer resident species of land birds than the mainland, and they have fewer the smaller and more remote that they are. Various of the island species have broader ecological niches than their mainland counterparts, and many are endemic. Evidence for these generalisations, which are now widely accepted, will be set out in the course of this book. To explain them, I maintain a theory, sketched in this opening chapter, which I cannot prove, but which I think fits the available facts better than any other. Its main emphasis is on ecological factors, whereas that of many previous workers has been on the difficulties of dispersal over the sea.

Broadly, the number of resident species of land birds on an oceanic island depends on its 'ecological poverty', the existing species virtually filling the available ecological niches, and leaving almost no 'room' in which potential new colonising species can establish themselves. In this context, the term 'ecological poverty' is deliberately vague. It takes account of the number of different kinds of habitat and local climate, whether there is humid as well as arid forest, or mountains as well as lowlands, the number of layers of canopy trees and of bushes in the forests, the range in size, edibility and seasonal abundance of the insects, fruits and seeds which comprise the main foods of land birds, and so on. Later research may show that some of these factors are much more important than others, and probably other factors are important which have not been included, but not enough is known to say more at present. The total number of species of land organisms of all types is probably in itself unimportant, but it is likely to be correlated with the degree of ecological poverty, and may at present be its only available indicator, so to that extent could be a useful guide. At one time I preferred the term 'ecological diversity' to 'ecological wealth', but do not now think it so satisfactory. Eventually, these and

other general terms should be superseded by knowledge of the particular factors involved in each case.

On this view, the avifauna of each island is stable, stable with
respect not only to the *number* of resident species, but also as to *which*
these are. It may reasonably be presumed that larger oceanic
islands tend to have more species of land birds than smaller ones
because they are ecologically richer—at least they are known to have
a greater variety of habitats and a larger number of species of land
organisms. Similarly, an oceanic island has a smaller avifauna than
an equivalent area of the mainland because it may be presumed to
be ecologically poorer. It is not known whether remoter islands are
ecologically poorer than nearer islands of similar size, but some
remoter islands are known to have fewer species of land organisms
than nearer ones, and also an extremely restricted variety of habitats,
so this could well be the case. Until this point has been established,
however, there will be a gap in the theory, because the tendency for
fewer species to be found on remote than on near islands is a critical
factor in island biogeography.

Some of the reasons that ecologically poorer islands have fewer
species of land birds than richer ones are obvious. Thus if a particular
type of habitat is absent from an island, many of the species adapted to
this habitat will probably be absent. Moreover, as pointed out in
Chapter 14, the area occupied by a habitat may be critical; it may
support a specialised species only if sufficiently extensive. Similarly,
there will tend to be more resident species of insectivorous birds if large
as well as small insects are present, but only if these larger species
are sufficiently numerous.

In addition to such particular points, it is an essential part of the
theory that, with ecological poverty, a small number of more generalised species tend to exclude in competition a greater number of more
specialised species. I regard this as the chief reason that the birds of
oceanic islands are not only fewer in number but also tend to have
broader ecological niches than their mainland counterparts. I first
appreciated this as a particular point in Darwin's finches, the
Geospizinae. On some of the small or remote Galapagos islands may
occur only one of two congeneric species which coexist on larger or
nearer islands, and it is then intermediate in beak or size between
the two elsewhere, presumably because, with ecological poverty, it
combines what is left of their respective feeding niches (Lack 1947).

But I did not appreciate that this might be the result of competitive exclusion, rather than of the chance failure of one of the two species concerned to reach the island in question, until I found that MacArthur and Levins (1967) had demonstrated theoretically that conditions exist in which a more generalised species, a 'jack-of-all-trades', could exclude through competition two specialists. In Darwin's finches, species with similar ecology are involved, but I now consider that a much more general tendency is important on oceanic islands, and that fewer species with broader niches may displace more species with narrower ones, without the involvement of exact, or even close, ecological counterparts. Indeed niches may be filled and divided in different ways on different islands.

A critical fact relating to this view is that land birds move between the mainland and oceanic islands, and between the islands of an archipelago, far more frequently than has generally been supposed, and evidence supporting this will be given later. For the reasons just given, the number of resident species on oceanic islands is small, not because few species have been able to reach them, but because nearly all those that have done so have been excluded through competition with the existing residents. But such exclusions would be extremely hard to observe in the field, and that is why their importance has hitherto been ignored. Because some ecological factors are obvious, we tend to think that all of them are, but in fact many are extremely hard to notice, especially if we are looking in the wrong direction at the time.

These views imply that, so far as land birds are concerned, oceanic islands are almost 'full' from the ecological standpoint. This does not mean that niches are filled in a similar way on an island and on the mainland simply by a reduction in the number of species of each type. If a particular mainland type has not reached an island, there is a a gap, but the niche concerned may be filled by some other type or, perhaps more usually, it may be divided between several other species, each of which also feeds in other ways. Nevertheless, although this view regards an oceanic island as 'almost ecologically full' so far as land birds are concerned, the word 'almost' is an important qualification. It may be hard for a further species to fit in, but it is not impossible, both through the slow processes of evolutionary adaptation among the species already resident, or through the arrival from elsewhere of a species able to displace one of the existing ones, or to carve out a niche for itself from among those of the existing species.

I tentatively suggest, also, that the high proportion of endemic birds on oceanic islands is not due primarily to the rarity with which further individuals of the species concerned arrive there, or to the length of time for which they have been resident (though the isolation of the population is essential), but to rapid adaptation where there are big differences in the ecological conditions. Usually the habitat on oceanic islands most different from those on the mainland is highland forest, and that is where most, but not all, the endemic species are found. Lowland habitats tend to be less peculiar, and that may be why they have fewer endemics, but this tentative idea needs precise study.

While I have not seen a previous interpretation of island avifaunas along these lines, the general principle behind it is not new. Comparative studies of the numbers of species in different environments, with special relation to land birds, have been made by MacArthur (*e.g.* 1965, 1969, 1972) and his pupils for over a decade, and they have related them to ecological factors (in one case, Puerto Rico, partly attributing the paucity of species on an oceanic island to such factors— MacArthur, Recher and Cody·1966). Similarly Orians (1969) has related the greater number of bird species in lowland than in montane tropical forest to ecological factors, as discussed in chapter 15. I am here merely suggesting that the much bigger reduction in numbers between oceanic islands and the mainland is explicable in terms of similar ecological factors.

An explanation in seemingly different terms was, however, proposed earlier by MacArthur and Wilson (1963, 1967) to account for the extremely small numbers of species of land birds on oceanic islands. In their view, land birds from elsewhere reach an oceanic island only rarely and at long intervals, and colonisation proceeds extremely slowly and almost by chance. The more remote the island, and to some extent the smaller the island, the smaller the chance of a new species reaching it, and hence the smaller the number of resident species there. At the same time, linked with their small populations, island species often become extinct, and such extinctions are more frequent the smaller the population and hence the smaller the island. As a result, there is for each island an equilibrium position for the number of resident species, where the frequency of new colonising species approximately balances the frequency of extinction among

the existing resident species, and this equilibrium position is determined primarily by the size of the island and its distance from other
land. In the letter referred to in the Preface, J. Diamond noted that
the rarity of colonisation and its occurrence by chance are not part
of the MacArthur/Wilson formulation, but have been added to it
by others.

From this view, it has been concluded that island avifaunas are
highly unstable, in the sense that the particular species present, though
not their total number, change repeatedly. For other reasons,
connected with the proportion of endemic species present, Mayr (1965)
reached a similar conclusion. It has also been concluded that oceanic
islands may be far from ecologically full, so that it is relatively easy
for a newcomer, once it has arrived, to establish itself, and because it
often finds few or no other species with similar requirements or adaptations, it tends to expand its ecological niche. Finally, because a newly
established population rarely has further contact with the ancestral
population, it tends to evolve endemic differences which, broadly,
are greater the longer that it has been on the island. As Mayr pointed
out, however, each island continues to receive new species, while
existing species, including endemics, become extinct, so there is
always a proportion of species present which have not had time to
evolve endemic differences.

On this latter theory the critical factor is the rarity of dispersal,
whereas I prefer to think it is ecological poverty, that chance is virtually
excluded, and that competition determines both the species which
colonise and the species which fail, and also the total number of
resident species. Chance may, however, play a part in determining
which of several possible species colonises first.

I hold my view for all *undisturbed* oceanic islands which have had
time to evolve natural forests and endemic land birds. It need not
hold for newly formed islands which have not yet attained ecological
stability, nor for an island like Krakatoa, still recovering from its
explosion, nor, in particular, for islands greatly disturbed by man.
On Hawaii, New Zealand or Mauritius, for instance, there have been
many recent changes in the land birds, but they are due to man, who
has cleared the natural forests, thus exterminating various native
bird species, and who has created new cultivated habitats to which
he has introduced land birds adapted elsewhere to cultivated land,
some of which may carry parasitic organisms devastating to native

birds. In the world as a whole, nearly all the land birds that have become extinct in the last 150 years lived on islands (Greenway 1967), but nearly if not quite all of them became extinct as a result of human disturbances. Land birds are much more vulnerable to man on islands than those on continents, especially because island forests occupy so small an area that, once destroyed, the birds have nowhere else to go. Under the impact of man, oceanic islands have a highly unstable avifauna, but we should, I consider, keep what has happened on disturbed islands out of our minds in considering the conditions on natural undisturbed ones. Enough is known, for instance, to say that the avifauna of Jamaica is virtually unchanged since at least 150 years ago.

In his last book, MacArthur (1972, pp. 79–81) particularly considered censuses taken by Diamond (1969) on the Channel Islands off California in 1968, which he could compare with previous counts in 1917. In the interval, there were big changes in the particular species present, but the total number of species on each island was about the same in both years (apart from a few exceptions, attributable to changes in vegetation). The MacArthur/Wilson model fits these findings extremely well. But as Diamond pointed out, the vegetation of the islands had been much modified by man already in 1917, and there have been later changes. Hence I do not think that conclusions drawn from the changes on these islands should be applied to un-disturbed oceanic islands on which the vegetation and the birds might have evolved together for thousands of years. I should add that, while I here differ fundamentally from MacArthur and Wilson (1963, 1967), their highly original re-appraisal of 'island biogeography' revitalised a supposedly dead subject, and I have re-read their short book of 1967 more times than any other on biology, because I keep finding further new and revealing biological insights in it.

The theory that I have outlined here applies to land birds. The extent to which it may apply to other types of land organism is beyond my competence to discuss. This is not so bad as it might seem, however, since the critical ideas concerning the factors influencing species diversity, both in different habitats, studied by MacArthur and his pupils, and on islands, by MacArthur and Wilson, were developed largely, and at the start almost entirely, in relation to land birds, and nearly all the classic demonstrations of the principles involved are taken from the records of ornithologists. Birds, being at or near the top of the food chain, might conveniently reveal what is happening in other types of organisms lower down.

While, however, differences in species diversity related to habitat or latitude might well depend on the same basic factors in land birds as in other types of land organisms, those concerned with the numbers of species on islands might be basically different in birds if the critical factor concerned is the power of dispersal over the sea. Some other types of organisms, such as fern spores or small insects drifted by the wind, or seed carried by frugivorous birds, probably cross the sea as frequently as do many types of land birds. But some others, notably true freshwater fish, cannot cross at all, others, such as large mammals or forest trees with heavy seeds, do so hardly at all, and in yet other groups, such as land reptiles, the process may occur but be much less frequent than in land birds. Hence the theory developed here for birds cannot apply, except in very modified form, to island faunas as a whole; a complete theory of island biogeography will need a much wider base than evidence drawn solely from birds. The reader may be reminded again, also, that a critical point in the theory is that more remote islands are ecologically poorer than less remote islands, but the fact is scarcely established, and the possible reasons for it are not known. In the past, bolder zoogeographers have often tried to fill gaps in knowledge by speculations, with unhappy results. But science is more surely advanced by acknowledging the existence of a gap due to ignorance than by concealing it with a faultily constructed bridge.

There have been two ways of studying the types of ecological problem discussed here, which Williams (1969) has termed the 'distant' and the 'close' views. The 'distant' view depends on *a priori* ideas, mathematical analyses and selected examples, and in the hands of masters has led to outstanding advances. But it has two weaknesses in lesser hands, first a tendency to concentrate on numbers of species rather than the particular species involved, and secondly, because nature is so various, one can with diligence find examples to illustrate almost any new idea. The 'close' view, in contrast, depends on the intensive study of a particular situation in all its aspects, from which conclusions are later drawn.

The 'close' view in this book is of the land birds of Jamaica, and to a lesser extent of the rest of the West Indies. My aim is to consider principles of evolution, ecology and zoogeography of interest to biologists in general, and the book is based on birds not merely because this is the group which I study, but because, as already mentioned, material from birds has proved particularly rewarding in relation to the types of problem under discussion. As already mentioned, I conclude that selection and 'ecological opportunity', not chance, determine which bird species settle on islands. It was likewise choice and ecological opportunity, not chance, which determined my spending my sabbatical leave of 1970–71 at the University of the West Indies in Jamaica. I do not wish to imply that my ideas on evolution on islands were fully formed before I went to Jamaica, but they had reached a stage (see Lack 1969a) where I realised that Jamaica might be the best possible area in which to continue my research, and my views were much modified as a result of the visit.

The special interest of the West Indies in the present context is that their land birds are at an intermediate stage between those of offshore islands with little endemism and those of the Galapagos or Hawaii where there have been adaptive radiations of endemic families or subfamilies. The West Indies are typical oceanic islands in that they have many endemic species independently derived from species colonising from elsewhere. Whether the islands themselves have peculiar features in relation to the kind of problems discussed in this book is hard to say when so little is known, but their geographical position is unusual for an oceanic archipelago in that there is mainland to north, west and south. Jamaica is also unusual, and here lies its special value, in that nearly one-fifth of the land is still covered by natural forest, and this includes representative areas of the three main types, namely arid lowland forest, wet midlevel forest and montane forest. Further, there are enough extant species of land birds (65) for meaningful analysis, only two species have become extinct since 1800, and human introductions are negligible.

My aim, then, is to discuss general principles on the basis of the land birds of Jamaica, but a complication here arises. When P.H. Gosse, F.R.S. produced his *Birds of Jamaica* in 1847, it was far ahead of its time, and remained one of the best bird books on any part of the world for at least half a century. But since Gosse's day, the birds of Jamaica have been little studied. The multitude of British amateur ornithologists among district officers, judges, soldiers, policemen, doctors, agricultural advisers and the like, who discovered so much about Indian and African birds between 1850 and 1950, did not appear in the West Indies. When in the field with my companions, therefore, we found ourselves studying what, from the ecological viewpoint, was an almost unknown birdlife.

This means that a second part of this book is needed, concerned primarily with the ecology and systematics of each Jamaican species. This is primarily of interest to the ornithologist, but has to be included as the basis on which the first part rests. It is, if you like, the price of taking a 'close' view, and while the general biologist need not read it, he will need to know something of the Jamaican land birds, as they come all through my discussion. To help him, I have put a conspectus of all these species in Table 1, to which he can refer whenever necessary. In addition, Kay Kepler has made a line drawing of every living species.

We ourselves came to know and love the Jamaican birds and the strange forests in which they live, and for reasons of this sort alone, a naturalist will prefer a 'close' to a 'distant' view. In addition it is, I suggest, through a 'close' view that biological principles are most likely to be uncovered; it is slower but, I think, more likely to be sound, though perhaps I hold the latter view because it is the method of working which I prefer.

TABLE 1. *Native Jamaican land birds, Pigeons to Passerines*

Name	Endemism	Wing (mm)	Culmen (mm)	Weight (g)	Natural habitat			Same species (or superspecies) resident on		
					low	mid	high	Mainland	Cuba	Hispaniola
COLUMBIDAE pigeons										
Columba leucocephala	—	190	17	(243)	R	R	S	+	+	+
Columba inornata	su	220	19		R	R	R	(+)	+	+
Columba caribaea	Sp	216	18			R	R	(+)	—	—
Zenaida macroura	—	136	13	(155)	R		r	+	+	+
Zenaida aurita	—	156	14	(126)	R	sW		+	+	+
Zenaida asiatica	—	156	20		R	(C)	(c)	+	+	+
Columbina passerina	su	82	11	35	R	R	r	+	+	+
Leptotila jamaicensis	su	157	17	162	R	R	R	+	—	—
Geotrygon montana	—	140	12	142	sW	R	R	+	+	+
Geotrygon versicolor	Sp	162	21	226		R	R	(+)	(+)	(+)
PSITTACIDAE parrots										
Ara sp.	?			Extinct				?		
Aratinga nana	Sp	140	22		R	R		(+)	(+)	—
Amazona collaria	Sp	184	26		f	R	f	(+)	(+)	(+)
Amazona agilis	Sp	171	24			R		(+)	(+)	(+)
CUCULIDAE cuckoos										
Coccyzus americanus	—	138	26	(63)	S			+	+	+
Coccyzus minor	su	133	28	(59)	R	w		+	+	+
Hyetornis pluvialis	Sp	126	45	(163)	r	R	r		—	(+)
Saurothera vetula	Sp	182	36		R	R	s		(+)	(+)
Crotophaga ani	—	151	31	(108)	R	(C)	(c)	+	+	+

Species	Code									
STRIGIFORMES owls										
Tyto alba	—	333	23		R	R	R	+	+	+
Pseudoscops grammicus	G	213	20		R	R	—	—	—	—
NYCTIBIIDAE potoos										
Nyctibius griseus	su	295	26		R	R	—	+	—	+
CAPRIMULGIDAE nightjars										
Chordeiles gundlachii	—	168	7		S	s	—	(+)	+	(+)
Siphonorhis americanus	Sp	132	12	Extinct			—	—	—	(+)
APODIDAE swifts										
Streptoprocne zonaris	—	202	9		F	F	R	+	+	+
Cypseloides niger	—	155	7	(33)	SF	SF	S	+	+	+
Tachornis phoenicobia	—	102	4	11	R	F	F	—	+	+
TROCHILIDAE hummingbirds										
Anthracothorax mango	Sp	74	27	7.7	R	E	(c)		—	
Trochilus polytmus	G	66	21	5.4	R	R	R		—	+
Mellisuga minima	su	37	10	2.2	R	R	R		(+)	+
TODIDAE todies										
Todus todus	Sp	47	18	6.7	R	R	R	—	(+)	(+)
PICIDAE woodpeckers										
Centurus radiolatus	Sp	134	36	(101)	R	R	R	—	(+)	(+)
COTINGIDAE becards										
Platypsaris niger	Sp	101	16		w	R	R	(+)	—	—

TABLE 1. (*cont.*)

Name	Endemism	Wing (mm)	Culmen (mm)	Weight (g)	Natural habitat			Same species (or superspecies) resident on		
					low	mid	high	Mainland	Cuba	Hispaniola
TYRANNIDAE flycatchers										
Tyrannus dominicensis	—	116	26	(53)	S	SE	(sc)	+	+	+
Tyrannus caudifasciatus	su	108	25	39	R	R	R	—	+	+
Myiarchus stolidus	su	85	19	21	R	E	R	—	+	+
Myiarchus barbirostris	Sp	73	12	12	R	R	R	(+)	—	—
Myiarchus validus	Sp	102	22	39	R	R	R	—	—	—
Contopus caribaeus	su	69	13	10	Ws	R	R	(+)	+	+
Elaenia fallax	su	68	10	14		r	wS	—	+	+
Myiopagis cotta	Sp	66	10	13	R	R	R	(+)	—	—
HIRUNDINIDAE swallows										
Kalochelidon euchrysea	su	110	4			R	R	(+)	—	+
Progne dominicensis	—	144	11		S	s	—	+	+	+
Petrochelidon fulva	—	102	7		R	R	w	+	+	+
MIMIDAE mockingbirds										
Mimus polyglottos	—	108	18	47	R	(C)	(c)	+	+	+
Mimus gundlachii	su	126	23	74	R			—	—	—
TURDIDAE thrushes										
Myadestes genibarbis	su	94	12	27	W	R	R	(+)	(+)	+
Turdus aurantius	Sp	123	24	81	R	R	R	—	—	—
Turdus jamaiensis	Sp	118	19	66	W	R	R	(+)	—	—

EMBERIZIDAE buntings

Ammodramus savannarum	su	57	11	17	R	(C)	E	+	−	+
Tiaris olivacea	—	51	9	9	R	E	R	+	+	+
Tiaris bicolor	—	53	10	11	R	E	E	+	−	+
Loxipasser anoxanthus	G	65	9	12	R	R	R	−	−	−
Loxigilla violacea	su	83	16	29	R	R	R	−	−	+

THRAUPIDAE tanagers, orangequit

Spindalis zena	su	97	14	43	sW	R	R	+	+	+
Euphonia jamaica	Sp	66	9	16	R	R	R	−	+	−
Euneornis campestris	G	71	14	17	R	R	R	−	−	−

PARULIDAE warblers, bananaquit

Dendroica petechia	—	65	11	11	R	—	—	+	+	+
Dendroica pharetra	Sp	63	11	11	W	R	R	−	−	−
Coereba flaveola	su	56	12	8.5	R	R	R	+	−	+

VIREONIDAE vireos

Vireo modestus	Sp	57	9	10	R	R	R	(+)	(+)	(+)
Vireo osburni	Sp	72	13	20	—	R	R	(+)	−	(+)
Vireo altiloquus	—	82	16	19	S	S	S	+	+	+

TABLE 1. (*cont.*)

Name	Endemism	Wing (mm)	Culmen (mm)	Weight (g)	Natural habitat low	mid	high	Same species (or superspecies) resident on Mainland	Cuba	Hispaniola
ICTERIDAE grackles, orioles										
Icterus leucopteryx	su	103	24	42	R	R	R	(+)	—	—
Nesopsar nigerrimus	G	101	29	39		r	R	—	—	+
Quiscalus niger	su	149	34		R	(C)		(+)	+	+
CORVIDAE crows										
Corvus jamaicensis	Sp	238	51			R		—	—	—

Notes (i) The sequence of birds is that in Peters. The nomenclature, including whether Jamaica has an endemic subspecies, is that in Peters, with the following exceptions: the species which Peters put in *Oreopelia*, *Zenaidura*, *Columbigallina* and *Nephoecetes* are merged in *Geotrygon*, *Zenaida*, *Columbina* and *Cypseloides* respectively; *Piaya pluvialis* and *P.rufigularis* are transferred to the genus *Hyetornis*; *Saurothera longirostris* and *S.vieilloti* are treated as full species, not subspecies of *S.vetula*, so that the last is an endemic Jamaican species, and *Siphonorhis brewsteri* is treated as a full species, so that *S.americanus* is an endemic Jamaican species; *Chordeiles minor gundlachii* and *Progne subis dominicensis* are treated as full species; I have separated *Centurus* from *Melanerpes*. Except for the last three, all these changes were included in Bond (1971). For simplicity I have treated the thrushes, buntings and tanagers as separate families.

(ii) The degree of endemism refers solely to Jamaica. Various other Jamaican birds are in genera, species or subspecies endemic to two or more of the Greater Antilles (see Part 2 for details). G means genus, Sp means species, su means subspecies.

(iii) The two measurements like all the rest in the book unless otherwise stated, are the means given by Ridgway for males. The weights are of birds trapped by A.W. Diamond in 1970–71 (pers. comm.), for males only when separable in the hand, otherwise for adults; a figure in brackets means only one individual weighed.

(iv) The habitats are based on our own observations. R means resident throughout the year, S means resident only in summer and W resident only in winter. Sporadic records outside the normal habitat are not included, but if a bird is regular, but local or very sparse, in the habitat concerned, it is shown by a small letter. E means present solely at edge of forest. (C) means present solely in cultivation, but it is in some cases hard to separate these two categories at midlevels and in the mountains. F means feeds but does not nest in the habitat concerned. Brackets means excluded from analyses, either because solely in cultivation or because based on past records and almost extinct there now (not seen there by us). A number of decisions are borderline, especially with respect to birds at edge and whether to classify a very scarce bird as present, regular but rare, or absent.

(v) In the three right-hand columns, + means that the same species, and (+) that a different species in the same superspecies, is found where indicated.

CHAPTER 2 · JAMAICAN BACKGROUND

GEOGRAPHICAL FEATURES, TYPES OF FOREST, METHODS OF OBSERVATION, BIRD NAMES

Early on the morning of 12 October 1970, a fortnight late owing to a British dock strike, our ship moved slowly into Kingston, which has one of the finest harbours in the world, and as a light mist dispersed, the whole line of the Blue Mountains came into view, forming a magnificent backdrop to the north. It was too hazy to see the montane forest on its steep slopes, but the arid lowland forest of the Hellshire Hills was clear to the west, and also the remains of the once extensive mangrove forests round the harbour itself. In the foreground was the unattractive town of Kingston, sprawling into the hills, with their 'ruinate' (that expressive Jamaican word) woodland, i.e. woodland disturbed and partly cleared by man with the larger trees removed by charcoal-burners.

SITUATION AND GEOLOGICAL HISTORY

The boundary of the West Indies as used here is shown in Fig. 1. Jamaica lies in latitude 18° N. and longitude 77° W. and is the third largest island in the archipelago, 230 km long from east to west and 80 km across at its widest, in area about 11,400 sq. km. As shown in Fig. 2, there is a mountain spine, starting with the limestone ridge of the John Crow mountains in the east, which rise to just over 1000 m, followed by the line of the Blue Mountains, made of igneous shales, which include Blue Mountain Peak at 2290 m, and then a series of lower limestone hills, Mount Diablo, Bull Head, the Cockpit Country and, near the west coast, Dolphin Head. The slopes, particularly in the Blue Mountains, are exceedingly steep, and nearly all the rivers are short and rapid.

Jamaica lies 150 km south of the much larger island of Cuba, and 180 km west of the larger and higher island of Hispaniola, and it is 650 km northeast of the nearest part of the mainland, in Honduras. It is an oceanic island, and it is now agreed that it was never connected

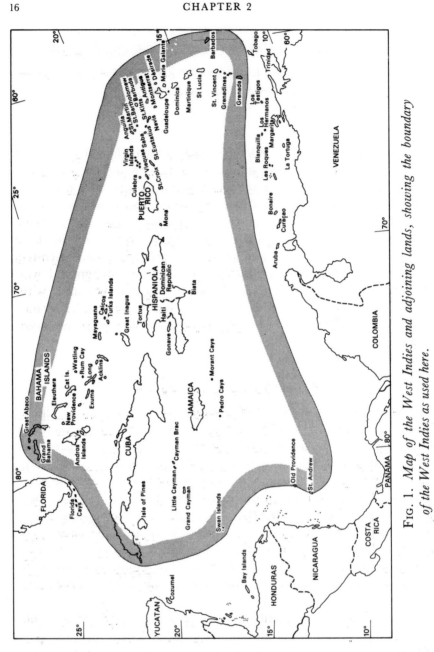

Fig. 1. *Map of the West Indies and adjoining lands, showing the boundary of the West Indies as used here.*

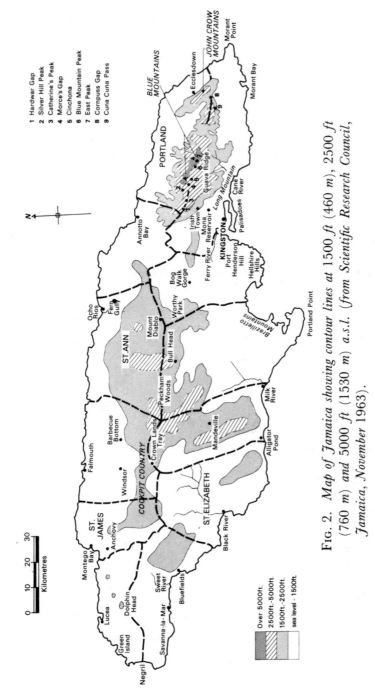

Fig. 2. *Map of Jamaica showing contour lines at 1500 ft (460 m), 2500 ft (760 m) and 5000 ft (1530 m) a.s.l. (from Scientific Research Council, Jamaica, November 1963).*

with the mainland or any large neighbouring island. Hence its animal and plant life must have reached it over the sea. As shown in Fig. 3, however, before the rise in sea level with the melting of much ice at high latitudes at the end of the last glaciation, some 10,000 years ago, part of the mainland, constituting the Honduras-Nicaraguan Bank, extended to within 400 km of Jamaica and there were three large low islands in between. Hence the sea crossing to Jamaica from the mainland would have been much shorter then than now. In this period, Central America had a temperate, not tropical, climate, so was probably inhabited mainly by birds like those in the southern

Fig. 3. *Map to show the present banks (dotted lines show depth of* 200 *m) which would have been dry land at the end of the last glaciation. Note especially the big extension of the mainland as well as the banks intervening between Honduras and Jamaica, and the Great Bahama Bank.*

parts of the United States today. As discussed later, most Jamaican birds are derived from northern, not southern, America.

According to Woodring (1954), the oldest rocks in Jamaica are the metamorphic shales of the Blue Mountains, probably formed near the start of the Cretaceous, while nearly all the rest are marine limestones laid down in the Eocene, apart from recent alluvial deposits. Land appeared above the sea in the Miocene, but the only fossil land animals, including a few mammals, are from the Quaternary. The absence of fossil birds is a serious handicap in any attempt to reconstruct the history of the avifauna.

CLIMATE

Jamaica has a subtropical climate. At the Hope Gardens in Kingston, at 150 m above sea level, the mean monthly temperature in 1969 varied between $23°$ and $27°C$, the lowest mean minima occurring in January and February, and the highest mean maxima in July and August. It is hotter than this in the arid lowlands near the south coast, and much cooler in the Blue Mountains. For instance, at Hardwar Gap at an altitude of 1200 m, the mean monthly temperature in December 1970 and January 1971 was just over $16°$ C, and the mean minimum $13°$ C (information from Brian Turner).

The average rainfall is shown in Fig. 4. Rain falls in every month, on average most heavily in October, and again heavily, but less so, in May. Other wet months are August, September, November and June, while the driest months are January, February and March. But the regime is very different in different years. During our stay, for instance, November was unusually wet, but all the other months were unusually dry, and in particular the summer rains almost failed, so that various lowland trees did not come fully into leaf until some heavy rain in August. In Jamaica, most rain is caused by rising air when the easterly trade winds reach the mountains, some by convection currents, and it falls mainly in the afternoon, and mainly on the high ground.

Because the prevailing winds are from the east, the highest rainfall is found in the John Crow Mountains, where figures from Jamaica's Scientific Research Council show that the annual average exceeds 500 cm, while the monthly average exceeds 37·5 cm in ten months of the year and 25 cm in the other two. The figures would be much

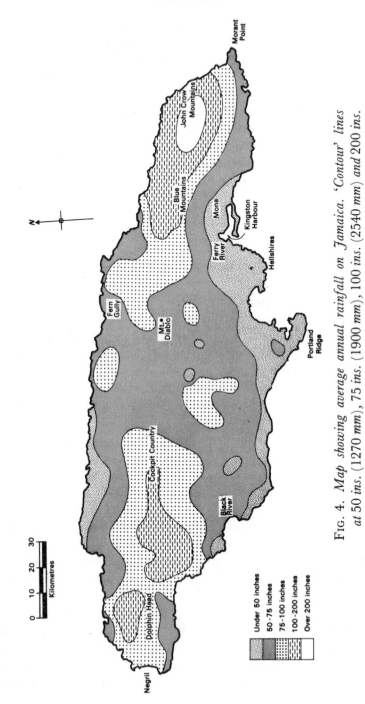

FIG. 4. *Map showing average annual rainfall on Jamaica. 'Contour' lines at 50 ins. (1270 mm), 75 ins. (1900 mm), 100 ins. (2540 mm) and 200 ins. (5080 mm) per annum. The wet months are August, September, October (very heavy), November, May (heavy) and June.*

higher on the almost inaccessible top of this range. Rainfall is also heavy, exceeding 250 cm in the year, in the northeast lowlands of Jamaica, in the Blue Mountains, in the highest parts of the Cockpit Country and at Dolphin Head in the west. At the other extreme, it is light in the southern lowlands between Kingston and the Black River, and also in a small area round Falmouth on the north coast, where it averages less than 125 cm in the year. The driest area is the Hellshire Hills, southwest of Kingston, with a monthly average of less than 12·5 cm in each month of the year except October, when it is less than 25 cm, and here less than 75 cm of rain falls in the whole year. Because it is wetter on the north than the south side of Jamaica, the vegetation differs on the two sides, and in particular, arid lowland forest is virtually confined to the south, while 'mid-level' wet limestone forest comes lower down in the north. Most of our observations were made on the south side of the island.

NATURAL VEGETATION

The main areas of natural forest that still exist on Jamaica, and the main areas where we studied them, are shown in Fig. 5. The following account is based on the full descriptions by Asprey and Robbins (1953), so that our own can be brief. I was also greatly helped while in Jamaica by conversations with Dr. Dennis Adams, whose new flora (1972) is here followed for plant names.

Natural Forest

There are three main kinds of natural forest: lowland arid limestone forest (5 in Table 2), found in parts of the southern lowlands; wet midlevel limestone forest (11), especially in the Cockpit Country, and very wet limestone forest (12) in the John Crow mountains; and montane forest (13), on shales in the Blue Mountains. Each of these kinds can be subdivided, and there are other minor types of woodland, set out in Table 2. Two other sorts of forest have gone, that on alluvial soils in some of the southern river valleys, and that in the wet limestone lowlands of the northeast, but perhaps neither was of great extent, and they were presumably intermediate in character between arid lowland and wet midlevel forest.

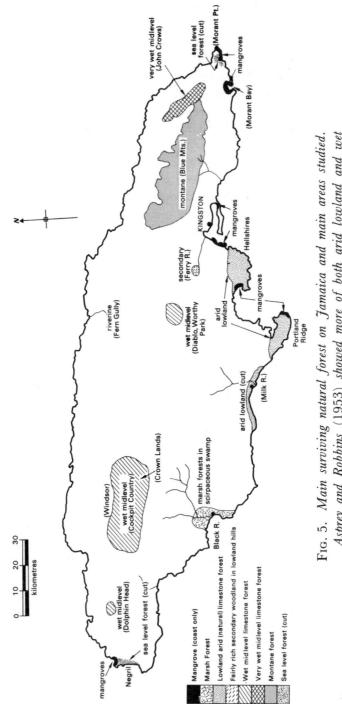

FIG. 5. *Main surviving natural forest on Jamaica and main areas studied. Asprey and Robbins (1953) showed more of both arid lowland and wet midlevel forest, but they included areas we considered now too much cut.*

Mangrove (coast only)

Marsh Forest

Lowland arid (natural) limestone forest

Fairly rich secondary woodland in lowland hills

Wet midlevel limestone forest

Very wet midlevel limestone forest

Montane forest

Sea level forest (cut)

Lowland forest; strand woodland west of Port Henderson Hill with the characteristic dildo cactus (*Stenocereus hystrix*) and scrubby acacia trees. Photograph: Paul Lack

Lowland forest; southern arid (natural) limestone forest in the Hellshire Hills showing the low thin-trunked trees and sparsely vegetated rocky ground. Photograph: Peter Lack

Midlevel forest; the Cockpit Country near Barbecue Bottom showing the typical caste-country skyline of steep towers with deep valleys
in between. Photograph: Andrew Lack

Midlevel forest; a cleared track in wet limestone forest at Crown
Lands, Cockpit Country, showing the tall trees and rocky ground.
Photograph: Catherine Lack

Midlevel forest; montane thicket by a stream near the top of the John Crow Mountains showing the density of low trees and their epiphytes. Photograph: Peter Lack

The trade wind clouds building up behind the main ridge of the Blue Mountains. Photograph: Paul Lack

Montane forest; the canopy of sclerophyll forest by the trail up to Blue Mountain Peak, showing the abundance of the greyish *Usnea* lichen. Photograph: Andrew Lack

Montane forest; cloud forest near Hardwar Gap showing the low trees covered with epiphytes especially bromeliads. Photograph: Andrew Lack

TABLE 2.   *Main types of forest in Jamaica, and main areas*
where studied

Type of Forest	Areas studied
Lowland	
1. Mangroves	Morant Point, Morant Bay, Kingston Harbour, edge of Hellshires
2. Strand woodland	Palisadoes (Kingston Harbour) (secondary)
3. Sealevel forest (liable to flooding)	Morant Point (partly cleared)
4. Marsh forest (in scirpaceous swamp)	Black River
5. (Southern) arid (natural) limestone forest	Hellshire Hills, Portland Ridge
6. Very arid ruinate	Port Henderson Hill (edge of Hellshires)
7. Arid ruinate woodland in hills (southern)	Long Mt. near Mona
8. Fairly rich secondary woodland in (southern) hills	above Ferry River
9. (Southern) riverine woodland	Mona, Ferry River (both secondary)
10. Northern riverine	Fern Gully
Midlevel	
11. Wet limestone forest (northern)	Mt. Diablo, Cockpit Country, Dolphin Head
12. Very wet limestone forest with montane thicket at top	John Crow Mountains
Montane	
13. Montane forest	Blue Mountains
typical	round Hardwar and trail to Morce's Gap
sclerophyll	parts of trail to Morce's Gap
cloud forest	above Hardwar and below Morce's Gap
elfin forest	top of Blue Mountain

Notes (i)   Bracketed words in the types of forest are usually omitted in the text when referring to the type of forest concerned.
(ii)   The localities listed are where the main studies were carried out, not a complete list.

Lowlands

1   *Mangroves* occur chiefly in southern Jamaica, in muddy inlets with calm shallow water. On the side inland from the sea, the trees *Laguncularia racemosa* and *Avicenna germinans* may reach a height of 12 m, with a closed canopy and no, or only a little, vegetation beneath, the ground usually being covered by salt water or drying mud. Most of the few bird species present are typical of arid limestone forest, but the resident warbler *Dendroica petechia* and the wintering water-thrush *Seiurus noveboracensis* are commoner in mangroves than anywhere else.

2   *Strand woodland* is often found as a narrow strip, perhaps 20 m wide, between an open shore and arid lowland forest. We made counts

in the secondary scrub along the Palisadoes, a sandy strip separating Kingston Harbour from the sea, with much *Coccoloba uvifera, Stenocereus hystrix* and acacias. This type of vegetation is too narrow to be of importance for birds, except that it appears to be the main natural habitat on Jamaica of the Northern Mockingbird *Mimus polyglottos*, which possibly spread from there to become one of the commonest species in wooded cultivation.

3 *Sea-level forest*, normally just above sea level and liable to flooding, provides a rather rich form of arid lowland forest and has the bird species typical of the latter, including several that are absent from the most arid parts. This type of forest occurs at Morant Point, but has been much cleared, and a small fragment remains at Negril.

4 *Marsh forest*, which occurs on slightly raised areas in the large freshwater swamp of the Black River, and is covered with the sedge *Cyperus giganteus*, is more unusual, and while it includes various typical lowland trees, the palms *Roystonea princeps* and *Calyptronoma occidentalis* are prominent, and so are the tall tree *Symphonia globulifera* and the peculiar *Grias cauliflora*, with leaves up to over a metre long. We visited this area only once, by boat in summer. It has birds typical of the richer lowland woods, and appears to be the main natural habitat of the ani *Crotophaga ani*, a common species of cultivation. The sedge marsh itself has almost no birds, except for waterbirds in the few ponds.

5 *Natural arid limestone forest.* Extensive areas of this type of forest still exist on the Hellshire Hills and on Portland Ridge, which rise from sea level to respectively 240 m and rather over 150 m above sea level and have an annual rainfall of less than 75 cm. This is a xeric scrub woodland, but the term 'scrub' may mislead an Englishman, for whom it usually means thorny bushes 3 to 7 m high. In the strange and beautiful forest under discussion, the trees in more sheltered places are often 12 m high, forming an open canopy, and there is a diversity of species, with *Bursera simaruba* standing above the rest, and the lower *Tecoma stans* and *Bauhinia divaricata* also prominent. Most of the trees have thin trunks and narrow or small leaves, many of them are at least partly deciduous, and thorns and spines are rare. Cacti are scarce except in open places. There is often a bush layer,

including small palms, but usually no ground vegetation, and often no soil or leaf litter, but the latter accumulates in sheltered areas and in crevices in the clinkered honeycomb limestone. In many places the jagged rocks and twisted branches and vines make walking extremely arduous, so our counts were done mainly from hunters' trails. The bird life is relatively rich, as can be seen from the counts in Appendices 1–3, and one species, the mockingbird *Mimus gundlachii*, is restricted to this type of forest.

6 *Very arid ruinate forest.* Similar arid forest extends west along the coast from Alligator Pond to Milk River, but here it has been much cut and forms only a narrow strip. There is also a larger area of it on Port Henderson Hill, an outlier of the Hellshires, where cacti are abundant in the clearings made by man, especially the columnar dildo *Stenocereus hystrix* and also the prickly-pear *Opuntia spinosissima*. The latter is a favourite flower of the hummingbird *Anthracothorax mango*. We made many counts here because it was a convenient site for mist-netting, but the trees rarely exceed 7 m in height, and various birds characteristic of the Hellshires themselves are absent.

7 *Arid ruinate woodland* covers large areas of the hills of the southern Jamaican lowlands. It has many of the bird species characteristic of natural lowland forest, but fewer; the number depending on the extent to which the larger trees have been removed and clearings have been made.

8 *Fairly rich secondary woodland in hills* occurs at between 60 and 120 m above sea level in a subsidiary valley above the Ferry River. It consists of a mixture of native and introduced trees up to 15 m high with higher emergents and a partly closed canopy, and the trees are less xeric and more mesic in character than those typical of ruinate woodland. It has evidently been left undisturbed for a long time and is one of the richest areas for forest birds that we found, so we made many counts there.

9 *Southern riverine woodland* must once have provided a rich lowland habitat, but now exists solely as secondary remnant. We made counts especially in a small but relatively rich area of it, near a stream from the Mona Reservoir much favoured by wintering warblers. This wood

adjoins the University, and should be preserved for biological study, but at present a few squatters are allowed to cut down the trees, to cultivate small plots and to keep pigs there. We also made counts along the Ferry River, where almost all the trees are of introduced species.

10 *Northern riverine*, with magnificent tall trees, has been preserved in a steep-sided valley, Fern Gully, at 120 to 270 m above sea level behind Ocho Rios. The closed canopy is at over 30 m, the light below is dim, and there is almost no understorey. The birds include some of those typical of midlevel forest, and the quail-dove *Geotrygon montana* is remarkably common. Unfortunately, though the valley itself has been preserved, the river has been diverted to make way for a trunk road, and the diesel fumes from the many lorries find it hard to escape from the valley floor.

Northern lowlands

Scarcely any woodland remains in the northern lowlands, and this has been heavily cleared. It is less arid than the ruinate woods of the southern lowlands, and has a few species down to sea level, such as the tanager *Spindalis zena*, which do not come so low in the south.

Midlevel

11 *Wet limestone forest*. The Cockpit Country in west-central Jamaica is the wildest part of the island, much of it still inaccessible, as it is almost impossible to walk through and there are few trails. It presents an extraordinary landscape of rounded hills and deep hollows, with occasional vertical cliffs bounding tall towers or deep valleys and is typical karst country, with underground rivers and caves. In the early morning, the screams of large flocks of parrots and parakeets and the chaotic 'jabbering' of the crow *Corvus jamaicensis* add to the wildness, while later in the day the tops of the hills are often covered in cloud and there is heavy rain. The cockpits are basins resulting from solution and erosion of the limestone, and may be 50 m deep and a kilometre or more across, but the dimensions vary greatly in different areas. They are bounded by steep slopes with hardly any soil, which lead up to dome-shaped tops, and in some places there are more conventional escarpments and deep long valleys. The annual rainfall is between 200 and 450 cm. In the cockpits themselves there is a deep bauxitic soil. The trees form a more or less closed canopy

at about 20 m, with emergent *Terminalia latifolia* and *Cedrela odorata* rising to 30 m, and they support lianas and many large bromeliads, especially *Hohenbergia* species. On the steep slopes, the closely growing trees with thin trunks reach only 10 to 12 m, but they are rather taller again on the tops.

Most of the high limestone areas in the centre of Jamaica are now cultivated, and the highest remaining wild forest in the Cockpit Country is to be found on a trail in from Troy and Crown Lands at 600 m, which descends gradually towards the north. We also entered along a trail from its lowest and most northerly part, at Windsor, rather below 100 m above sea level. As already mentioned, the north of Jamaica is much wetter than the south, and nearly all the birds typical of midlevels here descend to 100 m, being influenced by the type of forest, not by altitude as such. Finally we drove along the motor track at between 300 and 500 m which crosses the east side of the Cockpit Country above the big steep-sided valley of Barbecue Bottom, but the Bottom itself is cultivated, and the trees on parts of its slopes have been cut.

Since the Cockpit Country itself is distant from Kingston, most of our studies in midlevel wet limestone forest were made in the similar but much less extreme landscape on the southern and western slopes of Mount Diablo above Worthy Park, mainly at an altitude of around 450 m, but at times up to 300 m higher. Here, the bottoms have been cleared for grass pastures, but the woodland on the slopes and tops is natural, and the birds are almost the same as in the Cockpit Country itself. We are extremely grateful to the Clarks of Worthy Park Estate for permission to work there. We occasionally visited another area of wet limestone forest at Dolphin Head, at around 500 m above sea level, in the west of Jamaica, where much natural forest remains, though there has been some clearing. The birds are similar to those of the Cockpit Country, except that several of the large species are absent.

In the rest of the midlevel wet limestone country, cut-over forest often survives on the hills which, combined with grass pastures for cattle, reminded us of rural England. As in the lowlands, the naturalist may regret that much forest has gone, but he should rather be thankful that so much partly wooded country survives. We studied the birds in such disturbed areas on the Marshall's Pen Estate near Mandeville, thanks to the Suttons, also in Peckham Woods and a few other places.

Natural midlevel forest has most but not all of the lowland species and all the montane species, though a few of the latter are very local. In addition, the crow and one parrot are almost confined to it.

12   *Very wet limestone forest.* There is one further area of limestone on Jamaica, the John Crow mountains in the east, which, as already mentioned, are the first to meet the northeast trade wind and have the highest rainfall in the island. The types of forest and the birds show resemblances to both midlevel and montane forest, but are nearer to midlevel forest. We made counts on the east side above Ecclesdown, where strips of forest are mixed with cultivation, and on the west side at Cornpuss Gap at 600 m, where the John Crows meet the Blue Mountains, and there is a natural closed forest. The dark evergreen trees rise to 25 m or more, with a poor understorey, and in general appearence resemble the montane forest of sheltered parts of the Blue Mountains.

Above this rich lower forest, on the exposed ridge of the John Crows, there is a remarkable montane thicket, with trees some 4 to 6 m high, their narrow trunks covered in mosses. Clusias are prominent. It is extremely hard to travel through this vegetation, but on one summer day we scrambled to it with Dr. Jeremy Woodley and a local guide from Ecclesdown, using the bed of a stream which had cut small gorges, ledges, precipices and occasional deep pools in the limestone, and was at intervals crossed by twisted trunks or moss-covered branches, a miniature landscape which, as Jeremy Woodley remarked, would have suited the dwarves in Tolkien's 'Lord of the Rings'. Birds were scarce, and on the top itself we recorded only six species, the tody *T.todus,* hummingbird *Trochilus polytmus,* elaenia *E.fallax,* solitaire *Myadestes genibarbis,* vireo *V.modestus* and Bananaquit *Coereba flaveola,* with the bullfinch *Loxigilla violacea* a little below the top. This may not have been a full list, as we did not stay more than three hours. A similar group of species occurs in the equally stunted elfin forest on the exposed ridge between Blue Mountain Peak and the adjoining East Peak.

Montane

13   *Montane forest.* Extensive montane forest is found on the igneous shales of the higher slopes of the Blue Mountains, both on the long main ridge from Cornpuss Gap westward over Blue Mountain Peak

to Silver Hill Peak, and on the subsidiary ridge, southwest of Silver Hill Peak, on either side of Hardwar Gap. The latter area is close to Kingston, so most of our studies were made there, on trails at an altitude of around 1200 m, but we also walked regularly from Cinchona Gardens to Morce's Gap on the main ridge, on a trail at around 1500 m, once went to Cuna Cuna Gap, and three times to the top of Blue Mountain Peak. A walk along the main ridge of the Blue Mountains is spectacular, for the top is often only a few metres wide, with extremely steep slopes on either side, on the north a turmoil of whirling cloud in the trade wind, and on the south a dead calm.

The montane forest of Jamaica has sometimes been called rain forest, but the term is misleading as it is much less tall and luxuriant than typical lowland rain forest elsewhere. Asprey and Robbins (1953) called it 'lower montane rain forest', which Beard (1949) applied to a rather similar type of forest in the Lesser Antilles, but since there is no lowland rain forest or upper montane rain forest on Jamaica, this seems cumbersome. I have preferred to call it simply 'montane forest', but include under this term the more stunted types of mountain forest at higher altitude to which Beard and Asprey and Robbins gave special names.

Montane forest grows on the steep slopes on either side of the Blue Mountains, and its form varies greatly with the conditions. Typical montane forest occurs along the trail to Morce's Gap, for instance, in sheltered stream gullies where the trees form a closed canopy at 30 m, have moderately broad leaves and carry a small number of bromeliads and other epiphytes, and it is dark on the ground. But on the exposed flanks of the hills, at times only a few metres away, there is more open *sclerophyll forest*, with narrow-leaved trees only 6 to 7 m high, and grey *Usnea* lichens are the only prominent epiphytes. High up, again, a little below the Gap itself, which allows cloud to come through earlier in the day than elsewhere, there is a *cloud forest* of trees 12 m high with thick dark leaves, numerous epiphytic bromeliads and many tree ferns. There are similar contrasts on the subsidiary ridge above Hardwar Gap, but the trees are in general rather lower here. In this area, parts of the forest were felled in the distant past, but have re-grown with native forest trees, and but for the presence of old stone walls inside, it would be hard to tell this secondary from primary montane forest. There is also a spectacular small area of cloud forest near Hardwar Gap, with trees 10 m high,

almost completely covered in moss and bromeliads, and bromeliads
also grow over the fallen trunks and the ground, while tree ferns are
numerous. The black and white photograph does not convey a true
picture, because it omits the pervasive green light, especially after
cloud has descended around noon. Finally, on the top of the main
ridge, notably between Blue Mountain Peak and East Peak, there is a
narrow belt of *elfin forest*, a thicket with closely growing trees 4 to 5 m
high, with narrow twisted trunks covered in moss, but with hardly
any side branches and without large epiphytes such as bromeliads.
It is less tall, mossier and much denser than the montane thicket
on top of the John Crows, and occupies only a small area on Blue
Mountain Peak, though this or other variants of montane thicket
occur at intervals elsewhere on the main ridge. The elfin forest on
Blue Mountain is less extreme than that on the top of Puerto Rico,
which in some areas is less than a metre high, though it still looks like a
true forest if one gazes through its trunks from just above the ground.

Montane forest has fewer species of birds than either midlevel or
lowland forest. Two species, the elaenia *E. fallax* and the icterid
Nesopsar nigerrimus, are nearly confined to it, and so is the solitaire
Myadestes genibarbis for breeding, but these three species also breed
in the highest parts of the wet limestone forest.

MODIFIED LAND HABITATS

Much of the Hellshires and Portland Ridge have been spared from
destruction until now by their aridity, much of the Cockpit Country
by inaccessibility and the terrain, much of the montane forest by the
extremely steep slopes. Even so, each of these areas is being nibbled
away, by squatters who cultivate patches so soon as there is a trail,
and more drastically by foresters, who have clear-felled much montane
forest and re-planted with Caribbean Pine and eucalyptus, which
are extremely poor for native Jamaican animals, including birds.
Moreover there is now a plan to develop much of the Hellshires as
an extension of Kingston, a new road has been started into the Cockpit
Country from Crown Lands, and foresters, who might here, and elsewhere, be more pointedly called de-foresters, are active around
Hardwar Gap. How long the native birds of Jamaica will survive is
doubtful, though as yet only two species of land birds, a macaw and
a nightjar have become extinct, and two others, a pigeon and a swallow,

are rare. The record is, however, far better than that for nearly all other islands in the world, and could be maintained, since conservation could save the remaining species by keeping parts of the three main types of natural forest intact. Further, Jamaica has been almost completely spared the menace of introduced birds, though rats and the mongoose (introduced in 1872) have destroyed much.

As already remarked, much of the cultivated land is wooded and retains some of the forest birds. Particularly characteristic of wooded cultivation are the doves *Zenaida aurita* and *Columbina passerina*, ani *Crotophaga ani*, kingbird *Tyrannus dominicensis*, mockingbird *Mimus polyglottos*, and grassquit *Tiaris bicolor*. Except for the last, these are naturally lowland birds that have spread into the mountains where forest has been opened up.

The cultivated stands of coconuts and sugarcane in the lowlands and of bananas at midlevels have few birds, but the citrus orchards at midlevels attract a variety of species, which feed on the fallen fruits. The Botanic Gardens in Kingston at 150 m and Cinchona in the Blue Mountains at 1500 m also attract many birds. Grass pastures have few species, though the sparrow *Ammodramus savannarum* is here common.

MARSH AND WATER BIRDS

The natural swamps of Jamaica have been destroyed by man to a much greater extent than the forests, but anyway are poor in birds, as are the fast-flowing rivers, some of which have been tapped for water supplies. The few lakes and muddy estuaries are frequented chiefly by winter visitors and transients from North America, and their breeding species are the same as in similar habitats on the mainland. Finally there are a few seabirds, most of which breed on the small cays south of Kingston; big colonies are found only on the Pedro and Morant Cays, far offshore, which come outside the scope of this book.

The sea and shore birds are what the visiting birdwatcher first notices in Jamaica, but they are of the same species as on the mainland of Central America and are of no special interest from the biological viewpoint except for the contrast which they show with the landbirds in their degree of endemism. A full list of Jamaican breeding species other than those in the families from pigeons to passerines is set out in Table 3.

TABLE 3.   *Native Jamaican birds in the families grebes to terns*

PODICIPEDIDAE grebes	
Least Grebe	*Podiceps dominicus*
Pied-billed Grebe	*Podilymbus podiceps*
PROCELLARIIDAE petrels	
Black-capped Petrel	*Pterodroma hasitata*
PHAETHONTIDAE tropic-birds	
White-tailed Tropic-bird	*Phaëthon lepturus*
PELECANIDAE pelicans	
Brown Pelican	*Pelecanus occidentalis*
FREGATIDAE frigate-birds	
Magnificent Frigate-bird	*Fregata magnificens*
ARDEIDAE herons	
(Great Blue Heron)	*Ardea herodias* (or *cinerea*)
Green Heron	*Butorides virescens*
Little Blue Heron	*Florida caerulea*
Cattle Egret	*Bubulcus ibis*
(Common Egret)	*Egretta alba*
Snowy Egret	*Egretta thula*
Tricoloured Heron	*Hydranassa tricolor*
Black-crowned Night Heron	*Nycticorax nycticorax*
Yellow-crowned Night Heron	*Nyctanassa violacea*
Least Bittern	*Ixobrychus exilis*
THRESKIORNITHIDAE ibises	
Glossy Ibis	*Plegadis falcinellus*
White Ibis	*Eudocimus albus*
ANATIDAE ducks	
West Indian Tree Duck	*Dendrocygna arborea*
Ruddy Duck	*Oxyura jamaicensis*
Masked Duck	*Oxyura dominica*
CATHARTIDAE American vultures	
Turkey Vulture	*Cathartes aura*
ACCIPITRIDAE hawks	
Red-tailed Hawk	*Buteo jamaicensis*
FALCONIDAE falcons	
American Kestrel	*Falco sparverius*
ARAMIDAE limpkins	
Limpkin	*Aramus guarauna*
RALLIDAE rails	
Clapper Rail	*Rallus longirostris*
(Spotted Rail)	*Pardirallus maculatus*
Uniform Crake	*Amaurolimnas concolor*
Yellow-breasted Crake	*Porzana flaviventer*
Purple Gallinule	*Porphyrula martinica*
Common Gallinule	*Gallinula chloropus*
American Coot	*Fulica americana*
Caribbean Coot	*Fulica caribaea*
JACANIDAE jacanas	
Northern Jacana	*Jacana spinosa*

TABLE 3 (cont.)

CHARADRIIDAE plovers	
Thick-billed Plover	*Charadrius wilsonia*
Killdeer	*Charadrius vociferus*
RECURVIROSTRIDAE stilts	
Common Stilt	*Himantopus himantopus*
SCOLOPACIDAE sandpipers	
(Willet)	*Catoptrophorus semipalmatus*
LARIDAE gulls and terns	
Laughing Gull	*Larus atricilla*
Roseate Tern	*Sterna dougallii*
Bridled Tern	*Sterna anaethetus*
Least Tern	*Sterna albifrons*
Royal Tern	*Thalasseus maximus*
Brown Noddy	*Anous stolidus*

Notes (i)   Nomenclature follows Bond (1971).

(ii)   Breeding has not been proven for Great Blue Heron, Common Egret, Spotted Rail (now extinct) or Willet (of which A.W. Diamond and I saw a pair that behaved as if breeding). We proved breeding for the Least Tern in 1971.

(iii)   Extinct are the Black-capped Petrel, Uniform Crake and (if it ever bred) the Spotted Rail. The Caribbean Coot perhaps no longer breeds.

(iv)   The only endemic was the Uniform Crake, a Jamaican subspecies now extinct.

(v)   The Black Crake *Laterallus jamaicensis* has been claimed to have bred, but the evidence was rejected by Bond (1956).

(vi)   A few further seabirds breed on the Pedro and Morant Cays, but these are too far out to count as in Jamaica proper and are omitted here. The species nesting on the small cays off Kingston have, however, been included.

Only one out of the some forty of these species, an extinct rail, is endemic even at the level of the subspecies, whereas 28 of the 66 known land birds are endemic species.

MIGRATION

Most of the land birds which breed on Jamaica reside there throughout the year, but 7 species are summer visitors, the cuckoo *Coccyzus americanus*, nighthawk *Chordeiles gundlachii*, swift *Cypseloides niger*, kingbird *Tyrannus dominicensis*, elaenia *E.fallax* (a few stay), martin *Progne dominicensis* (a few stay) and vireo *V.altiloquus*. There are also a few wintering landbirds from the United States, including 18 species of parulid warblers discussed in Chapter 12, also the Yellow-bellied Sapsucker *Sphyrapicus varius*, catbird *Dumetella carolinensis* (scarce) and Indigo Bunting *Passerina cyanea* (local and mainly after midwinter).

Many other North American land birds occur as transients. In the latter connection we noted a number of arrivals between late December and mid-January of various North American passerine species which soon disappeared again, and were presumably migrants on passage, not winter visitors, despite the date. Various ducks and shore birds, briefly listed in Chapter 8, also come to Jamaica for the winter.

Apart from migration in and out of Jamaica, a number of the resident land birds have minor movements from higher to lower altitudes in winter and the reverse in summer, as shown diagrammati-cally in Fig. 6 (p. 40) and discussed under the species concerned in Part 2.

HABITAT COUNTS AND FEEDING OBSERVATIONS

We were out every day in the field except for the first two and last two days of our stay in Jamaica from mid October 1970 to mid July 1971. Since most of the forests that we wished to study were about two hours' drive from Kingston, we rose at 4.30 a.m. in winter and 3.30 a.m. in summer in order to reach them by the time of day at which birds are most active. Once there, we walked slowly along the trails, recording every bird seen, and in summer also every bird heard, and noting whenever a bird fed. The habitat counts are sum-marised in Appendices 1 and 2, and the feeding records under the species concerned in Part 2. The full data are deposited at the Edward Grey Institute of Field Ornithology, Oxford.

Most counts were made by at least two observers, who see more than one alone. For instance, in slow walks through montane forest at Hardwar Gap in winter, the number of land birds seen per hour was respectively 14.7, 20.6, 24.1 and 28.0 with 1, 2, 3 and 4 observers. The difference arises because, in thick forest, two observers a few feet apart usually look in different directions, and even if they look in the same direction, they have a rather different view through the leaves and branches, so tend to see different birds. We usually counted for two hours, sometimes three and rarely four, but the attention of the observer usually flags after a while. Further, birds become less active later in the morning in the hotter areas, though not usually in montane forest.

We walked at an average speed of about 0.8 km per hour, but did not keep to exact rates or distances, and stopped to record whenever we saw a bird feeding. If our return was along the same trail, we walked about four times as fast, and found that, then, we usually saw more ground-feeding birds than on the way out, presumably because, on slow walks, they usually saw us before we saw them, and quietly moved off into cover before we had come up with them. But at a fast walk it is much harder to see birds in thick vegetation. Hence the rate of walking affects the species seen. Further, since some species are heard more readily than seen, counts by eye and ear also give rather different results. In addition, the relative proportion of species recorded on slow walks is different from that of birds caught in mist-nets at the same place. Our counts therefore do not give a precise measure of the abundance of each species, but they do provide a much better record than a mere statement of 'common' or 'rare' would do. All of what has been said here may be obvious to experienced field workers, but during the last twenty-five years repeated attempts have been made to convert counts made on linear transects into quantitative censuses, and I consider that all such attempts are likely to produce serious errors. Some further difficulties in counting are discussed for the wintering warblers in Appendix 19 (p. 396).

Our feeding records, likewise, do not give a precise measure of the frequency of the ways in which each species feeds, since some kinds of feeding, for instance on fruits or by sallies for flying insects, are more conspicuous than others. When we saw a bird feeding, we recorded its height above the ground and its position in a tree only on the first occasion, but we made up to four or five records of its actual ways of feeding before we moved on to look for other birds.

BIRD NAMES

As explained in the notes to Table 1 (p. 14), the scientific names used in this book are those in the successive volumes of Peters' *Check-List of Birds of the World* for the passerines, but with a few minor changes in the non-passerines from Peters' earlier volumes. I should like to have followed the delightful vernacular names used by Gosse (1847), most of which are still in use in Jamaica today. But most of them do not show the biologist what kind of bird is involved. How many readers, for instance, will know that 'Hopping Dick' is a thrush and the 'Wild Pine Sergeant' an icterid, though these names are useful in indicating where the birds in question feed. The vernacular names created by Bond (1971) include the group name but do not always agree with those of Eisenmann (1961), many are not used in Jamaica, and in a book about Jamaica it is tiresome to have 12 out of 66 land birds in which the first name is 'Jamaican'. Moreover it is burdensome to have two Latin and two vernacular names for each species. I therefore decided to use simply the Latin name of each species, preceded by the group name to show the kind of bird involved. Bond's and the local vernacular names are included under each species in Part 2.

The brief description of Jamaica in this chapter omits, except by implication, the pleasure which we had in living there and working on an almost unknown ecology in natural surroundings. The lovely climate, dramatic scenery, strange forests, attractive birds, kind and courteous country people, the happy racially mixed marriages in the professional classes, and the high standard of scholarship in the University, far more than compensated for the few disadvantages, the threat of armed robbers, whom we did not ourselves meet, the impetuous drivers, and the inefficient machinery in our house. But behind all this, there is desperate poverty in town and countryside, for Jamaica, like the rest of the world, faces over-population, and it is hard to see how starvation is to be avoided. Yet once a week, sometimes from shacks so poor that it was hard to believe that anyone could live there, mothers turned out clean and beautifully dressed, if far too many, children in their Sunday best.

Visits of a few days each were paid to various other Caribbean islands, including Trinidad, Tobago, Grenada, St. Vincent, Barbados, St Lucia, Antigua, Puerto Rico and Grand Cayman, and I had nearly three weeks on Dominica, as set out with dates in the acknowledgments. These visits enlarged my experience but were, of course, much too short for research, except on the habitats of the land birds on Dominica.

SUMMARY

This chapter describes the geographical features of Jamaica, and especially the types of natural forest, summarised in Table 2, together with the localities where we made most of our studies. The breeding species other than the landbirds (already set out in Table 1) are listed in Table 3. Our methods of counting are discussed, and so are the reasons for not using vernacular names for the birds.

CHAPTER 3 · HABITATS OF JAMAICAN LAND BIRDS

It is fortunate indeed that enough remains of each of the three main types of forest on Jamaica for us to have been able to determine the natural habitat of each of the land birds. As described in the previous chapter, these three distinctive types of forests growing on lowland arid limestone, midlevel wet limestone and montane shale respectively, are determined by variations in the altitude, rainfall and type of soil. To save space, I have often referred to them in this chapter simply as 'lowland', 'midlevel' and 'montane' respectively, but the reader should keep in mind that, as stressed earlier, altitude is not the sole factor concerned. In particular, forest typical of midlevels occurs much lower down on the wet north than on the dry south of the island, and as high up as montane forest where the underlying rock is limestone, not shale, as in the John Crow mountains.

If, before I visited Jamaica, I had been asked which of the three, the arid lowlands, wet midlevels or mountains, held most species of resident birds, I would probably have guessed the wet midlevels. In fact, omitting species which occur solely in cultivation at the level concerned, there are a similar number at midlevels and in the lowlands. The totals are set out in the top lines of Table 4. All regular species have been included, but if scarce species together with those restricted to forest edge and those which feed but do not breed at the level concerned are omitted, then the lowlands have more species than midlevels (see note ii, Table 4). There are fewer species in the mountains, as elsewhere in the tropics, but the difference is much smaller on Jamaica than on the mainland, as discussed in Chapter 15.

It is not easy to say which type of forest has the greatest number of individual birds, because visibility and other factors affecting the numbers counted differ so much in different types of forest (see, for instance, the comments in Appendix 19, p. 396). We recorded most birds per hour on walks through parts of the wet midlevel forest and in the rich secondary woodland of the lowland hills above the Ferry

Table 4. *Analysis by habitat of Jamaican land birds*

	Summer	Winter
	Number of species	
	Summer	Winter
Total species analysed	65	59
Total in arid lowlands	53	51
Total in wet midlevels	54	51
Total in mountains	42	39
Restricted to arid lowlands	10	8
Restricted to wet midlevels	2	2
Restricted to mountains	0	0
Only in lowlands and at midlevels	11	10
Only at midlevels and in mountains	10	6
In lowlands, at midlevels and in mountains	32	33
Proportion restricted to one level	18%	17%
Proportion resident at all three levels	49%	56%

Notes (i) The figures are based on all the entries under habitat in Table 1 except those bracketed because, at the level concerned, the species is solely in cultivation. Totals are smaller in winter than summer owing to the departure of the summer visitors, while winter visitors which do not breed on Jamaica are excluded.

(ii) The figures include all the species normally resident at the level concerned. Almost all of them live in forest. If scarce though regular species (shown by a small letter in Table 1), those which in forest are solely at the edge (E), and those which feed but do not breed at the level concerned (F) are omitted, the total for lowlands, midlevels and mountains respectively are 46, 42 and 35 for the summer and 47, 42 and 31 for the winter, while the proportion restricted to one level is 42 per cent in summer and 34 per cent in winter, and the proportion resident at all three levels is 31 per cent in summer and 41 per cent in winter.

River, and fewest per hour in montane forest (as can be seen from the figures in Appendices 1 and 2), but little weight can be attached to these figures as they stand, and I could see no way of adjusting them to different conditions.

Each of the main types of forest can be subdivided, and as shown in Appendix 3, in the lowlands we saw most species in winter in riverine woodlands and the secondary woodland above the Ferry River, and these are also among the lowland habitats richest for birds in summer. Similarly we saw more species in tall humid than open sclerophyll montane forest or montane thicket, but did not keep precise records, as these types of forest so often intergrade after a short distance along a trail. Ruinate woodland normally has fewer species than natural forest at the same level.

BREADTH OF HABITAT OF EACH SPECIES

A habitat-altitude diagram has been prepared in Fig. 6 for each of

the extant Jamaican land birds. This and all the other information
on particular species in this chapter is documented under the species
concerned in Part 2.   Fig. 6 is schematic, and altitudes should not be
read precisely, because the birds are influenced primarily by the type
of vegetation, which also depends on rainfall and type of soil, as

FIG. 6. *Altitudinal ranges of Jamaican birds in natural forest in summer.*

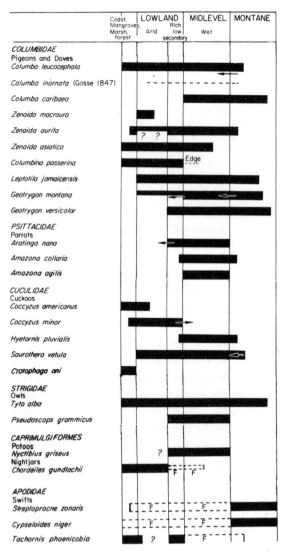

Fig. 6 continued

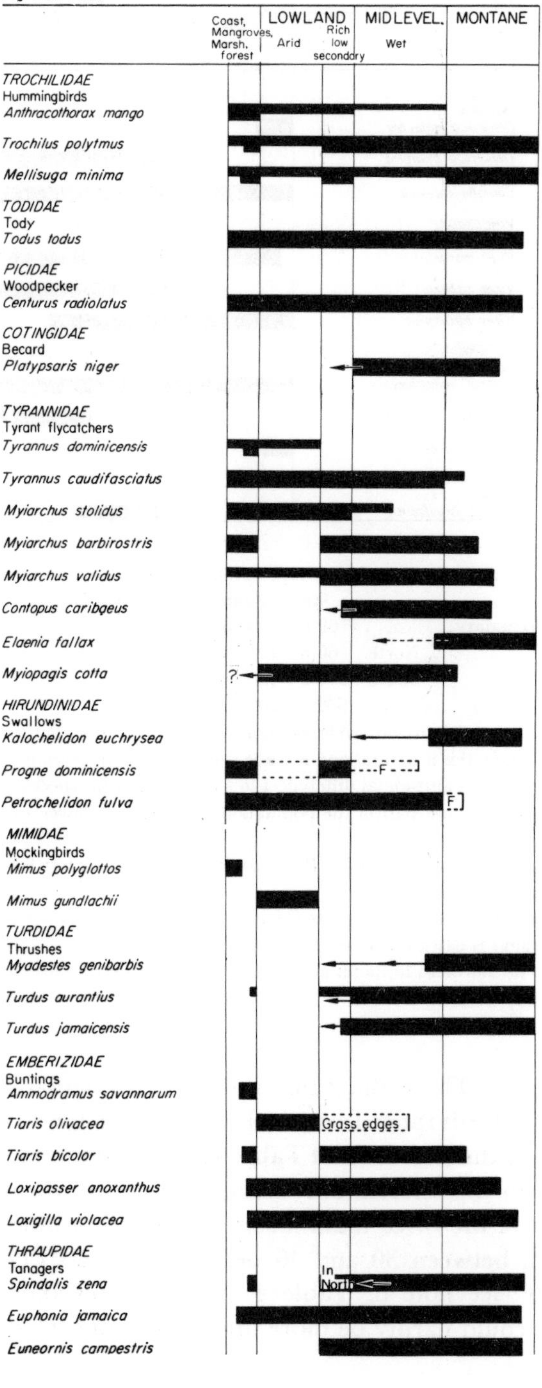

	Coast, Mangroves, Marsh, forest	LOWLAND Arid	Rich low secondary	MIDLEVEL. Wet	MONTANE

TROCHILIDAE
Hummingbirds
Anthracothorax mango

Trochilus polytmus

Mellisuga minima

TODIDAE
Tody
Todus todus

PICIDAE
Woodpecker
Centurus radiolatus

COTINGIDAE
Becard
Platypsaris niger

TYRANNIDAE
Tyrant flycatchers
Tyrannus dominicensis

Tyrannus caudifasciatus

Myiarchus stolidus

Myiarchus barbirostris

Myiarchus validus

Contopus caribaeus

Elaenia fallax

Myiopagis cotta

HIRUNDINIDAE
Swallows
Kalochelidon euchrysea

Progne dominicensis

Petrochelidon fulva

MIMIDAE
Mockingbirds
Mimus polyglottos

Mimus gundlachii

TURDIDAE
Thrushes
Myadestes genibarbis

Turdus aurantius

Turdus jamaicensis

EMBERIZIDAE
Buntings
Ammodramus savannarum

Tiaris olivacea

Tiaris bicolor

Loxipasser anoxanthus

Loxigilla violacea

THRAUPIDAE
Tanagers
Spindalis zena

Euphonia jamaica

Euneornis campestris

Fig. 6 continued

	Coast, Mangroves, Marsh, forest	LOWLAND		MIDLEVEL	MONTANE
		Arid	Rich low secondary	Wet	
PARULIDAE Warblers *Dendroica petechia*	⇐▭				
Dendroica pharetra				⇐▬▬▬▬▬▬	
Coereba flaveola	▬▬▬▬▬▬▬▬▬▬▬▬▬				
VIREONIDAE Vireos *Vireo modestus*	▬▬▬▬▬▬▬▬▬▬▬▬				
Vireo osburni				▬▬▬▬▬▬▬	
Vireo altiloquus	▬▬▬▬▬▬▬▬▬▬				
ICTERIDAE Icterids *Icterus leucopteryx*	▬▬▬▬▬▬▬▬▬▬▬▬▬▬▬				
Nesopsar nigerrimus				▬▬▬▬▬	
Quiscalus niger	▬▬				
CORVIDAE Crow *Corvus jamaicensis*				▬▬▬	

Notes (i) The altitudinal range of each type of forest varies with aspect and rainfall:
Lowland arid.................. 0m— 200m a.s.l. in the south
Rich lowland secondary......... 100m— 300m
Wet-Midlevel............North 60m—1200m
South 300m—1200m
Montane....................... 600m—2000m

(ii) The ranges refer solely to natural forest, not wooded cultivation, but wood-edge is included (and specified) where this is natural and not due solely to human clearing.

(iii) Bar width denotes altitudinal differences in abundance of the species.

(iv) The arrows mean that part of the population descends to a lower altitude in winter (and in one species rarely ascends).

(v) A double interrupted line labelled F means feeding is regular but breeding does not take place at the altitude concerned.

(vi) A single interrupted line is used for *Columba inornata* because the species is almost extinct, and its former range is based on Gosse (1847).

(vii) Ranges in the northern lowlands are not shown. In general they are similar to those of rich lowland secondary on the south side.

already noted. These diagrams show, in particular, how many of the Jamaican birds range from the lowlands through to the mountains. The figures in the lower half of Table 4 show that this applies to roughly one half of them, whereas only about one-fifth of them are restricted to only one of the three main levels. Even with a more rigorous type of selection, between 30 and 40 per cent of the species occur at all three levels (see note ii, Table 4). Yet the lowlands and the Blue Mountains could hardly be more different from each other in climate or in the type of forest which they support, and it is almost incredible to the visiting birdwatcher that they should have so many species of birds in common.

In contrast, however, there are four Jamaican land birds which are even more restricted in habitat than to just one of the three main levels, the dove *Zenaida macroura* to arid ruinate woodland with grassland near sea level in the southwest, the cuckoo *Coccyzus americanus* to marsh forest and probably arid ruinate woodland near sea level, the mockingbird *Mimus gundlachii* to the thicker parts of natural arid lowland forest and the warbler *Dendroica petechia* to mangroves, arid woodland near the shore and the borders of rivers near sea level. It is also possible that the ani *Crotophaga ani*, mockingbird *Mimus polyglottos* and grackle *Quiscalus niger* were formerly restricted in their natural habitats on Jamaica, but they are now widespread in cultivation. Similarly in montane forest the icterid *Nesopsar nigerrimus* is restricted to the more humid parts rich in small bromeliads. But these few species are the exception; nearly all Jamaican species have broad habitats.

COMPARISON WITH DOMINICA

To see whether broad habitats are characteristic of other West Indian islands, we made a similar, but inevitably brief survey of the land birds on one of the small mountainous islands. For this purpose we chose the magnificent Dominica, indeed it virtually chooses itself, since it has much more extensive forests than any other of the Lesser Antilles, of which it is the last that can be visualised as Columbus saw them, and on Mount Diablotin in the north it might still be possible to walk from the shore to the peak through forest the whole way.

Dominica is a little closer than Jamaica to the nearest mainland, 550 compared with 650 km, but this is rather misleading because the mainland in question is South America and, as discussed in Chapter 11, Dominica probably received many of its birds from the north. It is much smaller than Jamaica, 800 compared with 11,400 sq. km, and rather lower, rising to 1450 m compared with 2260 m. It has four main types of forest: the lowland leeward semi-deciduous is less arid than that on Jamaica; the lowland windward evergreen persists only as a few remnants, so that our species-list for it is incomplete; the

midlevel rain forest is grander than anything on Jamaica; and the
montane thicket is reminiscent of that of the John Crow mountains
(Beard 1949).

Our observations, set out in Appendix 4, justify only the bald
summary in Table 5, which shows that rather over half of the resident
species of land birds on Dominica occur in both the lowlands and the
highlands, if anything a higher proportion than on Jamaica, yet the
forests in question are as dissimilar from each other as are those of
Jamaica. Note ii to Table 5 shows that more species reside in the semi-
arid lowlands than in rain forest and more in rain forest than in
montane thicket.

TABLE 5.   *Habitat distribution of land birds on Dominica*

	Number of species
Both lowland and highland forest (including 2 not seen by us)	22 (56%)
Lowland forest and cleared edges of highland	4
Solely lowland forest	5 (28%)
Solely lowland cultivation	2
Solely highland forest	6 (15%)

Notes   (i) **Based** on our field observations in June 1971 and 1972 summarised in the two parts
of Appendix 4 (p. 366). Lowland forest includes the semi-arid leeward and very small areas of
the evergreen windward; highland forest includes midlevel rain forest and montane thicket
on the tops.
(ii) Of the 39 resident species of land birds, 32 are in the leeward lowlands (but 2 solely in cultivation), about 27 in rain forest and about 19 in montane thicket (on the assumption that of the
two species that we did not see, one lives in lowland forest and rain forest and the other in lowland
forest, rain forest and montane thicket). The lowland windward forest is too fragmentary for a
complete species list.

COMPARISON WITH HONDURAS

The situation on the two islands is in marked contrast to that on the
mainland. Fortunately a full survey of the habitats of the birds on
the nearest part of the mainland to Jamaica, namely Honduras,
has been made by Monroe (1968). His tables give only the typical
species for each habitat, but he set out full details under each species,
from which I made the appropriate additions, which Monroe kindly
checked *in litt*. Appendix 5, summarised in Table 6, shows that there
are more types of forest in Honduras than on the islands, and that
about 60 per cent of the breeding species are restricted to only one
type of forest. Nearly all the other species are found in only two,
occasionally three, different types of habitat at the same altitude

TABLE 6. *Habitats of breeding land birds (pigeons to passerines) in Honduras (based on Monroe 1968)*

A. SUMMARY

		Number of species	
(a) solely one habitat		249	(64%)
(b) edge of lowland dry and humid forest		59	(15%)
(c) more than one habitat at same altitude		57	(15%)
(d) lowland and montane		24	(6%)

B. DETAILS
(a) *Solely one habitat*

(1) lowland rain forest		
(including 45 spp. also in low montane)		144
(2) lowland monsoon and vega (deciduous)		4
(3) lowland pine, including pine savanna		5
(4) lowland arid forest		
(including 5 spp. solely on islands)		20
(5) mangroves		2
(6) marshes		1
(7) cloud forest		47
(8) highland pine-oak forest		19
(9) highland steppe		3
(10) highland aerial feeders		4

(b) *Edge*

(11) edge of lowland arid and humid forest	59

(c) *More than one habitat at same altitude*

(1,2) lowland rain forest and vega	14
(2,4) vega and lowland arid forest	17
(2,3,4) vega, lowland pine and lowland arid	1
(3,4) lowland pine and arid forest	3
(4,5) lowland arid and mangroves	1
(7,8) montane, i.e. cloud forest and pine-oak	21

(d) *Lowland and montane habitats*

(1,7) lowland rain and cloud forest	7
(1,2,7) lowland rain, vega and cloud forest	1
(1,2,7,8) lowland rain, vega, cloud forest and pine-oak	1
(2,7) vega and cloud forest	1
(2,8) vega and highland pine-oak	1
(3,4,8) lowland pine, lowland arid and highland pine-oak	1
(3,4) lowland pine and highland pine-oak	12
TOTAL	389

C. TOTALS FOR SOME FOREST HABITATS

Lowland rain forest	167
Monsoon forest and vega	39
Lowland arid forest (including mangroves and pine)	62
Montane forest (cloud and pine-oak)	111
All lowland forest	235 (+ 59 edge)

Notes (i) Low montane forest is not counted as a separate habitat because it is transitional between lowland rain forest and montane forest and so is its bird population, and no species is confined to it.

(ii) The basis of these figures is the set of tabulations by Monroe (1968), modified as shown in Appendix 5.

(most of them in the lowlands). Only 6 per cent occur in both the
lowlands and the mountains, compared with about 50 per cent of
the resident species on Jamaica or Dominica. It is reasonable to link
at least part of this big difference with competition for habitat between
the 389 resident species of land birds in Honduras compared with
only 65 species on Jamaica.

COMPETITIVE EXCLUSION BY A DIFFERENCE IN HABITAT

On the mainland, most congeneric species of passerine birds, and
many of other land birds, occupy separate habitats, presumably
through competitive exclusion (Lack 1971). My analysis of Monroe's
data suggests that this holds for just over half the congeneric species
of land birds in Honduras with respect to the types of habitat set out
in Table 6, namely to 115 out of a possible 222 species pairs, or 52
per cent. Moreover this is a minimal figure, for it is likely that other
pairs of species are separated by a difference in habitat within one of
these main forest types, and any such pairs would not be separated
in my analysis.

On Jamaica, in contrast, only 2 out of the 20 possible congeneric
pairs of species are separated by a difference in habitat, and one of
these may not be due to competitive exclusion. The clearest case is
that of the two mockingbirds in the genus *Mimus* of which *M.gundlachii*
is restricted to more or less closed natural arid lowland forest and
M.polyglottos to open arid woodland, including strand woodland
and the wood-edge, and the two species are seen together solely at the
boundary of their respective habitats. Secondly, of the two resident
Dendroica warblers, *D.petechia* breeds solely in mangroves and in arid
or riverine woodland near sea level, and *D.pharetra* solely in montane
forest and high up in midlevel forest. They are leaf-gleaners of similar
size, so each might possibly be excluding the other from its habitat,
but this seems unlikely since competitive exclusion is certainly not
responsible for the boundary between them, where there is a large
area of arid lowland woodland in which neither occurs. The other
genera with more than one species on Jamaica, not separated by habitat,
are *Columba* (3), *Zenaida* (3), *Geotrygon* (2), *Amazona* (2), *Coccyzus* (2),
Tyrannus (2), *Myiarchus* (3), *Turdus* (2), *Vireo* (3) and *Tiaris* (2).

Competitive exclusion in relation to habitat is important only
where the species concerned have similar feeding habits and so cannot

coexist, while the same holds for exclusion by geographical range. In mainland birds, exclusion by range or by habitat is normally found only between congeneric species, but on oceanic islands it is found at times between species in different genera, presumably because feeding niches on islands tend to be broader, and thus species in different genera may be potential competitors. I earlier gave examples of this which had resulted in exclusion by geographical range for various island birds, including some in the West Indies (Lack 1971). Similarly there are two possible examples on Jamaica of competitive exclusion with respect to habitat between species which feed in a similar way but are in different genera. Neither, however, is at all certain. First, of the two large hummingbirds, *Anthracothorax mango* lives chiefly in open lowland forest and *Trochilus polytmus* chiefly in closed lowland forest and in the highlands, so that they are at least partly separated by habitat; but they meet in parts of the lowland forest and *A.mango* is so much larger that it may be suspected that they also differ significantly from each other in their feeding. Secondly, the two swallows *Petrochelidon fulva* and *Kalochelidon euchrysea* appear to feed similarly, and while *P.fulva* breeds in the lowlands and the limestone hills, but not in the Blue Mountains, *K.euchrysea* used formerly to breed in the highest parts of the limestone hills and presumably also in the Blue Mountains (where it was common). Hence these two species might have been separated from each other by altitude, though with an overlap in the high limestone hills. *K.euchrysea,* however, is nearly extinct, so it is not possible to check this.

FACTORS LIMITING HABITAT

I stated in Chapter 1 that many workers (once including myself) have attributed the broad ecological niches of land birds on remote islands to the failure of other species with similar feeding habits to reach the islands in question; whereas I now attribute it to a tendency for fewer species with broader niches to oust a greater number of more specialised species under conditions of ecological poverty. I find it hard to conceive that the latter principle is in operation directly in relation to the broad habitats of the Jamaican land birds. However, with at the most only four pairs, and very possibly only one pair, of Jamaican land bird species limited in habitat through competitive exclusion, one must anyway seek elsewhere for the main factors limiting their habitats. Far and away the most likely limiting factor to be involved is their feeding requirements, each species occurring wherever its feeding requirements allow it to survive (nesting requirements might have a very secondary influence in the swallow *Petrochelidon fulva*, which uses holes in limestone). If this view is correct, then the unusually broad habitats of the Jamaican land birds may be simply a result of broad feeding niches and if the competition between species is for food, then I can understand that a smaller number of generalised species might be excluding a greater number of specialists. But the evidence available in this chapter does not allow one to decide whether this view, or the failure of many mainland species to reach Jamaica, is the more likely factor to be concerned.

HABITATS OF SAME OR CLOSELY RELATED SPECIES ON JAMAICA AND IN HONDURAS

It is of interest to see whether the general trend for broader habitats on Jamaica than on the mainland in Honduras holds for the species which they have in common. The summary in Table 7 shows that 6 of the 15 species concerned have similar habitats. But four, the pigeon *Columba leucocephala*, the dove *Leptotila jamaicensis*, the Bananaquit *Coereba flaveola* and evidently the owl *Tyto alba*, which are restricted to the lowlands in Honduras, are also regular at midlevels and in the mountains on Jamaica. A fifth species, the dove *Geotrygon montana*, restricted to humid forest in Honduras, on Jamaica occurs not only in humid forest but is regular, though scarce, in arid lowland forest (and common in the semi-arid lowland leeward forest on Dominica). A sixth species, the warbler *Dendroica petechia*, restricted to mangroves on the mainland, breeds not only in the mangroves but also in riverine and arid forest near the sea on Jamaica. In two other species, the cuckoo *Coccyzus minor* and the swift *Streptoprocne zonaris*, there are minor differences in habitat between the two countries; whether this also applies to the potoo *Nyctibius griseus*, is uncertain.

A similar comparison can be made between Jamaican species and species in the same species-group in Honduras. It is tempting to include as many of such pairs of species as possible, but I have used strict criteria, as set out in the footnote to Table 8. Of the 16 cases involved, the habitat is similar in 4. In 7 others, a species which in Honduras is restricted to the lowlands extends to the mountains

TABLE 7. *Habitats of native Jamaican birds which also breed in Honduras*

Species	Forest habitat in Jamaica	Habitat in Honduras
pigeon *Columba leucocephala*	low, mid, high	(4) lowland arid (isles)
dove *Zenaida asiatica*	low, (mid)	(4) lowland arid
dove *Columbina passerina*	low	(4) lowland arid
dove *Leptotila jamaicensis*	low, mid, (high)	(4) lowland arid (isles)
dove *Geotrygon montana*	low, mid, high	(1) lowland rain forest up to lower cloud forest
cuckoo *Coccyzus minor*	low (not mangroves)	(5) mangroves (and (4) arid low elsewhere)
ani *Crotophaga ani*	low (marsh forest)	(4) lowland arid (isles)
owl *Tyto alba*	low, mid, high	(11) open lowlands, dry and humid
potoo *Nyctibius griseus*	low, mid	(11) open wooded lowlands, dry and humid
swift *Streptoprocne zonaris*	high (air)	(11) open lowlands (air)
swift *Cypseloides niger*	high (air)	(10) highlands (air)
bunting *Ammodramus savannarum*	low (grassland)	(3) lowland pine savanna (grass)
grassquit *Tiaris olivacea*	low, mid (edge)	(11) middle heights, grassland
warbler *Dendroica petechia*	low (mangroves, riverine)	(5) mangroves
bananaquit *Coereba flaveola*	low, mid, high	(11) rain forest edge and second growth

Notes (i) Figures in brackets refer to habitats in Table 6.

(ii) Habitats in Honduras are from Monroe (1968), except for *Coereba flaveola*, which is too rare there for evaluation, so for this species I have given the habitat in other parts of Central America. Note that *Coccyzus minor*, in Honduras in mangroves, is in other parts of Central America also in arid lowland woodland.

on Jamaica, namely the pigeon *Columba inornata,* the woodpecker *Centurus,* the flycatchers *Myiarchus* and *Myiopagis,* the two pairs of *Vireo* species and the oriole *Icterus;* an eighth, the parakeet *Aratinga,* extends to the highest parts of the midlevels on Jamaica, so might well be included in this group. Two other lowland species in Honduras breed on Jamaica only at midlevels and in the mountains, namely the becard *Platypsaris* and pewee *Contopus* (and both descend to the lowland hills of Jamaica in winter). The *Amazona* parrots have a more restricted habitat on Jamaica than in Honduras. The altitudinal range of the nighthawk *Chordeiles* is also wider in Honduras than on Jamaica, presumably owing to its preference for pinelands, which

TABLE 8.   *Habitats of native Jamaican birds and of species in same species-group in Honduras*

Jamaican species	Habitat in Jamaica	Honduran species	Habitat in Honduras
pigeon *Columba inornata*	low, mid, high	*C.flavirostris*	(1,2) rain forest, vega
pigeon *Columba caribaea*	mid, high	*C.fasciata*	(8) high pine-oak
parrots *Amazona agilis* *A.collaria*	mainly mid	*A.albifrons*	(2,4) vega, lowland and high arid
parakeet *Aratinga nana*	low, mid	*A.astec*	(1,2) open rain forest, vega
nighthawk *Chordeiles gundlachii*	low, (mid) open	*C.minor*	(3,8) lowland and high pine
woodpecker *Centurus radiolatus*	low, mid, high	*C.aurifrons*	(2,4) vega and lowland arid
becard *Platypsaris niger*	mid, high	*Platypsaris (aglaiae)*	(2,4) vega and lowland arid
flycatcher *Myiarchus barbirostris*	low, mid, high	*M.tuberculifer*	(11) open woodland, mainly lowland
flycatcher *Contopus caribaeus*	mid, high	*C.cinereus*	(2,4) open vega and lowland arid
flycatcher *Myiopagis cotta*	low, mid, high	*M.viridicata*	(2,4) open vega and lowland arid
martin *Progne dominicensis*	low, (mid)	*P.chalybea*	(11) open lowlands
mockingbird *Mimus polyglottos*	low (cultivation)	*M.gilvus*	(4) lowland arid
solitaire *Myadestes genibarbis*	mid, high	*M.unicolor*	(7,8) cloud forest
vireo *Vireo modestus*	low, mid, high	*V.pallens*	(5) mangroves (and (4) lowland arid elsewhere)
vireo *Vireo altiloquus*	low, mid, high	*V.magister*	(4,5) mangroves, lowland arid
oriole *Icterus leucopteryx*	low, mid, high	*I.pustulatus*	(4) lowland arid

Notes   (i) Figures in brackets refer to the habitats given in Table 6.

(ii) Of these pairs, the species of parakeet *Aratinga*, nighthawk *Chordeiles*, elaenia *Myiopagis* and mockingbird *Mimus* are so close that some authors treat the Jamaican and Honduran birds as conspecific. Nearly all the rest are generally accepted as being in the same species-group. This includes the becards *Platypsaris*, all the species of which are allopatric, though the specific mainland ancestor of the Jamaican bird is uncertain. The two pewees *Contopus*, together with the Lesser Antillean species, were at one time in a separate genus *Blacicus*. For the solitaires *Myadestes*, I have used my own judgement. Bond linked the Jamaican thrush *Turdus jamaicensis* with the Central and South American *T.albicollis* (*sens. strict.*). The latter is not in Honduras, where occurs the closely related *T.assimilis,* which various authors treat as conspecific; but it is not very like *T.jamaicensis,* so I thought it best to exclude it. Further details of species relationships are set out in Part 2.

(iii) For a similar analysis of the habitats in Honduras of species or related species also found on Cuba or Hispaniola, but not Jamaica, see Table 20, p. 137.

occur in both lowlands and mountains in Honduras.

In summary, of the Jamaican species which also occur, or have a closely related species, in Honduras, about half have broader habitats on Jamaica, in nearly all cases because a species confined to the lowlands in Honduras extends from the lowlands to the mountains on Jamaica. There is also one species which lives in humid forest in Honduras, but which also extends to arid lowlands on Jamaica, and several other species show minor differences in habitat. In about one quarter of the species the habitat is similar in the two lands.

HABITAT IN RELATION TO ENDEMISM

In Chapter 1 a tendency for the endemic birds of oceanic islands to be found especially in montane forest was mentioned, and Ricklefs (1970) found that this holds on Jamaica. The figures set out in Table 9, though small, support this view, for 81 per cent of the endemic species occur in the mountains, compared with only 45 per cent of the forms

TABLE 9. *Habitat in relation to endemism of Jamaican birds*

	Number of resident species in summer				
	Endemic Jamaican species	Endemic Jamaican subspecies	Not endemic to Jamaica	Total	Endemic Antillean genus
Only arid lowlands	0	5	5	10	0
Only wet midlevels	2	0	0	2	0
Lowlands and midlevels	3	2	6	11	1
Midlevels and mountains	7	3	0	10	2
Lowlands, midlevels, mountains	14	9	9	32	10
Total	26	19	20	65	13

Note Based on the information in Table 1.

which are not endemic (the figure for the endemic sub-species being similar to that for those which are not endemic).

Ricklefs claimed further that the Jamaican forms which are not endemic tend to have broader habitats than the endemic species, but the figures in Table 9 show that this is not so, for only 8 per cent of the endemic species, but 25 per cent of the forms that are not endemic, are restricted to one of the three main habitats on Jamaica (the figure for the endemic subspecies again being similar to that for those which are not endemic).

In this analysis, endemism was considered in relation to Jamaica alone, but some species which are not endemic to Jamaica belong to genera endemic to the Antilles, so might reasonably have been included among the endemics. The figures in the right-hand column of Table 9 show that 12 of the 13 species concerned occur in the mountains and 10 of them have broad habitats, ranging from the lowlands to the mountains, while none are restricted to a single habitat.

It is reasonable to link the high degree of endemism in the montane species to montane forest being the most peculiar habitat on Jamaica, because of which one might expect its birds to be the most different from those elsewhere. In contrast, the arid forest of the lowlands has close counterparts on the other Greater Antilles and on the mainland. I cannot suggest why so many of the endemic species, and of the species in endemic Antillean genera, should have broad habitats. (This fact is contrary to the view developed by Ricklefs (1970) and Ricklefs and Cox (1972), on the taxon cycle in Jamaican birds, in which they postulate that the endemic species tend to lose their formerly broad habitats.)

OTHER SPECIES THAN THE RESIDENT PIGEONS TO PASSERINES

The land birds which visit Jamaica for the winter, most of which are parulid warblers, present so many different problems from the breeding species that they are treated separately in Chapter 12. Most of them, like the native Jamaican birds, have broad habitats.

At least most of the raptorial, marsh and water birds on Jamaica listed in Table 3 have habitats similar to those they have on the mainland. I noted, however, that while the Turkey Vulture *Cathartes aura* is widespread at all altitudes in open forest, cultivation, villages and towns on Jamaica, on Trinidad it is restricted to the forested hills and the Black Vulture *Coragyps atratus*, absent from Jamaica, is the common species of the cultivated lowlands and the towns (Herklots 1961). The relationship between these two species elsewhere would be worth study. Also the Limpkin *Aramus guarauna*, restricted in various other lands to lowland swamps, on Jamaica also occurs in midlevel wet limestone forest, where it was formerly widespread in the west (Gosse 1847) and we saw it in the John Crow mountains.

SUMMARY

A habitat altitude diagram is set out for all 65 extant species of land birds. On Jamaica, lowland arid forest and midlevel wet forest support a similar number of resident species, but there are fewer species in the mountains. Here and on Dominica, about half the species of land birds occur in both lowlands and mountains, whereas in Honduras only 6 per cent do so. The more restricted habitats of the Honduras birds are presumably due, at least partly, to the much greater number of resident species in Honduras and the resulting competition. Thus in Honduras over half the congeneric species are segregated from each other by habitat, compared with at most four and perhaps only one pair of species on Jamaica. The broad habitats of the Jamaican birds are probably limited by their feeding requirements; but a very few species have restricted habitats. Of the Jamaican species also present in Honduras, or with a closely related species present there, about half have broader habitats on Jamaica, nearly all of these being species of the arid lowlands in Honduras which extend from there into the mountains on Jamaica. A higher proportion of the endemic Jamaican species, and of the species in endemic Antillean genera, than of the species that are not endemic, occur in the mountains, and they also tend to have broader habitats than those which are not endemic, many of them extending down to the lowlands.

The Jamaican and Dominican land birds have broader habitats than those in Honduras, which is linked with the much greater number of species in Honduras; but the available evidence does not enable one to decide whether the paucity of species on the islands is due to fewer generalised species excluding more specialists through competition, or to the failure of many further species to reach the islands through difficulties of dispersal.

CHAPTER 4 · COMPETITION FOR FOOD

In view of what was said in the previous chapter, it looks as though competition for food might be the key factor in determining which species of land birds occur on Jamaica. Unfortunately, while in a year's visit the main habitat of each species can be determined with reasonable certainty, it takes much longer to establish its food requirements. Indeed, the feeding habits of the species in a single genus could well make a full year's study, particularly if it was critical to analyse potential competition between similar species. Hence the findings in the present chapter are tentative. Nevertheless, the differences in feeding between many of the species are so great that generalisations are possible which, I consider, throw light on the central problems discussed in this book.

In the discussion which follows, all references to the foods of particular species are documented in the annotated list in Part 2 under the species concerned, and to save space, this point is not repeated again. We studied feeding particularly in the small species (i.e. the species included in the standard sequence in the families from swifts to passerines inclusive). We did this primarily by observations on how and where the birds feed, and we also collected any fruits that we found them taking when these were accessible (and often they were not); but we did not make stomach analyses or attempt in other ways to identify the insects and other animal foods, nor, though we observed throughout the year, did we make special observations on foods brought to the young. We did not study critically the feeding of the large birds (i.e. those in the sequence of families from pigeons to nightjars inclusive, or the crow) the more so because, owing to their shyness, they do not often allow themselves to be seen feeding for long.

The main types of feeding and food are summarised in Table 10 for the species which depend on animal prey and in Table 11 for those which eat mainly plant foods. Out of the 66 known land birds (the total is 66, not the 65 used in the previous chapter, because the extinct parauque *Siphonorhis americanus* can reasonably be included among the animal feeders), 29 depend on animal food, 22 on plant matter, normally fruit or seeds, and 15 take both many insects and much plant matter (normally fruit or nectar).

PREDATORS ON VERTEBRATES

In the families from pigeons to passerines inclusive, the only species which prey mainly on vertebrates are the two owls, *Tyto alba*, which feeds on rats and some birds in open country, and *Pseudoscops grammicus*, which feeds on mice and beetles in forest. Hence they differ from each other, and also from the three raptorial species (not treated here), the carrion-feeding vulture *Cathartes aura*, the large hawk *Buteo jamaicensis* and the small falcon *Falco sparverius*. In addition lizards form part, but probably only a small part, of the prey of the cuckoos, notably *Saurothera vetula*, of the three largest flycatchers and of the grackle *Quiscalus niger*.

PREDATORS ON INSECTS

All the species which take many insects are included in Table 10, irrespective of whether they also take much vegetable matter. Fruit, where included, is usually a subsidiary diet. The special interest of this section is to see whether each species depends primarily on different sources of food from every other. As already stressed, our information is much too sparse to determine this with certainty. On the other hand, the principle of competitive exclusion is now so firmly established for birds, especially insectivorous birds (Lack 1971), that suggestive evidence is of value. As will be seen, the available evidence favours the view that each species is segregated from the rest, omitting a few species whose feeding habits are little known, and there is no evidence whatever pointing in the opposite direction, to suggest that any two insectivorous Jamaican birds depend on the same main source of food. In the summary which follows, it is assumed that the only *potential* competitors of each species are those set out under the same sub-heading for feeding in Table 10.

TABLE 10.   *Feeding methods of Jamaican land birds which prey mainly on
animals (primarily on insects except for the two owls)*

Crepuscular: 5 spp.

    owl *Tyto alba*
    owl *Pseudoscops grammicus*
    potoo *Nyctibius griseus*
    nightjar *Chordeiles gundlachii*
    nightjar *Siphonorhis americanus*

Diurnal hawking: 6 spp.

    swift *Streptoprocne zonaris*
    swift *Cypseloides niger*
    swift *Tachornis phoenicobia*
    martin *Kalochelidon euchrysea*
    martin *Progne dominicensis*
    martin *Petrochelidon fulva*

Flycatching, *i.e.* sallying from perch into air: 2 spp.

    flycatcher *Tyrannus dominicensis*
    flycatcher *Contopus caribaeus*

Pouncing, *i.e.* sallying from perch to ground: 1 sp.

    flycatcher *Tyrannus caudifasciatus*

Leaf-snatching, *i.e.* sallying from perch to leaf: 8 spp.

    tody *Todus todus*
    becard *Platypsaris niger* (and fruit)
    flycatcher *Myiarchus stolidus*
    flycatcher *Myiarchus barbirostris*
    flycatcher *Myiarchus validus* (and fruit)
    flycatcher *Elaenia fallax* (and fruit)
    flycatcher *Myiopagis cotta*
    solitaire *Myadestes genibarbis* (and fruit)

Gleaning from leaves or twigs: 10 spp.
    cuckoo *Coccyzus americanus*
    cuckoo *Coccyzus minor*
    cuckoo *Hyetornis pluvialis*
    cuckoo *Saurothera vetula*
    warbler *Dendroica petechia*
    warbler *Dendroica pharetra*
    bananaquit *Coereba flaveola* (and nectar)
    vireo *Vireo modestus*
    vireo *Vireo osburni*
    vireo *Vireo altiloquus* (and fruit)

(cont.)

TABLE 10 (cont.)

From trunks, under bark, or in epiphytes: 3 spp.

    woodpecker *Centurus radiolatus*
    oriole *Icterus leucopteryx* (and fruit)
    icterid *Nesopsar nigerrimus*

On ground: 6 spp.

    ani *Crotophaga ani* (and rarely fruit)
    mockingbird *Mimus polyglottos* (and fruit)
    mockingbird *Mimus gundlachii* (and fruit)
    thrush *Turdus aurantius* (and fruit)
    thrush *Turdus jamaicensis* (and fruit)
    grackle *Quiscalus niger*

Minute insects off leaves or in air: 3 spp.

    hummingbird *Anthracothorax mango* (and nectar)
    hummingbird *Trochilus polytmus* (and nectar)
    hummingbird *Mellisuga minima* (and nectar)

Notes (i) Each species is entered only once, under its commonest method of feeding on animals. (ii) In all, 29 species depend primarily on animals, and another 15 on animals and either fruit or nectar.

Crepuscular feeders

Of the 5 species, the two owls have already been considered. The potoo *Nyctibius griseus* takes large insects on the wing near trees at dusk, while the much smaller extinct parauque *Siphonorhis americanus* presumably took much smaller insects in woodland at dusk. The nighthawk *Chordeiles gundlachii* differs in habitat, and hawks in the open.

Diurnal hawking

Of the 6 species, the two large swifts *Streptoprocne zonaris* and *Cypseloides niger* and the large martin *Progne dominicensis* hunt mainly in the open above the trees, the two swifts especially over the mountains, but descending to the lowlands at dawn, dusk or with rain, the martin chiefly in the lowlands and not normally feeding with the swifts. The two swifts, which differ in size, are almost certainly separated by where they feed, as detailed in the annotated list.

The other three diurnal hawking species are much smaller and much more capable of manoeuvre in flight. They take insects close to vegetation, the swift *Tachornis phoenicobia* with rapid wingbeats and dashing twists and turns, and the two swallows in more leisurely fashion, which suggests that they depend on different prey from the small swift, which in any case does not usually feed in company with them. The two swallows were partly separated by habitat, *Kalochelidon euchrysea* in the mountains and *Petrochelidon fulva* lower down, but *K.euchrysea* is almost extinct, so the possible differences between them cannot now be studied.

Flycatching, Pouncing

Of the three flycatchers comprising these two groups, the large *Tyrannus dominicensis* flies out from a perch in open wooded country into the open to take large insects in the air, and the much smaller *Contopus caribaeus* flies out from a perch inside the forest to take small insects in the air well below the canopy, while the large *Tyrannus caudifasciatus* flies out from a perch at the wood-edge, usually to take a large insect off the ground.

Leaf-snatching

Watching from a perch and then sallying out to take an insect off a leaf on a nearby tree or bush by snatching or hovering is a common method of feeding in the tropics (Orians 1969). It enables larger passerine birds than the warblers to take insect prey, particularly, perhaps, on the outer edges of trees. There are 8 species in this group on Jamaica. Of these the tody *T.todus* is a specialist, looking upward from a perch well below the canopy and flying to take an insect, often of relatively large size, from the underside of a broad leaf. It taps a different source from the other seven leaf-snatchers. Five of the latter are flycatchers, of which the three species of *Myiarchus* differ from each other markedly in size of beak and presumably size of prey, and partly in habitat and ways of feeding, while the two elaenias *Elaenia fallax* (a summer visitor) and *Myiopagis cotta*, are yet smaller, and are separated from each other largely by habitat. Probably each of these five depends on a different main source of food, as set out in more detail in Part 2 and Table 44 (p. 295). The becard *Platypsaris niger* also takes insects by snatching, but we rarely saw it feed, which probably means that it takes larger (and hence scarcer) prey than the flycatchers. Finally, the solitaire *Myadestes genibarbis* depends in part on leaf-snatching, but also flycatches and pounces, and it takes much more fruit than the flycatchers (except *E.fallax*). As explained in Part 2, we saw it taking insects too rarely for critical comment, but it feeds at least in part on different sources from the flycatchers. In all, 8 of the 66 Jamaican land birds are mainly leaf-snatchers, which is less than half the proportion found by Orians (1969) in five lowland and one lower montane forest in Costa Rica, but a similar proportion to that which he found in a high montane forest. So it may be noted that all 8 of the Jamaican species concerned breed in montane forest, but 5 of them also in lowland forest.

Leaf and twig gleaners

In this group of 10 species, we did not study the feeding of the four large species, all cuckoos, which take their prey from leaves or twigs while perched. However, the big, rather short, beak of *Hyetornis pluvialis,* the long dagger-shaped beak of *Saurothera vetula* and the smaller beak of *Coccyzus minor* are so different from each other that they are presumably adapted to mainly different types of prey. The fourth species, *Coccyzus americanus,* is a scarce summer visitor to part of the habitat of *C.minor,* and it is not known whether, or how, it might be separated from it.

Of the three small narrow-beaked leaf-gleaners, the two warblers are separated from each other by habitat, *Dendroica petechia* being found near the coast and *D.pharetra* in the highlands. The Bananaquit *Coereba flaveola* occurs in many habitats where both of them are absent and also differs from them in taking much nectar; nor did we see it gleaning for insects from the same types of leaves as did the warblers, but its insect diet needs further study to determine the extent to which it differs from them. The three vireos have thicker beaks than the warblers or Bananaquit, and probably take mainly larger insects. *Vireo altiloquus,* a summer visitor, takes large caterpillars and other insects in the leaves of the canopy, while *V.modestus* and *V.osburni* hunt below the canopy, taking insects off both leaves and twigs and finding them less frequently than the warblers. The larger *V.osburni* has a much thicker beak than *V.modestus,* so is presumably adapted to different types of prey.

Tree-climbers

All three tree-climbers are specialists, the woodpecker *Centurus radio-latus* excavating in wood like most others of its family, the oriole *Icterus leucopteryx* stripping off bark for the insects under it, and the icterid *Nesopsar nigerrimus* rummaging among epiphytes in montane forest.

Ground-feeders

Of the 6 species in this group the grackle *Quiscalus niger,* ani *Crotophaga ani* and mockingbird *Mimus polyglottos* feed in wooded grassland, the first two also in fields. We did not study their prey, but their beaks are so different in size and shape that they are clearly adapted to take different types of prey, the grackle often by probing in the soil. The other mockingbird, *M.gundlachii,* which lives inside natural lowland arid forest, is separated by habitat from *M.polyglottos* at the edge, and both are separated by habitat from the two forest thrushes. Of the latter, *Turdus aurantius* is the larger, with a longer beak, and it feeds more on the ground in the open than *T.jamaicensis,* but it is not at all clear whether, and if so how, these two thrushes might differ in diet.

Hummingbirds

All three hummingbirds feed on much smaller insects than any other Jamaican birds, and they take them in the air or off vegetation by hovering. The small *Mellisuga minima* perhaps feeds on smaller insects than the two larger species, *Anthracothorax mango* and *Trochilus polytmus.* The two latter are separated from each other largely by habitat, in open lowland and other types of forest respectively, but *A.mango* is also the larger, so might differ in diet as well.

This summary, amplified for particular species in the annotated list, provides suggestive evidence that each insectivorous bird species in Jamaica depends on a different main source of insect prey from every other; and I would reiterate that there is no positive evidence for thinking that any two species are not ecologically segregated, though all the species, and some in particular, need further study.

There are many more large insects in the tropics than at temperate latitudes (Schoener and Janzen 1968), and in conformity with this, there is a much higher proportion of large-beaked insectivorous birds in the tropics, the median size of the exposed culmen being 16 mm for tropical species, but only 11.8 mm for the species of temperate latitudes (Schoener 1971). It can be seen from the figures in Table 1 that the median figure for all Jamaican insectivorous species is near to 16 mm. Schoener also reported, though without precise figures, that montane has mainly smaller-beaked species than lowland tropical forest and there is a similar tendency on Jamaica.

TABLE 11.   *Main foods of Jamaican land birds which feed mostly on plants*

A. The smaller species

Fruit: 4 spp.

bullfinch *Loxipasser anoxanthus*
bullfinch *Loxigilla violacea* (probably seeds in fruit)
tanager *Spindalis zena*
tanager *Euphonia jamaica* (especially mistletoes)

Seeds: 3 spp.

finch *Ammodramus savannarum*
grassquit *Tiaris olivacea*
grassquit *Tiaris bicolor*

Fruit and nectar: 1 sp.

Orangequit *Euneornis campestris*

Fruit and insects (included in Table 10): 10 spp.

becard *Platypsaris niger*
flycatcher *Myiarchus validus*
flycatcher *Elaenia fallax*
mockingbird *Mimus polyglottos*
mockingbird *Mimus gundlachii*
solitaire *Myadestes genibarbis*
thrush *Turdus aurantius*
thrush *Turdus jamaicensis*
vireo *Vireo altiloquus*
oriole *Icterus leucopteryx*

Nectar and insects
(included in Table 10): 4 spp.

hummingbird *Anthracothorax mango*
hummingbird *Trochilus polytmus*
hummingbird *Mellisuga minima*
bananaquit *Coereba flaveola*

(*cont.*)

TABLE 11 (*cont.*)

B. The larger species,
not critically studied

pigeon *Columba leucocephala* (fruit, seeds)
pigeon *Columba inornata* (fruit, seeds)
pigeon *Columba caribaea* (fruit)
dove *Zenaida macroura* (seeds)
dove *Zenaida aurita* (seeds)
dove *Zenaida asiatica* (seeds, fruit)
dove *Columbina passerina* (seeds)
dove *Leptotila jamaicensis* (seeds)
dove *Geotrygon montana* (seeds, fallen fruit)
dove *Geotrygon versicolor* (seeds, fallen fruit)
parakeet *Aratinga nana* (fruit, seeds)
parrot *Amazona collaria* (fruit, seeds)
parrot *Amazona agilis* (fruit, ? seeds)
crow *Corvus jamaicensis* (fruit, ? seeds)

Notes (i) Each species is entered under only one heading, and there are some borderline cases.
(ii) In all, 22 species depend primarily on vegetable matter, primarily fruit or seeds, and another
14, also included in Table 10, eat fruit or nectar and many insects.

FRUGIVOROUS PASSERINE BIRDS

Whereas each insectivorous species takes mainly different prey, the
frugivorous birds of Jamaica overlap extensively with each other in
the fruits which they take. In north temperate regions, many species
that are normally segregated from each other in feeding, join to eat
fruits, but there, fruits constitute only a small fraction of the food
supply and are only temporarily superabundant (Lack 1946). The
situation in the tropics is different, in that fruits are available throughout the year (though each species of tree may have its own season), and
many more species of birds eat fruits. On Jamaica, for instance, one
third of the land birds include a substantial proportion of fruit in
their diet. Further, Snow (1971) has pointed out that whereas insects
are adapted for concealment (or distastefulness) from birds, fruits are
adapted for conspicuousness, as it is in the interests of their species
that birds should eat them. This leads to an unusual situation with
respect to potential competition for food among frugivorous birds.
In Trinidad, for instance, Snow and Snow (1971) found that nearly
all the species of tanagers depend on the same species of fruits, but
that each is separated in its diet from every other by its alternative

insect prey, with the exception of one of the euphonias, which does not take insects and specialises on the fruits of mistletoes, which the other tanagers do not take. Our much smaller number of observations suggest that the situation is similar among the frugivorous birds on Jamaica, though there are a few puzzling cases.

In Table 12, I have set out the passerine species on Jamaica which include a substantial proportion of fruit in their diet, and in Appendix 6 (p. 370) I have set out for these and a few other small species all the species of wild fruits which we saw them take. Each number in the table corresponds to one individual bird, irrespective of how many individual fruits we saw it take at the time. This shows the

TABLE 12. *Jamaican passerine species which take a substantial proportion of fruit in their diet*

Species	Number of feeding observations	Percentage on fruit	Main other foods
Platypsaris niger	few	?	insects off leaves
Myiarchus validus	38	32	insects off leaves
Elaenia fallax	75	36	insects off leaves
Mimus polyglottos	few	small?	insects on ground
Mimus gundlachii	few	small?	insects on ground
Myadestes genibarbis	50	68	insects, perhaps mainly off leaves
Turdus aurantius	71	41	invertebrates on ground
Turdus jamaicensis	few	large?	includes invertebrates on ground
Tiaris bicolor	53	28	grass seeds on ground
Loxipasser anoxanthus	80	54	flowers, seeds (not grass seeds)
Loxigilla violacea	119	81	flowers, seeds (not grass seeds)
Spindalis zena	116	78	flowers, leaves
Euphonia jamaica	81	63	flowers, leaves
Euneornis campestris	162	41	nectar
Coereba flaveola	187	24	nectar, insects off leaves
Vireo altiloquus	89	55	insects off canopy leaves
Icterus leucopteryx	88	16	invertebrates under bark

Note P.niger and M.gundlachii were seen feeding too rarely for any reliable figures. M.polyglottos and T.jamaicensis were seen to take fruits on 32 and 49 occasions respectively, but were recorded feeding in other ways too rarely for a reliable proportion of the feeds on fruits to be calculated. For E.jamaica, E.campestris and C.flaveola, feeds on introduced plants were excluded (see Part 2 for the figures when they are included). For most species, the proportion seen taking fruit was not necessarily the true proportion, as some of them, especially M.genibarbis, are more conspicuous when feeding on fruits than insects.

big overlap in fruit diet between the different species. For instance, one of the commonest fruits in the arid lowlands is that of the tree *Bursera simaruba,* which we recorded taken by 13 of the bird species included in Appendix 6, and in addition by two large resident species, the parakeet *Aratinga nana* and grackle *Quiscalus niger,* and three species of migrant warblers. The fruits of the tree *Pithecellobium unguis-cati,* observed beside Mona reservoir, were almost as popular, being taken by 8 of the bird species included in Appendix 6, and in addition by two migrant buntings and three migrant warblers, while the dove *Zenaida aurita* picked the fallen fruits off the ground. In the wet limestone midlevels, the fruits of the *Fagara* species were especially popular, and all 10 bird species recorded in Appendix 6 taking *Fagara martinicensis,* as well as parakeets *Aratinga nana,* were once seen together in the same tree. Likewise the 8 species seen on *Fagara elephantiasis* were in the same tree. Again in the Blue Mountains, the most popular fruit was that of *Alchornea latifolia,* which we recorded taken by 9 different species of birds. The records in Appendix 6 show that various other kinds of fruits were taken by from 4 to 6 species of birds. Indeed, almost the only fruits which we did not see taken by several species of birds were those which we rarely saw taken at all.

To this last statement, however, there is one important exception. The berries of mistletoes Loranthaceae are eaten almost exclusively by the euphonia *Euphonia jamaica.* As already mentioned, the genus *Euphonia* is specialised for mistletoes and this holds for the Jamaican species. *E. jamaica* is thereby segregated ecologically from every other species on the island, but we should add that, like many other species, it also took the fruits of *Pithecellobium unguis-cati,* and also of *Guazuma ulmifolia,* which was popular with the parakeet *Aratinga nana.* Two other preferences in Appendix 6 may be noted, that of the elaenia *Elaenia fallax* for the fruits of the myrtle *Myrica cerifera,* which might be important as we rarely saw it taken by other species of birds, and that of the solitaire *Myadestes genibarbis* for melastomes, which were, however, taken by many other birds.

How, if they eat mainly the same species of fruit, are the 17 species of frugivorous species in Table 12 separated from each other in diet, if they are? As already mentioned, *Euphonia jamaica* differs from all the rest in specialising on mistletoe berries, so can be excluded from further consideration. So can the 10 species which, in addition to fruit, take many insects since, as discussed in the previous section, each of them probably has a mainly different insect diet from every other (though more evidence is needed to establish this point). Two other species, the grassquit *Tiaris bicolor* and the Bananaquit *Coereba flaveola*, take too little fruit to be regarded as serious competitors for it (though they eat enough for inclusion in Table 12), and are considered later under the seed-eaters and nectar-eaters respectively.

This leaves four species which eat primarily fruits and other plant foods. The 'bullfinch' *Loxipasser anoxanthus* also takes tree flowers and many seeds. It favours the seeds of acacias and of Compositae herbs, which we did not record for other species, either for the larger bullfinch *Loxigilla violacea,* or for the three small seed-eating species which eat grass seeds, discussed later. Probably, therefore, it is separated from all the rest. *L.violacea,* in particular, is much larger, its culmen being 1·44 times and its weight 2·4 times those of *L.anoxanthus,* a greater proportionate difference than those normally found between coexisting congeners which might compete for food (*cf.* the figures in Table 13). Further, *L.violacea* is larger, with a larger beak, on Jamaica, where it coexists with *L.anoxanthus,* than in the rest of its range (Hispaniola and the Bahamas), where *L.anoxanthus* does not occur, which suggests that it may have evolved into a larger bird on Jamaica through character displacement, to avoid competition with *L.anoxanthus.*

The bullfinch *Loxigilla violacea* presents a more puzzling situation with respect to the tanager *Spindalis zena,* since about four-fifths of the observed diet of both these species consists of fruits, often of the same species (see Appendix 6). They differ in their alternative diet, *S.zena* eating leaves, especially in the last quarter of the year, and buds, and *L.violacea* eating various seeds, but both take these other foods to so small an extent that they can hardly provide a critical means of segregation. However, though they often take the same species of fruits, we did not see them feeding in the same tree, even, for instance, when both were feeding on *Alchornea latifolia* on the same day, which suggests that they might be attracted to the fruits at a different stage of ripeness. Further, *L.violacea* has an extremely strong and thick finch-like beak, which looks adapted, like that of the European Hawfinch *Coccothraustes coccothraustes,* for crushing seeds. I tentatively suggest that *L.violacea,* like *C.coccothraustes* may visit fruits primarily to obtain their seeds, but *S.zena* for the fruits themselves, and that this is how they might be segregated. This possibility needs checking in the field; however, we did not think of it while in Jamaica even when the mist-netters complained that *L.violacea* has an extremely painful bite!

Probably, therefore, both 'bullfinches' *L.anoxanthus* and *L.violacea* are separated in diet from every other species. The tanager *Spindalis zena* is in a different position, however, because though it depends on fruits to a much greater extent than any other species (except *L.violacea*), the fruits that it takes are those taken by many other species as a supplement to their main diet. How, under these circumstances, it might be segregated ecologically requires further study.

A similar but more complex situation is presented by the Orange-quit *Euneornis campestris*. Two-fifths of its recorded diet consists of fruits, nearly all of which are commonly taken by other species, but it is separated in diet from all these other species because its main alternative is nectar, which they do not take. On the other hand, as discussed in the next section, the main flowers which it visits for nectar are also visited regularly by other nectar-eating species, but it is separated from the latter in feeding because they do not take an appreciable quantity of fruit. Hence *E.campestris* differs from every other Jamaican species in that it eats mainly fruits and nectar, but it is doubtful whether it can be regarded as segregated ecologically when there are other species which eat the same species of fruits and further species which visit the same species of flowers. We have no reason to think that *E.campestris* has, in addition, a source of food peculiar to itself.

NECTAR-EATERS

As well as the Orangequit *Euneornis campestris*, just discussed, four other Jamaican species eat large quantities of nectar, namely the Bananaquit *Coereba flaveola* and the three species of hummingbirds. The wild, but not the introduced flowers which we saw these birds visiting are set out in Appendix 7 (p. 374), which shows that they overlap greatly with each other. Indeed the main differences in the species of flowers visited that are apparent in Appendix 7 might really be due to differences in the birds' habitats. *E.campestris*, for instance, is absent from the arid lowlands, and the hummingbird *Anthracothorax mango* from the mountains, so they do not visit the flowers common in these habitats respectively. In addition, the tiny hummingbird *Mellisuga minima* does not visit some of the larger flowers available in its habitat that are visited by the two larger hummingbirds, but it overlaps extensively with them on the smaller flowers.

Hence the five nectar-eaters are not separated from each other by the flowers which they visit; but *E.campestris,* as already noted, differs from the other four (though not from various other Jamaican birds) in taking much fruit, while the main diet of the other four consists of insects, and their possible means of segregation has been discussed in a previous section.

THE SMALL SEED-EATERS

Of the three small seed-eating species, the sparrow *Ammodramus savannarum* lives in open grassland and so is separated by habitat from the grassquits which live in wooded grassland. The two grassquits differ because *Tiaris olivacea* takes seeds direct from the grass heads, whereas *Tiaris bicolor* seeks mainly fallen seeds on the ground and also feeds to some extent in trees (Pulliam 1969, see also Part 2.)

THE LARGER VEGETARIAN SPECIES

The larger vegetarian species (Part B, Table 11) were not studied critically. As can be seen from the figures in Table 1, various of them differ greatly in size, and hence presumably in diet from each other.

SEGREGATION OF CONGENERIC SPECIES
THROUGH FEEDING

As shown in the previous chapter, only two out of a possible 20 pairs of congeneric Jamaican land birds are segregated from each other through a difference in habitat. If, as I consider (Lack 1971), competitive exclusion is the rule in birds, then all the other pairs are presumably segregated from each other by their feeding. As mentioned earlier in this chapter, a marked difference in feeding methods separates the two species of flycatchers in the genus *Tyrannus,* the two grassquits *Tiaris* and the vireo *V.altiloquus* from *V.osburni* or *V.modestus* (but not *V.modestus* from *V.osburni*). At least partial differences in feeding stations also separate the three species of flycatchers in the genus *Myiarchus* (see Table 44 p. 295).

Insufficient information is available for the other congeneric

TABLE 13. *Differences in size between the congeneric Jamaican land birds*

Smaller species	Larger species	Measurement of larger as ratio of smaller	
		culmen	body-weight

A. Coexisting species not known to differ markedly in feeding methods

Smaller species	Larger species	culmen	body-weight
Columba leucocephala	*C.inornata*	1.11	
Columba leucocephala	*C.caribaea*	1.06	
Columba caribaea	*C.inornata*	1.06	
Zenaida macroura	*Z.aurita*	1.08	
Zenaida macroura	*Z.asiatica*	1.54	
Zenaida aurita	*Z.asiatica*	1.43	
Geotrygon montana	*G.versicolor*	1.75	1.6
Amazona agilis	*A.collaria*	1.08	
Coccyzus americanus	*C.minor*	1.08	
Myiarchus barbirostris	*M.stolidus*	1.19	1.8
Myiarchus barbirostris	*M.validus*	1.38	3.3
Myiarchus stolidus	*M.validus*	1.16	1.9
Turdus jamaicensis	*T.aurantius*	1.26	1.2
Vireo modestus	*V.osburni*	1.78	2.0

B. Coexisting species which differ markedly in feeding methods

Smaller species	Larger species	culmen	body-weight
Tyrannus caudifasciatus	*T.dominicensis*	1.04	1.4
Tiaris olivacea	*T.bicolor*	1.04	1.2
Vireo modestus	*V.altiloquus*	1.78	1.9
Vireo osburni	*V.altiloquus*	1.23	0

C. Species in separate habitats

Smaller species	Larger species	culmen	body-weight
Mimus polyglottos	*M.gundlachii*	1.28	1.6
Dendroica pharetra	*D.petechia*	0	0

Notes (i) The ratios are calculated from the figures in Table 1.

(ii) Hutchinson (1959) considered culmen ratios of 1.2 to 1 or more as typical for co-existing congeners on islands. For culmen-length, Schoener (1965) grouped all Greater Antillean congeners (irrespective of whether they co-exist in the same habitat or feed similarly). He considered a ratio of 1.14 to 1 as large and found that the ratio was higher than this in 56 per cent of the species-pairs and higher than 1.24 per cent in 44 per cent of them. The figures in Part A of this table are similar. In contrast, Schoener found that the corresponding proportions for North and Middle American mainland birds in the same families are 32 per cent over 1.14 and 18 per cent over 1.24 *i.e.* a smaller proportion of mainland than island species differ to an important extent in length of beak.

(iii) For body-weight, Diamond (1972) found that in New Guinea the average difference between co-existing congeners is 1.9, with usual limits of 1.5 to 2.5 and extremes of 1.3 and 2.7. The mean for the six figures in Part A of this table is similar.

(iv) Note that there can be a big difference in size between congeners segregated by habitat, as shown by the mockingbirds *Mimus* spp. in Part C, but this is irrelevant to their potential competition if they are segregated by habitat (though the size difference might, of course, be related to habitat).

species, but a further clue is given by their relative sizes (Table 13), since it is now generally accepted that coexisting congeneric species of birds which differ markedly in size from each other also differ in their feeding.

Hutchinson (1959) concluded that a difference in culmen-length ratio of at least 1.2:1 is characteristic of coexisting congeneric island species which are segregated in feeding. If a difference of this order may be accepted as an indication of segregation by feeding, this holds for the dove *Zenaida asiatica* in comparison with both its two congeners, for the two doves in the genus *Geotrygon*, for the flycatchers *Myiarchus barbirostris* and *M.validus* (and almost for each of these species with the middle-sized *M.stolidus*), for the two thrushes in the genus *Turdus* and for the two vireos *V.modestus* and *V.osburni*. To these might be added the two *Amazona* parrots because, though they differ little in length of culmen, they differ in depth of beak (see p. 259). This leaves five other congeneric pairs in Part A of Table 13, four of pigeons and one of cuckoos, which are similar in size, and in which the possible means of segregation by feeding are not known.

In Darwin's finches Geospizinae and the Hawaiian sicklebills Drepanididae, differences in size, with corresponding differences in food, were evolved through adaptive radiation within the archipelagoes concerned. Probably a difference in size is one of the easiest means of evolving coexistence through ecological segregation. Even in the simple case of Darwin's finches, however, the size differences in question are not related solely to size of food items but also, in the genus *Geospiza*, to hardness of seeds (Bowman 1961) and in the genus *Camarhynchus* to feeding methods (Lack 1971).

In contrast to Darwin's finches, nearly all of the West Indian congeners which differ from each other in size are derived from different mainland species and it was presumably on the mainland that they evolved the size differences in question. Schoener (1965) found that, among congeneric species, a higher proportion of the West Indian species, than of the greater number of species on the mainland, show a big size-difference (see note ii to Table 13). It is not clear whether this is because the species with bigger differences in size are those most likely to establish themselves in the West Indies, as suggested by Grant 1969 (see also p. 140), or because any differences in size tend to be intensified through competition for food after arrival, and both factors might be involved. Whatever the origin of these differences, their existence fits the view that the island species have broader feeding niches than their mainland congeners. This is an extremely important point, for which one would have liked to have had more than statistical evidence, and it should be pursued further by comparative feeding studies in the islands and on the mainland; but Schoener has provided the first step.

DIFFERENCES IN FEEDING IN SAME SPECIES ON JAMAICA AND THE MAINLAND

The feeding habits on the mainland of the Jamaican species also present there, are in most cases too poorly known to allow comparisons to be made. There are, however, two instances in which the Jamaican bird probably has a broader range of feeding station or methods. First, the Jamaican representative of the white-eyed vireo group, *V.modestus*, feeds in both bushes and trees, whereas the North American representative *V.griseus* feeds primarily in the understorey (Hamilton 1962). (The second Jamaican vireo of white-eyed stock, *V.osburni*, likewise feeds in both bushes and trees.) Secondly, the mainland species closest to the Jamaican oriole *Icterus leucopteryx* is *I.pustulatus*, which is a typical oriole and eats mainly fruit and some nectar (Beecher 1950). The Jamaican species likewise eats both fruit and nectar, but its main food consists of invertebrates obtained by stripping bark from twigs, linked with which it has evolved a thicker beak than its mainland relatives. So far as known, *I.pustulatus* does not feed by stripping bark.

As considered in the previous chapter, about half of the Jamaican species also found on the mainland, or with a close relative there, have broader habitats on Jamaica. The proportion which have broader feeding habits on Jamaica might be expected to be smaller, however, since J.M.Diamond (1970) found that, on various Pacific islands with relatively few resident species, broader habitats have been evolved much more often than broader feeding niches. For instance, the small island of Karkar, 16 km off New Guinea, has 49 species in common with New Guinea itself. In the absence of many other New Guinea birds, 11 of these 49 have expanded their altitudinal range, 9 upward and 2 downward, 12 have expanded their habitat, 9 from second growth into forest, 2 from coastal habitats into the interior, and one from the interior to the coast. But only one has expanded its foraging range, a swift hunting inside the forest on Karkar in the absence there of any

Rhipidura flycatcher, and only one has expanded its diet, a grassland finch eating insects as well as seeds in the absence of a grassland warbler.

This is the situation on one of New Guinea's nearby islands, but in archipelagoes far to its east, differentiation has proceeded further, and there a modification in feeding habits has occurred more often, primarily in species which have evolved corresponding morphological adaptations. The same might possibly have occurred in some of the Jamaican birds, but perhaps only in those now so differentiated that their mainland ancestor is uncertain, so the point would be hard to establish. However, the icterid *Nesopsar nigerrimus* feeds on insects by rummaging in epiphytes. It is almost certainly descended from *Agelaius* or *Icterus* stock, and no species in either of these genera feeds in that kind of way. This species is, however, one of the most peculiar on Jamaica, and there might be no others which have diverged so much in feeding.

ARE ALL THE AVAILABLE NICHES FILLED?

One of the key questions in relation to the feeding of Jamaican birds is whether all the available niches are filled. There seems, however, to be no direct way of determining whether an ecological niche exists unless a bird is filling it. Hence I can see no way of answering this question directly, though important indirect evidence bearing on it will be discussed in Chapter 6 and later.

To illustrate the difficulty, a few puzzling points from the feeding of Jamaican birds may be mentioned. Jamaica has two species of *Amazona* parrots and two vireos of white-eyed stock, and since the two members of each pair differ in size of beak from each other, they are presumably segregated from each other in their feeding. But the adjoining islands of Cuba and Hispaniola each have only one *Amazona* parrot and one vireo of white-eyed stock. Is this because, by chance, Jamaica has received two invasions from the mainland of each of these stocks, or because there is not 'ecological room' for two species of each on these other islands owing to some undetected ecological gap? I can see no way of answering this question on the available evidence. Similarly Jamaica has three species of *Myiarchus* flycatcher, a large, a medium and a small, but Cuba and Hispaniola each have only the medium-sized species. I end on this puzzling note in order to stress how little is yet known about the feeding requirements of West Indian birds, and of the general ecological conditions. But I hope to show later that, nevertheless, one can proceed further in the general argument than these negative points might suggest is possible.

SUMMARY

The available information suggests that each of the Jamaican land birds which takes primarily animal food depends on different food resources from every other. The small seed-eating species are also segregated. On the other hand apart from the euphonia, which specialises on mistletoes, the fruit-eating species overlap greatly with each other in the species of fruits taken; but most of them also eat many insects, and are probably segregated from each other by their insect diet. Of two species in which four-fifths of the observed feeding records were on fruits, one perhaps takes the seeds rather than the fruits themselves. The other, which eats a much higher proportion of fruits than any other species, eats the same fruits as the others do, and it is not known how it might be segregated in diet, if it is. One further species differs from every other in eating much fruit and much nectar, but both the fruits and the flowers in question are taken by other species of birds, so its possible segregation is doubtful. This and the other nectar-eating species are not segregated from each other by the flowers which they visit.

Various congeneric species which are probably segregated by feeding differ markedly from each other in size, and Schoener (1965) showed that the size differences in question are larger in the West Indies than among the greater number of mainland congeners, suggesting that feeding niches are broader in the island than in the mainland birds. In two instances a Jamaican bird has a broader feeding niche than the same or a closely related species on the mainland. It is not possible to determine directly whether all the available feeding niches on Jamaica are filled, and many puzzling problems concerning feeding remain to be resolved.

CHAPTER 5 · STABILITY OF THE AVIFAUNA
EXTINCTIONS, INTRODUCTIONS, WANDERERS, AND ENDEMISM

JAMAICA 150 YEARS AGO

Thanks to Gosse (1847), to his knowledgeable correspondent Mr. Hill of Spanish Town, to the MSS and illustrations left in earlier years at the Institute of Jamaica by Dr. Robinson (many of which were used by Gosse), and to the rather later observations in the mountains of Jamaica by another of Gosse's correspondents Osburn (1859–60), we have an exceptionally good idea of the birds present on Jamaica in the first half of the nineteenth century. There are even earlier published records from the eighteenth century, but these are too incomplete to be of much value.

These records show that in the last 150 years only two species of land birds in the families from pigeons to passerines inclusive have become extinct on Jamaica, both of them over a century ago. First, there was probably a small green macaw *Ara* sp. (see discussion on p. 252). Macaws, formerly widespread in both Greater and Lesser Antilles, are now everywhere extinct in the West Indies (Greenway 1967). Secondly, the endemic parauque *Siphonorhis americanus* was last collected in the southern lowland hills near Linstead in 1859. The only other species in the genus, on Hispaniola, survives. There are no facts bearing on why either of the Jamaican species should have become extinct.

Two other Jamaican land birds are nearly extinct, the pigeon *Columba inornata*, probably due in part to shooting, and the swallow *Kalochelidon euchrysea*, for unknown reasons, as it lives, apparently undisturbed by man, in the mountains. Two further species outside the pigeons to passerines have become extinct, namely the crake *Amaurolimnas concolor* and the petrel *Pterodroma hasitata* (the latter probably as the result of the introduction of the mongoose in the second half of the nineteenth century).

In the same period, no land bird in the families from pigeons to passerines has colonised Jamaica. Of the birds in other families,

73

however, the Cattle Egret *Bubulcus ibis* has done so. It evidently reached South America from the Old World in the late nineteenth century; after a pause it spread northward, and reached Jamaica early in the 1950s, where it is now widespread in cattle pastures and also visits the sugar cane fields when the crop is lifted. It follows cattle for the insects which they disturb, and we have even seen one following a man with a mowing machine up the grass verge of a road in suburban Kingston. It is present solely in man-modified habitats, and its establishment is obviously linked with the creation by man of a new ecological niche on Jamaica through the introduction of cattle in grassland.

Hence during the last 150 years, there have been hardly any changes in the resident species of land birds on Jamaica. The island has experienced nothing like the extinctions and colonisations that are implied to take place on remote islands by MacArthur and Wilson (1963, 1967). Perhaps Jamaica is larger and more accessible to birds than the type of island they had in mind, but even so, it is an oceanic island in the usual meaning of the word.

This stability is in marked contrast to what J.M. Diamond (1971) reported for the island of Karkar, 16 km off New Guinea and 370 sq. km in area. His own survey in 1969, compared with that of an experienced collector in 1914, suggests that, between these years, at least 5 out of a possible 43 lowland species became extinct and that there were a corresponding number, at most 11, of new species which colonised the island. This rapid turnover fits well with the MacArthur/Wilson theory, but is so different from the stable situation on Jamaica over a much longer period of years that I suggest that great caution is needed in applying Diamond's results to oceanic islands. In comparison with Jamaica Karkar is, of course, extremely small and extremely close to land, nor has it the many endemic species characteristic of Jamaica. I wonder, therefore, whether the instability implied by the MacArthur/Wilson equations holds good only for small or offshore islands. The results for Jamaica, on the other hand, fit my idea of the stability of the avifaunas of oceanic islands.

The stable situation in the land birds of Jamaica is also in marked contrast with that on oceanic islands greatly disturbed by man, such as Hawaii, and the latter cannot be taken as a model for what happens under natural conditions. Probably the main factor in the survival of the Jamaican birds has been that sufficient of their natural habitats has survived up to the present time.

HUMAN INTRODUCTIONS

A few land birds have been introduced to Jamaica by man, but with one possible exception they have had a negligible influence on the native birds. Domestic pigeons *Columba livia* stay round their dovecotes and are not found feral, even in cultivated land. Just over a century ago another domesticated dove, '*Streptopelia risoria*', was sometimes seen in company with wild *Zenaida asiatica* (March 1863–64), but there are no later records of it. The Guiana Parrotlet *Forpus passerinus* was introduced about 1918 and is now widespread in wooded cultivation in the lowlands and also occurs at midlevels, but is at times seen in natural forest, though to an unimportant extent. The European Starling *Sturnus vulgaris* was introduced about 1903, spread slowly at first but in recent years rapidly, and is now widespread in pastures with scattered trees in the lowlands, with some at midlevels, but it is not found in natural habitats. The Troupial *Icterus icterus* was at one time partly naturalised but is now extinct (Scott 1891–3, Bangs and Kennard 1920). The English Sparrow *Passer domesticus* was introduced about 1903 near Annotto Bay on the north coast and spread a short way, but it has now greatly declined, the last published record refers to 1966 (Agar 1966) and we looked in vain for it in 1971. Finally the Saffron Finch *Sicalis flaveola* was introduced well before 1847 and is now widespread in lowland cultivation with very short grass and scattered trees, with some at midlevels, especially near houses, but it is not in natural or even ruinate woodland. Of birds outside the families from pigeons to passerines, the Bobwhite Quail *Colinus virginianus* was introduced about 1747, flourished until the middle of the 19th century, but only a few were surviving by the end of the century (Scott 1891–3) and it is now extinct, an attempt to reintroduce it in 1953 having failed. Another sporting bird, the Guineafowl *Numida meleagris*, flourished in the 18th and the first part of the 19th centuries, and there were still a few at the end of the 19th century (Scott 1891–3), but it is now extinct.

That no introduced bird, with the partial exception of the parrotlet, occurs in natural habitats on Jamaica might perhaps be attributed to competition with the native species, but the evidence is insufficient to evaluate this point, particularly since, anyway, most of the introduced birds are not species that would be expected to flourish in natural forest.

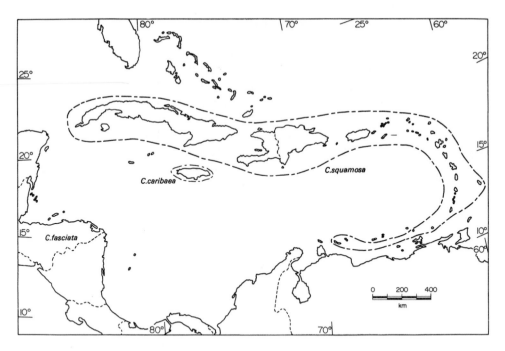

Fig. 7. *Range of:* (*i*) Columba caribaea, *which is confined to Jamaica,* *with a close relation* (Columba fasciata) *in Central America; and of* (*ii*) Columba squamosa *which replaces* C.caribaea *in the rest of the Antilles, extending also to several islands off South America.*

WANDERERS TO JAMAICA

Traditionally the stability of the Jamaican avifauna in the last 150 years would be ascribed to the rarity with which birds from the mainland or other islands wander there. A few wanderers have in fact been recorded, but there have been so few birdwatchers on Jamaica that it is hard to know whether the rarity of such records is due to the paucity of wanderers or the paucity of ornithologists. By including sight records of such species in the present book, I appreciate that I am infringing on the American tradition that a species should not be accepted for a country's list unless supported by a collected specimen, and this qualification does not apply to several of the wanderers I mention. On the other hand, the evidence that they provide for wandering is too important for the records to be suppressed. I have not attempted to evaluate them critically, which is the task of the avifaunist.

A record for the Red-necked Pigeon *Columba squamosa* is unquestionable since, apart from old reports of this species by hunters to Gosse (1847) and Scott (1891–3), there is a specimen shot on Portland Ridge in September 1953 (see p. 249). This species occurs on all the mountainous Greater and Lesser Antilles except Jamaica, while only Jamaica supports the montane pigeon *Columba caribaea*. The two are not exact ecological equivalents since *C.squamosa,* unlike *C.caribaea,* at times occurs in the lowlands, but the circumstantial evidence provided by Fig. 7 strongly suggests that each excludes the other from its breeding range. Here, then, is a probable example of a potential colonist which is excluded through competition with a local resident species.

A small mainland dove *Scardafella inca* was seen in Westmoreland in August 1963 by Harvey and Cruikshank, Harvey (1968), both experienced observers, and they also reported past records of one dead in August 1906 and another seen in the late autumn of 1934 in the same county by B.Williams. Bond doubted these records.

Two green woodpeckers were seen on 5 and 7 January 1957 near Anchovy on the north coast, and could hardly have been anything except the Cuban endemic species *Xiphidiopicus percussus* (L.Salmon pers. comm.). The same observer reported two further woodpeckers in this area, one individual of *Dendrocopos villosus* (which is resident in the Bahamas and in North and Central America) in January 1957 and one of the North American *Dryocopus pileatus* on 13 and 14 September 1958. It would be hard to mistake these latter species for others, and both, of course, look very different from the sole Jamaican woodpecker, but there are no collected specimens from Jamaica.

An old record of the honeycreeper *Cyanerpes cyaneus* was attributed by Bond (1956) to an escape from captivity, but this species breeds on Cuba as well as in Central America, so might perhaps have been a wild wanderer.

Finally the four ornithological Lacks had close views of two separate individuals of the Hispaniolan Crossbill *Loxia leucoptera megaplaga,* first of a nearly unstreaked grey-green individual on Guava Ridge on 17 December 1970 and later of a much more streaked grey-green one near Hardwar Gap on 15 April 1971, while a pink male was seen on Guava Ridge on 16 April 1971 by Professor I.M. and A. Goodbody. All three birds were feeding on the small cones of an introduced species of pine. The white wingbars were clearly seen, excluding the possibility of *Loxia curvirostra* from the mainland. Under normal circumstances, I would not trust a subspecific identification in the field, but the beak of *L.l. megaplaga* is so thick compared with that of the North American subspecies that there is no doubt in our minds as to the form involved. Crossbills are well known wanderers, and if the Jamaicans had planted the Hispaniolan pine instead of the Caribbean pine from Honduras, there might well, by now, have been a new breeding species on the island. Unfortunately the cones of the Caribbean Pine are too large for a crossbill to tackle, and the birds that we saw were feeding on old pines introduced before the present plantations of Caribbean Pine.

I am not including North American passage migrants as true wanderers, and a Pine Warbler *Dendroica pinus* which my wife and I saw at Negril on 5 April 1971 was doubtless in this category, but as the species also breeds on Hispaniola, it had just possibly wandered from there.

Of land birds outside the families from pigeons to passerines inclusive, at least three species of raptors have also wandered to Jamaica, the Black Vulture *Coragyps atratus* several times between 1847 and 1861, also the Brazilian Eagle *Hypomorphnus urubitinga* and perhaps other species (March 1863–66), while a Crested Caracara *Polyborus cheriway*, a species resident on Cuba and the mainland, was seen in August 1963 by Miss L. Salmon (pers. comm.).

There are, of course, many other land birds from the mainland which regularly visit Jamaica, over twenty species staying there in some numbers for the winter, at least as many more being regular on spring or autumn passage, and many others occurring occasionally (*cf.* Bond 1971). These, admittedly, are birds which breed in the United States and are on their way to or from their winter quarters further south. But we tend to take their temporary presence on Jamaica too much for granted. Their 'home' may be North America, but obviously they are able to reach the island, and it is reasonable to presume that they would have evolved local populations there if any individuals had stayed to breed and could have, on average, raised more young than on their present breeding grounds. That they do not stay implies that any which attempt to do so are eliminated by natural selection. If Jamaica were empty of all birds, some of these migrants would surely be able to breed there, so it is reasonable to attribute the absence of at least some of them to competitive exclusion by native Jamaican birds.

WANDERERS FROM THE WEST INDIES TO NORTH AMERICA

As already pointed out, the rarity of birdwatchers in the West Indies makes it hard to evaluate the importance of the few records of wanderers there. Fortunately for the present discussion, however, there is one part of the New World where birdwatchers are common, namely the United States, and here, especially in Florida, so many typical West Indian land birds have been seen in recent years that the old idea that island birds rarely wander must be discarded. The records concerned are set out in Table 14. In part A are listed the 10 species which need not have travelled to Florida further than from the Bahamas, at their nearest only 100 km away, though some of them may have come further, of course. But though the sea crossing involved is short, these species (except in recent years the ani *Crotophaga ani*) do not breed in the United States, so they have wandered north of their normal range and outside, so to speak, their 'avifaunal limit', for most of them breed only in the Bahamas and Greater Antilles.

The other 12 species, listed in Part B of Table 14, travelled further, some of them much further, indeed two of them as far as Nova Scotia, while another travelled at least as far as from Puerto Rico to Texas. Even though birdwatchers are common in the United States, these records must constitute a minute fraction of the number of West Indian land birds making such journeys. One critic of this manuscript thought that 'minute fraction' was too strong a term to use under the circumstances, but it certainly is not when one considers the number of hours of each day, and the proportion of the land surface of eastern North America, actually covered by bird-watchers in the course of, say, a year. It is now well known that whenever the number of bird-watchers increases, so does the number of rare birds seen; to take only one recent example, various species of North American shore-birds which prior to the 1939–45 war were considered extremely rare visitors to Britain are now known to occur almost annually.

I therefore think it safe to conclude that West Indian landbirds wander not infrequently from their home land, and if they go north-ward to the United States, probably they also go in other directions,

TABLE 14.   *Records of Greater Antillean and Bahaman Birds in U.S.A.*
and Canada

A. Florida records of species which could have come from the Bahamas

   (i)   dove *Zenaida aurita zenaida*
  (ii)   dove *Geotrygon chrysia* (species restricted to Bahamas and Greater Antilles)
 (iii)   ani *Crotophaga ani* (now breeds Florida)
 (iv)   hummingbird *Calliphlox evelynae* (Bahaman endemic species)
  (v)   flycatcher *Tyrannus caudifasciatus* (species restricted to Bahamas and Greater Antilles)
 (vi)   swallow *Callichelidon cyaneoviridis* (Bahaman endemic species)
 (vii)   grassquit *Tiaris b.bicolor* (several records)
(viii)   warbler *Geothlypis rostrata* (Bahaman endemic species)
 (ix)   bananaquit *Coereba flaveola behamensis* (several records)
  (x)   tanager *Spindalis zena* (Bahaman form of species restricted to Bahamas and Greater Antilles)

B. Longer journeys

   (i)   pigeon *Columba squamosa*: 2 Florida Keys October 1896 and May 1929 (the species is almost restricted to Greater and Lesser Antilles) (Sprunt 1954).
  (ii)   dove *Geotrygon montana*: Florida Keys December 1888, May 1923, February 1952 (could have come from Greater Antilles or Central America) (Sprunt 1955).
 (iii)   cuckoo *Coccyzus minor nesiotes* (the subspecies on Jamaica and Hispaniola): one old record for Florida Keys (Sprunt 1955).
 (iv)   swift *Tachornis phoenicobia*: 2 Key West, Florida, July-Aug. 1972 (P.Sykes pers. comm.) (the species is restricted to Cuba, Hispaniola and Jamaica)
  (v)   hummingbird *Chlorostilbon ricordii* (probably Cuban subspecies): one Florida October-November 1943 (Sprunt 1955). Same species near Cocoa, Fla., October 1964 (*Audubon Field Notes*).
 (vi)   hummingbird *Orthorhyncus cristatus exilis* (the subspecies on Puerto Rico, Virgins and most of Lesser Antilles): one Texas February 1967 (Pulich 1968).
 (vii)   flycatcher *Tyrannus dominicensis sequax* (Cuban form): 6 Florida Keys April-May 1890 (Sprunt 1955).
(viii)   flycatcher *Myiarchus stolidus sagrae* (Cuban form): one Alabama September 1963 (Miles 1963) (the species is restricted to the West Indies).
 (ix)   swallow *Petrochelidon fulva cavicola* (Cuba form): Florida Keys, March 1890 and June 1939 (Sprunt 1955); also 9, one identified as *P.f.fulva*, May-June 1968, one seen June 1969 and one collected May 1971, in Nova Scotia (*American Birds*). (Different subspecies of this species occur on the mainland.)
  (x)   martin *Progne dominicensis cryptoleuca* (Cuban form): two Florida, May 1858 and undated (Sprunt 1955).
 (xi)   oriole *Icterus dominicensis*: Nova Scotia May 1971 (*American Birds*). (The species is restricted to the Bahamas and Greater Antilles.)
 (xii)   icterid *Agelaius humeralis*: two Florida Keys February 1936 (Sprunt 1955). (The species is restricted to Cuba and Hispaniola.)

Note   A record of the Cuban finch *Melopyrrha nigra* in August-September in Florida was rejected by Bond as a probable escaped captive, and similarly records of the Cuban grassquit *Tiaris canora* in Florida (Sprunt 1955) were rejected as escaped captives, together with one misidentified specimen, by Austin (1963).

between the islands of the West Indies, or to Central America, where they are unlikely to be seen by birdwatchers. One may similarly postulate a traffic from Central America to the islands. Wandering is, of course, typical of birds throughout the world, and Scotland's Fair Isle has become a mecca for British birdwatchers because so many rarities are seen there, including species from North America and eastern Asia, but the number which alight on the island must be tiny compared with those passing annually over Britain. However, the species concerned are migrants, and it has become accepted that they, and especially the juveniles, are liable to go off-course. The most remarkable feature of the West Indian birds recorded in North America is that they are resident island species, many of them confined to a few of the islands in the archipelago, and many of them represented by endemic forms which are presumably adapted to their environment. Hence they are among the last species which one would have expected to wander. As already stressed, too, the number seen must constitute a minute fraction of those that do wander. Nevertheless, the frequency of such wandering must not be exaggerated. We ourselves recorded only one wandering species on Jamaica during our ten months' stay although we were out almost every day in the field. Similarly the Keplers recorded only two, both swifts, during their three years on Puerto Rico. Wandering is uncommon, but it is far less rare than previous workers have supposed. In particular, it is common enough to mean that the relatively small number of resident species on Jamaica cannot be attributed to the rarity with which newcomers arrive there. Newcomers must be presumed to be prevented from settling, in which connection competition from the resident species is presumably an important factor involved.

ENDEMISM

If island birds wander to the extent suggested by the evidence in the preceding section, then one's ideas on endemic island forms need modification. How can these forms preserve their identity if the related forms from which they were presumably evolved continue to arrive not infrequently? In this connection it may be noted that Jamaica has an unusually high proportion of endemic forms, even for an oceanic island; out of 66 named land birds (pigeons to passerines), 5 are in endemic monotypic genera and another 22 are endemic species, making 27 endemic species in all, or 41 per cent of the total. Further, of the other 39 species, 19 are represented on Jamaica by endemic subspecies, and 12 of these belong to species confined to the West Indies. Endemism is also high, though not so high as this, on Cuba, Hispaniola and Puerto Rico.

Unless I were wrong in supposing that wandering is fairly frequent, the only possible answer, I suggest, is that the endemic forms are so well adapted to the islands where they live that, when further individuals of the ancestral form arrive from outside, they are quickly eliminated in competition, and if any of them should survive long enough to interbreed, any resulting hybrids also fail to survive competition. At the present day, of course, many of the endemic forms are now so distinctive that the possibility of interbreeding with putative ancestors from elsewhere no longer arises, but there would have been a stage in the past when such interbreeding would have been possible, to which the same argument would have applied.

This raises the question of the origin of such endemic forms in the first place. When it was supposed that mainland birds reach islands extremely rarely, it could be presumed that island populations had a long period of complete isolation in which to evolve hereditary differences. Genetic isolation is, of course, essential for the evolution of new subspecies, and how can they evolve if newcomers from the ancestral population arrive as frequently as I now suggest? The answer, I consider, is a problem of rates. Adaptive hereditary differences will spread in a population provided that selection for them is sufficiently strong to outweigh their potential dilution through the arrival of newcomers from outside. Even though birds wander to islands more frequently than formerly supposed, they do not do it that often, and their temporary isolation will be sufficient for the evolution of hereditary differences provided that a sufficiently strong selective advantage is involved. On this view, selection for hereditary differences will tend to be stronger the greater the environmental differences to which the island population is subjected compared with the ancestral population from which it was derived.

As mentioned earlier, we tend to think that on an oceanic island the endemic species are those which have been there longest, *i.e.* in our thinking we subconsciously emphasise the length of the period of potential isolation, and not the strength of the selective forces involved. The situation on Jamaica shows the weakness of this view.

Presumably when it first appeared above the sea, Jamaica provided suitable habitats for coastal and marsh birds, later for birds of arid lowland scrub, and only much later, as it continued to rise, for birds of highland forest. But of the 41 resident or probably resident water and marsh birds on Jamaica today (*i.e.* all those in Table 3, p. 32 except the three raptors), only one, an extinct rail, was an endemic subspecies, and there are no endemic species in the list. This provides a remarkable contrast with the land birds (pigeons to passerines) already mentioned, since only 2 per cent of the species in Table 3, compared with 70 per cent of the land birds in Table 1, are endemic at least at the level of the subspecies. Yet the water and marsh birds were surely not the most recent species to colonise Jamaica, and may, as just noted, have been the first.

I also suggested that the birds of arid lowland forest may have colonised at an early stage. But as can be seen from Table 9, the 10 species confined to this habitat on Jamaica include no endemic species, and only half of them are endemic subspecies. So the degree of endemism is lower in this group than in those in any other land habitat on Jamaica. Further, it is next lowest among the 11 species that live solely in the lowlands and at midlevels, which include 3 endemic species and another 2 endemic subspecies. In contrast, endemism is highest among the birds confined to midlevels and the mountains, where 9 of the 12 are endemic species, and the other 3 are represented by endemic subspecies. Endemism is also fairly high in those which extend from the lowlands to the highlands, where 14 of the 32 species are endemic. Probably the habitat on Jamaica least like those anywhere else is montane forest, so these findings fit my suggestion that the degree of endemism in island birds is related primarily to the degree of ecological difference to which they are subject, and to which they have evolved, and not to the length of time for which they have lived on the island concerned. (This view applies, of course, only to long-established oceanic islands, since an island must have been in existence for long enough to provide the necessary conditions.)

The lack of endemism in the water and shore birds of Jamaica may be reinforced if any of them move rather regularly between the different islands, or between the islands and the mainland, as some of them might. One land bird, the pigeon *Columba leucocephala*, is also known to move fairly often between different islands, and as might be expected under these circumstances, it is not divided into subspecies. Whether any other land birds make such movements is not known.

SUMMARY

The number of resident species of land birds on Jamaica has remained almost the same during the last 150 years, with only two extinctions and no new natural arrivals. This is in marked contrast to the big changes among the land birds on oceanic islands greatly disturbed by man, and also to Diamond's findings for those of the small island of Karkar off New Guinea. The stability of the Jamaican avifauna can be attributed to the continuing presence of sufficient of the main natural habitats of the island. The few bird species successfully introduced by man remain in man-modified habitats, with the partial exception of a parrotlet.

There are a few records of birds wandering to Jamaica from elsewhere, but birdwatchers are too few for it to be known how much weight should be attached to such records. In addition, Jamaica is visited annually by many migratory species which breed in North America, at least some of which might presumably have evolved local breeding populations if they were able to raise young more successfully there than elsewhere. Further, there are now records of over twenty West Indian resident species wandering to North America, and these must constitute a minute fraction of the birds which wander between the mainland and the islands, or between the islands. The idea that land birds from elsewhere rarely reach oceanic islands like the West Indies has to be abandoned. This probably means that newcomers are excluded from settling through competition with the existing residents, and hence that competition is responsible for the relatively small numbers of resident island species.

The degree of endemism among Jamaican land birds is high. It is extremely low in the marsh and water birds and, among the land birds, is lowest in those restricted to the lowlands and highest in those restricted to midlevels and the mountains. Yet the last group were presumably the latest of the Jamaican birds to evolve. It is suggested that the degree of endemism depends primarily on the degree of environmental difference to which an island population has been subject in comparison with the population from which it was derived, and that it is not closely correlated with the length of time for which a species has lived on the island concerned.

CHAPTER 6 · HUMMINGBIRDS OF THE WEST
INDIES or ARE ALL THE NICHES FILLED?

The evidence in the previous chapter suggests that land birds move more often between the mainland and the West Indies, and among the islands, than previously believed; and that many potential colonists having arrived on the islands, have been unable to establish themselves there, probably because competitive exclusion by the existing resident species has been an important factor preventing them from settling. Hence it is likely that competitive exclusion is partly responsible for the small number of resident species on each island. It is a much bigger step, of course, to suggest, as I did in the first chapter, that virtually all the potential ecological niches for land birds on each island are filled, and that competitive exclusion (under conditions of ecological poverty) is the *primary* factor responsible for the small number of resident species on each island. Moreover, as I pointed out in Chapter 4, I can see no certain way of discovering that an ecological niche exists except that there is a bird species filling it, and hence no way of showing that all the available niches are filled.

THE PLAIN TALE OF THE HUMMINGBIRDS

Nevertheless the argument can be taken a stage further through comparison of the situation on different islands, and the hummingbirds of the West Indies provide a particularly good example. Jamaica, it will be recalled, has three species, a small one which lives in both lowlands and highlands, a large one in the open lowlands, and a medium-large one in the highlands and in closed lowland forest. The adjoining island of Hispaniola likewise has three species, one small and two larger, which occupy broadly similar ecological niches (though with minor differences), so does Puerto Rico, and so do nearly all the mountainous Lesser Antilles. On the other hand, each of the lowlying islands of the West Indies has only two species, a small and a large, the large highland species of the mountainous islands being absent. This situation would not be remarkable if the three species involved were the same throughout the archipelago, but they are often different. A few of the replacements are merely island forms of an orginal colonist which have become sufficiently distinct to be called separate species, but many others are not closely related to each other. In all, 9 or 10 different kinds of hummingbirds have colonised the West Indies, so the fact that there is just one small species and one large lowland species on each island, and an additional large species on each mountainous island, can hardly be due to coincidence, and strongly implies that this is the number for which there is 'ecological room'; that any further species of hummingbirds that try to settle are excluded by those already present.

The natural scene is never completely simple, and there are complications and exceptions to this account, but before they are discussed, the key point should be firmly emphasised. To repeat, the lowlands of each West Indian island are occupied by a small and a large species of hummingbirds, and the highlands by the same small lowland species but a different large species. Further, though the small species, the large lowland species and the large highland occupy similar ecological niches on different islands, they are often of different origin, from which, to me, it follows that these are the number and ecotypes of hummingbirds for which there are niches on each island, and that no further species of hummingbirds can find a place, *i.e.* the available niches are filled. I also conclude that the small species can coexist with either of the two larger ones because it is adapted to sufficiently different food resources, and that the two large species are separated by habitat through competitive exclusion. (It may be added that hummingbirds probably do not compete seriously for food with any other West Indian birds, except that the widespread Bananaquit *Coereba flaveola* often visits the same species of flowers for nectar.)

So far as the distribution of hummingbirds is concerned, the West Indies may be considered as providing two habitats, the semi-arid forest of the *lowlands*, and the humid forest (rain forest and montane thicket) of the *highlands*. The islands are of two main types, lowlying and mountainous, and only the latter have the highland habitat. The mountainous islands, each with three species of hummingbirds, are, in the Greater Antilles, Jamaica, Hispaniola and most of Puerto Rico, and in the Lesser Antilles, Saba, St Eustatius, St Kitts, Nevis, Montserrat, Guadeloupe, St Lucia, St Vincent and Grenada. The lowlying islands, each with two species of hummingbirds, are Great Abaco, Grand Bahama and Andros in the Bahamas, the Isle of Pines off Cuba, Gonave off Hispaniola, Vieques and Culebra off Puerto Rico, Anegada, Tortola, St John, St Thomas and St Croix in the Virgin Islands and Anguilla, St Martin, St Bartholomew, Barbuda, Antigua, Désirade, Marie Galante, Barbados and the Grenadines in the Lesser Antilles. The critical factor determining whether two or three species of hummingbirds are present is not island-area, for the mountainous islands in question vary from 12 to 80,000 sq. km in area, but altitude, for in the preceding list all the islands that reach an altitude of 600 m have a third species, whereas the islands that do not reach this height have only two. Altitude is critical because it brings in the additional habitat of humid forest and an additional species of hummingbird adapted to it.

The exceptional islands

A few islands, the reader will have observed, were omitted from these lists, but only a few. First, the Bahamas other than the three already specified each have only one species of hummingbird, while Cuba, though mountainous and the largest of the West Indies, has only two. I cannot account for this, but it may be noted that these are the northernmost of the West Indies and that the number of species of hummingbirds resident on the American mainland declines dramatically at higher latitudes. Thus while Mexico has 44 species, Florida has only·one, the same number as in most of the Bahamas. Perhaps the decrease in the Bahamas and Cuba is somehow linked with the trend for a smaller number of species at higher latitudes, which is general in land birds, but it forms too big a subject to be discussed in this book.

Secondly, Puerto Rico has five species of hummingbirds, a standard set of three on most of the island (which is mountainous), while the lowlying northeast corner is occupied solely by two different species, namely those characteristic of the nearby Virgin Islands. Hence Puerto Rico is not an exception if the main mountainous island and the lowlying northeast corner can be regarded as two separate islands, the special interest of this situation being that there is no separation by a sea barrier, which strongly suggests that competitive exclusion is involved. Study has not been made of the possible ecological differences between the northeast and the rest of Puerto Rico which might account for the success of one pair of lowland species in the northeast and another pair in the rest of the island. Possibly the situation is of recent origin, because formerly the large lowland species of most of Puerto Rico, *Anthracothorax dominicus*, was also resident on St Thomas, St John and Anegada in the Virgin Islands, but now the

TABLE 15.   *Hummingbirds of the West Indies*

Name	Range	Mean for males (mm)	
		wing	culmen
1. Smallest species			
Calliphlox evelynae	Bahamas	39	16
Mellisuga helenae	Cuba	28	10
Mellisuga minima	Hispaniola, Jamaica	35–37	10
Chlorostilbon maugaeus	Puerto Rico (not NE)	49	14
Orthorhyncus cristatus	NE Puerto Rico, Virgins,		
	Lesser Antilles	49	10
2. Rather small highland species			
Cyanophaia bicolor	Dominica, Martinique	60	17
3. Medium to large lowland species			
Chlorostilbon ricordii	Bahamas, Cuba	53	17
Anthracothorax mango	Jamaica	74	27
Anthracothorax dominicus	Hispaniola	63	23
	Puerto Rico (not NE)	68	24
Sericotes holosericeus	NE Puerto Rico, Virgins,		
	Lesser Antilles	61	22
4. Medium to large highland species			
Trochilus polytmus	Jamaica	66	21
Chlorostilbon swainsonii	Hispaniola	56	17
Anthracothorax viridis	Puerto Rico	65	24
Eulampis jugularis	mountainous Lesser Antilles		
	(not Grenda)	74	23
Glaucis hirsuta	Grenada	66	35

Notes   (i) Measurements from Ridgway.

(ii) The typically lowland species *S.holosericeus* also occurs in highland rain forest on Grenada, and so does *A.dominicus* on Hispaniola but not Puerto Rico. *T.polytmus* occurs not only in the highlands but in closed lowland forest.

(iii) In rain forest, *C.swainsonii*, *G.hirsuta* and *C.bicolor* feed primarily below the canopy.

large lowland species of the Lesser Antilles, *Sericotes holosericeus*, has replaced it there (C. and A. Kepler *in press*), and it is this same Lesser Antillean species that replaces *A.dominicus* in northeastern Puerto Rico.

Thirdly, two of the largest islands in the Lesser Antilles, Dominica and Martinique, have the same three species as most of the other mountainous Lesser Antilles, but in addition a rather small fourth species, *Cyanophaia bicolor*, which lives in humid forest. How this extra species fits in there, but not on other islands, is a mystery. Difficulties of dispersal could hardly be involved, since Dominica and Martinique are about as far apart as is each from the next large island to the north and south respectively.

Finally, the Cayman Islands and Mona have no resident hummingbirds, I cannot suggest why. Hence there are a few, but only a few, exceptions to the trend described at the start of this chapter. There are further differences, however, since the counterparts which replace each other on different islands are not identical in morphology or ecology. The situation is summarised in Table 15 and Figs. 8 to 10.

THE SMALL SPECIES

As shown in Fig. 8, there are 5 small species of hummingbirds in the West Indies, one on the Bahamas, one on Cuba, one on Jamaica and Hispaniola, one on most of Puerto Rico, and the fifth in N.E. Puerto Rico, the Virgin Islands and the Lesser Antilles. The Cuban species is in the same genus as that on Jamaica and Hispaniola, and presumably of common origin, but the other four species are in different genera, look dissimilar and probably colonised the West Indies independently of each other. Since they replace each other geographically and no two are found on the same island, they are sufficiently alike in their requirements to exclude each other, but as can be seen from Table 15, they differ fairly markedly in size, ranging from the Cuba "bee hummingbird", which is the smallest bird in the world, to the more moderate sized Puerto Rican species. (In the latter, incidentally, male and female differ fairly markedly in size of beak and feeding habits, so that the two sexes have partly separate ecological niches; C. and A. Kepler 1973.)

Each of these small species lives in both lowlands and highlands, with a preference for open rather than closed forest. There is, however,

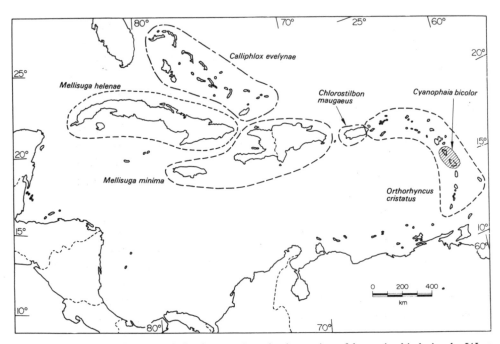

FIG. 8. *Ranges of the five small endemic species of hummingbirds in the West Indies, and also of the fairly small montane species* Cyanophaia bicolor.

one partial exception; the Lesser Antillean species *Orthorhyncus cristatus* occurs in highland humid forest on most of the mountainous islands in the chain, but does not do so on Dominica, though even there it occurs in cultivated clearings in the highlands. This is linked with the presence on Dominica of the fairly small 'extra' species *Cyanophaia bicolor*, mentioned in the preceding section, which lives in the understorey of the rain forest and in montane thicket, and evidently displaces *Orthorhyncus cristatus* there. (The situation on Martinique, the only other island with *C.bicolor*, has not been studied.)

THE LARGE LOWLAND SPECIES

As can be seen from Fig. 9, there are four medium to large lowland species in the West Indies, one on Cuba and some of the Bahamas, one on Jamaica, one on Hispaniola and most of Puerto Rico, and the fourth in N.E. Puerto Rico, the Virgin Islands and the Lesser

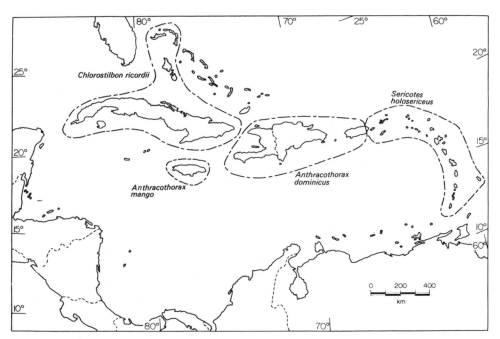

FIG. 9. *Ranges of the four medium or large lowland species of endemic hummingbirds in the West Indies.*

Antilles. Hence except for the last, they are divided up among the different islands differently from the small species. The species on Jamaica is in the same genus as that on Hispaniola with Puerto Rico, but looks so different that it might be of independent origin from the mainland, where the genus concerned, *Anthracothorax*, also occurs (though there is only one species of it in Central America). The other two large lowland species are in separate genera and look very different from each other, so probably colonised the archipelago independently.

As can be seen from Table 15, the four large lowland species differ from each other in size. Indeed, that on Cuba and some of the Bahamas is so small that I put it in this group only because it occurs in the lowlands alongside a much smaller species. Moreover, its nearest relative is a congener on Hispaniola which lives in the highlands. I could not discover from the literature whether this Cuban species also lives in the highlands; but if it does, it might well be that it is really the Cuban representative of the highland species, and that the species missing from Cuba is a large lowland species, in the absence of which the highland species has come lower down.

There are further complications, since the large lowland species on Jamaica is primarily in open forest, and the larger species of the highlands, *Trochilus polytmus*, also occupies the closed lowland forest. Again, while the large lowland species *Anthracothorax dominicus* of Puerto Rico is there restricted to the lowlands (except in man-made clearings high up), on Hispaniola the same species is regular in both lowlands and highlands. This is linked with the fact that the highland species of Hispaniola feeds solely under the canopy, and the resulting gap in its potential feeding station is filled by *A.dominicus*, which on Hispaniola feeds in the canopy of the highland forest. The same happens with the fourth large lowland species, *Sericotes holosericeus*, on Grenada. On the other mountainous islands of the Lesser Antilles, *S.holosericeus* occurs with the highland species *Eulampis jugularis* and is restricted to the lowlands; but on both Dominica and St Vincent we observed *S.holosericeus* occasionally visiting the highlands, and conversely *Eulampis jugularis* occasionally visiting the lowlands, usually, it must be admitted, where man had planted exotic trees with attractive flowers. Even so, each of these species evidently has the potentiality for occurring in the altitudinal zone of the other, and the fact that, nevertheless, they generally live apart, notably when breeding, is presumably due to competitive exclusion. On Grenada, however, *Eulampis jugularis* is replaced by a different highland species, *Glaucis hirsuta* which, unlike *E.jugularis*, feeds solely under the canopy (as it also does in Trinidad—Snow and Snow 1971). On Grenada, but no other island, *Sericotes holosericeus* feeds regularly at the edges and in the canopy of the highland humid forest. Doubtless it would do the same on others of the Lesser Antilles were it not excluded there by *Eulampis jugularis*. The latter species has wandered to Grenada, and that it does not breed there is presumably because it is excluded by *Glaucis hirsuta*, but why this should happen only on Grenada is not known.

This survey shows that the four medium to large lowland species differ from each other fairly markedly in their ecology, and as can be seen from Table 15, they also differ in size. Yet no two of them breed in the same area, so evidently they are sufficiently alike to exclude each other.

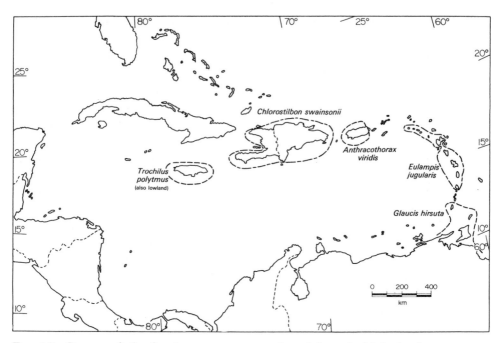

FIG. 10. *Ranges of the five large montane species of hummingbirds in the West Indies. Mainland range of* Glaucis hirsuta *is not shown.* (Chlorostilbon ricordii, *shown on Fig. 9, occurs perhaps also in the mountains on Cuba.*)

THE LARGE HIGHLAND SPECIES

In Fig. 10 are shown the ranges of the 5 large highland species. The species on Jamaica also occurs in closed lowland forest, the species on Hispaniola feeds solely under the canopy, the species on Puerto Rico is in the same genus as the lowland one on this island, and presumably evolved within the Greater Antilles, the fourth species occupies the mountainous Lesser Antilles except Grenáda, and the fifth species, on Grenada, feeds solely under the canopy. Once again, therefore, the replacing species differ somewhat from each other in their ecology, and also in size, but they are evidently similar enough to exclude each other from their respective ranges.

COMPETITIVE REPLACEMENT

As can be seen from Table 15, there are, in all, 15 species of hummingbirds in the West Indies, in 10 genera. Fourteen of these are endemic species, the exception being *Glaucis hirsuta*, a South American species found in the West Indies solely on the southernmost island of Grenada. Six of them are in endemic genera, namely *Mellisuga, Orthorhyncus, Cyanophaia, Sericotes, Trochilus* and *Eulampis*, and the classification of the hummingbirds is so difficult that it is not possible to say from what mainland genera these might be derived (though *Mellisuga* is thought to be close to *Calypte*). Bond has also suggested that the two large Lesser Antillean species in the genera *Sericotes* and *Eulampis* might have diverged from a common ancestor within the West Indies, but this is doubtful. Since representatives of three mainland genera, *Calliphlox, Chlorostilbon* and *Anthracothorax* have also colonised the West Indies, this means that there have been 10, or if *Sericotes* and *Eulampis* are of common origin, 9 successful colonisations of the West Indies from outside.

Hence to get only two species on each lowlying island and three on each mountainous island has involved considerable selection and reduction, which is presumably still maintained. As a recent example, one large lowland species has been replaced by another in the Virgin Islands, as has already been mentioned; it may be wondered whether this might be linked with recent changes in the vegetation or other conditions in the Virgin Islands due to man.

Further evidence that exclusion is still maintained is provided by the fact that there are records of hummingbirds moving between the islands and beyond them. As already set out in Table 14 (p. 80), three West Indian species have been recorded in North America, the Bahaman *Calliphlox evelynae*, the Bahaman and Cuban *Chlorostilbon ricordii* twice, and the Lesser Antillean *Orthorhyncus cristatus* once, the last species at least 3300 km. from where it was raised. Further, within the Lesser Antilles, *Eulampis jugularis* has been seen on both Barbados and Grenada, respectively 160 km. and 110 km. from its nearest breeding station on St. Vincent, and also on Antigua, Barbuda, Desirade, Iles des Saintes and Bequia, also outside, but nearer to, other islands where it breeds (Danforth 1934, Bond 1966, 1971). The large lowland species *Sericotes holosericeus* breeds on all the Lesser Antilles, so would not be recognised as a wanderer if it moved from one of these islands to another, but it has been seen at sea between Montserrat and Antigua and between some of the Grenadines (Clark 1905). Finally, four South American species have been recorded in the Lesser Antilles.

Florisuga mellivora, Amazilia tobaci and *Chrysolampis mosquitus* have been recorded some 120 km. away from their nearest breeding station on Tobago, the first on Carriacou in the Grenadines and the other two on Grenada. Similarly *Anthracothorax viridigula*, which breeds in Trinidad, has been seen on Union Island in the Grenadines (Clark 1905, Bond 1966, 1971). Evidently these, and doubtless further mainland species, are prevented from settling in the West Indies by the resident species.

It will be asked why, if hummingbirds wander between the islands, so many as 15 species should persist there. Why are there not the same two or three species on every island? The answer must, I consider, be competitive displacement, each species having the advantage over potential rivals on the island or islands where it occurs. The different islands of the West Indies differ to some extent from each other in their forests and the other conditions which they provide. Further, as already noted, the replacing species differ somewhat from each other in both their morphology and their ecology. One can hardly attribute their morphological and other differences to chance, and it is perhaps through these differences, linked with differences in the ecological conditions on the different islands, that each is the most efficient where it resides. While, however, there are such differences, the replacing species are sufficiently similar to exclude each other.

Perhaps a more intriguing question is how, if hummingbirds wander as much as they do, so many different species should have evolved in the West Indies in the first place. This is the question already raised for island birds in general in the previous chapter, but the situation is carried to an extreme in the hummingbirds, since 14 of the 15 species present are endemic to the West Indies, as are 6 of the genera. I can only suggest, as before, that if inter-island wandering is much more frequent than formerly supposed, then the time needed to evolve a separate species might be much shorter than formerly supposed, especially if selection for differentiation is strong; and selection is likely to be strong where ecological differences are great, as they might well be between an oceanic island and the mainland. Recognisable differences between bird populations of the same species can evolve within fifty years even on a continent (Johnston and Selander 1964 for the House Sparrow *Passer domesticus*), and perhaps might do so more rapidly on an island.

There is the further possibility that some of the species are different on different islands because the first mainland hummingbird to arrive happened to be different and, once it had evolved to the local conditions, was thereafter able to exclude potential newcomers with rather similar ecology. But this is speculative.

COMPARISON WITH MAINLAND

The continental island of Tobago has twice as many resident species of hummingbirds as Grenada, only 120 km away, just as it has twice the number of land birds altogether, and the possible reasons for this will be considered in Chapter 11. It may be added that 4 of the 6 Tobagan species have occurred on or near Grenada, *Glaucis hirsuta* being resident there and three others have occurred as stragglers (see p. 94). Trinidad has 16 species of hummingbirds (Herklots 1961), and Venezuela about 90 species (Phelps 1958).

In Central America, for comparison with the 3 species of hummingbirds on Jamaica and the 2 on Cuba, Honduras has 37 species (Monroe 1968) and Mexico 44 (Friedmann *et al.* 1950). As shown later, the proportionate reduction in the number of species on Jamaica compared with Honduras is much higher in hummingbirds than in the land birds as a whole. In North America, however, the number of species of hummingbirds greatly declines, and as already noted, there is only one resident species in Florida.

SUMMARY

Nine or ten different forms of hummingbirds have colonised the West Indies, and are divided into 15 different species. Yet nearly every lowlying island has just one small and one large resident species, and nearly every mountainous island has just one small species, which occurs in both lowlands and highlands, together with one large lowland and one large highland species. This situation cannot be ascribed to chance and may reasonably be attributed to all the potential ecological niches for hummingbirds on each island being filled.

There are a few exceptions to the general trends, notably the presence of an extra small species in the highlands of Dominica and Martinique, and the absence of a third species from the mountainous island of Cuba. Puerto Rico has five species, but is not a true exception since three are on the main mountainous island and two are apart from them in the northeast corner. This shows that replacement can occur without any obvious geographical barrier, presumably through competitive exclusion.

Five small species replace each other on different islands, so do four large lowland species and five large highland species. Some of the replacing species are in different genera, and they differ from each other to some extent in morphology and ecology, yet are sufficiently alike to displace each other. It may be through their minor differences, linked with differences in the ecological conditions on different islands, that each is the most efficient where it resides. In the last fifty years, one large lowland species has replaced another in the Virgin Islands.

Inter-island movements are frequent, but endemism is higher than in any other group of West Indian land birds, suggesting that the evolution of island forms may be rapid. It is likely to be rapid where there is strong selection for change in relation to ecological differences.

CHAPTER 7 · GEOGRAPHICAL DISPLACEMENT

The weight to be attached to the example of the hummingbirds depends on the extent to which they are representative or exceptional among West Indian land birds. The fact is that there is no other family of land birds in which so many different species have colonised the archipelago but so few are present on any one island. However, the phenomenon of geographical displacement, on which this fact depends, is widespread on a smaller scale in other land birds, and provides further evidence that the available niches may be full.

DEFINITION

I use the term 'geographical displacement' for the replacement on different islands of one species by another, not closely related, with similar but not identical ecology, the inference being that the replacement is due to competitive exclusion. Closely related species on different islands are not in question, as they probably arose as geographical forms of a common ancestor and evolved where they now occur. In cases of geographical displacement, the species must be sufficiently alike in ecology to exclude each other, but sufficiently different for each to be the most efficient on its particular island, and the islands must therefore be sufficiently different from each other to allow this. The similarities in ecology are usually obvious, but the postulated differences, between both the species and the islands, have not usually been observed, and their existence rests on inference.

A simple example was given in Chapter 5. As shown in Fig. 7 (p. 76), the widespread Caribbean pigeon *Columba squamosa* is replaced on Jamaica by the endemic *C.caribaea*. These two species are of different origin, *C.squamosa* being closest to various other Caribbean species and *C.caribaea* to the Central American *C.fasciata* (see p. 238). They are of similar size and both live in humid forest, but they do not have identical ecology, since *C.squamosa*, unlike *C.caribaea*, descends to the arid lowlands. The absence of *C.squamosa* as a resident on Jamaica is not due to its failure to reach it, as it has occurred several times; so it is evidently unable to survive there, for which competitive exclusion by *C.caribaea* is a likely cause. But the evidence for this is circumstantial, as it is for the other cases of geographical displacement discussed in this chapter. However, there are so many such instances that it would be hard to invoke coincidence to explain them all. Further examples of geographical displacement were given in the previous chapter for the hummingbirds, many of them involving species in different genera, and in their case also, competitive exclusion is probably involved.

It is tempting to attribute glibly any case where rather similar species replace each other on separate islands to geographical displacement. Before reaching such a conclusion, however, one must discover, first, whether the species concerned are not island forms derived from a common ancestor, and secondly whether they are, broadly, ecological counterparts; both difficulties are illustrated by the Greater Antillean thrushes discussed later. In addition to the three hummingbirds already discussed, at least 9 of the 66 species of Jamaican land birds are displaced geographically in part of their West Indian range by a congener, not closely related, with similar ecology, and at least 2 more are displaced by a species of a different genus. There may well be a few other instances, but I have omitted any where I had doubts about either the taxonomy or ecology of the birds concerned. That at least one-fifth of the land birds are concerned might represent an unusually high proportion for an island in an oceanic archipelago, but I have not attempted to produce comparable figures for other archipelagoes, because detailed knowledge of both systematics and ecology is needed in order to do so, as discussed earlier. If the proportion is unusually high, it may be noted that the big arc of mainland round much of the West Indies provides a large pool of potential colonists from which bird species with similar but not identical ecology might be drawn. More important, it has to be presumed that various of the West Indian islands are sufficiently different from each other to mean that one member of this particular pool is the most successful on one island, another on another.

GEOGRAPHICAL DISPLACEMENT BETWEEN SPECIES
WHICH COEXIST ON THE MAINLAND

Further details about the species discussed in this and the following
sections are given under the species concerned in Part 2. Of special
interest are species which replace each other on different West Indian
islands but which coexist on the mainland, where they differ in ecology.
For instance the Jamaican oriole *Icterus leucopteryx*, also on St Andrew
and formerly Grand Cayman, is most closely related to the Central
American species *I.pustulatus*, which Beecher (1950) put in the subgenus
Icterus (*sens. strict.*), a group of thicker-beaked orioles which eat mainly
fruit and some nectar. The habitat, at least in Honduras, is arid forest,
chiefly in the lowlands (Monroe 1968).

As shown in Fig. 11, a different species of oriole, *I.dominicensis*,
replaces *I.leucopteryx* on Cuba, some of the Bahamas, Hispaniola and

FIG. 11. *Geographical replacement in the Greater Antilles of two endemic
orioles in the genus* Icterus, *derived from different mainland species. Three
Lesser Antillean species derived from* I.dominicensis *are also shown.*

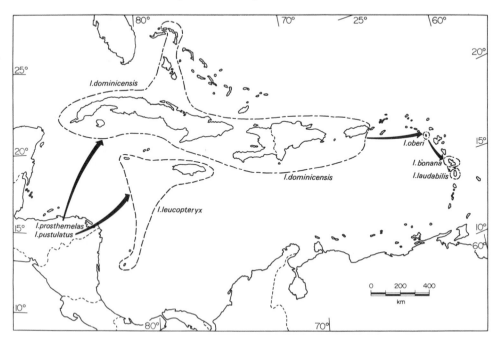

Puerto Rico. It is most closely related to a different mainland species, *I.prosthemelas*, which Beecher (1950) put in the subgenus *Bananivorus*, a group of narrower-beaked orioles which eat mainly nectar and some fruit. At least in Honduras, *I.prosthemelas* lives in lowland rain forest (Monroe 1968). The differences in diet and habitat between these two mainland species enable both of them to occur there. On the other hand there is only one species of *Icterus* on any one island in the West Indies. Hence both of the island species have broader habitats and diets than their mainland ancestors, for each occurs in both the arid lowlands and the humid highlands; further, the Jamaican bird has a thicker beak than its mainland ancestor and eats mainly insects from under the bark, but also fruit and some nectar. Nothing significant seems on record for the diet of *I.dominicensis* on Cuba or Hispaniola, but the Puerto Rican form, like the Jamaican, has evolved a thicker beak and includes many insects in its diet (Wetmore 1927). One cannot reasonably attribute all these changes to coincidence, and the most likely explanation is that, though two mainland species of orioles have colonised the West Indies, there is 'ecological room' for only one on any one island, and that one has there evolved a broader or coarser niche than its mainland ancestor. Why one mainland species should have settled on Jamaica and a different species on the other islands is not known. (I have added to Fig. 11 the ranges of three other island species of orioles found on Montserrat, Martinique and St. Lucia respectively; it is generally agreed that these are distinctive forms derived from *I.dominicensis*.)

A very similar situation is provided by two species of parakeets in the genus *Aratinga*, of which the ranges are shown in Fig. 12. Jamaica has the endemic *A.nana*, which is extremely close to the Central American *A.astec*, a species which, at least in Honduras, occurs in lowland rain forest, vega and open wooded cultivation, both humid and arid (Monroe 1968). But the closely related parakeets of the other Greater Antilles, *A.euops* of Cuba and *A.chloroptera* of Hispaniola and formerly Mona and probably Puerto Rico, belong to a different subgenus of *Aratinga*, of which *A.holochlora* is the mainland species living nearest to these islands and which, in Honduras, occurs in montane forest (Monroe 1968). Whether the two mainland species *A.astec* and *A.holochlora* also differ significantly from each other in diet is not recorded. In any case, though both occur on the mainland,

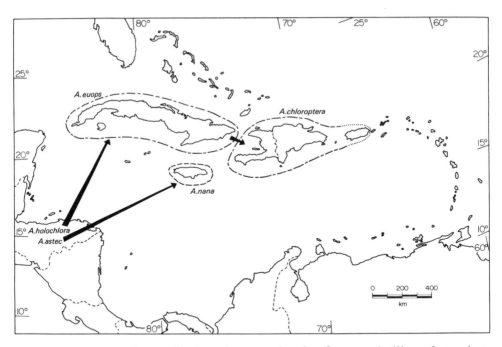

Fig. 12. *Geographical replacement in the Greater Antilles of parakeets* Aratinga *derived from different mainland species.*

there is evidently room for only one of them on any one island in the Greater Antilles.

The story is essentially the same in the two West Indian solitaires *Myadestes*, the ranges of which are shown in Fig. 13. The Cuban species *M.elisabeth* is probably derived from *M.obscurus*, whereas *M.genibarbis* of Jamaica, Hispaniola and some of the Lesser Antilles is nearest to a different mainland species *M.unicolor*. The two mainland species differ in habitat, *M.obscurus* living in montane pine-oak and *M.unicolor* in cloud forest and lower montane forest (Monroe 1968). Whether they also differ in feeding is not known. Once again, therefore, two species have colonised the Greater Antilles, but there is evidently room for only one species on any one island, though in Honduras there is room for two, one in each of the two different types of montane forest. (Fig. 13 also shows a curious gap in the eastern part of the range of *M.genibarbis*, since it is absent from Puerto Rico and Guadeloupe; it is hard to see why this should be, as both islands have good humid forest.)

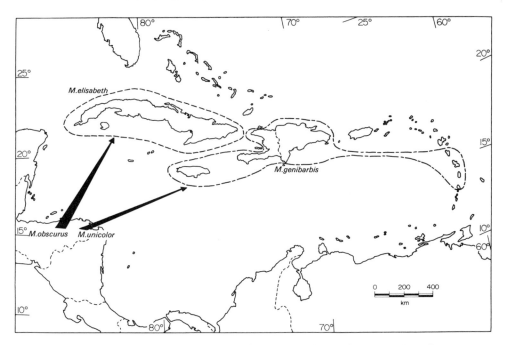

FIG. 13. *Geographical replacement in the Greater Antilles of two species of solitaire* Myadestes, *probably derived from different mainland species. Note also the interrupted range of* M.genibarbis *in the east.*

As many as four species of melanerpine woodpeckers have colonised the West Indies, but there is only one on each island (Fig. 14). The fifth species, *Melanerpes herminieri*, on Guadeloupe, is close to that on Puerto Rico and was presumably derived from it, so does not represent a fifth colonisation. As shown by Selander and Giller (1963), the Jamaican Woodpecker *Centurus radiolatus* is closest to the Golden-fronted Woodpecker *C.aurifrons*, which is widespread in Central America, where it occurs in semi-open situations in the arid lowlands and monsoon forest (Monroe 1968). It also occurs in Mexico and part of southern U.S.A., north of which it is replaced by the closely related Red-bellied Woodpecker *C.carolinus*, with a very small zone of overlap. The latter species, which lives in heavy forest, is that nearest to the Cuban species, *C.superciliaris*, which also occurs on Grand Cayman and some of the Bahamas. Since *C.aurifrons* and *C.carolinus* replace each other geographically on the mainland, it was to be expected that the species derived from them in the Greater

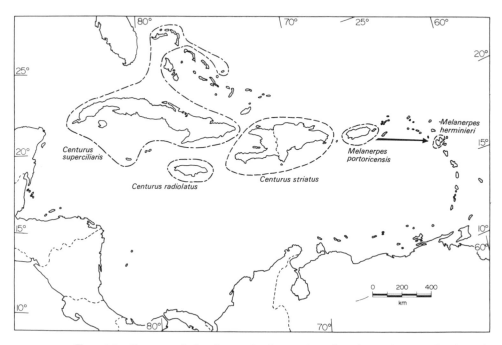

FIG. 14. *Ranges of the five endemic species of melanerpine woodpeckers in the West Indies.*

Antilles would do the same. The third species, *Centurus striatus*, which occurs on Hispaniola, though also derived from *Centurus*, is so distinctive that its immediate ancestor is unknown; probably it represents an earlier colonisation of the Greater Antilles by a member of this genus. The fourth species, *M.portoricensis*, on Puerto Rico, differs in that it belongs to the genus *Melanerpes* (with which *Centurus* is often merged, including by Peters). The Puerto Rican bird seems about equally close to two mainland species of *Melanerpes*, the Acorn Woodpecker *M.formicivorus*, found in montane pine-oak forest and locally in lowland pine in much of Central America (Monroe 1968), also in part of Mexico and western U.S.A., and the Red-headed Woodpecker *M.erythrocephalus*, found in light woodland in eastern and central U.S.A. Hence *M.formicivorus* occurs in Central America with the putative ancestor of the Jamaican species, and *M.erythrocephalus* in eastern U.S.A. with the putative ancestor of the Cuban species; so whichever is the ancestor of the Puerto Rican species, it coexists on the mainland with one of the *Centurus* species of the Greater Antilles.

The two members of each of these pairs differ from each other to an important extent in habitat and, probably more important, in feeding, since the species of *Centurus* feed like typical woodpeckers by excavating in wood (Bent 1939, Selander and Giller 1959), whereas *M.erythrocephalus* and *M.formicivorus* obtain many flying insects by sallying out from a perch and pick others off the surface of bark, and both also take many acorns. Hence, while on the mainland these pairs of species are able to coexist through differences in diet and habitat, there is evidently room for only one of them on each West Indian island. It would seem that the Puerto Rican species has changed its habits more than the species of *Centurus*, for so far as observations go, it excavates in wood and in general behaves like a typical woodpecker (C. and A. Kepler pers. comm.).

One further Puerto Rican species is involved in a case of geographical displacement, for though two species of nightjars in the genus *Caprimulgus* have colonised the Greater Antilles, there are none on Jamaica. The endemic Puerto Rican species *C.noctitherus* is closely related to the mainland Whip-poor-Will *C.vociferus* and the endemic Cuban and Hispaniolan species *C.cubanensis* to the mainland Chuck-Will's Widow *C.carolinensis*. These two mainland species live together in the eastern United States, but how they might there be separated from each other ecologically is not clear from the published literature; once again, the species derived from them in the Greater Antilles are on separate islands. There is a parallel case in the Lesser Antilles, where *Caprimulgus rufus* is found on St Lucia and *Caprimulgus cayennensis* on the adjoining island of Martinique, whereas both species occur on the South American mainland, where their possible means of ecological separation are not known. This genus is not otherwise represented in the Lesser Antilles.

It may be added that the occurrence on Puerto Rico of a species derived from *Caprimulgus vociferus* and another from *Melanerpes* (sens.-strict.) also shows that, while some mainland species probably spread gradually from island to island in the Greater Antilles, here are two which either made a direct crossing of at least 1500 km from the mainland to Puerto Rico, or else later died out on the intervening islands.

There is yet one other case of two species which coexist on the mainland but occupy separate islands in the Greater Antilles, but the two are in different genera and differ so much from each other

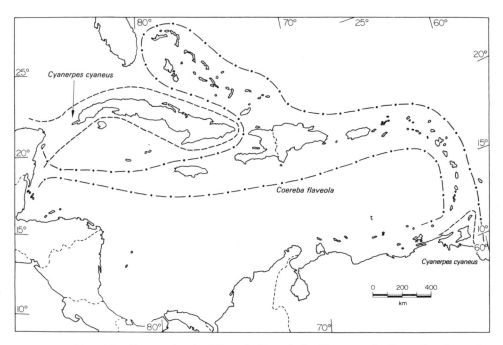

FIG. 15. *Ranges in the West Indies of the Bananaquit* Coereba flaveola *and the honeycreeper* Cyanerpes cyaneus, *which coexist in Central and South America (where ranges not shown).*

in appearance and feeding that it is hard to believe that they can really displace each other by competitive exclusion. These are the two honeycreepers, the Bananaquit *Coereba flaveola*, which is probably the commonest bird throughout the West Indies except for its absence from Cuba and the Caymans, and the Red-legged Honeycreeper *Cyanerpes cyaneus*, which in the West Indies is confined to Cuba, as shown in Fig. 15. Their geographical replacement seems too remarkable to be due to coincidence. Where they coexist on Trinidad they are separated by their diet, because *C.flaveola* feeds to a much greater extent on nectar and finds most of its insect prey on the underside of leaves, whereas *C.cyaneus* feeds to a much greater extent on fruit and takes insects chiefly from twigs and the upper sides of leaves (Snow and Snow 1971). Critical observations of this type have not been made in the West Indies, and observations are particularly needed for *C.cyaneus* on Cuba. Hence a firm judgement should be suspended, but there is an *a priori* case for thinking that they exclude each other on the islands where, it should be remembered, they are the sole species filling the 'honey-creeper' niche (except on Jamaica, where there is also the Orangequit *Euneornis campestris*).

In this section, then, have been cited six examples, in orioles, parakeets, solitaires, woodpeckers, and two in nightjars, with a seventh possible case in honeycreepers, in which two species which occur together on the mainland replace each other geographically on separate islands in the Greater Antilles, presumably because, in the simplified ecological conditions on the islands, there is a niche for only one species of the type concerned. For these species, therefore, the available niches appear to be full, as they do in the hummingbirds. Further, in at least some of these cases, the island species has a broader habitat or broader feeding habits than its mainland ancestor. Had there been only one such example, it might have been ascribed to coincidence, but with six or seven, it seems reasonable to conclude that competitive displacement is involved. There are not so many examples of it as in the West Indian hummingbirds, but there is the advantage that the mainland ancestors of the species discussed in this section are known; it is also known that the ancestors of the island species not only occur on the mainland together but also that, in most cases, they there differ from each other in ecology.

The examples in the previous section were singled out because the mainland representatives of the island species concerned are known. Jamaican species are involved in several other cases. The ancestor of the distinctive Jamaican Crow *Corvus jamaicensis* is not known, but according to Johnston (1961) the ecological counterpart on Cuba, *C.nasicus*, is closely related to the widespread Common Crow *C. brachyrhynchos* of North America, while the counterpart on Hispaniola and formerly Puerto Rico, *C.leucognaphalus*, is related to a different mainland species, the White-necked Raven *C.cryptoleucus*, which just overlaps in range with *C.brachyrhynchos* near the Mexican border, and extends down into Mexico. Probably, therefore, the crows should be regarded as another example of geographical displacement, but it was omitted from the previous section because the relationships of the island to the mainland forms have been disputed (see p. 351).

The species (or superspecies) of flycatcher *Myiarchus stolidus* occurs throughout the West Indies, to which it is endemic, except for the two southernmost islands of Grenada and St. Vincent, where it is replaced by another endemic species, *M.nugator*, derived from the South American mainland species *M.tyrannulus*, which looks similar and fills a similar niche. The interest of this case lies not so much in the fact of geographical displacement, but in the careful taxonomic study needed by Lanyon (1967), who used voice as well as morphology, before the systematics of the island forms concerned could be interpreted. Had I used the classification of previous workers, I would have drawn wrong conclusions about where geographical displacement is involved in this group.

Euphonias, as mentioned in Chapter 4, specialise on the fruits of mistletoes Loranthaceae, so it is unlikely that there would be room for more than one species on each West Indian island. In fact, as shown in Fig. 55 (p. 330), there is only one on each, the widespread mainland species *Euphonia musica* occurring on Hispaniola, Puerto Rico and many of the Lesser Antilles, but being replaced on Jamaica by the endemic *E.jamaica*, the mainland ancestor of which, although not known, is not close to *E.musica*.

THRUSHES *Turdus*

At first glance, the situation in thrushes of the genus *Turdus* (with which I have included here the related Lesser Antillean genus *Cichlherminia*) is similar to that in the hummingbirds. Seven different species have colonised the West Indies, but no island has more than two resident species, suggesting that this is the most for which there is ecological room. To bring about such a situation there must have been much exclusion, presumably involving competition; but the story is not simple, at least in the Greater Antilles, because various of the species involved are not ecological counterparts, and further, their systematic relationship to each other is uncertain. The interest of this example is as much in illustrating difficulties in interpretation as in the facts themselves. The ranges of the West Indian thrushes are shown in Fig. 16.

In the Lesser Antilles, the story is straightforward. The two southernmost islands of Grenada and St Vincent have two South American species, *T.nudigenis* in lowland wooded cultivation and *T.fumigatus* in humid forest, so they are separated by habitat.

T.fumigatus does not extend to the islands further north, where it is replaced in humid forest by the endemic *Cichlherminia lherminieri* (which on St Lucia also lives in lowland windward forest, a habitat now destroyed on the other islands). *C.lherminieri* coexists with the lowland *T.nudigenis* on St. Lucia, is absent from Martinique, coexists with a different lowland species *T.plumbeus* on Dominica, and is the only thrush on Guadeloupe and Montserrat. *T.nudigenis* is the only thrush on Martinique where, as on St Lucia, it was first reported only in 1951, and there are no thrushes on the rest of the Lesser Antilles. (It seems possible that the absence of *C.lherminieri* from Martinique and of *T.plumbeus* from all the Lesser Antilles except Dominica might be due to human disturbance, but there is no evidence for this.)

In view of what happens in the Lesser Antilles, one might have expected to find a lowland and a highland species on each of the mountainous islands of the Greater Antilles. In fact, *T.plumbeus* is the sole species of thrush on Cuba and Puerto Rico, and also on most of Hispaniola, and on all three of these islands it extends from the arid lowlands to the humid highlands. It is also found on the northern Bahamas and Cayman Brac, and the distinctive *T.ravidus* of Grand Cayman, now extinct, was probably a well-marked island form of it. There are only two islands in the Greater Antilles with two species of thrush. Hispaniola, in addition to *T.plumbeus*, has the endemic *T.swalesi* which is confined to humid forest high up on one mountain, Morne La Selle. Jamaica has *T.aurantius*, extending from the more humid parts of the lowlands to the mountains, and *T.jamaicensis* restricted to the highlands.

As can be seen from Fig. 16, *T.aurantius* and *T.plumbeus* are on separate islands, and they might be sufficiently similar in their ecology to exclude each other, even though *T.plumbeus* is common in the arid lowlands, a habitat without a thrush on Jamaica. However, their mainland ancestors are not known, and it is just possible that they were derived from the same original colonist, in which case geographical displacement need not be involved. *T.jamaicensis* and *T.swalesi* are also on separate islands, but though both are montane, they are not ecological counterparts, so cannot be excluding each other. The very local *T.swalesi* feeds much on the ground, where its habits and long tail recall those of the Jamaican *T.aurantius*, to which Wetmore and Swales (1931) related it, while *T.jamaicensis* has a short tail and different stance, and probably different feeding habits. Why, in the

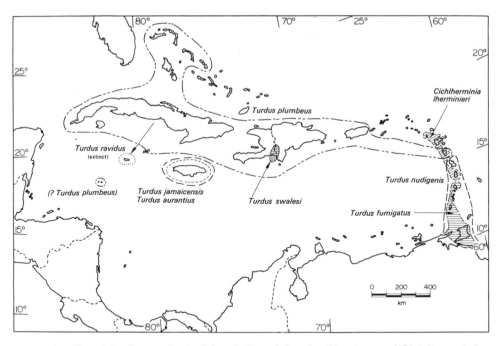

FIG. 16. *Ranges in the West Indies of thrushes* Turdus *and* Cichlherminia. (*Mainland ranges of* T.nudigenis *and* T.fumigatus *not shown.*)

Greater Antilles, only Jamaica accommodates a short-tailed thrush and only Hispaniola has two long-tailed ground-feeding hopping species is not known. This example shows the danger of deducing from the replacement on separate islands of congeneric species that geographical displacement is necessarily involved.

To conclude, though seven species have colonised the archipelago, there are not more than two West Indian thrushes on any one island; competitive exclusion evidently plays an important part in their distribution, but the extent of competition cannot be fully elucidated until more is known of the ecology and the systematic relationships of the Greater Antillean species.

There is one further genus, that of the parulid warblers *Dendroica*, with many species in the West Indies, but few on any one island. However, geographical displacement probably plays little part, as various of the highland species are probably descended from one original colonist, and various of the other species are separated from each other by habitat, as discussed in Chapter 10.

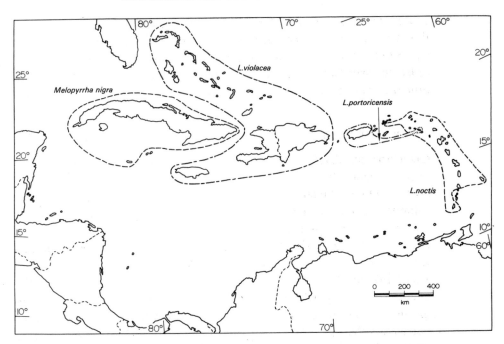

FIG. 17. *Ranges in the West Indies of the three species in the endemic West Indian bullfinch genus* Loxigilla *and the Cuban and Cayman endemic* Melopyrrha nigra. L.portoricensis *is now extinct on St Kitts.*

FURTHER INTERGENERIC EXAMPLES

Most species of the pigeon family Columbidae are the same on Jamaica, Hispaniola and Cuba (apart from the replacement of *C.caribaea* by *C.squamosa* already discussed p. 77), but Jamaica is the only one of the three with the ground-feeding *Leptotila jamaicensis,* while Hispaniola and Cuba have the quail-dove *Geotrygon chrysia,* absent from Jamaica (see Fig. 30, p. 243). Both *L.jamaicensis* and *G.chrysia* live in arid lowland forest, but too little is known to say whether or not they are ecological equivalents.

A case involving the bullfinch genus *Loxigilla* is much more likely. As shown in Fig. 17, this endemic West Indian genus has three species, *L.violacea* on Jamaica, Hispaniola and the Bahamas, *L.portoricensis* on Puerto Rico (and formerly St Kitts, see p. 153), and *L.noctis* in the Lesser Antilles. Cuba, instead, has the endemic *Melopyrrha nigra,* which is also on Grand Cayman. *Melopyrrha* is not closely related to

Loxigilla and is probably derived from the mainland genus *Sporophila*, though it is of similar size and has a similarly shaped beak to *Loxigilla* and is probably an ecological equivalent. Hence while a firm judgement must be suspended until *M.nigra*'s feeding habits are known, geographical displacement is probably involved.

REPLACEMENT BY MEMBERS OF THE SAME SPECIES-GROUP

Geographical displacement through competitive exclusion has not been discussed here in relation to the ranges on separate islands of species which started as geographical forms of the same original colonist, since they may well have evolved where they now live. Even so, however, competitive exclusion may be involved. For instance, though *Loxigilla noctis* probably evolved in the Lesser Antilles and *L.portoricensis* on Puerto Rico, each perhaps wanders at times to an island inhabited by the other, in which case it is then probably eliminated in competition. In that case, the present ranges of these species are reinforced by geographical displacement, and there is no essential difference, except in their origin, from the displacement of unrelated species discussed in this chapter. Further, one need not assume that the Lesser Antillean *L.noctis* evolved on all the islands where it now occurs. It may have evolved locally and spread later, in which case the boundaries of its range at a later stage have probably been determined by competition with the other species.

The most complex example in the Greater Antilles of closely related species which live on adjacent islands is that of the members of the white-eyed vireo group, the ranges of which are set out in Fig. 18. Some of these species are more distinctive than others, indeed the Hispaniolan species was at one time classified among the flycatchers Tyrannidae, but it is generally agreed that all of them belong to the white-eyed vireo group, of which *V.griseus* and *V.pallens* are the mainland representatives in, respectively, northern and central America. However, the precise relationships of these forms to each other and to the mainland species are not known. Doubtless most of them evolved on the islands where they now live. It seems unlikely, however, that this should have happened on every island throughout the discontinuous range of *V.crassirostris*, which occurs on the Bahamas, the Caymans and Old Providence, and in this species at least, subsequent geographical displacement has presumably been involved.

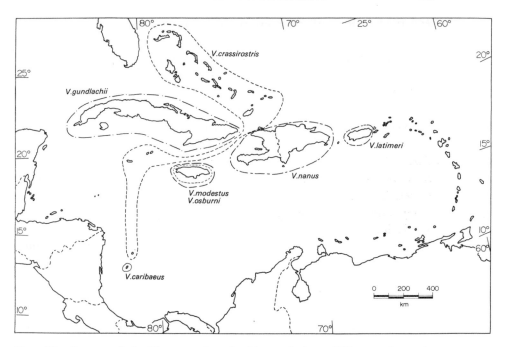

FIG. 18. *Ranges of Antillean species of white-eyed vireos* (Vireo griseus + V.pallens *stock*). *Note* (*i*) *that there are two species solely on Jamaica; and* (*ii*) *the discontinuous range of* V.crassirostris. *The mainland ranges of* V.griseus *and* V.pallens *are not shown.*

(The different problem of the existence of a second species on Jamaica is discussed in Chapter 8.)

As just pointed out for *Loxigilla* each of these vireos may at times wander onto an island where another is resident, and is then probably eliminated in competition; so even if it evolved on the island where it now occurs, its present range is probably reinforced by geographical replacement. The same probably holds for other island species derived from one original colonist.

SUMMARY

The term 'geographical replacement' is used here primarily for the replacement on different islands of one species by an unrelated species with similar but not identical ecology, through competitive exclusion. In several instances, two mainland species have colonised the West Indies but there is only one on any one island. The mainland species differ in ecology, but evidently are too alike to coexist in the ecologically poorer conditions on the islands, where ecological niches tend to be broader. These examples also provide further evidence that the niches available for island land birds are full. At least one-fifth of the Jamaican land birds are involved in geographical displacement in part of their West Indian range, and some examples involve species in different genera. In addition, while island species descended from a common ancestor may have evolved where they now live, the boundaries of their present ranges are probably reinforced by competitive exclusion, and may in some cases have been determined by geographical displacement subsequent to their speciation.

CHAPTER 8 · COMPARISON OF JAMAICA
WITH CUBA AND HISPANIOLA

The examples in the two preceding chapters show how much can be learned from comparing various types of land birds on different islands of the West Indies. The aim of this chapter is to put such selected comparisons into perspective by giving an overall picture of the land birds of Jamaica in relation to those on the adjoining large islands, Cuba, 150 km to the north, and Hispaniola 180 km to the east, themselves 90 km apart. Cuba has an area of some 114,000 sq. km, ten times that of Jamaica, rises to 2000 m and at its nearest point is only 200 km from the nearest mainland. Hispaniola is 80,000 sq. km in area, rises to 3200 m, and is 1100 km from Central America. Jamaica it will be recalled is 11,400 sq. km in area, rises to 2260 m and is 650 km from Central America. The number of species of land birds (pigeons to passerines) on each of these islands is very similar, 66 on Jamaica, 68 on Cuba and 73 on Hispaniola. (One further species, the mockingbird *Mimus gundlachii,* occurs on cays just north of Cuba, and another, the thrasher *Margarops fuscatus,* on the small island of Beata, just off southern Hispaniola, but in neither case on the major island.)

BIRD SPECIES IN COMMON

The Jamaican species also found on Cuba or Hispaniola are marked by a ' + ' in the two right-hand columns of Table 1, brackets indicating a different but very closely related species (in the same super-species). Including the latter, 34 species are in common, just over half the Jamaican land birds. They are of two types, those which also occur on the mainland, where many of them are widespread, and those typical of the West Indies which are absent from, or only just reach, the mainland.

SPECIES IN COMMON BETWEEN JAMAICA, CUBA AND
HISPANIOLA, AND ALSO PRESENT ON PART OF THE MAINLAND

The following 18 species are in this category:

dove *Zenaida macroura*   swift *Streptoprocne zonaris*
dove *Zenaida aurita*   swift *Cypseloides niger*
dove *Columbina passerina*   flycatcher *Tyrannus dominicensis*
dove *Zenaida asiatica*   martin *Progne dominicensis*
dove *Geotrygon montana*   swallow *Petrochelidon fulva*
cuckoo *Coccyzus americanus*   mockingbird *Mimus polyglottos*
cuckoo *Coccyzus minor*   grassquit *Tiaris olivacea*
ani *Crotophaga ani*   warbler *Dendroica petechia*
owl *Tyto alba*   vireo *Vireo altiloquus*

In addition, two pairs of Jamaican species, the parrots *Amazona collaria* and *A.agilis* and the white-eyed vireos *Vireo modestus* and *V.osburni*, are represented by very closely related species, but only one of each, on Cuba, Hispaniola and part of the mainland respectively. Hence the number of species in this category comes, in all, to 22.

SPECIES FOUND ON JAMAICA, CUBA AND HISPANIOLA BUT
NOT ON THE MAINLAND

The following 9 species are in this category (though the pigeon *Columba leucocephala* and tanager *Spindalis zena* reach offshore islands):

pigeon *Columba leucocephala*   flycatcher *Myiarchus stolidus*
pigeon *Columba inornata*   flycatcher *Contopus caribaeus*
nighthawk *Chordeiles gundlachii*   tanager *Spindalis zena*
swift *Tachornis phoenicobia*   grackle *Quiscalus niger*
flycatcher *Tyrannus caudifasciatus*

In addition, 5 Jamaican species are represented by a very closely related species on Cuba and Hispaniola but not on the mainland (in hummingbird *Mellisuga minima* by the same species on Hispaniola and a congener on Cuba):

dove *Geotrygon versicolor*   tody *Todus todus*
cuckoo *Saurothera vetula*   woodpecker *Centurus radiolatus*
hummingbird *Mellisuga minima*

Hence there are, in all, 14 species in this category, all of them being species endemic to the West Indies, and several of them being in genera endemic to the West Indies. Otherwise, the species common to all three islands call for little comment, except that it is perhaps surprising to find that, in islands so near to each other, only about half the species on each island are shared with the other two islands, even when extremely closely related species (in the same species-group) are included as the same species.

The following 8 Jamaican species also occur on Hispaniola, but not on Cuba:—

potoo *Nyctibius griseus*
flycatcher *Elaenia fallax*
swallow *Kalochelidon euchrysea*
solitaire *Myadestes genibarbis*
bunting *Ammodramus savannarum*
grassquit *Tiaris bicolor*
bullfinch *Loxigilla violacea*
bananaquit *Coereba flaveola*

To these should be added the hummingbird *Mellisuga minima,* listed in the previous section because there is a closely related species on Cuba. There are also two species in genera confined to Jamaica and Hispaniola with separate species on each, namely (the Jamaican species) the cuckoo *Hyetornis pluvialis* and the nightjar *Siphonorhis americanus*. (It may be added that Peters treated the Jamaican and Hispaniolan species of the cuckoo *Saurothera* as conspecific, which would have provided a 12th case, but in this treatment he has not been followed by later workers.)

These 11 species are a mixed lot. Four of them, the potoo *N.griseus,* the bunting (or sparrow) *A.savannarum,* the grassquit *T.bicolor* and the Bananaquit *C.flaveola,* also occur on the mainland (though *T.bicolor* only in South America). It is hard to see why the potoo and the bunting, both present in Central America, should be absent from Cuba, which is much nearer to the mainland than either Jamaica or Hispaniola. The grassquit *T.bicolor* is replaced on Cuba by an endemic congener, *T.canora,* the relationship of which to *T.bicolor* is uncertain. The Bananaquit is apparently replaced on Cuba by the Honeycreeper *Cyanerpes cyaneus,* as discussed in Chapter 7. Likewise of the species in this group not found on the mainland, the bullfinch *L.violacea* is replaced on Cuba by the endemic *Melopyrrha nigra* (see p. 111), the solitaire *M.genibarbis* by a congener, not very close to it, *M.elisabeth* (see p. 102), and the hummingbird *M.minima* by a congener *M.helenae,* which is probably closely related. The remaining four species are without related species or ecological equivalents on Cuba, three of them in genera restricted to Jamaica and Hispaniola, namely the cuckoo *Hyetornis*, nightjar *Siphonorhis* and swallow *Kalochelidon*, and the fourth species, *Elaenia fallax* very distinctive.

This link between Jamaica and Hispaniola is remarkable in that Jamaica has no species in common with Cuba that is absent from Hispaniola. It is also remarkable that four forms otherwise widespread in the Greater and Lesser Antilles should be replaced by different forms on Cuba, namely the solitaire *M.genibarbis*, grassquit *T.bicolor*, bullfinch genus *Loxigilla* and Bananaquit *C.flaveola*.

SPECIES ON JAMAICA AND SOME OTHER ISLANDS, BUT NOT CUBA OR HISPANIOLA

There are only three species in this category, the dove *Leptotila jamaicensis*, also found on Grand Cayman, St Andrew and in Yucatan, the mockingbird *Mimus gundlachii*, also found on cays off the north coast of Cuba and in most of the Bahamas except Grand Bahama and Great Abaco, and the oriole *Icterus leucopteryx*, also found on St Andrew and (now extinct) Grand Cayman. The discontinuous range of the

FIG. 19. *Range in the West Indies of the Mocking bird* Mimus gundlachii.

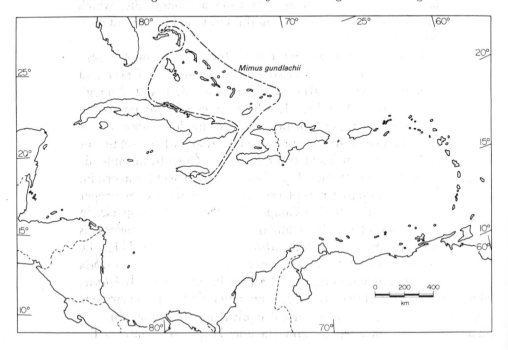

mockingbird *M.gundlachii* (Fig. 19) is remarkable. Occurring on most of the Bahamas, it is also, though local, on Jamaica, being there confined to lowland arid forest. One would think that there would have been somewhere suitable for it on the main island of Cuba. Nor is there any unrelated ecological equivalent to it on either Cuba or Hispaniola. Of the other two species in the group, the dove *L.jamaicensis* is perhaps replaced on Cuba and Hispaniola by *Geotrygon chrysia* (see p. 111) and the oriole *I.leucopteryx* is replaced by a different species of oriole (see p. 100).

SPECIES RESTRICTED TO JAMAICA

Finally, there are another 17 species peculiar to Jamaica. This is fewer than the number of endemic species, 27, because 10 of the latter have already been included in one of the previous categories under species with a closely related species on Hispaniola and Cuba. Of the 17 species peculiar to Jamaica, 7 have an ecological equivalent, but not very closely related, on Hispaniola, and usually also Cuba, namely:

pigeon *Columba caribaea*   thrush *Turdus aurantius*
parakeet *Aratinga nana*   euphonia *Euphonia jamaica*
hummingbird *Anthracothorax mango*   crow *Corvus jamaicensis*
hummingbird *Trochilus polytmus*

Much more remarkable, from the ecological viewpoint, is the existence of 10 further species peculiar to Jamaica which have no apparent ecological equivalent on Cuba or Hispaniola. These are:

owl *Pseudoscops grammicus*   thrush *Turdus jamaicensis*
becard *Platypsaris niger*   bullfinch *Loxipasser anoxanthus*
flycatcher *Myiarchus barbirostris*   Orangequit *Euneornis campestris*
flycatcher *Myiarchus validus*   warbler *Dendroica pharetra*
flycatcher *Myiopagis cotta*   icterid *Nesopsar nigerrimus*

To these should be added the second species of *Amazona* parrot and the second in the white-eyed vireo group, since there is only one of each of these in Cuba and Hispaniola.

As mentioned later in this chapter, there is a corresponding group of species on Cuba, and another on Hispaniola, which likewise have no ecological equivalents on either of the other two islands. On the conventional view that land birds rarely reach islands, one could expect such irregularities in distribution on the grounds that colonisa-

tion is very much the result of chance. But the situation can hardly
be so simple as this.

The Jamaican species concerned are a varied group. They include
three species, the becard *P.niger* and the flycatchers *M.barbirostris* and
M.cotta, which are close relatives of mainland species, indeed the two
latter have sometimes been treated as conspecific with the corresponding mainland species. So they have made the relatively long sea
crossing of 650 km. from the mainland to Jamaica but not the smaller
additional 150 to 180 km which would take them on from Jamaica
to Cuba or Hispaniola. Since they are so like their mainland relatives,
they are perhaps of recent origin on Jamaica. At the other extreme,
the Orangequit *Euneornis campestris* is so peculiar that even the bird
family to which it belongs is uncertain, and the icterid *Nesopsar
nigerrimus* is sufficiently unusual for its nearest relatives among the
icterids to be unknown. If they have been long enough in Jamaica to
evolve such big differences, surely they should have had time to reach
other islands?

Two further species, the second *Amazona* parrot and the second
member of the white-eyed vireo group are probably the result of
'double invasion' of Jamaica by the same mainland stock. But the
occurrence of double invasion implies mobility, so if difficulties of
dispersal had been critical, it is hard to understand why there should
not have been double invasions of the same stocks on Cuba and
Hispaniola. The two Jamaican parrots differ in depth of beak, the
two vireos in overall size, which presumably enables each to coexist
on Jamaica without eliminating the other, but there is no obvious
reason why the same should not have happened on the other two
islands. Another group of Jamaican species differentiated by size
is that of the *Myiarchus* flycatchers, of which the middle-sized *M.stolidus*
is on all three islands, but Jamaica, and only Jamaica, has, in addition,
a large and a small species.

One can make similar comments about the remaining species
unique to Jamaica. Either my interpretation of the small number of
bird species on oceanic islands is wrong and, after all, they get there
only rarely by chance, or we are extremely ignorant about the factors
limiting the range of bird species. I suggest that the latter alternative
is the more likely to be involved. For instance the becard genus
Platypsaris occurs through Central America and just reaches the
southern United States. Why should it stop there? I doubt if a reason-

able answer can be given, and if we are ignorant in this case, why not also for the factors limiting the range of the genus in the West Indies? The fact that Jamaica is an island gives its limitation there particular prominence, but from the biological viewpoint it may be no more remarkable than its limitation in range on the mainland. Perhaps, therefore, the facts presented in this chapter chiefly illustrate our ignorance as to what limits the ranges of bird species. Even so, it seems surprising that so many as 12 of the 66 Jamaican land birds should be without close relatives or ecological counterparts on the two large adjoining islands only 150–180 km away.

SPECIES COMMON TO CUBA AND HISPANIOLA BUT NOT ON JAMAICA

Including extremely closely related species which replace each other on adjacent islands as belonging to the same form, Hispaniola has about as many land birds in common with Cuba that are absent from Jamaica as it has with Jamaica that are absent from Cuba. Nine species come in this category:

pigeon *Columba squamosa*	thrush *Turdus plumbeus*
dove *Geotrygon caniceps*	oriole *Icterus dominicensis*
dove *Geotrygon chrysia*	icterid *Agelaius humeralis*
owl *Asio stygius*	crow *Corvus palmarum*
nightjar *Caprimulgus cubanensis*	

Of these, the pigeon *C.squamosa* is widespread in the West Indies and is displaced by *C.caribaea* on Jamaica (see p. 77), the dove *G.caniceps* is a geographical representative of the Jamaican *G.versicolor* and like it lives in highland forest, the dove *G.chrysia* is possibly replaced on Jamaica by an ecological equivalent in *Leptotila jamaicensis* (see p. 250). The large owl *A.stygius* is also on the mainland, but has no equivalent on Jamaica. There are also no equivalents on Jamaica of the nightjar *C.cubanensis*, icterid *A.humeralis* or small crow *C.palmarum*, but the thrush *T.plumbeus* and oriole *I.dominicensis* are replaced on Jamaica by congeners that are not closely related.

In addition, Cuba and Hispaniola, but not Jamaica, share closely related species which replace each other geographically in the parakeets (*Aratinga euops* and *A.chloroptera*), trogons (*Priotelus temnurus* and *Temnotrogon roseigaster*) and hummingbirds *Chlorostilbon* (*C.ricordii* and *C.swainsonii*). As already discussed, the parakeets and hummingbirds have their ecological counterparts, not closely related, on Jamaica, but the trogons do not. Indeed, Cuba and Hispaniola are the only islands in the West Indies on which this family is present, providing as peculiar a situation as that of the cotingid family (*i.e.* the becard), present solely on Jamaica.

SPECIES ON HISPANIOLA BUT NOT JAMAICA OR CUBA

As already mentioned, Hispaniola has 73 species of land birds, 7 more than Jamaica, and 25 of them are absent from Jamaica and Cuba. They fall into two groups, those respectively with and without a closely related species on Jamaica or Cuba. The 9 with a closely related species on one or both the other islands have already been mentioned in previous lists, so need not be discussed further, except to point out that Hispaniola has two species of *Todus*, each of the other islands only one. The two todies differ in the width of their beaks and in other ways, and pose the same question as Jamaica's two *Amazona* parrots and two white-eyed vireos, namely why, in each case, there should be two species on just the one island. The other Hispaniolan species with close relatives on one or both of the other islands include species in the parrot genus *Amazona*, cuckoos *Hyetornis* and *Saurothera*, nightjar *Siphonorhis*, hummingbird *Chlorostibon*, trogon, woodpecker *Centurus* and *Vireo*. These other 16 species, without close relatives on Jamaica or Cuba, are:

owl *Speotyto cunicularia*	tanager *Phaenicophilus poliocephalus*
owl *Asio flammeus*	tanager *Calyptophilus frugivorus*
woodpecker *Nesoctites micromegas*	warbler *Dendroica pinus*
palm-chat *Dulus dominicus*	warbler *Microligea palustris*
thrush *Turdus swalesi*	warbler *Xenoligea montana*
bunting *Zonotrichia capensis*	finch *Carduelis dominicensis*
euphonia *Euphonia musica*	finch *Loxia leucoptera*
tanager *Phaenicophilus palmarum*	crow *Corvus leucognaphalus*

Of these, the two owls, the bunting *Z.capensis*, the euphonia, the warbler *D.pinus* and the crossbill *L.leucoptera* are mainland species, the last some thousands of miles from its next nearest breeding area in northern North America. The crow *C.leucognaphalus* was also present formerly on Puerto Rico. The other 9 species are endemic to Hispaniola, together with another 10 species from previous lists, making 19 species in all, fewer than on Jamaica. The piculet *Nesoctites micromegas* is much larger than any other species in this subfamily, which is not otherwise represented in the West Indies. The palm-chat *Dulus* is placed in a family of its own, perhaps related to the waxwings Bombycillidae. The thrush *Turdus swalesi* is closely related to the Central American montane species *T.rufitorques*. The tanagers *Phaenicophilus* and *Calyptophilus* and the warblers *Microligea* and *Xenoligea* are in genera endemic to Hispaniola. The cardueline finch is the only member of its genus in the West Indies. The crow is close to a North American species.

This group of species poses the same question as that of the group peculiar to Jamaica, as to how they can be present on Hispaniola but not the adjacent islands. Is this due to dispersal between the islands being rare and random, or to the absence of particular ecological requirements? The absence of three of the Hispaniolan species from Jamaica is readily explained by the absence there of their particular requirements, since the warbler *Dendroica pinus*, the finch *Carduelis dominicensis* and the crossbill *Loxia leucoptera* live in montane pine forest on Hispaniola and there is no natural pine forest on Jamaica. The rarity of movement from one island to another is also unlikely to be involved in the absence of the crossbill from Jamaica because three were seen during our stay (see p. 77), and similarly the owls *Speotyto cunicularia* and *Asio flammeus* have occurred on Cuba, though they do not breed there. Hence the absence of at least five species from a particular island is likely to be due to the absence there of its ecological requirements, and if the latter factor is involved in five cases it may well be due to ignorance that we cannot see how it may be involved in many others. Hence I see no need, on present evidence, to invoke difficulties of dispersal as an important factor in the situation.

SPECIES ON CUBA BUT NOT JAMAICA OR HISPANIOLA

The following 10 species, present on Cuba but not Jamaica or Hispaniola, are also on some of the Bahamas and/or Cayman Islands:

parrot *Amazona leucocephala* (also Bahamas, Caymans) (closely related species on Jamaica and Hispaniola)

cuckoo *Saurothera merlini* (also on Bahamas) (related species on Jamaica and Hispaniola)

hummingbird *Chlorostilbon ricordii* (also on Bahamas) (related species on Hispaniola)

woodpecker *Colaptes auratus* (also on Caymans and mainland)
woodpecker *Centurus superciliaris* (also on Bahamas and Caymans) (close relation on mainland and fairly close relation on Jamaica)
flycatcher *Tyrannus cubensis* (also on Bahamas)
bunting *Melopyrrha nigra* (also on Caymans) (replaces *Loxigilla*)
warbler *Dendroica pityophila* (also on Bahamas)
icterid *Agelaius phoeniceus* (also on Bahamas and mainland)
crow *Corvus nasicus* (also on Bahamas) (close relation on mainland)

The following 22 species are, in the West Indies, restricted to Cuba: three of them are also on the North American mainland, the other 19 are endemic to Cuba:
dove *Starnoenas cyanocephala*
macaw *Ara tricolor* (extinct)
parakeet *Aratinga euops* (close relations on Hispaniola and mainland)
owl *Gymnoglaux lawrencii*
owl *Glaucidium siju*
hummingbird *Mellisuga helenae* (congener on Jamaica and Hispaniola)
trogon *Priotelus temnurus* (close relative on Hispaniola)
tody *Todus multicolor* (close relatives on the other Greater Antilles)
woodpecker *Nesoceleus fernandinae*
woodpecker *Xiphidiopicus percussus*
woodpecker *Campephilus principalis* (also mainland)
wren *Ferminia cerverai*
solitaire *Myadestes elisabeth* (close relative on mainland, congener on other Greater Antilles)
gnatcatcher *Polioptila lembeyei*
bunting *Torreornis inexpectata*
grassquit *Tiaris canora* (replaces *T.bicolor*)
vireo *Vireo gundlachii* (representative of white-eyed vireo group)
honeycreeper *Cyanerpes cyaneus* (apparently replaces *Coereba flaveola*)
warbler *Teretistris fernandinae*
warbler *Teretistris fornsi*
icterid *Sturnella magna* (also on mainland)
icterid *Dives atroviolaceus* (close relatives on mainland)

Most of the more interesting species in these two lists for Cuba have already been discussed in previous sections and for most of the others the comment in brackets after the name of the species should suffice. They show that Cuba, like Jamaica and Hispaniola, has some species that are very different from any on either of the other two islands. It may be particularly noted that Cuba has as many as five species in the woodpecker family, compared with only one on Jamaica and two on Hispaniola. It also has 10 species of raptorial birds (Falconiformes), compared with only 3 on Jamaica and 4 on Hispaniola. Are there really 10 separate niches for such species on Cuba, and 5 for woodpeckers, when Jamaica supports respectively only 3 and 1 species in these groups of birds? It seems unlikely, but raptorial birds fly strongly, so the difficulties and chances of dispersal are unlikely to be the cause of the different number of species on each of these islands. A similar question is posed by the presence of 8 species of flycatcher on Jamaica compared with only 5 on each of Cuba and Hispaniola, and of 5 species of tanager on Hispaniola but only two on Cuba and Jamaica (with the possible addition of the peculiar Orangequit *Euneornis* on Jamaica). There is scarcely need to stress further our ignorance of the ecology of West Indian land birds, and until at least as much is known about those of Cuba and Hispaniola as of those on Jamaica, it would be unrewarding to discuss the problem further.

SUMMARY

About half the species of land birds resident on Jamaica are also resident on both Cuba and Hispaniola, rather over half of them also being present on part of the mainland and the rest being typical West Indian birds. About 11 species (including geographical forms classified as separate species, but extremely closely related) are common to Jamaica and Hispaniola but absent from Cuba, and a similar number are common to Cuba and Hispaniola but not Jamaica; but none are in common between Jamaica and Cuba but not Hispaniola.

The most remarkable feature in a comparison of the land birds of Jamaica, Hispaniola and Cuba is that each of those islands has ten or more species with no close relatives and no ecological counterpart on either of the other islands. This could be attributed either to dispersal over the sea being rare and random, or to some of the ecological requirements of the species concerned being absent from the islands where they do not occur. The latter explanation holds for at least five Hispaniolan species, three of which are there restricted to montane pine forest, a habitat lacking on Jamaica, and three of which (including one in montane pine forest) have wandered to one of the other two islands. I therefore think it likely that these gaps in range are due to missing ecological requirements rather than to difficulties of dispersal, but more cannot be said until more is known of the ecology of the Cuban and Hispaniolan land birds.

CHAPTER 9 · ORIGIN OF
JAMAICAN LAND BIRDS

Certainty about the likelihood of when the Jamaican species of land birds originated is not possible, one difficulty being that there is no fossil record; but on a broad general level, much can be inferred from the continental families present in and absent from Jamaica, and, at the particular level, from the distribution on the mainland of the present Jamaican species and of any very close relatives.

EVIDENCE OF ORIGIN FROM BIRD FAMILIES IN THE GREATER ANTILLES

In the classic study of zoogeography by Sclater (1858), the American continent was divided into two regions, and when the theory of evolution came later to be accepted, these were recognised as centres of evolutionary divergence, namely the North American (Nearctic) and South American (Neotropical) respectively, the boundary between them coming around what is now Panama when there was a sea gap. The latter was closed by a land bridge formed near the end of the Tertiary Period, probably some two million years ago. Presumably as a result of this, the land birds of South America include a large number of families that are still restricted or almost restricted to this continent (or sub-continent), though many but not all of them have a few species in Central America, mainly in lowland rain forest. These families include, among non-passerines, the oilbirds Steatornithidae, potoos Nyctibiidae, jacamars Galbulidae, puffbirds Bucconidae, and toucans Ramphastidae; and among passerines, the wood-hewers Dendrocolaptidae, ovenbirds Furnariidae, ant-thrushes Formicariidae, manakins Pipridae and cotingas Cotingidae, together with some very small families, the Conopophagidae, Rhinocryptidae and Phytotomidae, and some very small subfamilies, the Oxyruncinae, Cyclarhinae and Vireolaniinae (which various modern workers consider should be treated as families). Only two families generally believed to have evolved primarily in South America have spread far north in North America, namely the hummingbirds Trochilidae and tyrant flycatchers Tyrannidae, and they have evidently been there sufficiently long to have evolved endemic North American genera.

Of all these primarily South American families, only the humming-birds and tyrant flycatchers are strongly represented in the West Indies, and in view of what has just been said, these could as easily have reached the islands from Central as from South America. From all the other families, there are just two West Indian species, the potoo *Nyctibius griseus* on Jamaica and Hispaniola and the becard (a cotingid) *Platypsaris niger*, solely on Jamaica. But the potoo belongs to the only species in its family, and the cotingid to the only genus in its family, that have spread so far north on the mainland as Mexico. Hence these species could have colonised Jamaica from the mainland to the west rather than the south; indeed they almost certainly did so since, had they come from South America, one might have expected them to occur in some of the Lesser Antilles, which they do not.

Almost no bird families are restricted in range to North America, from which Mayr (1946) argued that the members of families originating in North America have spread more actively into South America than have those originating in South America into North America. But certain families seem typically North American and probably originated there, including the mockingbirds and thrashers Mimidae, vireos Vireonidae, and New World warblers Parulidae. Two other groups well represented in the Greater Antilles, the tanagers Thraupidae and troupials Icteridae, are now well represented in both North and South America and might have originated from either, but Mayr (1946) thought it more probable that they started in North America and had a secondary radiation in South America.

In the classical zoogeographical subdivisions of the world's faunas already referred to, the West Indies were placed in the South American (Neotropical) not North American (Nearctic) subdivision, but without critical evidence. In view of the evidence on the families of land birds present and absent there, Bond (1936) was clearly right in postulating that the main colonisation of the Greater Antilles has been from bird families of North not South American origin, and his conclusion has been generally accepted. Further, when Mayr (1946) pointed out that there must have been an avifauna adapted to the tropical conditions in the southernmost part of North America prior to the formation of the Panamanian land bridge with South America at the end of the Tertiary period, Bond (1948) postulated that most of the West Indian birds probably came from this avifauna. Since the formation of the land bridge, climatic conditions on the Central American mainland have oscillated between tropical and temperate, and presumably there were corresponding variations in the bird species living in that part of the mainland nearest to Jamaica (from which part, if not most, of the Jamaican avifauna was drawn).

RANGES OF JAMAICAN LAND BIRDS ON THE MAINLAND

Partly because of the climatic shifts just noted, the present ranges on the mainland of the Jamaican species which also occur there, and of species closely related to those on Jamaica which also occur there, are not of much significance. But the figures set out in Appendix 8 show the predominance on Jamaica of species now present in Mexico (35) or the lands between Mexico and Panama, here designated as Central America (32), with fewer in North (22) or South America (22). As already noted however, little should be argued from these figures as they stand, because some species occur in all four mainland areas, while a few are so restricted on the mainland that they almost certainly reached it from the West Indies and not the other way about. In addition, many species probably extended further south or less far north during the cool period ending with the last glaciation, and 21 species, in Part C of Appendix 8, are not present, or are not represented by closely related species, on the mainland. In general, however, the figures support the view that most Jamaican birds colonised it from among those now living in central America or Mexico.

SPECIES WHICH PROBABLY COLONISED JAMAICA FROM THE SOUTH

Probably 6 species, set out in Table 16, colonised Jamaica from the south. All of these are regular in northern South America and common through the Lesser Antilles, except for one represented there by a closely related species, and they are all absent from or very local in Central America. All of them are widespread in the Greater Antilles,

TABLE 16. *Species which in probably colonised Jamaica from the south*

	Status of species (or close relatives) in:			
	northern South America	Lesser Antilles	Central America	Cuba
ani *Crotophaga ani*	common	common	scarce local	present
flycatcher *Tyrannus dominicensis*	common	common resident	absent	summer visitor
grassquit *Tiaris bicolor*	common	common	absent	absent
bananaquit *Coereba flaveola*	common	common	local	absent
vireo *Vireo altiloquus*	mainly winter visitor	common	absent (close relative local)	present
grackle *Quiscalus niger*	closely related *Q. lugubris*	closely related *Q. lugubris* (abundant)	closely related *Q. nicaraguensis* (very local)	present

except that two are absent from Cuba, which suggests (p. 106) that by the time that they had got so far north, ecological equivalents had evolved on Cuba and were able to exclude them, as proposed by Bond (1963).

This evidence strongly suggests that the birds in question spread up from the south, and it is interesting that three of them, the ani *Crotophaga ani*, flycatcher *Tyrannus dominicensis* and vireo *Vireo altiloquus*, have just reached Florida on the North American mainland by this route. Since the ani is so much a bird of cultivation, it is possible that its spread has been partly, if not wholly, due to the spread of cultivation by man, and the same might apply to a more limited extent to the flycatcher *Tyrannus dominicensis*.

COLONISATION FROM NORTH OR WITHIN THE GREATER ANTILLES

There are no strong reasons for thinking that any Jamaican species colonised it from North America, since the species which might conceivably have come from this direction also occur in Mexico and Central America.

Four Jamaican species are most closely related to West Indian forms of unknown origin. The bullfinch *Loxigilla violacea* belongs to an endemic West Indian genus (see Fig. 17, p. 111 for its range, and for its displacement on Cuba by an unrelated endemic genus). The smaller *Loxipasser anoxanthus* is closest to *Loxigilla*. The flycatcher *Tyrannus caudifasciatus* is one of the 'grey kingbirds', the relationships of which are not fully understood (see Part 2). The mockingbird *Mimus gundlachii* is closest to the widespread *M.polyglottos/gilvus* group. A fifth species might be added, since the flycatcher *Elaenia fallax* is otherwise known only from Hispaniola, but on both islands it is mainly a summer visitor, and its winter quarters and nearest mainland relatives are unknown.

JAMAICAN COMPARED WITH HONDURAN BIRDS

Clearly, the land birds of Jamaica have more in common with those on the mainland to the west than to anywhere else. But even the most superficial inspection shows that those on Jamaica are not a representative sample of those on the mainland. The differences are best brought out by a quantitative analysis, but it would be extremely difficult to use for this purpose the birds of the whole area Mexico south to Panama inclusive. I have therefore selected for comparison the birds of Honduras, not because it is more 'typical' than any other land in Central America but because of the analyses by Monroe (1968). In addition, it is the nearest part of the mainland to Jamaica (650 km) and provides a diversity of habitats.

Comparison by families

As shown in Table 17, the representation of land birds by families on Jamaica is very different from that in Honduras. For all the families from pigeons to passerines combined, the number of species on Jamaica is 17 per cent of that in Honduras, which gives one a yardstick for the individual families. Many families have too few species in Honduras to provide a reliable figure, but in the 11 with at least 14 breeding species, the representation on Jamaica is unusually high in only one, the pigeons Columbidae (63 per cent), and three are not represented at all. It is near the average in the flycatchers Tyrannidae, buntings and cardinals Emberizinae, warblers Parulidae and icterids Icteridae, lower in the tanagers Thraupinae, very low in the hummingbirds Trochilidae and woodpeckers Picidae, and there are no representatives

TABLE 17. *Comparison by families of birds in Jamaica and Honduras—*
pigeons to passerines

Family	Number of species in Jamaica	Number of species in Honduras	Jamaican species as percentage of Honduran species
pigeons Columbidae	10	16	63
parrots Psittacidae	3 (+1)	13	23 (31)
cuckoos Cuculidae	5	7	71
barn owls Tytonidae	1	1 }	15
other owls Strigidae	1	12 }	
potoos Nyctibiidae	1	2 }	43
nightjars Caprimulgidae	2	5 }	
swifts Apodidae	3	7	43
hummingbirds Trochilidae	3	37	8
trogons Trogonidae	0	8	0
kingfishers Alcedinidae	0	4	0
motmots Momotidae	0	6	0
todies Todidae	1	0	—
jacamars Gulbulidae	0	1	0
puffbirds Bucconidae	0	3	0
toucans Ramphastidae	0	5	0
woodpeckers Picidae	1	14	7
wood-hewers Dendrocolaptidae	0	14	0
ovenbirds Furnariidae	0	8	0
ant-thrushes Formicariidae	0	19	0
manakins Pipridae	0	6	0
cotingas Cotingidae	1	13	8
tyrant flycatchers Tyrannidae	8	40	20
swallows Hirundinidae	3	3	100
dippers Cinclidae	0	1	0
wrens Troglodytidae	0	15	0
mockingbirds Mimidae	2	3	67
thrushes Turdinae	3	12	25
Old World warblers Sylviinae	0	3	0
tree creepers Certhiidae	0	1	0
buntings, cardinals Emberizinae	5	27	19
tanagers, honeycreepers Thraupinae	3	25	12
New World warblers, bananaquits Parulidae	3	15	20
pepper-shrikes Cyclarhinae	0	1	0
shrike-vireos Vireolaniinae	0	1	0
vireos Vireoninae	3	6	50
icterids Icteridae	3	17	17
finches Fringillidae	0	3	0
crows Corvidae	1	9	11
TOTAL	66 (+1)	383	17

of the wood-hewers Dendrocolaptidae, ant-thrushes Formicariidae, or wrens Troglodytidae.

One cannot place much reliance on the figure for families which have only a few species present in Honduras, but Jamaica seems strongly represented in the cuckoos Cuculidae, the nightjar order Caprimulgiformes, swifts Apodidae, swallows and martins Hirundinidae, mockingbirds Mimidae and vireos Vireoninae, and is not represented at all in many other families, including most of those represented in Central America but regarded as of South American origin. Among the latter however, there are one potoo and one cotingid in Jamaica.

As regards families other than those from the pigeons to passerines inclusive, the information in Table 18 shows that Jamaica is strongly represented in all wading and freshwater birds (69 per cent of the total of 36 species in Honduras) but is poorly represented in the raptors (9 per cent) and has no gallinaceous birds or tinamous.

An obvious suggestion for these differences is that some kinds of birds have a much greater ability than others to fly across the sea. For instance it might be argued that swifts Apodidae and swallows Hirundinidae are strongly represented on Jamaica because they have good powers of flight, whereas tinamous and gallinaceous birds are absent because they can fly only a short way before needing to rest, and woodpeckers and wrens are poorly represented because they do not fly long distances, as indicated by their short rounded wings. Actually the example of the woodpeckers has to be discarded, because though Jamaica has only one species, adjoining Cuba has 5, 36 per cent of the number in Honduras, which is double the proportion for all land birds present there.

While, however, there are a few families the presence or absence of which on Jamaica could support the idea of a correlation with flying abilities, this cannot be the explanation for most observed

Notes for Table 17   (i) Monroe (1968), used here for Honduras, followed a rather different classification of passerine families from Peters, but the changes should be clear from my use of vernacular names above. For my purposes, it seemed simplest to treat the Turdinae and Sylviinae as separate families, likewise the Cyclarhinae, Vireolaniinae and Vireoninae, and likewise the Thraupinae (including 4 Dacninae) and Emberizinae (including the Cardinalinae). *Coereba* has been included in the Parulidae.

(ii)   Four other families in Honduras are represented in the Greater Antilles but not on Jamaica, namely the trogons Trogonidae, wrens Troglodytidae, Old World warblers Sylviinae and finches Fringillidae.

TABLE 18. *Comparison between Jamaica and Honduras of freshwater and marsh birds, and of land birds other than pigeons to passerines (Seabirds are excluded)*

Group or groups	Number of species in Jamaica	Honduras	Jamaican as percentage of Honduran species
tinamous Tinamidae	0	4	0
gallinaceous birds Galliformes	0	14	0
raptors Falconiformes	3	c.32	9
grebes, darters, cormorants, ducks, all freshwater swimmers	3	7	43
herons, ibises etc. Ciconiiformes	10	15	67
rails etc. Gruiformes	8	10	80
waders (not gulls or terns) Charadriiformes (part)	4–5	4	100
Total for all land and freshwater birds (*i.e.* including those in Table 17)	94–95 (+1)	469	21

differences. Jamaica is only 650 km from the mainland, a distance which does not seem beyond the flying capacity of most Honduran birds in the families from pigeons to passerines. Moreover this distance was only 400 km, with two large intervening islands, prior to 10,000 years ago, when many of the birds concerned might have colonised Jamaica (see p. 18). Further, at least two types of birds with good powers of dispersal are poorly represented on Jamaica, first the Falconiformes (Table 18), which are strong fliers, and secondly the hummingbirds (Table 17), which have been recorded outside their normal range more often than any other family of birds in the Caribbean, as discussed in Chapter 6. Again, the cuckoos Cuculidae are strongly represented on Jamaica, but one does not usually think of these short-winged birds as strong fliers (though in fact the migratory species make long journeys)

Comparison by avifaunal region

As already mentioned, certain bird families are present in Honduras which are of South American origin, including the potoos Nyctibiidae, hummingbirds Trochilidae, trogons Trogonidae, jacamars Galbulidae, puffbirds Bucconidae, toucans Ramphastidae, wood-hewers, Dendrocolaptidae, ovenbirds Furnariidae, ant-thrushes Formicariidae, manakins Pipridae, cotingids Cotingidae, flycatchers Tyrannidae, pepper-shrikes Cyclarhinae, and shrike-vireos Vireolaniinae, which together comprise 148 species. But they are represented on Jamaica by only 13 species, or 8 per cent, which is under half the proportion for all land birds. Moreover, as already noted, there are relatively more species of hummingbirds and flycatchers in North America than of other families of South American origin, and if they are omitted, the Honduran total of species drops to only 81, the Jamaican to only 2 (less than 2 per cent), a potoo and a becard.

Families of North American origin are hard to recognise as such, as already discussed, but they include the motmots Momotidae, mockingbirds Mimidae, vireos Vireoninae, warblers Parulidae and probably the tanagers Thraupinae and icterids Icteridae, which together include 72 species in Honduras and 14 (19 per cent) on Jamaica. Hence the Jamaican representation for these families is slightly above the average for all land birds and decidedly higher than for the South American element. As already mentioned, however, it is doubtful whether the tanagers and icterids originated in North America, and the hummingbirds and flycatchers, which originated in South America, have had a secondary radiation in North America, so these figures do not mean much. Many other families resident in Honduras were not included in this analysis owing to doubts as to their zoogeographical position (though Mayr thought that most are probably of North rather than South American origin in the New World).

The only clear-cut point emerging from this section is that most South American families except the flycatchers Tyrannidae are under-represented on Jamaica compared with Honduras. However this is at least partly explicable through the under-representation of rain-forest birds on Jamaica, as discussed in the next section.

Representation by habitat

The most striking differences in the representation of Honduran birds on Jamaica are found in relation to habitat. For an analysis of this factor however, one can use for the Jamaican side only those species present in or closely related to another species present in Honduras, which reduces the available Jamaican total to 31, just under half of those present there (meaning that the overall reduction

TABLE 19.   *Comparison by habitat in Honduras of those Honduran land birds present on Jamaica*

Habitat in Honduras (as in Table 7)	Number of species in that habitat in Honduras	Species or closely related species from that habitat on Jamaica		Additional species from that habitat on Cuba or Hispaniola
		Number	Proportion	
1 lowland rain forest	144	0	0	1
2,1 lowland vega, and vega with rain forest	18	2	11%	1
4(& 5) lowland arid forest (and mangroves)	23	11	48%	
2 & 4 vega and lowland arid	18	5	28%	
11 edge of lowland arid and humid forest	59	7	12%	4
7–8 montane forest (cloud and pine-oak)	87	2	2%	4
3(3 & 4) 3 & 8 lowland pine (including pine with lowland arid) and lowland with highland pine	21	2	10%	2
1 & 7–8 lowland rain to montane forest	11	1	9%	1
6,9,10 lowland marsh, highland grassland, highland aerial	8	1	13%	1
Total	389	31	8%	14

Notes   (i) The totals of species in Honduran habitats are in Table 6, the habitats in Honduras of Jamaican species and of extremely closely related species are in Table 7.

(ii) A single number under habitat refers to one habitat in Table 6. Two numbers joined by '&' refer to those species which occur in both the habitats so joined but not in only one of them.

in Jamaican land birds to be used in this section for comparison with Honduras is 8 per cent, not 17 per cent as in Table 17). This leaves so few species present in some of the Honduran habitats that they have been grouped together in Table 19.

The birds living in one habitat in Honduras, lowland arid forest, are strongly represented on Jamaica (with 48 per cent, compared with the overall 8 per cent), and so are those which occur in both lowland forest and vega (with 28 per cent). The lowland arid forest of Jamaica is apparently rather like that of the mainland.

In contrast, no species restricted to the lowland rain forest on Honduras is resident on Jamaica, which can be attributed to the absence of true rain forest on the island. (Parts of the highland forest on Jamaica are sometimes called rain forest but are not really similar, see p. 29). However, one Honduran species found primarily in lower montane rain forest, but extending both down to lowland rain forest and up to lower cloud forest, the dove *Geotrygon montana*, occurs on Jamaica. Since many of the species in Honduras that are of South American origin live in lowland rain forest, the paucity of Jamaican species of South American origin might really be due to the absence there of species from lowland rain forest, and not to their being of South American origin as such.

Jamaica also has a poor representation (2 per cent) of species which live in Honduras in montane forest, solely the pigeon *Columbia caribaea*

TABLE 20.   *Land birds on Cuba (C) or Hispaniola (H), but not Jamaica, which breed, or have a closely related species breeding, in Honduras*

Species		Habitat in Honduras
A. Same species		
bunting *Zonotrichia capensis* (H)		(7) cloud forest edge
tanager *Euphonia musica* (H)		(2,7,8, part of 1) mid-level rain forest, vega, montane forest
honey-creeper *Cyanerpes cyanea* (C)		(2, edge of 1) vega, edge of lowland rain forest
icterid *Agelaius phoeniceus* (C)		(6) marshland
icterid *Sturnella magna* (C)		(3,8) low and high grassland (with pines)
B. Closely related species		
macaw *Ara tricolor* (C)	*A.macao*	(11) lowland open forest, humid and arid
parakeet *Aratinga chloroptera* (H) and *A.euops* (C)	*A.holochlora*	(7,8) montane forest
hummingbird *Anthracothorax dominicus* (H)	*A.prevostii*	(11) lowland open forest, humid and arid
hummingbird *Chlorostilbon swainsonii* (H) and *C.ricordii* (C)	*C.canivetii*	(11) lowland open forest, humid and arid
solitaire *Myadestes elisabeth* (C)	*M.obscurus*	(8,7) montane forest (mainly pine-oak)
thrush *Turdus swalesi* (H)	*T.rufitorques*	(8) montane pine-oak forest
warbler *Dendroica pityophila* (C)	*D.graciae*	(3,8) lowland and montane pine
oriole *Icterus dominicensis* (H, C)	*I.prosthemelas*	(1) lowland rain forest
icterid *Dives atroviolaceus* (C)	*D.dives*	(11) lowland open humid and arid forest

Note   The habitats of these species on Cuba and Hispaniola have not been studied critically, but appear to be broadly similar to those of the same or related species on the mainland.

(close to Honduran *C.fasciata*) and the solitaire *Myadestes genibarbis* (close to Honduran *M.unicolor*). In addition however, it has the dove *Geotrygon versicolor*, probably close to the mainland species *G.costaricensis*, which lives in montane forest in Costa Rica, south of Honduras.

The birds from the other habitats in Honduras have a near average representation on Jamaica, somewhat higher in the case of forest edge, but the total numbers of species involved are too small for the percentages to be reliable.

I have set out in Table 20 the habitats in Honduras of those species of land birds also found on Cuba or Hispaniola but not Jamaica. This brings in another 14 species, the totals for which are in the right hand column of Table 19. There are no further additions for lowland arid forest, simply because the species in this habitat on Cuba and Hispaniola also occur on Jamaica. The biggest additions are four more species from the forest edge, particularly of arid forest, and four more montane species, namely a parakeet, another solitaire, a thrush and, at the edge, a bunting.

There is also one additional species, an oriole, from lowland rain forest. Various workers have argued that rain-forest birds have rarely colonised oceanic islands because they have relatively weak powers of flight, whereas the birds of lowland arid habitats frequently do so because they are more mobile. There may be a little truth in this, but another possible explanation is that oceanic islands do not usually have humid forest similar to rain-forest on the mainland, but do usually have lowland arid scrub forest similar to that on the mainland; so that in the one case the birds find an unsuitable, in the other a suitable, habitat if they reach the islands.

It has also been claimed that the birds of montane forest are exceptionally sedentary. Yet as just mentioned, three montane forest birds from Central America have colonised Jamaica, and another four have colonised either Cuba or Hispaniola. This suggests that, when there is a vacant ecological niche, the birds appear. On the other hand, at least one montane species on Jamaica is descended from a lowland species on the mainland, namely the vireo *Vireo osburni*, derived from the white-eyed *V.griseus* group, and the same holds for two further species which are primarily highland, namely the becard *Platypsaris niger* and the flycatcher *Contopus caribaeus*. It also holds for at least 8 species on Jamaica which range from the lowlands, through midlevel, to montane forest, including the pigeons *Columba leucocephala* and *C.inornata*, the dove *Leptotila jamaicensis*, the wood-pecker *Centurus radiolatus*, the flycatcher *Myiarchus barbirostris*, the vireos *Vireo altiloquus* and *V.modestus* and the oriole *Icterus leucopteryx*.

Since some Jamaican land birds probably colonised first in the arid lowlands and later spread from there into the highlands, it is interesting to know whether the same has held in the forest trees themselves. At my request, Dr. D. Adams analysed a sample of the common tree species growing in Jamaica between 1000 and 2000 m (*viz.* the 32 in the left-hand column of p. 400 in Asprey and Robbins (1957), of which 12 are endemic, 6 Caribbean, mainly in the Greater Antilles, and 14 are tropical American). He concluded that the common montane trees of Jamaica have either evolved locally from groups that are already montane, or have spread from montane regions elsewhere without change. Hence the montane trees did not evolve their montane habit on Jamaica, as some of the birds probably did.

Comparison may be made with the land birds in three other areas. On Timor in Southeast Asia, there is a monsoon montane forest which probably originated recently in the cool period at the end of the last glaciation. This forest has been colonised exclusively by montane birds from the Malaysian region further north, although the arid lowlands of Timor are inhabited primarily by birds of Australo-Papuan origin (Mayr 1944). As pointed out by Mayr, in the cool period in question a montane avifauna existed relatively close to Timor in the north, but there was no such avifauna in the Australasian region to the south. Secondly, of the birds on the isolated mountain block of Pantapuir in Venezuela, three-fifths are derived from the birds of other mountains in South America, while two-fifths are most nearly related to species in the adjacent tropical lowlands, which have become adapted to higher altitudes (Mayr and Phelps 1967). Here, the proportion of species previously adapted to mountains is probably higher than on Jamaica. Thirdly, the less clear-cut situation in the Lesser Antilles will be discussed in the next chapter.

As already mentioned, Table 19 covers only 31 of the 66 Jamaican land birds. Two other species, the second parrot and the second white-eyed vireo, were omitted because they are presumed products of double invasion by the same mainland species, but they might have been scored separately instead of only once for each pair, thus raising the total for species derived from arid forest by two. Six other

Jamaican species breed on the mainland north of Honduras, the doves *Zenaida macroura* and *Z.aurita* and the cuckoo *Coccyzus americanus* in lowland arid forest, the flycatcher *Tyrannus dominicensis* in mangroves and arid scrub, the swallow *Petrochelidon fulva* in open country near limestone caves and the tanager *Spindalis zena* on Cozumel, an island of arid scrub forest off Mexico; their inclusion would raise yet further the proportion of Jamaican species which live in arid lowland forest on the mainland. (However, two of them, the flycatcher *T.dominicensis* and the tanager *S.zena* probably colonised the mainland from the West Indies, not the other way about.) Yet another species, the quail-dove *G.versicolor*, is close to a montane species which breeds only south of Honduras. Even with these additions, however, there are many Jamaican species of which the habitats of their mainland ancestors are not known, and these include various of the endemic species, four of which are primarily highland species on Jamaica and another 8 of which range from the lowlands to the mountains. Had the mainland ancestors of these species been known, their inclusion might well have modified the picture presented in this section, especially for the proportion of montane species and a corresponding reduction in the proportion of Jamaican species derived from the arid lowlands of the mainland.

Comparison by feeding and by size

Information on the feeding of land birds in Honduras is too inadequate for a quantitative comparison with that of the same or closely related species on Jamaica. However if, crudely, each family of Honduran birds is grouped under the type of food most frequently taken, and the number of species in each group is counted, then the proportion of insectivorous, frugivorous and seed-eating birds in Honduras is broadly similar to that on Jamaica.

As already discussed in Chapter 4, various congeneric species in the West Indies differ from each other in size or size of beak, probably an adaptation to a difference in feeding. Grant (1969) attributed this to the West Indian species being derived, not from a random sample of those on the mainland, but from those which differ markedly in size of beak from each other. However, there are not enough figures to discuss this idea in relation to Jamaica compared with Honduras.

SUMMARY

Most Jamaican land birds were probably derived from the North American avifauna in Central America, two from South American genera probably after they had spread into Central America, while probably six species arrived from the south via the Lesser Antilles. The species on Jamaica are not a random sample of those on the nearest mainland, with respect to either bird-family or habitat.

Of the families with at least 15 species in Honduras, Jamaica has a high proportion of pigeons Columbidae, and also of wading and freshwater birds, and a low proportion, or none, of hummingbirds Trochilidae, ant-thrushes Formicariidae and wrens Troglodytidae, also of Falconiformes. Probably various other families are also disproportionately represented on Jamaica, but with so few Honduran species to form a reliable basis of comparison it is hard to be sure. The differences between families do not vary strongly in parallel with their powers of flight.

A comparison of the habitats in Honduras of the 31 Jamaican species and very closely related species that occur there shows that the birds of lowland arid forest are disproportionately strongly represented on Jamaica, whereas birds of lowland rain forest are scarcely represented at all. This might be because lowland arid forest is the Jamaican habitat most like a mainland one, and Jamaica does not have lowland rain forest.

Species from montane forest in Honduras are under-represented on Jamaica, but this is a little misleading, since one other Jamaican bird comes from montane forest in Costa Rica, and four other species of the montane forest in Honduras are represented on Cuba or Hispaniola, but not Jamaica. The birds of the highland forests on Jamaica are derived partly from species restricted to montane forest on the mainland, and partly from birds of lowland arid forest on the mainland which doubtless started in a similar habitat on Jamaica and later spread up from there into the wet highland forest. The mainland ancestors of various other Jamaican highland species are not known. Too little is known to compare quantitatively the feeding habits of the Honduran land birds which respectively have, and have not, colonised Jamaica.

CHAPTER 10 · NOTES ON THE
LESSER ANTILLES

The land birds of the Lesser Antilles present both parallels with, and important differences from, those of Jamaica, so though I paid only brief visits to the islands (see p. 36), selected problems are considered here. The Lesser Antilles (Fig. 1, p. 16) are a chain of small islands running roughly north and south for 700 km, from Anguilla in the north, separated by rather over 100 km from the Virgin Islands, to Grenada in the south, 126 km from Tobago. Of the six largest islands, considered from north to south, the first five, namely Guadeloupe, Dominica, Martinique, St Lucia and St Vincent, are each some 40 km from the next in the chain, and in sight of each other; there is then a gap containing the low-lying Grenadines and finally Grenada. The main islands are volcanic and mountainous, with scrub forest in the lowlands and humid forest higher up, and there are also low-lying islands covered in natural scrub forest. The vegetation has been described by Beard (1949). Much has been cleared for cultivation, and a few land birds have become extinct notably on Barbados, and also various parrots on Guadeloupe and elsewhere.

A list of 70 species of land birds represented by specimens in collections, based on the summary in Bond (1956, 1971) is set out in Appendix 9. Information given in its various columns shows that 11 of these species are widespread in the Caribbean, occurring on the mainland of Central and South America and in the Greater Antilles. Another 13 are otherwise wholly on the South American mainland, and another 7 otherwise solely in the Greater Antilles. Hence the Lesser Antillean birds' ranges are varied. The greatest number of species on any one island is 42, on St Lucia.

HABITAT

The island least disturbed by man is Dominica, and it is still so beautiful that it ought to be a world nature reserve. Our analysis of birds in relation to the four main types of forest on Dominica is set out in Appendix 4. This showed that rather over half of the land birds reside on both lowland semi-arid and highland humid forest, a rather higher proportion than on Jamaica and in marked contrast to the Central American mainland (p. 43), where the overlap is extremely small. Similar counts in the much more disturbed conditions of St Lucia (A.W. Diamond 1973), St Vincent (Lack *et al.* 1973) and Grenada (Lack and Lack 1973) gave results similar to those for Dominica. They fully support the view that birds have broad habitats on remote oceanic islands.

The proportion of species in each habitat, or which occur in both lowlands and highlands, in any particular island is somewhat different from that in the Lesser Antilles as a whole, because some species are widespread and others are restricted to only one island. For the group as a whole, only 26 out of the 70 species, or 37 per cent, occur in both lowlands and highlands. Of the 25 species restricted to the lowlands, only 3 are endemic, whereas of the rest, which occur in the highlands, 22 out of the 45, almost half, are endemic, 11 of them occurring in both lowlands and highlands, and 11 solely in the highlands. As on Jamaica, therefore, most of the endemic species are in the highlands.

A few species show modifications in habitat on different islands. Thus the cuckoo *Coccyzus minor*, restricted to the arid lowlands or mangroves on the mainland, also occurs in humid forest on Dominica (personal observations), St Lucia (Diamond 1973), St Vincent (Lack *et al.* 1973) and Grenada (Lack and Lack 1973), though it is scarce there.

The ranges of the small swifts in the genus *Chaetura* are shown in Fig. 20. The endemic *C.martinica* breeds in the humid forest, which is its main feeding area. But it also feeds regularly in the lowlands on Dominica and St Lucia though not on St Vincent, where a South American species *C.brachyura* breeds and feeds in the lowlands. Further south, on Grenada, *C.martinica* is replaced by an extremely closely related South American species *C.cinereiventris*, which likewise feeds and breeds in the highlands but also feeds in the lowlands. No other species of *Chaetura* breeds on Grenada. *C.cinereiventris* also resides on Tobago, but so also does *C.brachyura*, breeding in the lowlands as on St Vincent, and here *C.cinereiventris* is restricted to the highlands for feeding, like *C.martinica* on St Vincent. Why *C.brachyura* should breed among these islands solely on St Vincent and Tobago is not known.

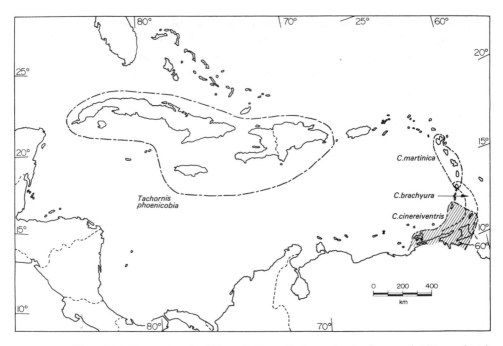

FIG. 20. *Range in the West Indies of the endemic Lesser Antillean Swift* Chaetura martinica, *and the island (but not mainland) range of* C.cinereiventris, *which is in the same superspecies. The range of* Tachornis phoenicobia *is also shown.*

It also feeds to some extent in the highlands, but only well above the forest canopy, whereas *C.martinica* and *C.cinereiventris* feed mainly among the trees, hence below *C.brachyura*. Here *C.martinica* and *C.cinereiventris* are separated in feeding from *C.brachyura* by height above the trees in the highlands and by geographical displacement in the lowlands.

The thrasher *Margarops fuscatus* is common in humid forest. On Dominica (personal observations) and St Lucia (Diamond 1973), it is extremely sparse in the lowlands and is there restricted to sheltered areas with tall trees, for instance in the river valleys. But from Antigua northward it is also typical of semi-arid lowland scrub forest. Its curious range (Fig. 21) suggests that it spread from the Lesser Antilles northward to the Bahamas, the only species known to have done so.

Finally, as shown in Fig. 22, the parulid warbler *Dendroica adelaidae* occurs in the Lesser Antilles solely on St. Lucia in both lowland scrub

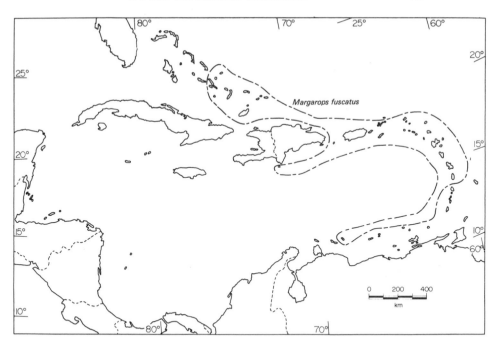

Fig. 21. *Range in the West Indies of the thrasher* Margarops fuscatus.

forest and humid forest, and on lowlying Barbuda in lowland scrub forest. Outside the Lesser Antilles, it occurs on Puerto Rico, but solely in lowland scrub forest, being replaced in humid forest, there by a different species, *D.angelae*, though there is an altitudinal gap without either species. It is also present on low-lying Vieques, inevitably in lowland scrub forest. This is the most curious example of a discontinuous range in a West Indian bird. The presence of *D.adelaidae* in the humid forest on St Lucia can be linked with the absence from this island of any other leaf-gleaning forest warbler. As shown in Fig. 23, St Vincent to the south has *Catharopeza bishopi*, and Dominica and Guadeloupe to the north have *Dendroica plumbea*. Martinique, however, has no comparable species and here *D.petechia*, normally a bird of mangroves and coastal scrub, enters the humid forest (Diamond 1973). Here, then, are two further examples of species with broader habitats in the absence of congeners. The puzzle is to know why they should occur only on St Lucia and Martinique respectively, and not elsewhere. *D.adelaidae* is also of interest, because it is close to, and probably derived from the mainland species *D.graciae*, which frequents pine forest. Hence the establishment

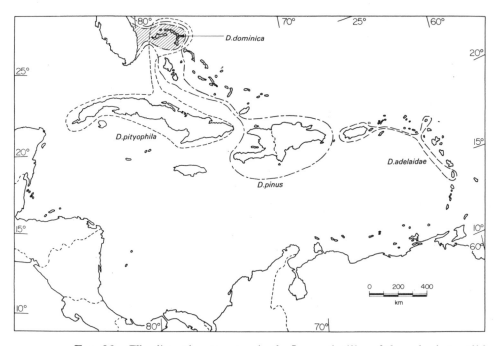

FIG. 22. *The discontinuous range in the Lesser Antilles of the endemic parulid warbler* Dendroica adelaidae *(derived from* D.graciae *of the mainland). Also the range in the Greater Antilles of another endemic parulid warbler* Dendroica pityophila, *independently derived from* D.graciae, *and of the two other pine-frequenting warblers of the West Indies* D.dominica *and* D.pinus.

of *D.adelaidae* in the West Indies has in itself involved a change in its habitat, since there is no pine forest in Puerto Rico or the Lesser Antilles. As mentioned elsewhere another endemic West Indian parulid, *D.pityophila*, is also derived from *D.graciae* and frequents pine forest in Cuba and some of the Bahamas. It is so different from *D.adelaidae* that it presumably represents a separate colonisation of *D.graciae* stock from the mainland. Its range is shown in Fig. 22, together with those of two other pine-frequenting warblers in the West Indies which also breed in North America, namely *D.pinus* and *D.dominica*.

Bridgetown, Barbados is a well-developed town and it is interesting to see that here, to a greater extent than anywhere else in the West Indies, the bullfinch *Loxigilla noctis* is a town sparrow and the dove

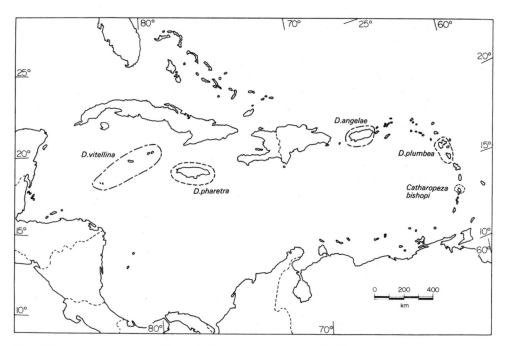

FIG. 23. *Ranges in the West Indies of other endemic* Dendroica *and* Dendroica-*like warblers* (*see also Fig.* 22). D.pharetra *and* D.angelae *are probably related, also perhaps* D.plumbea *and* C.bishopi.

Zenaida aurita is a town pigeon, and both hop down freely among the traffic. Here and on several other islands, both the bullfinch *Loxigilla noctis* and the Bananaquit *Coereba flaveola* visit sugar bowls on hotel tables. More unusually, the large pigeon *Columba squamosa*, nearly exterminated by hunters, found a refuge in the tall trees of the small cathedral close in Bridgetown, where it has now built up a population and is spreading outward. Hence West Indian birds have begun to adapt themselves to urban conditions.

ENDEMISM

Twenty-three of the 70 Lesser Antillean species are restricted to the archipelago, and two more, both hummingbirds, are otherwise found only on the northeastern tip of Puerto Rico. Including these two latter as Lesser Antillean endemics, 36 per cent of the species are endemic, a smaller proportion than on Jamaica (p. 81), or in the West Indies as a whole.

Twelve of the 25 endemic species are each restricted to only one island, but 4 of these are parrots and 3 are extremely closely related species of orioles, *Icterus*, which replace each other geographically and are clearly derived from the Greater Antillean species *I.dominicensis* (see Fig. 11, p. 100). Among neither the endemic nor the other species are there the marked differences to be seen in the species present on adjacent islands and so typical of the Greater Antilles. This is probably linked in some way with the fact that the larger islands of the Lesser Antilles are about twice as near to each other as are Jamaica, Hispaniola, Cuba and Puerto Rico, but how the greater isolation of the latter might produce this effect is not known. As noted, there are about a dozen species on each of Jamaica, Cuba and Hispaniola without any relation or ecological equivalent on either of the other islands. Only two species pose a similar problem in the Lesser Antilles, the long-beaked shrub-feeding warbler *Leucopeza semperi* and the Black Finch *Melanospiza richardsoni*. Both of these are confined to St Lucia and there are no comparable species elsewhere. Do their ecological niches not exist on other islands? A few other curious gaps 'exist, involving several islands. Why, for instance, should there be an oriole *Icterus* solely on three islands in the Lesser Antilles, namely Montserrat, Martinique and St Lucia? Such interrupted ranges are highly characteristic of island birds.

ORIGIN OF LESSER ANTILLEAN AVIFAUNA

It is not possible to say from where the widespread Caribbean species, i.e. those found in Central and South America and the Greater Antilles, colonised the Lesser Antilles. There is equal doubt about some of the highly distinctive species, notably the endemic parrots. Species found solely in the Lesser Antilles and northern South America are assumed to have colonised from South America, while species found solely in the Lesser and Greater Antilles, with, in addition, some sort of link with Central America, are assumed to have colonised from the northwest. I have included among the latter the endemic parulid warblers and thrashers as both belong to primarily North American families. On this sort of basis I have set out in the last column in Appendix 9 the probable area of origin of each of the Lesser Antillean land birds;

TABLE 21. *Probable area of origin of Lesser Antillean land birds*

Probable origin from	Number of species		
	solely in lowlands	in highlands (many also in lowlands)	Total
South America	17 (65%)	11	28 (40%)
N.W. (Greater Antilles and Central America)	4	15	19 (27%)
Unknown	5	18	23 (33%)

Note Based on data in Appendix 9.

but so many cases are doubtful that it is hard to make a firm quantitative analysis of these findings, which are summarised in Table 21.

Clearly, however, there have been sizeable contributions to the Lesser Antillean avifauna from both ends of the chain, at least 40 per cent from South America and at least 27 per cent from the Greater Antilles; but with so many species of unknown origin it is not safe to say that the greater contribution has been from South America. What is clear, however, is that most of the species confined to the lowlands in the Lesser Antilles are of South American origin, at least 65 per cent. In contrast, of the species which occur in the highlands, rather more of those of known origin have come in from the north than the south, but the number of unknown origin exceeds either of those totals. Those of unknown origin which live in the highlands include many of the Lesser Antillean endemic species. Of the latter which are of known origin, many more probably came in from the north than the south, so probably the same holds among those of unknown origin.

Much fuller documentation is needed, but it looks as though there is a genuine difference here between the lowland and highland species of the Lesser Antilles. This could well be linked with the nature of the highland forest—that of the Lesser Antilles has many resemblances to that of Puerto Rico. Further, the forest birds of the Greater Antilles are already adapted to a depauperate environment and have relatively broad ecological niches, so would find it relatively easy to settle in the even more depauperate forest of the Lesser Antilles. In contrast, the nearest humid forest on the South American mainland is lowland rain forest, with each of many bird species holding a highly specialised niche. Such species would probably be poorly adapted to the depauperate humid forest of the Lesser Antilles. This illustrates a point made earlier for Jamaican land birds, that the birds which have established themselves are not a random sample of those available outside, but those which find ecological conditions most suitable.

As many as 7 of the 28 Lesser Antillean species of South American origin are, in the Lesser Antilles, confined to Grenada, and another 5 do not come further north than St Vincent. In general, as shown in Table 22, species originating from South America fall away towards the north in the Lesser Antilles. It has been suggested by others that this is because colonisation occurs slowly and many of the species have not yet had time to spread the whole way. I suggest, instead, that it is mainly because of the differences in climate and habitat, the southern lowlands of Grenada being so much more arid than the rest of the Lesser Antilles that various South American species can survive there but not further north, and that this holds to a lesser extent for St Vincent. There is no similar variation in the birds of northern origin.

Actually four species which entered the Lesser Antilles from South America have been spreading north during the present century. The dove, *Zenaida auriculata*, long established on Grenada, was first recorded on St Vincent in 1961 (Schwarz and Klinikowski 1963), and is still confined to the dry southeast of the island with open fields and scrub; it reached the south end of St Lucia more recently (Bond 1971). The mockingbird *Mimus gilvus* was first recorded on Dominica in arid man-modified scrub woodland in 1961 (D.B. Wingate pers.-comm.) and is also now on Guadeloupe (Guth 1971, Bond 1971). The thrush *Turdus nudigenis* was first recorded on St Lucia and Martini-

TABLE 22.   *Species on six main Lesser Antilles in relation to direction of entry*

| Island | Latitude | Number of species which probably entered from | |
		south	northwest
Guadeloupe	16°N.	11	10
Dominica	15°15 N.	11	11
Martinique	14°50 N.	14	11
St. Lucia	13°50 N.	15	12
St. Vincent	13°N.	18	8
Grenada	12°N.	23	3

Note Based on information in Appendix 9, for 28 species entering from south and 19 from north.

que in 1951, in both of which it frequents wooded cultivation (Bond 1956). Finally, the cowbird *Molothrus bonariensis* was first recorded for the Lesser Antilles in the Grenadines in 1899, then on Grenada in 1901, Barbados in 1916, St Vincent in 1924, St Lucia in 1931 and Martinique in 1949 (Bond 1956), and finally on Puerto Rico in 1955, on all of which it frequents dry grassland (Gracey 1957).

These four instances might appear to go against the principle that island avifaunas are stable, but I advocate the latter view solely for natural habitats, and all four of these species have established themselves in habitats opened up by human cultivation. Another new colonist was shown to us by Dr. Earle Kirby on St Vincent, the grass finch *Sicalis luteola*, which is now established and breeding on the grassland of the airport; it arrived after a recent hurricane, presumably from Barbados, where it was earlier introduced successfully by man.

The observations by Beard (1949) on the forest trees of the Lesser Antilles show a different pattern of colonisation from that here suggested for the land birds. In the semi-arid lowlands, two-fifths of the flora consists of widely ranging tropical species, there are only 12 per cent of endemics, and of the rest, about twice as many species have entered the Lesser Antilles from the north, from Puerto Rico, as from the south. The situation in the humid forest is strikingly different, some 42 per cent of the species being endemic (most of these being on several islands), while of the rest only slightly more have entered from Puerto Rico than from South America. Similarly of the montane trees, about half are endemic and of the rest, two are widely distributed, 6 entered from Puerto Rico and three from South America. The possible reasons for these striking differences between the forest trees and the forest birds should be studied in detail. The seeds of nearly all the rain forest species were probably transported there by birds or bats.

EXTRA POINTS OF INTEREST

A few points about particular Lesser Antillean species may be added which reinforce examples of ideas discussed earlier. The two South American nightjars, *Caprimulgus rufus* on St Lucia and *C.cayennensis* on Martinique, add a further example to those given for the Greater Antilles (p. 105), of species which replace each other geographically on different islands in the West Indies, but coexist on the mainland;

how they might be separated ecologically on the South American mainland is not known.

The two flycatchers *Myiarchus stolidus* on the Lesser Antilles south to St Lucia and *M.nugator* on St Vincent and Grenada, provide an example of geographical replacement between species in different superspecies (Lanyon 1967, but following Bond 1971 for nomenclature).

Another endemic West Indian flycatcher, *Elaenia martinica* has a range without parallel among other West Indian birds (Fig. 24). Typically a bird of lowland scrub forest, it also occurs in humid forest in the southern Lesser Antilles, and on two of them, Grenada and St Vincent, is perhaps becoming restricted to this habitat owing to competition with a mainland species, *E.flavogaster*, but the situation, studied by Crowell (1968 and in prep.) is not altogether clear (see also Lack *et al.* 1973, Lack and Lack 1973).

The four monotypic genera of thrashers characteristic of the Lesser Antilles are of unknown origin. The range of *Margarops fuscatus* extends to Puerto Rico and the Bahamas (Fig. 21). *Allenia fusca* is

FIG. 24. *Range in the West Indies of the flycatcher* Elaenia martinica.

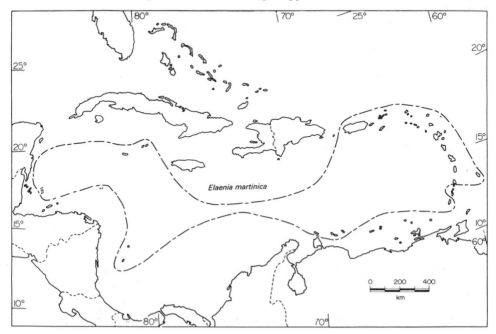

another generalised thrush-like species, and like the specialised Trembler *Cinclocerthia ruficauda*, is found almost throughout the Lesser Antilles, but not outside them, in both lowlands and highlands. It climbs along branches and up vertical trunks, and searches for invertebrates, including at the base of the bracts of large bromeliads (Zusi 1969). Finally *Ramphocinclus brachyurus* is restricted to the lowland forest of the windward side on Martinique and St Lucia (Diamond 1973), where it searches for invertebrates in the leaf litter on the ground. The thrashers are a North American family, but there are none in the Greater Antilles (except for *M.fuscatus* as above), and how these species reached the Lesser Antilles, and whether, in part at least, they diverged after their arrival, is not known.

The bullfinch *Loxigilla noctis* is endemic to the Lesser Antilles (see Fig. 17, p. 111). St Kitts, but no other island, formerly had a second species, *L.portoricensis*, which is also found on Puerto Rico. The St Kitts form is now extinct, possibly due to predation of its nests by an introduced monkey. *L.noctis* on St Kitts has a mean length (in mm.) of wing 69, culmen 13.2 and depth of beak 8.9. On Puerto Rico, the corresponding measurements of *L.portoricensis* are 90, 16.5 and 14.0 mm; but they were much larger on St Kitts, namely wing 100, culmen 20.8 and depth of beak 17.0 mm. The larger size on St Kitts was presumably evolved as a result of potential competition with *L.noctis*, which, incidentally, is not smaller on St Kitts than elsewhere (measurements of adult males from Ridgway 1901). This is a good example of character displacement, except that only one of the two species concerned was affected.

SUMMARY

On any one island in the Lesser Antilles, about half the species of land birds occur in both arid lowlands and humid highlands, a much higher proportion than on the mainland. Good examples of a species with a wider habitat on an island where a congener is absent than on another where it is present occur both in swifts of the genus *Chaetura* and in warblers of the genus *Dendroica*.

Twenty-three of the 70 Lesser Antillean species are endemic and two more are almost so, but reach northeastern Puerto Rico. Most of the endemic species live in the humid highlands.

Nearly all of the Lesser Antillean species confined to the lowlands originated from South America, as a number of them are restricted to the southern islands of the archipelago. Probably more of the Lesser Antillean species of humid forest came in from the north than the south, which might be linked with those from the Greater Antilles already being adapted to a depauperate forest.

CHAPTER 11 · THE WEST INDIAN
AVIFAUNA

The term 'avifauna' is often used for the birds of any specified area, and I have so used it for the birds of Jamaica in this book. But sometimes it is given a more precise meaning, for the birds of a large area within which the birds are similar to each other, and outside which they are very different. In particular, it has been so used for the six great zoogeographical regions of the world, the Palaearctic, Nearctic, Oriental, Ethiopian, Australasian and Neotropical, each of which can be distinguished through its peculiar families of birds (though the Palaearctic and Nearctic less clearly than the others).

A WEST INDIAN AVIFAUNA

Is there a West Indian avifauna in this special sense? If so, then presumably the islands have been sufficiently isolated from the mainland to allow its separate evolution, which must again raise the role of isolation in evolution on islands. Discussion will, as in the rest of the book, be restricted to land birds, because the marsh, water, freshwater and seabirds, and the raptors of the West Indies are not peculiar to it, but are widespread in the New World tropics.

At the level of the bird family, there is no justification for speaking of a West Indian avifauna, for of the 30 families (pigeons to passerines) represented, only two are endemic, and both are small. First the palmchats Dulidae consist of a single species, *Dulus dominicus*, confined to Hispaniola; and secondly the todies Todidae consist of a single genus *Todus*, with two species on Hispaniola and one each on Jamaica, Cuba and Puerto Rico. Neither family has a clear affinity with other birds.

At lower taxonomic levels however, endemism is high, for of the 108 genera represented, 39 (36 per cent) are endemic, and of the 210 species represented, 151 (72 per cent) are endemic. (The figures refer to the West Indies as defined later.) These figures are higher than for any other archipelago of comparable geographical position, and it therefore seems justifiable to speak of a West Indian avifauna. It should perhaps be added, however, that 19 of the endemic genera and 90 of the endemic species are each confined to a single island.

DETERMINATION OF BOUNDARIES

In determining the boundaries of the West Indian avifauna, it is important to classify each species as 'West Indian', 'South American' and so on, so as to be able to recognise islands with a substantial proportion of West Indian forms and keep them inside the boundary, while excluding the rest. Appendix 10 lists the main West Indian islands with some of their geographical features.

It has been difficult to determine just which species are 'West Indian', but after trial and error, I decided that definition must be rigid, and that no species should be called 'West Indian' if it breeds anywhere on the mainland, even if its present range suggests that it colonised the mainland from the West Indies, rather than the other way about. For, once one admits one small exception, others immediately appear.

Particular difficulty arises over five species characteristic of the West Indies which also breed on one or a few islands off the mainland, but not on the mainland itself. These, set out in Table 23, I have put in a special category. Whether they colonised the offshore islands from the West Indies, or the other way about, cannot certainly be determined, but in either case, here are five species of land birds which have successfully colonised across the big sea gap between the West Indies and the offshore islands of the mainland, but not over the far shorter sea gap between the offshore islands and the mainland.

TABLE 23.   *Typically West Indian species found also on islands near the mainland*

Species	Also on islands off
pigeon *Columba leucocephala*	Florida and Central America
pigeon *Columba squamosa*	South America
flycatcher *Elaenia martinica*	Mexico and Central America
thrasher *Margarops fuscatus*	South America
tanager *Spindalis zena*	Mexico

At least in their case, the breeding range is presumably determined by ecological, not geographical, barriers. And if this holds in their case, why not for species confined to the West Indies proper for which, hitherto, the sea barrier has been thought all-important?

It is particularly difficult to determine whether the vireo *Vireo altiloquus* is a 'West Indian' species. It occurs throughout the West Indies, and also on a few offshore islands, and so would have been placed in the same category as those in Table 23, except that it also breeds in southern Florida. It is virtually certain that it colonised Florida from the West Indies, and not the other way about, but if one therefore classifies it as a West Indian species, other less definite exceptions have to be considered. Two such are the dove *Zenaida aurita*, typically West Indian and on islands off Honduras and Mexico, but also local on the mainland of Mexico; and the dove *Leptotila jamaicensis*, which is also on the mainland of Mexico. The only possible procedure is to classify such species as 'West Indies and mainland', but to qualify them in the text where this would be misleading.

The Bahamas, the Northern boundary

The northern boundary of the West Indies consists of the low-laying

TABLE 24. *Northern and western boundaries of the West Indian avifauna*

Range elsewhere besides the island or islands named	Number of species found on			
	Bahamas	Swan I.	Old Providence	St Andrew
Solely Antilles	17	1	1	1
Solely Antilles and offshore islands	3	1	2	2
Antilles and mainland	16	2	7	9
Solely mainland (North America for Bahamas, Central America for rest)	4	—	1	1
Endemic	3	—	—	1
Totals	43	4	11	14

Notes (i) Based on Appendices 11–13.
(ii) Of the Bahaman species found both in the Antilles and on the mainland, 3 are not on the mainland of North America, hence so far as the Bahamas are concerned, they could have been classed as West Indian. On the other hand, one of the endemic Bahaman species is so close to a North American species that it might have been added as a fifth species otherwise North American.

Bahamas, beyond which lies Florida. The 43 resident land birds of
the Bahamas are listed in Appendix 11 and summarised in Table 24.
From their geographical position, it might have been supposed that
the Bahaman birds would be a mixture of North American and
West Indian species. In fact, they are overwhelmingly West Indian.
Only four North American species, a woodpecker, a nuthatch, a
gnatcatcher and a parulid warbler, are present in the Bahamas but
on none of the other West Indies, though a fifth species could be added,
since the endemic warbler of the Bahamas is closely related to a North
American species. In contrast, the Bahamas have 17 West Indian
species and 3 more found in the Antilles and offshore islands, none
of which are resident in North America. Nearly all the remaining
species are common to the West Indies and the adjoining North
American mainland so are not important to this discussion.

The Western boundary

Some of the offshore islands close to Yucatan and Honduras have
some of the species set out in Table 23, but the rest of their birds are
Mexican or Central American, and they are clearly outside the West
Indies faunistically. Swan Island, further offshore, has only four
species of land birds, set out in Appendix 12. One of these is *Dendroica
vitellina*, an endemic warbler (range shown in Fig. 23), and none
is a mainland species absent from the West Indies; so Swan Island
can reasonably be included with the West Indies.

Old Providence and St Andrew, further south, included by Bond
in the West Indies, are marginal, since as shown in Appendix 13,
each has only one typically West Indian species, a vireo on Old Providence and the Jamaican oriole *Icterus leucopteryx* on St Andrew, whereas
on the other hand both have a mainland species of hummingbird
not found in the West Indies. I have, however, followed Bond in
including them.

Aruba, Curaçao, Bonaire, the Southern boundary

Bond was clearly right to exclude from the West Indies the Dutch
islands of Aruba, Curaçao and Bonaire, which lie off Venezuela, even
though two of them are just outside the 100-fathom line. As shown in
Table 25 and Appendix 14, their main link with the West Indies

consists of 3 species found in the West Indies and also on offshore islands near South America, to which a fourth species, the vireo *Vireo altiloquus*, can be added (see note (ii) to Appendix 14). To set against these, there are 11 South American species not found in the West Indies, to which can be added 2 more species found in South America but nowhere in the Lesser Antilles (though they are found in the Greater). The remaining 11 species are widespread on the mainland and in the West Indies.

The Southeast boundary, Grenada

Grenada has a sufficient number of Antillean species to be included faunistically in the West Indies, though it has a stronger continental (in this case South American) element than any other West Indian island. As shown in Table 25 and Appendix 15, 6 South American

TABLE 25.   *Southern and southeastern boundary of the West Indian avifauna*

Range elsewhere besides the island or islands named	Number of species found on		
	Aruba Curaçao Bonaire	Grenada	Tobago
Solely Antilles	0	6	0
Antilles and offshore islands	3	2	0
Antilles and mainland	13	20	13 + 7
South America	11	6	50
Endemic	0	1	0
Totals	27	35	70

Notes (i) Based on Appendices 14–16.

(ii) The vireo *Vireo altiloquus* (on Aruba, Curaçao, Bonaire and Grenada), and dove *Zenaida aurita* (on Grenada) and the martin *Progne dominicensis* (on Grenada and Tobago) should for these islands be included with the West Indian element, since they do not occur on the mainland of South America, but only much further north, in Florida and Mexico.

(iii) On Grenada, the endemic dove *Leptotila wellsi*, and two species endemic to Grenada and and St. Vincent, are most closely related to South American species, so should be included with the South American element. So should several of the 20 species classified as 'Antillean and mainland', since they are in South America, Grenada and only some of the southern Lesser Antilles (see Appendix 15 for details).

(iv) Of the 20 Tobagan species found on the mainland and in the Antilles, 7 are separated in the Table as they are not typically West Indian, being found there only on the southernmost islands of Grenada and/or St. Vincent.

species occur on Grenada but nowhere else in the West Indies, to which may be added the only species endemic to Grenada, a dove closely related to a South American species. Moreover, 2 Grenadian species found solely in the West Indies are endemic to Grenada with St Vincent and are derived from South American species, while of the 20 Grenadian species found on the Antilles and the mainland, 6 are, on the mainland, solely in South America and 4 of them are either restricted to the southern Lesser Antilles or have recently spread north. On the other side, the West Indian element includes the other 4 species found solely in the Antilles, also the 2 found solely on the Antilles and offshore islands, and at least 3 of 20 found in the Antilles and on the mainland (because they are on the mainland solely in the north). On this reckoning, the South American element out-numbers the West Indian element on Grenada, but the 3 endemics, though derived from South America, might with equal justice be reckoned as West Indian, which would make the contributions from the two areas equal, and virtually no typically West Indian species occur south of Grenada.

If extremely closely related species which replace each other geographically are counted as one, as many as 15 of the 35 species of land birds resident on Grenada are also resident on Cuba or the Bahamas, 2500 km to the northwest, at the opposite end of the West Indies.

The Southeast boundary, Tobago

Tobago lies only 120 km southeast of Grenada and looks very similar. The two islands are similar in size (around 300 sq. km). Tobago is a little lower (580 m cf. 840 m), and both are about 150 km from the South American mainland, though Tobago is only 35–40 km from the island of Trinidad, which is virtually part of the mainland (see Appendix 10). They also have a similar climate and similar cultivated crops. Yet their birdlife could hardly be in greater contrast (Table 25 and Appendix 16), that of Tobago being South American, and that of Grenada West Indian, though with a strong South American element. The faunal boundary between them I propose to call 'Bond's line', after James Bond, who has spent so much of his life studying the birds of the West Indies. It is a dramatic experience to fly from the one island to the other, as we did in August 1971, for it takes only a few minutes. The marked difference in the land birds is not apparent at the airports, since the birds of cultivation are similar, but it is clear so soon as one enters the forests.

In the first place, Tobago has twice as many species of land birds as Grenada, 70 compared with 35. The Tobagan birds that are not in the West Indies are summarised by families in Appendix 16 and the species can be determined from the list by Bond (1970). Present on Tobago but absent from the Lesser Antilles are representatives of the typically South American families of potoos Nyctibiidae, trogons Trogonidae, jacamars Galbulidae, wood-hewers Dendrocolaptidae, ovenbirds Furnariidae, ant-thrushes Formicariidae, cotingas Cotingidae and manakins Pipridae, which between them provide 13 of the species on Tobago which are not on Grenada; but the majority of the Tobagan species absent from Grenada are widespread elsewhere.

Some of the latter, for instance the woodpeckers Picidae, with 3 species on Tobago, are not represented on Grenada, while other families are much less strongly represented there. Thus there are 10 species of flycatchers on Tobago, but only 4 on Grenada, 6 species of humming-birds Trochilidae compared with 3 on Grenada, and so on. One family, the pigeons Columbidae, is represented more strongly on Grenada, with 6 species, than on Tobago with 5, but this family is strongly represented throughout the West Indies.

Eighteen species are common to Tobago and Grenada, of which 11 are widespread species in South America and the Lesser Antilles. One, the martin *Progne dominicensis*, is widespread in the West Indies but on the mainland is solely in Mexico, so may be reckoned as 'West Indian' so far as Tobago is concerned; it is the sole West Indian element in its avifauna. Another 6 species are found on the mainland and in the Lesser Antilles, but in the latter are restricted to Grenada, and one other is restricted to Grenada with St. Vincent, so are part of the South American element on Grenada. The species in common between Tobago and Grenada comprise one-quarter of the Tobagan avifauna, but one-half of the Grenadian, because its total is smaller.

That Grenada, so close and looking so similar, should have only half the number of species of land birds resident on Tobago, raises in acute form the problem of the number of species on islands. Tobago is a continental island, apparently cut off early in the Pleistocene, whereas Grenada arose as a volcano from the sea and has never been connected with the mainland. But it is hard to believe that a sea gap of only 150 km should have made all that difference to its land birds.

Moreover, if the land bridge between Tobago and the mainland has been all-important with respect to its land birds, why should Tobago have only about one-third of the 205 or so species resident on nearby Trinidad (Herklots 1961)? Most naturalists would, I think, be prepared to explain this difference in terms of ecology rather than dispersal by saying that compared with Tobago, Trinidad has a greater variety of habitats available for land birds, and that at least some of these habitats are richer than their equivalents on Tobago. If an explanation in terms of ecological factors is acceptable for this difference, then I see no *a priori* reason why it should not be equally acceptable to explain the proportionately smaller difference between the avifaunas of Tobago and Grenada. Tobago has richer forests floristically than Grenada (Beard 1944, 1949), and they are likely to provide ecological niches for a greater number of land birds than on Grenada. In that case, Tobago's former land connection with the mainland is of considerable significance, since neither rain-forest trees (Carlquist 1966), nor various other kinds of plants and animals, normally cross sea gaps. The Tobagan forest is, in essence, South American, that on Grenada is Antillean. As shown in the previous chapter, the highland forest birds of the Lesser Antilles are, at least in large part, derived from those of the Greater Antilles, not South America.

Hence even though land birds may not find it hard to cross the 150 km of sea between South America and Grenada, the former land bridge to Tobago may have been critical in determining its richer bird life. In general, of course, land birds are more numerous on continental than oceanic islands, but often comparisons have to be made between islands of very unequal size, in the Gulf of Guinea, for instance, between the continental Fernando Po and the much smaller oceanic islands of Principe, San Tomé and Annobon, as noted in Chapter 14. The special value of Tobago in such a discussion is that, except in having a former land connection, it is so similar in climate, size and other geographical features to the nearest oceanic island of Grenada.

ENDEMISM IN LAND BIRDS OF OTHER ARCHIPELAGOES

It may be concluded that there is a West Indian avifauna with defined geographical boundaries. One further question should, however, be asked, namely whether any part of the West Indies has such distinctive land birds that it should be treated as a separate avifauna. The only area that might possibly be considered in this connection is the Lesser Antilles, but their many links with the rest of the archipelago, shown in the previous chapter, rule out this possibility.

It is rare to find an endemic family of birds confined to an oceanic archipelago, but there is one in the Hawaiian Islands, the sicklebills Drepanididae, and a subfamily, Darwin's finches, the Geospizinae in the Galapagos. The West Indies have, in fact, two endemic families, but both are small, and their evolution is in no way comparable with the adaptive radiations of the sicklebills or Darwin's finches.

The degree of endemism at the generic and specific levels in the land birds of other oceanic archipelagoes is compared in Table 26. The figures for the West Indies of 36 per cent of endemic genera and 72 per cent of endemic species are exceeded in the Hawaiian Islands,

TABLE 26. *A comparison of endemism of land birds on various archipelagoes*

Archipelago or island-group	Distance from nearest mainland or large island (km)	Number of genera	Percent endemic	Number of species	Percent endemic
West Indies	100–200	108	36	208	72
Hawaii	3300	18	83	33	97
Galapagos	1000	13	39	25	80
Tristan (and Gough)	2800 (3200)	3	100	4	100
New Hebrides (and Banks)	450	32	3	42	19
Fiji	450	31	13	45	44
Samoa	800	22	5	26	35
Philippines	350	90	7	193	49
Gulf of Guinea Is	220–340	31	10	41	54
Canaries (and Madeira)	100 (700)	27	0	35	17

Note Land birds are those in the families from pigeons to passerines inclusive. Extinct species, provided collected, have been included, introduced species excluded. The species lists are derived from standard works. The number of endemic genera and species differs somewhat in different classifications but I have used Peters' 'Check-List' wherever possible, supplemented by other modern treatments. A few differences in classification would not seriously affect the figures. The two distances for the Tristan archipelago refer respectively to South Africa (and in brackets South America, from which the land birds probably came). The Mascarene Islands of Mauritius Réunion and Rodriguez may well have had a higher proportion of endemic species than at most of the islands in this Table; but some species became extinct before they were collected, and there are other doubts, so that I was unable to make a satisfactory list.

the Galapagos and the Tristan group (but the last has few land birds). These three groups of islands are much further from other lands than are the West Indies, and are in a class by themselves so far as endemic land birds are concerned, especially in view of the adaptive radiations in the Hawaiian and Galapagos Islands already mentioned.

In all the other oceanic archipelagoes for which I could find reliable lists of land birds, the degree of endemism is much lower than in the West Indies, even though most of these archipelagoes are further than the West Indies from other lands (Table 26). This might suggest that it has been unusually difficult for land birds to reach the West Indies (and if they came from Central America they would have had to come against the prevailing easterly trade winds). On the other hand, the West Indies have been colonised by a larger number of species of land birds than have the other archipelagoes, which might suggest that it has been unusually easy for land birds to reach them. Not enough is known about the possible factors involved to resolve this anomaly at the present time, but at least it may be noted, once again, that isolation has an influence but it may be complex.

THE ZOOGEOGRAPHICAL REGIONS

The importance of isolation is clear, even though the way in which it works is not, and a really high degree of endemism is found, in fact, only in the remotest archipelagoes. Similarly the great zoogeographical regions of the world have been isolated geographically from each other. These six regions were first recognized and defined in terms of birds by P.L. Sclater (1858), but were later shown to apply to mammals and other groups, and they have stood the test of further research up to the present time. Later discussion has chiefly concerned two subsidiary points, first whether the Palaearctic and Nearctic have sufficiently similar types of birds to be grouped in one avifauna, the Holarctic, and secondly, where the boundary between the Oriental and Australasian regions should be drawn (Wallace's and other lines). The basic question of why there should be just six, or perhaps only five, zoogeographical regions has rarely been considered. (Sclater, writing before the 'Origin of Species', postulated that they represented six separate centres of animal creation.)

The six regions are broadly separated from the rest by sea, except for the Palaearctic from the Ethiopian by desert and from the Oriental by desert and mountains. Hence geographical barriers must have played a critical part in the separation of these avifaunas, even though birds regularly travel between one faunal region and another. Thus every year birds which breed in the Palaearctic spend the winter in the Ethiopian and Oriental regions, and others which breed in the Nearctic spend the winter in the Neotropics. Further, the recent increase in birdwatchers has shown that the passage of birds from the New to the Old World across the Atlantic is not an extremely rare event to be reported in the ornithological journals on every occasion, but involves scores and probably hundreds of birds every year. The basic premise is the same for the West Indies, that its minor avifauna could hardly have come into existence without isolation, although birds regularly cross the geographical barriers concerned.

The importance of such barriers in the formation of faunal regions is shown by the closing of the sea gap between South and North America with the formation of the Panamanian land bridge in the late Tertiary, some two million years ago. Prior to this, as shown by fossil evidence, the mammal faunas of North and South America were almost entirely different, but afterwards they mingled to a great extent (Simpson 1940). It is reasonable to infer that the land birds of the two continents did the same. As already mentioned repeatedly, at least a dozen bird families of South American origin, which presumable evolved there in isolation, occur at the present time in small numbers in Central America. It seems absurd, however, to suppose that at least some of these birds could not have crossed from South into North America by flight before the Panamanian land bridge was formed. Further, two other families which are agreed to be of South American origin, the hummingbirds Trochilidae and the flycatchers Tyrannidae, have spread in relatively large numbers into North America. If they crossed before the formation of the land bridge, why did not the others? Mayr pointed out that some birds are 'good colonisers', especially those of semi-arid regions which have strong flight and are forced to travel at intervals, since in part they live in temporary habitats; whereas various other birds are 'bad colonists', notably those of humid forest, which have relatively weak flight and do not need to move out of their habitat.

I therefore wonder whether the main factor checking the earlier spread of South American birds into Central America was not their inability to cross the sea gap, but the absence of suitable habitats for them in Central America until after the Panamanian land bridge had allowed the South American rain forest and perhaps other habitats to spread there. As already mentioned, rain forest trees do not become established across large water gaps, owing to their large and heavy seeds (Carlquist 1966), so the South American rain forest could hardly have reached Central America before the land bridge was formed. However various flycatchers live in open woodland, as do some hummingbirds, so it is possible that these two families would have been less dependent on the presence of South American habitats for their survival than the other families, and so could have spread into Central America ahead of them. This is speculative, but it suggests the possibility that, for the great zoogeographical regions, the factor isolating the land birds may not have been a geographical barrier to bird dispersal but an ecological barrier to colonisation, dependent on the vegetation.

When a particular type of forest has been isolated, with its birds, for a long time, the birds will tend to evolve closely interlocking ecological niches, and this will make it hard for birds from elsewhere to establish themselves there. This argument was developed earlier for the highland forests of Jamaica, but it applies equally to the far richer forests and far more complex birdlife of the great zoogeographical regions. In tropical Africa, for instance, Moreau (1966) attributed to this factor the virtual segregation of the avifauna of the lowland and montane evergreen forests, even though they come in contact with each other at their margins. He also attributed to it the inability of the wintering Palaearctic migrants in Africa to exist in lowland rain forest, although many of them are forest species in their summer homes. This interlocking of niches will make for stability in forest avifaunas both on continents and on remote islands, but with this difference, that conditions on the continents favour the survival of many species with specialised ecological niches and remote islands favour relatively few species with broad niches. Hence to a casual observer the island forests will not look so 'full', but this, I suggest, is deceptive.

There is the further point that, once a bird species has become closely adapted to a particular type of forest, and once other species in other types of forest have evolved closely interlocking ecological niches, it will be almost impossible for the one to survive outside its own type of forest—hence natural selection will favour a strongly sedentary habit. That is perhaps why some forest species of white-eyes *Zosterops* in the Solomon Islands replace each other on islands only 5 to 6 km apart, a distance which they could fly in a few minutes (Mayr 1942). It is especially in humid forest, with its relatively stable conditions, that one may expect each species to be closely adapted and hence to evolve sedentariness; and it is especially in semi-arid habitats which are liable to big changes in conditions that mobility will be advantageous; and this is probably why forest birds may be 'bad' and birds of semi-arid habitats 'good' colonists.

SUMMARY

The land birds of the West Indies may be termed an 'avifauna' in the special sense of a group of birds very different from those of surrounding areas, and the boundaries of the area can be clearly defined. The proportion of endemic genera and species is higher in the West Indies than in any other archipelago a similar distance from other land, and the number of resident species is also higher. Endemism is higher only in extremely isolated archipelagoes, such as the Hawaiian and Galapagos.

Tobago, a continental island only 120 km from the oceanic island of Grenada, and of similar size with a similar climate, has twice as many species of land birds. This can hardly be attributed to Tobago's former land bridge favouring bird dispersal, and is probably linked with it having a much richer forest than Grenada. The richer forest can be attributed to the former land bridge.

The distinctive avifaunas of the great zoogeographical regions are a result of geographical barriers, but the latter probably did not themselves isolate the land birds through difficulties of dispersal. It is possible that the land birds were isolated by an ecological barrier to colonisation through restriction of the main types of forest.

CHAPTER 12 · THE WINTERING WARBLERS

Up to this point in the book, all the evidence has run in the same direction, to the conclusion that dispersal of land birds to and between the West Indian islands is relatively frequent, that the natural habitats are nearly 'ecologically full', and that the small number of resident species of land birds is due largely to the fact that, with the reduced ecological diversity on such islands, a few generalised species tend to exclude a larger number of specialists. However, one important group of Jamaican land birds has not yet been considered, namely the wintering parulid warblers from North America. At least at first sight, the evidence which this group presents appears to refute the above views, since a large number of related species of warblers pour into the Jamaican forests, which can hardly, therefore, be 'ecologically full', and it is obviously easier for these migrants, which anyway travel long distances over the sea, than for resident species to disperse through the islands. Earlier I have discarded the view that dispersal is the critical factor in determining how many species of land birds occur on an island: but here is a group of a large number of species for which dispersal is easy apparently contradicting this view. Detailed study (Lack and Lack 1972) shows, however, that the problem is not nearly so simple as this brief statement might suggest. The probable answer is that competitive exclusion is still effective, but that it operates at a very different level for these wintering warblers than for other species, a point which raises further problems.

THE SUMMER AND WINTER VISITORS TO JAMAICA

There are 7 species which visit Jamaica only in summer, namely the cuckoo *Coccyzus americanus*, the nighthawk *Chordeiles gundlachii*, the swift *Cypseloides niger*, the kingbird *Tyrannus dominicensis*, the elaenia *Elaenia fallax* (mainly), the martin *Progne dominicensis* and the vireo *Vireo altiloquus*. Of these, the nighthawk, the swift, the kingbird and the martin depend on airborne insects, which become scarce in winter, while the cuckoo and the vireo eat large caterpillars, probably also scarce or absent in winter. As to be expected, none of them is replaced in winter by equivalent species from the north, though a number of North American hirundines come through on passage and stay a while.

There are 21 species of regular wintering land birds from North America, of which 18 are parulid warblers. Of the other 3, the Yellow-bellied Sapsucker *Sphyrapicus varius* is a fairly common woodpecker which bores numerous small holes in native trees, and especially in the introduced eucalyptus, to get the sap. No native Jamaican bird obtains its food in this way. (The aberrant tanager *Euneornis campestris* regularly, and the Bananaquit *Coereba flaveola* occasionally, insert their beaks into holes made by the sapsucker to get at the sap, so does the wintering Cape May Warbler *Dendroica tigrina*.) The second wintering species other than the warblers, is the Catbird *Dumetella carolinensis*, a very scarce migrant found in the thicker parts of the arid lowland forest. Its size and shape suggest that it might perhaps compete with the mockingbirds *Mimus* spp., but the latter feed more in the open, and anyway the Catbird is too scarce to be a serious competitor and co-exists with the Mockingbird in North America. The third species is the Indigo Bunting *Passerina cyanea*, which is a local and scarce seed-eater occurring mainly after the winter solstice, and it probably has little impact on the native birds.

THE WINTERING WARBLERS

The 18 wintering parulid warblers form a substantial proportion of the Jamaican avifauna in winter, for including the two resident species, the Yellow *Dendroica petechia* and the Arrow-headed *D.pharetra*, they comprise two-fifths of all the passerine species resident on the island at this season. Indeed, warblers formed about one quarter of all the individual passerine birds that we counted on our winter walks, and one third of those in natural forest (Appendix 17).

The species which regularly spend the winter in Jamaica are set out in Table 27. These birds are familiar to American ornithologists by their vernacular names, so I have used these in the text, and for consistency, have done the same for the two native Jamaican species, which are also included in all the Tables, as they must be reckoned as potential competitors with the winter visitors. But the observations

TABLE 27.　*The warblers present in Jamaica in winter*

| | | Mean length (mm) | | Winter habitat | | |
		wing	culmen	low	mid	high
Residents						
Yellow Warbler	*Dendroica petechia*	65	10.6	+		
Arrow-headed Warbler	*Dendroica pharetra*	63	11.3	+	+	+
Winter visitors						
Black-and-White Warbler	*Mniotilta varia*	69	11.4	++	+	+
Swainson's Warbler	*Limnothlypis swainsonii*	70	15.0	+	+	+
Worm-eating Warbler	*Helmitheros vermivorus*	69	13.7	+	+	+
Tennessee Warbler	*Vermivora peregrina*	65	9.6	×		×
Parula Warbler	*Parula americana*	61	9.9	++	+	(E)
Magnolia Warbler	*Dendroica magnolia*	60	9.0	+	(E)	(E)
Cape May Warbler	*Dendroica tigrina*	66	9.8	+	(C)	(C)
Black-throated Blue Warbler	*Dendroica caerulescens*	65	9.4	+	+	+
Myrtle Warbler	*Dendroica coronata*	74	10.0	×		×
Black-throated Green Warbler	*Dendroica virens*	64	9.9	+	+	+
Yellow-throated Warbler	*Dendroica dominica*	67	13.8	(C)		(C)
Prairie Warbler	*Dendroica discolor*	58	9.4	++	+	(E)
Palm Warbler	*Dendroica palmarum*	65	9.9	+	(E)	(E)
Ovenbird	*Seiurus aurocapillus*	73	11.7	+	+	+
Northern Waterthrush	*Seiurus noveboracensis*	77	12.7	+		
Louisiana Waterthrush	*Seiurus motacilla*	81	13.2	+	+	+
Common Yellowthroat	*Geothlypis trichas*	53	10.5	+	+	+
American Redstart	*Setophaga ruticilla*	64	8.5	+	+	+

Notes (i) Mean lengths of wing and culmen are from Ridgway (1902).
(ii) Under habitat, + means regular, ++ abundant, with more than 15 counted per 10 hours of walking, × regular but very scarce, (C) mainly in wooded cultivation, (E) at forest edge in introduced trees or (Palm Warbler) grassland.
(iii) The Yellow Warbler and Arrow-headed Warbler do not overlap in habitat in the lowlands, since the Yellow is in mangroves and coastal woodland, the Arrow-headed in the richest woodland of the lowland hills.

on the native species in this chapter refer solely to the period from October to the end of March, when the winter visitors are present, and not to the summer.

Table 27 shows that 10 of the 20 warbler species concerned are in the genus *Dendroica*, and all of them are very similar in overall size (as indicated by wing-length and length of beak). The other 10 species are in 8 genera, but these genera are all fairly close to *Dendroica* and the morphological differences are small compared with those between, for instance, the different genera of resident passerine birds in the West Indies. Therefore, 20 rather similar species in a single family of birds live in Jamaica in winter. The greatest number in any other family is 10 pigeons Columbidae, and in any passerine family 8 flycatchers Tyrannidae, but these are much more diverse than the 20 warblers.

The first, and perhaps the most important, point to determine is whether each of these 20 species is ecologically separated from every other. At first sight it seemed to us almost impossible that they could be, especially the leaf-gleaning species, but detailed study showed that at least nearly all, and probably all, are in fact segregated. MacArthur (1958) showed that, in summer, 5 species of *Dendroica* in spruce forest in northeastern North America are separated ecologically from each other in unusually subtle ways, by their feeding stations, and the same holds for many of them in their winter quarters, though some of the differences are obvious.

Differences in habitat

The summary in the right-hand part of Table 27 shows that in natural forest 12 of the 20 species are regular in both the lowlands and highlands, this including two scarce species, the Tennessee and Myrtle. Another, the Yellow-throated Warbler also occurs in lowlands and highlands but mainly in introduced trees. Of the others, 5 are confined to the lowlands and the other 2 to low and midlevels, except that some of these 7 are in the highlands at the forest edge in introduced trees of wooded cultivation. The evidence on which this summary is based consists of the counts in Appendices 17 and 18. Difficulties in assessing total numbers from such counts are discussed in Appendix 19, supplemented by comparisons between numbers seen on slow and fast walks, and at the forest edge compared with the interior, in Appendix 20, and comparisons between numbers seen and numbers mist-netted in Appendix 21.

Only two species are completely segregated from each other by habitat, namely the two residents, the Yellow Warbler in mangroves and the coastal strip of scrub forest, and the Arrow-headed in the forests of the mountains, midlevels, and the richest parts of the lowland hills.

TABLE 28.   *Positions of insects when captured for food by warblers resident or wintering in Jamaica*

	No. of observed feeds on insects	Percentage of insect feeds from						
		broad leaves	conifer needles	bromeliads	air	ground	twigs, boughs	flowers, fruits
Yellow	67	**76**			9	7		7
Arrow-headed	377	**92**		3	3	**96**	3	3
Black-and-White	246	11	2	2	7	6	**70**	3
Swainson's	26	4					20	8
Worm-eating	60	**69**		3	2		7	5
Parula	461	**87**			11		11	6
Magnolia	178	**73**			11		4	4
Cape May	198	**81**		1	17		13	8
Black-throated Blue	350	**46**	2		5	15	6	3
Black-throated Green	354	**61**	26				11	8
Yellow-throated	61		**72**	8	5		11	2
Prairie	305	**84**	2		15	1		
Palm	81	9				**77**	5	
Ovenbird	106	1				**94**		
Northern Waterthrush	55	2				**98**		
Louisiana Waterthrush	53					**100**		
Common Yellowthroat	96	**65**				11	19	5
American Redstart	322	28			**64**	×	8	

Notes   (i) Of the 60 observed feeds for the Worm-eating, 75 per cent were on dead and 18 per cent on living vegetation, while for 7 per cent this point was not recorded. Of the 27 feeds on broad leaves of the Black-and-White, 30 per cent were on dead and 70 per cent on living leaves. The 5 feeds of the Yellow Warbler on the 'ground' were actually on insects taken off the surface of water.

(ii) The Cape May Warbler is different from all the other species in that many of its feeds were on fruits (14% of total feeds) and nectar (15% of total feeds). In the table the figures are the percentages of the insect feeds only. Most other warblers did not take any fruit or nectar, and the only two species in which the proportion of feeds on either of these items exceeded 4 per cent were the Parula (6 per cent on fruits) and Black-throated Green (5 per cent on fruits).

(iii) The two rare warblers, the Tennessee and the Myrtle, are not included.

Broad differences in feeding

The four specialists

All the parulid warblers in Jamaica feed predominantly on small insects, though the Cape May supplements them with an appreciable amount of fruits and nectar (29% of its feeds—see Table 28, note ii). Table 28 summarises the places from which each species obtains its insects, and at once separates out four specialists and five ground-feeding species, which may be discussed first, before the harder problem of the leaf-gleaners is investigated.

Four species are specialists in the sense that no other Jamaican species feeds in the same way in the same habitat. The **Black-and-White Warbler** *Mniotilta varia*, which is common in all types of forest from the lowest and most arid to the highest and most humid, feeds primarily by creeping up and down and along trunks, branches and twigs of all sizes, taking insects from bark and crevices. It occasionally follows termite trails, or climbs damp rocks or vertical banks with short vegetation. Rarely, it takes an insect off a leaf or catches one in the air that it has disturbed. It fills a niche very similar to that of the North America Tree-creeper *Certhia familiaris*, but it is less specialised, has a shorter bill and does not support itself with its tail. In late summer it interacts strongly with the Brown-headed Nuthatch *Sitta pusilla* (Morse 1970).

The **Worm-eating Warbler** *Helmitheros vermivorus* is in all types of natural forest except mangroves. Its vernacular name is a misnomer, for it does not feed on the ground, but low in the trees. It is the only species which feeds primarily by probing among clusters of dead hanging leaves, and also on dead twigs, in which it sometimes excavates or pulls off bark. We often saw it single out the only patch of dead leaves among many living ones.

The **Common Yellowthroat** *Geothlypis trichas* is, so far as Jamaica is concerned, a specialist because of the habitat it frequents for feeding, being the only species in the lush herb layer, usually between a half and one metre high, which grows at the edges of lowland swamps and parts of the montane forest, and at times elsewhere. In the lowlands it is also found at times in damp woodland with thick bushes or low trees but no herb layer. It feeds on insects primarily in this herb layer, but occasionally in bushes, or even in trees up to 10 m above the ground.

Finally, the **American Redstart** *Setophaga ruticilla* is widespread in all types of natural woodland, especially in the lowlands in mangroves, sea-level forest and riverine woodland, but it is scarce in the mountains. It is the only warbler in Jamaica which takes almost all its insect prey from the air, by quick short flights and hops among the twigs, especially where there are a few leaves, often just under the canopy, but also lower down, and even on the ground, flashing its tail, flicking its wings, and darting out to take an airborne insect, usually within a few centimetres of vegetation. The Magnolia sometimes feeds in a similar way, but much more often gleans from leaves. The others which occasionally take insects from the air are in different habitats and do not flick their tails. No native Jamaican species takes insects in a similar way.

The ground-feeding species

The five ground-feeding species are also separated clearly from each other, as summarised in Table 29. **Swainson's Warbler** *Limnothlypis swainsonii* is regular in lowland woods and montane forest with thick

TABLE 29.   *Differences in feeding habitat preferences of ground-feeding warblers wintering in Jamaica*

	Swainson's Warbler	Palm Warbler	Ovenbird	Northern Waterthrush	Louisiana Waterthrush
Forest floor	**77**	2	30	—	—
Ground at forest edge	—	11	20	—	9
Mud in or beside shallow water					
(a) lowlands	—	—	—	**89**	—
(b) midlevels	—	—	—	—	38
(c) highlands	—	—	2	—	—
Rocks by water	—	—	5	9	**53**
Short grass with scattered trees	—	**48**	8	—	—
Other ground records					
(unspecified)	20	15	28	—	—
Herbage	4	9	7	2	—
Air	—	15	—	—	—

Notes   (i)   Feeds of Northern Waterthrush from off mud beside shallow water included 9 per cent from off *Victoria regia* water-lily leaves in Botanic Garden.
(ii) Proportion of aerial feeds by Palm Warbler is probably exaggerated, as these are most conspicuous, and we could not always record normal feeds on the ground.

undergrowth, and also in the tall dark forest with a dense canopy, but no undergrowth, of Fern Gully. It is an extremely retiring species, most often seen on fast walks through the forest, presumably because on slow ones it had usually moved off into cover before we came up. It stays in thick cover, feeding by rummaging with its very long beak in leaf litter, sometimes probing and sometimes tossing leaves aside. It feeds similarly in North America (Meanley 1966). When disturbed, it flies up from the ground into low vegetation, but we never saw it feed there.

The **Palm Warbler** *Dendroica palmarum* occurs chiefly in the lowlands, in open grassland with scattered trees, but we occasionally saw it in the highlands, once on the grassy top of Blue Mountain. It is the only species which feeds primarily on insects on the ground in short grass in the open. It occasionally takes an insect off herbage or in the air, but the proportion of such feeds recorded in Table 29 is misleadingly high, as we did not always record normal feeds on the ground.

The **Ovenbird** *Seiurus aurocapillus* is common on the forest floor of all types of natural forest from sea level to the mountains, even including mangroves where the mud has dried. It normally feeds where there is thick tree cover overhead, though, unlike Swainson's Warbler, it comes out on to the forest trails and tracks. In lowland forest it feeds on dry ground, among leaf litter and stones, and the Northern Waterthrush takes its place on muddy ground; but it occurs all through the wet montane forest, where the Northern Waterthrush is absent. It differs from Swainson's Warbler in picking its food off the surface with its shorter beak, rather than probing or tossing leaves, and it will also feed in drier places than Swainson's.

The **Northern Waterthrush** *Seiurus noveboracensis* is abundant in mangroves and regular but scarce in lowland woods on muddy ground, usually near standing water or a muddy stream. We also found it on wet tracks through wooded cultivation in the very wet limestone forest of the John Crow mountains, up to 240 m above sea level, but nowhere else as high as this. In winter in Venezuela, likewise, it depends on damp earth, quiet waters and woody cover (Schwarz 1964). It feeds by picking small invertebrates off mud or extremely shallow water. One in the Kingston Botanic Garden fed regularly from off the large leaves of the introduced waterlily *Victoria regia*.

Finally the **Louisiana Waterthrush** *Seiurus motacilla* is regular in rather small numbers on rocky streams and rivers through forest, chiefly at midlevels and in the mountains, but also in the lowlands, where it has a niche similar to that of the Grey Wagtail *Motacilla cinerea* in Europe, taking insects while standing on rocks beside or in the water, and it wags its. tail up and down in a similar way. In the lowlands, where the Northern Waterthrush is on mud by still water, the Louisiana Waterthrush is confined to rocks near running water (except for one on the *stonework* of a pond in the Kingston Botanic Garden). Also, at 500 m beside the Hermitage Reservoir, well above the altitude frequented by the Northern Waterthrush, it behaves as the latter does in the lowlands, hunting regularly on mud and beside shallow standing water. Hence it is separated from the Northern Waterthrush. As a curiosity, one fed regularly on a tarmac road through montane forest where a small stream splashed onto it and made the surface wet.

Thus the five ground-feeding warblers in Jamaica are clearly separated from each other. The difference can be striking, as when in a lowland wood we once saw a Louisiana Waterthrush standing on a rock in midstream, only two metres from a Northern Waterthrush at the muddy edge and six metres from an Ovenbird on dry ground under the trees. Since all three were in the same wood, it is hard to know whether to classify them as differing in habitat or feeding station.

In Trinidad, 1600 km southeast of Jamaica, the Northern Waterthrush is the only species of *Seiurus* which regularly spends the winter, and here I saw it not only on mud in mangroves, as in Jamaica, but also on the dry floor of lowland forest, like the Ovenbird in Jamaica, while Dr. A. Lill, my companion in the field, informed me that it is also regularly beside rocky streams in the montane forest, like the Louisiana Waterthrush in Jamaica. Hence in Trinidad it occupies niches which in Jamaica are divided among the three species of *Seiurus*. Many examples are given in this book, and they have been reported from other islands for many years, of resident species with a wider niche in the absence of congeners, but this appears to be the first known case involving a winter visitor.

The leaf-gleaning warblers

We now come to the much more complicated problem of the leaf-gleaning warblers. There are 11 species altogether, and I have thought it best, in this discussion, to take the easiest first, rather than keeping to the systematic sequence in Tables 30–32, which summarise much of the relevant information. (Note that two leaf-gleaning species, the Tennessee and Myrtle Warblers, are omitted from some of these tables because they are so scarce.)

The resident **Yellow Warbler** *Dendroica petechia* is easily separated as it is the only common leaf-gleaning warbler in mangroves, where it takes nearly all its food off the leaves. (The figures for feeds off the ground and in the air in Table 28 are misleadingly high as we did not always record normal feeds for this species.)

The other resident species, the **Arrow-headed** *Dendroica pharetra*, is clearly separated by habitat from all the other leaf-gleaners except the two Black-throated Warblers, because it is commonest in montane forest. Here it takes insects primarily off the rather thick evergreen leaves of forest trees; this separates it from the Black-throated Green, which at this altitude feeds from off the small leaves of sclerophyllous trees and junipers. The Black-throated Blue, however, feeds regularly from off the same broad types of leaves as the Arrow-headed, but is separated from it mostly by its ways of feeding, though also partly by habitat, as it occurs in the lowlands, where the Arrow-headed is absent. The Arrow-headed usually feeds fairly high above the

TABLE 30. *Heights at which feeding observed in resident or wintering leaf-gleaning warblers in Jamaica*

	Number of observations	Mean height (metres)	Stand. dev. (metres)
Yellow	17	5.6	4.5
Arrow-headed	107	6.8	4.1
Parula	131	6.4	3.6
Magnolia	49	6.3	3.3
Cape May	39	7.6	3.5
Black-throated Blue	152	4.5	4.0
Black-throated Green	81	7.8	4.0
Yellow-throated	11	8.6	4.7
Prairie	93	5.3	4.0

Note Each individual bird was recorded only once, at the height at which it was first seen feeding. It was not recorded for successive feeds.

TABLE 31. *Part of tree in which feeding observed in resident or wintering leaf-gleaning warblers in Jamaica*

	Number of observations	Percentage of recorded feeds in			
		lowest quarter	second quarter	third quarter	top quarter
Yellow	13	0	31	23	46
Arrow-headed	76	4	28	30	38
Parula	105	4	28	31	38
Magnolia	46	7	50	22	22
Cape May	38	0	18	34	48
Black-throated Blue	67	6	36	30	28
Black-throated Green	72	1	24	32	43
Yellow-throated	11	0	36	36	27
Prairie	59	3	34	21	42

Notes (i) Each individual bird was recorded only once, at the height at which it was first seen feeding.
(ii) Trees under 3 m high were excluded as too low for the above subdivisions to be very meaningful.

ground, both below and from the underside of the canopy, and typically spends much time searching and peering about from one perch on a twig, ready to stretch further from its perch than the Black-throated Blue. The latter, in contrast, changes its perch much more often in its searching through the leaves, and indeed takes nearly half its food from twigs, the ground or the air (Tables 28 and 32) as well as tending to feed lower down in the trees (Table 31). Hence though these two species at times feed alongside each other, they are in the main separated by their feeding stations and feeding methods.

Since much has just been said about the **Black-throated Blue Warbler** *Dendroica caerulescens*, it may conveniently be taken next. In Jamaica it is common in rich lowland forest, in midlevel and in montane forest; but it is virtually absent from arid lowland forest, which partly separates it from various common leaf-gleaners of the lowlands. Much more important, it is separated from all the other leaf-gleaners (except the Arrow-headed, already discussed) by its preference for feeding from off broad thick leaves of forest trees, and this holds even in the lowlands. This also separates it from the Black-throated Green, which is the only other regular leaf-gleaner in montane

TABLE 32.   *Position of tree-feeding and herbage-feeding resident of wintering Jamaican warblers when capturing insects*

	Percentage of feeds			
	while perched	in flight	while hovering	with a flutter from a perch
Yellow	81	16	3	—
Arrow-headed	96	3	×	×
Black-and-White	93	7	1	—
Worm-eating	100	—	—	—
Parula	95	3	2	×
Magnolia	79	12	6	3
Cape May	75	11	14	—
Black-throated Blue	71	18	8	2
Black-throated Green	79	5	14	3
Yellow-throated	98	—	2	—
Prairie	82	5	11	2
Common Yellowthroat	99	1	—	—
American Redstart	15	81	3	1

Note   The total numbers of insect feeds for each species are given in Table 28. × less than 1.0%.

forest. Its other feeding characteristics were noted in the previous paragraph. It is clearly segregated from all other species.

The **Black-throated Green Warbler** *Dendroica virens* is regular in forest at all altitudes. In montane forest, we saw it feeding especially from off juniper needles. No other species feeds regularly in the junipers. It also feeds in introduced pines, but at times, such as when eating fruits, in natural forest, especially sclerophyll forest. It feeds by picking insects off the needles of junipers and pines, especially at the tips of the canopy and side branches, usually when perched, but commonly also when hovering (as in summer—MacArthur 1958, Morse 1967). The Yellow-throated feeds regularly in the introduced pines, but probes with its relatively long beak into the base of the needles, and so utilises a source of food different from that of the Black-throated Green. The Black-throated Green is also regular in the lowlands, chiefly in small-leaved mimosaceous trees, which are also frequented by the Prairie Warbler. These two species are, however, largely separated by habitat, since the Black-throated Green is absent from sealevel forest and nearly all the arid lowland forest where the

Prairie is commonest (Appendix 21); and where both occur together, the Black-throated Green tends to feed in the top half of taller trees than those preferred by the Prairie (Tables 30 and 31).

The **Yellow-throated Warbler** *Dendroica dominica*, though nowadays associated in Jamaica chiefly with introduced pines, was known on the island to Gosse (1847), so is not a new arrival due to man providing an alien species of tree. It is regular both in the lowlands and the mountains. In the lowlands, we saw it several times on trees in the Botanic Garden, probing on these occasions with its beak among the small narrow leaves of the common native xerophytic species of *Tillandsia* ('Spanish Moss') which covered the trees in question. In the highlands, as already noted, it probes in the base of pine needles. It is clearly separated by its feeding method from all the other species.

The **Prairie Warbler** *Dendroica discolor* is the commonest leaf-gleaning warbler in all types of lowland woodland except rich secondary, where it is relatively scarce (Appendix 21). It occurs especially in more open parts and where scrubby mimosaceous trees predominate. It is scarce at midlevels, and in the mountains is found chiefly at the forest edge in introduced trees. It feeds by moving rather rapidly from perch to perch, taking insects off leaves at the tips of sidebranches and of the canopy, especially on trees with a low open canopy, usually from a perch but often by hovering. The ways in which the Prairie Warbler is separated from the Black-throated Green have already been discussed under that species, and its separation from various species yet to be mentioned will be discussed under them.

The other common leaf-gleaner of the lowland forest is the **Parula Warbler** *Parula americana*. It is scarce at midlevels, and in the mountains is found only at the edge in introduced trees. It is commonest in the richer damper woods, and not the arid types preferred by the Prairie. This is due to the preference of the Parula for feeding in trees with broad thin leaves, not in small-leaved mimosaceous trees. It also prefers the upper half of the taller and denser trees, and unlike the Prairie often feeds near the trunk and on creepers; further, it moves rather slowly through the vegetation, and rarely feeds by hovering. Hence the two species are largely separated from each other, but we did not appreciate this until near the end of the winter, so did not make enough observations on the critical points for our full satisfaction. On spring passage in North America, as in winter in Jamaica, it prefers taller trees than does the Prairie (Parnell 1969).

In North America in summer, it evidently feeds more from the tips of trees, at least in conifers, than it does in Jamaica (Morse 1967, 1971), but we did not see it frequent conifers in Jamaica.

The **Magnolia Warbler** *Dendroica magnolia* is rather scarce in Jamaica. Like the Parula too, it usually feeds in trees with thin broad leaves, but it prefers rather taller trees and feeds lower down in them, usually between one quarter and half way up (compare Tables 30 and 31). Further, it moves much more rapidly from perch to perch

TABLE 33. *Main manner of ecological separation in leaf-gleaning warblers resident or wintering in Jamaica*

	Yellow	Arrow-headed	Parula	Magnolia	Cape May	Black-throated Blue	Myrtle	Black-throated Green	Yellow-throated
Arrow-headed	H	Arrow-headed							
Parula	H	H	Parula						
Magnolia	H	H	PS	Magnolia					
Cape May	H	H	LPS	LSN	Cape May				
Black-throated Blue	H	(H) S	(H) LS	(H) LS	LSN	Black-throated Blue			
Myrtle	H	(H) L (P)	LP	LP	PS	LPS	Myrtle		
Black-throated Green	H	(H) L	LPS	LPS	LSN	LPS	PS	Black-throated Green	
Yellow-throated	H	H	HLP	LS	LSN	LPS	PS	LS (N)	Yellow-throated
Prairie	H	H	LP	LS	HSN	(H)LPS	P	H (P) ?	HL

Notes   (i) H (habitat) means separation by whether in mangroves, lowland dry forest, midlevel forest, montane forest, or parkland.

L (type of leaf) means separation by feeding mainly on narrow mimosaceous leaves, broad thin leaves, broad thick leaves, pine needles or juniper needles.

P (part of tree) means separation by feeding mainly in upper or lower part of tree, near trunk or on terminal twigs.

S (feeding station) means separation by whether or not, in addition to insects taken off leaves from a perch, many are taken in the air, or from twigs, or on the ground; for those feeding in conifers, it also means whether or not taken at base of needles by probing.

N (nectar and fruit) means separation by whether or not, in addition to insects, much fruit and nectar are taken.

(ii) If separation by habitat is clear-cut, only H is put in table, though there may also be important differences in feeding. If H is followed by other letters, it means that there is only partial separation by habitat and that other factors are important in the area of coexistence. If a letter is placed in brackets, it means that the difference in question is less important than others.

(iii) The Tennessee Warbler is omitted because of its scarcity.

than the Parula and takes a higher proportion of insects off twigs and a much higher proportion in the air (Tables 28 and 32). It also has a shorter beak than the Parula, which suggests that it picks off insects, whereas the Parula may work for them. In its aerial feeding, it recalls an American Redstart. Hence it is separated by its feeding methods from the Parula, and from all the other species by its preference for trees with broad thin leaves. It feeds lower in the trees than the Parula also in the United States (Morse 1967, 1971).

The **Cape May Warbler** *Dendroica tigrina* is rather scarce in lowlands, midlevel and highlands, and occurs chiefly at the wood-edge and in parkland, and hence often in areas partly cleared by man. It usually feeds in small-leaved trees (but not conifers), preferring much higher trees than the Prairie and feeding high up in them (Tables 30 and 31). It travels rather slowly through the trees, and unlike the other leaf-gleaners, it may peck repeatedly, even twenty times, at the same leaf, suggesting that it is taking extremely small but plentiful insects such as aphids. It not infrequently takes insects in the air (Table 28) or by hovering (Table 32) and eats many more small fruits and much more nectar than the other species (Table 28, note ii). It also sucks sap from holes bored by the Yellow-bellied Sapsucker, as it does in the United States (Foster and Tate 1966), and it comes to hummingbird feeders in gardens. These various points help to separate it from all the other species.

The **Myrtle Warbler** *Dendroica coronata* comes much later to Jamaica than the other species, nearly all of which we had seen by early November, whereas we did not see our first Myrtle Warbler until 10 January. In some years it is said to be a common transient, but only a few ever stay for the winter. We regularly saw four in mimosaceous trees in wooded cultivation in the lowlands near Kingston, also one in sclerophyll forest and two in introduced pines in the mountains. The preferred types of tree might bring it into potential competition with the Cape May or Black-throated Green, but the latter are smaller (Table 27) and feed in the terminal twigs of the canopy or side branches, not lower down like the Myrtle, a difference which also holds on its breeding grounds (MacArthur 1958), where it does more flycatching than the others and may for this reason come into competition with the American Redstart (D. Morse *in litt.*). Hence it is probably separated from these other species in winter by its feeding stations, but anyway is too scarce to be a serious competitor.

The other scarce species is the **Tennessee Warbler** *Vermivora peregrina*, which is regular in small numbers in both lowland riverine woodland and montane forest, where it takes insects off both large and small leaves of trees. We saw too little of it to see whether it is a potential competitor with other species, but it is too scarce to be important.

This survey strongly suggests that all 10 of the common leaf-gleaning warblers present in Jamaica in winter are segregated ecologically from each other, and the other (the Tennessee) is too scarce to be a serious competitor. One species, the Yellow, is separated from all the rest by habitat, and habitat is a subsidiary factor separating several other species; but the main differences between all of them are in the type of leaf from off or among which they prefer to feed (small, broad and thin, broad and thick, or coniferous, dead or alive, the position in the tree where they hunt (at the tips of branches, or near the trunk, or in the lower parts), and whether in addition to taking insects off leaves they also take an appreciable proportion from twigs, the ground or the air. These points are summarised in Table 33. Whether the differences in question suffice for the full ecological separation of each species was not possible to determine in a single year's study, but they might well suffice, and there is no evidence suggesting that any two species seriously compete for the same food resources. I might repeat that their ecological separation was by no means obvious when we were first confronted with this array of species.

Competition

It was suggested at the start of this chapter that the abundance of wintering warblers appears to refute the idea that the island habitats are 'ecologically full' and hence that other species might be excluded through competition. But this analysis of the feeding habits of the warblers shows with reasonable certainty that each is ecologically isolated from every other, and this can only be a result of competitive exclusion. Hence the remarkable point is not the absence of competition, but that the level at which it is operating in the wintering warblers is very different from that in the resident species.

Two further points show that this is the correct interpretation. First, in addition to the 18 regular wintering species already discussed, at least another 12 North American warblers have occurred in Jamaica as transients. We ourselves saw a Prothonotary *Protonotaria citrea*, a Blue-winged *Vermivora pinus*, a Nashville *Vermivora ruficapilla*, several Blackburnians *Dendroica fusca* and Blackpolls *Dendroica striata*, and a Pine Warbler *Dendroica pinus*. Six further species have been recorded in recent years by members of the Gosse Bird Club, namely the Golden-winged *Vermivora chrysoptera*, Cerulean *Dendroica cerulea*, Chestnut-sided *Dendroica pennsylvanica*, Bay-breasted *Dendroica castanea*, Kentucky *Oporornis formosus* and Hooded *Wilsonia citrina* (per Roger W. Smith). Moreover Jamaica is underwatched ornithologically, so there are probably yet other species which occasionally occur there, and which have been recorded on nearby islands. Since these further 12 species have reached Jamaica, and several of them do so regularly, at least some of them would presumably stay for the winter if they could survive there, and much the most likely factor preventing their survival is the potential competition from the 18 regular winter resident species.

Secondly, 14 species of parulid warblers breed in Honduras, compared with only 2 on Jamaica, a reduction to 14 per cent, which is close to the average reduction in the number of all passerine species breeding in the two areas (see Table 17, p. 132). In winter, about 30 North American parulid species are regular in Honduras (Monroe 1968), compared with 18 on Jamaica, a reduction to only 60 per cent. This difference corroborates the different outcome of competitive exclusion at the two seasons, but it emphasises that there is a reduction in the number of species on the island compared with the mainland, presumably the result of competitive exclusion. The 30 species which spend the winter in Honduras include 13 of those regular on Jamaica, but not Swainson's, Parula, Cape May, Black-throated Blue or Prairie (though most of these have occurred as transients in Honduras) and so are presumably excluded from there in winter by some of the other species.

Only one other West Indian island has been studied sufficiently for a full list of wintering warblers to be given. Puerto Rico has 11 species, 7 being regular in the humid forest, namely Black-and-White, Worm-eating, American Redstart, Parula, Cape May, Black-throated Blue and Louisiana Waterthrush, and 4 more in the lowlands, namely

the Common Yellowthroat, Prairie, Ovenbird and Northern Waterthrush (C. and A. Kepler pers. comm.). The only difference from
Jamaica in habitat use is the absence of the Ovenbird from humid
forest, but this forest is much wetter on Puerto Rico than in much
of the Blue Mountains of Jamaica. Several of the species that are
regular in Jamaica but missing from Puerto Rico have been recorded
there occasionally, and it would be interesting to know why they are
not regular. Further south, enough is known to say that far fewer
warbler species spend the winter in the Lesser Antilles, where on
brief visits in March to St Vincent and Grenada we saw only American
Redstart, Northern Waterthrush and, once, a Cape May, but we
were there for too short a time for this to be considered a full list. At
the least, however, no other species were common there then. The
factors determining the numbers of species of resident land birds
on islands have in recent years attracted much attention, but those
determining the numbers of species of winter visitors have not even
been mentioned.

The final question is why, since most of them live there for over
half of every year, at least some of the 18 regularly wintering warblers
on Jamaica do not stay to breed there. Presumably they would do
so if, on average, they could raise more young in Jamaica than in
North America, and possibly they would do so if they could raise
young at all in Jamaica. They must be prevented from doing so by
ecological factors, and in particular, presumably, by the absence of
suitable food for their young. Evidently, there are ecological niches
for only two breeding species on Jamaica, the Arrow-headed in the
highlands and the Yellow in mangroves, coastal and riverine forest,
with a large gap between them of arid lowland forest where no warbler
breeds (unless the Bananaquit *Coereba flaveola* be considered one).

What happens in Jamaica in summer in the ecological niches
of the wintering warblers after they have left? Apart from the Yellow
Warbler moving up into riverine woodland, their habitats are not
filled by any resident Jamaican species. In summer, no passerine
species searches the mud in mangroves like the Northern Waterthrush does, or the sides of rocky streams like the Louisiana Waterthrush, or the forest floor like the Ovenbird and Swainson's Warbler.
It is harder to say whether the leaf-gleaners are replaced to any
extent, but the Bananaquit *Coereba flaveola* gleans leaves for insects
more frequently in summer than winter, perhaps to provide food

for its young, and the same might apply to other species. Here is
another problem deserving further research.

The origin of the ecological differences between the wintering warblers

A subsidiary question is where the Jamaican warblers evolved the
differences critical for their ecological separation. What is known
of the species in question shows that, in general, their habitats and
feeding habits are similar both on Jamaica in winter and on their
northern breeding grounds in summer. This holds, for instance, with
respect to the habitats of the Northern and Louisiana Waterthrushes
and the Common Yellowthroat. The Black-throated Blue, which
prefers to feed in trees with broad thick leaves on Jamaica, breeds in
heavy broadleaved forest in North America. The Yellow-throated,
which feeds in pines or *Tillandsia* on Jamaica, likewise breeds in pine
forest or where there is much *Tillandsia*, primarily in southern North
America. The Black-throated Green frequents conifers in the two
regions, though it also breeds in deciduous forest north of the range of
Tillandsia. However, some of the other species which normally breed in
conifers in North America, notably the Tennessee, Magnolia and
Cape May, do not normally frequent them on Jamaica in winter.

Further, the feeding methods and feeding stations are generally
similar on Jamaica and on the breeding grounds in the Black-and-
White, Swainson's, the Ovenbird and the American Redstart, while
comparison with the observations of MacArthur (1958) and Morse
(1967) shows that the more subtle differences in feeding between the
Magnolia, Cape May, Myrtle and Black-throated Green likewise
hold good in both winter and summer. Again as in Jamaica, the
Parula feeds higher in the trees than the Prairie, at least on passage
in North America. For various other species, quantitative observations
on feeding are not available for the breeding season, but general
descriptions are consistent with what we observed on Jamaica, except
possibly to some extent for the Parula and Yellow-throated (*cf*. Morse
1967, 1968, Ficken *et al*. 1968).

In general, then, the habitats and feeding habits of the species
concerned are typical for them throughout the year. They determine
which species can survive the winter on Jamaica, but it need not
follow that they were evolved in the winter rather than the summer
range. However, various of the species concerned do not meet in

summer. Four of them, the Black-and-White, Ovenbird, Common Yellowthroat and American Redstart are widespread in summer in eastern North America, and also the Parula except that it does not breed so far north. But seven other species breed primarily in the coniferous forests of Canada and northeastern U.S.A., namely the Tennessee, Magnolia, Cape May, Myrtle, Black-throated Green, Palm (more typically a bog species) and Northern Waterthrush, though several breed quite far south. The range of the Black-throated Blue extends less far north and somewhat further south than those of the seven northern species, and it lives in broad-leaved not coniferous forest. The remaining five species, Swainson's, Worm-eating, Yellow-throated, Prairie and Louisiana Waterthrush, breed in eastern U.S.A. omitting the northeast, so when breeding come into minimal contact with the seven northern species which they meet on Jamaica in winter. This might suggest that at least some of the feeding adaptations of each species have been evolved to achieve segregation from each other in their winter quarters. In any case the result is a large number of coexisting species with subtle differences in feeding and this is conformable with competition on continents, but not on islands. Hence judgement should be suspended, and at least for the time being, it seems best to regard their adaptations as evolved for survival in competition with other parulid species in both winter and summer.

In at least one instance, however, a habitat preference has been modified in the winter quarters, since as already mentioned (p. 176), the Northern Waterthrush is on Jamaica confined to mud by still waters in the lowlands, whereas on Trinidad it also occupies the habitats of the related, but absent, Ovenbird and Louisiana Waterthrush on Jamaica.

In both their summer and winter quarters, the American parulid warblers often feed in groups with other species, which travel together through the forest, each species taking its own particular foods in its particular feeding stations. Such 'foraging parties' are absent from Jamaica, but since this curiosity is irrelevant to the main theme of the book, I have relegated discussion of it to Appendix 22.

OTHER WINTERING SPECIES IN JAMAICA

As already mentioned, only three other species of North American land birds regularly spend the winter on Jamaica, and two of them are scarce. Hence the pouring in of the parulid warblers is not, at least in this area, typical of winter visitors as a whole, but is unique to one family. The parulids are also highly unusual in summer, as already mentioned, in the subtlety of their segregation by feeding, and in autumn are the predominant migrant of the North American east coast. Perhaps, therefore, this chapter is concerned with the peculiarities of a family of birds, as much as with a difference between winter and summer visitors in general, but since the proportion of parulid species breeding on Jamaica (although only two in number) compared with Honduras is similar to that for other passerine species, it is at least partly a problem peculiar to wintering. Further study is needed in other parts of the world to take this problem further.

There is a partial parallel in the shore birds of Jamaica. As set out in Table 3, p. 32, only one species in the family Scolopacidae, *Catoptrophorus semipalmatus*, possibly breeds in Jamaica, and this doubtfully and rarely, since Dr. A.W. Diamond and I found in summer only the one pair of Willets calling as if breeding. But in winter, in addition to many more Willets, we saw many Common Snipe *Capella delicata* (*gallinago*), Spotted Sandpiper *Actitis macularia*, Greater Yellowlegs *Tringa melanoleuca*, Lesser Yellowlegs *Tringa flavipes*, Least Sandpiper *Erolia minutilla*, Semipalmated Sandpiper *Ereunetes pusillus*, Sanderling *Crocethia alba* and American Dowitcher *Limnodromus griseus*, another 8 species, together with a few others, such as the Solitary Sandpiper *Tringa solitaria* and Stilt Sandpiper *Micropalama himantopus*, more rarely, nearly all of which breed in the arctic and subarctic. In view of the earlier discussion on whether the parulid warblers may have evolved their ecological differences in their summer or winter quarters, it is interesting that Holmes and Pitelka (1968) concluded that, at least in the four shore birds which they studied in Alaska, the differences in beak and size are adapted to the winter not the summer range. Hence there is a partial parallel here to the situation in the parulid warblers; but the scolopacid waders are peculiar in that nearly all of them breed in or near the arctic where there is temporarily abundant, if not super-abundant, food for the young (and certainly no such food supply would be available for their young on Jamaica in summer), and spend the whole of the rest of the year, including the summer when they are not breeding, on tidal mudflats, brackish or freshwater lakes and marshes further south (cf. Lack 1971). The parulid warblers, on the other hand, breed over a wide area of the temperate regions and retain their feeding specialisations in summer. Also Morse (1968, 1971) has indirect evidence suggesting that the food problem may be severe at selected times (e.g. during incubation) for the parulid warblers, and that they show differences in foraging depending on the species composition. The problem of the arctic waders is, of course, common to the whole world, not peculiar to Jamaica.

Perhaps a similar situation is also found in the duck family Anatidae. Three species breed on Jamaica (Table 3), but in winter we also saw Mallard *Anas platyrhynchos*, Pintail *Anas acuta*, Green-winged Teal *Anas crecca*, Blue-winged Teal *Anas discors*, American Wigeon *Anas americana*, Shoveler *Anas clypeata*, Ring-necked Duck *Aythya collaris* and Lesser Scaup *Aythya affinis*, while Bond (1971) also listed the Gadwall *Anas strepera*, another 9 species, all of which leave for the summer.

SUMMARY

Excepting one family of birds, only three species of land birds regularly winter on Jamaica, but in that family there are 18 species of parulid warblers, which comprise a substantial proportion of the whole avifauna at this season, and distort the overall picture for native Jamaican land birds of a paucity of species in all families.

The two resident species, and at least 17 of the 18 winter visitors (the other being scarce) are segregated ecologically from each other, one of the resident species by habitat and a few other species partly by habitat, but most of them by their feeding stations and feeding methods. The differences between the leaf-gleaning species are much more subtle than those between native Jamaican passerine birds in other families, but are typical of parulid warblers in their summer quarters (*cf*. MacArthur 1958). They allow many more related species to coexist in winter on Jamaica than do so among the native birds. Nevertheless, competitive exclusion must be in operation, for a further 12 parulid species have occurred on Jamaica as transients, and they presumably do not stay for the winter because excluded by those that do so. Further, 30 parulid species spend the winter in Honduras, so that, compared with the mainland, there is a reduction on Jamaica, but only to 60 per cent, compared with a reduction to 14 per cent in summer. Competitive exclusion must be in operation, but with a very different result for the wintering parulid warblers than for any other

Jamaican land birds. It is also noteworthy that none of the 18 regular winter visitors to Jamaica stay on to breed; this is presumably because they are prevented from doing so by ecological factors. The extent to which the problem raised here is peculiar to the family Parulidae requires study in other areas, but, at least there is no parallel among the other land birds wintering in Jamaica, though there is a partial, but only partial, parallel in the scolopacid waders.

CHAPTER 13 · THE OTHER LAND ORGANISMS

Repeatedly in previous chapters the evidence would have been strengthened, and the argument might have been changed, if one had known whether the findings for the land birds hold, or do not hold, in other types of land organisms on Jamaica—but the knowledge is not there, at least in an available form. The biologist cannot use raw data on groups outside his own speciality, for they need critical evaluation. Even if a simple species list is involved, he needs to know whether the author's concept of the species, or his use of generic names, are comparable with those of the author of a similar list for a different island; while the more subtle questions concern an ability to identify the mainland ancestors of the Jamaican species, or to specify their habitats on the mainland.

In the hope that some readers of this book may seek to relate the findings in their own group to mine in birds, I have here set out a series of questions for which the answers would be valuable. Incidentally, they also provide a summary of some of the findings on Jamaican birds.

1 Do the species in your group conform with the new model for an island fauna proposed in Chapter 1? In particular do they form, or appear to form, a stable group of relatively few species, each with a relatively broad ecological niche, which might prevent other species from colonising?

2 Do the species in your group tend, in general, to have broader habitats on Jamaica than in Central America? In particular, do many of them range from arid lowland to humid montane forest on Jamaica? Where the same species occurs on Jamaica and on the mainland, does it have a broader habitat on Jamaica?

3 Are most of the species endemic to Jamaica in the highlands, or in both lowlands and highlands, and are most of those that are not endemic in the arid lowlands?

4 Are rather few closely related species segregated ecologically from each other by habitat and rather many by feeding, compared with the mainland?

5 Is there evidence for wandering from the mainland to Jamaica, or from Jamaica to other areas?

6 How does the proportion of endemic species and genera in your group compare with the high figure for land birds and the low figure for water birds on Jamaica?

7 Is the number of resident species on each island correlated with its area, its altitude, or with the number of bird species? Are the variations different in different families or orders, and are they somewhat different in the Lesser from the Greater Antilles?

8 What proportion of the Jamaican species are (a) widespread in the Caribbean, (b) spread through, but restricted to, the Greater Antilles, or perhaps the Greater and Lesser Antilles, and (c) peculiar to Jamaica? Have the Jamaican species more in common with those of Hispaniola than Cuba?

9 Do you find any species which replace each other on different islands in the Greater Antilles (presumably by competitive exclusion because they are ecological equivalents) but which are derived from (or belong to) different mainland species which coexist there and differ in ecology? Do you find other species on Jamaica which have no ecological equivalents on other islands, and even belong to families not represented on other islands?

10 Did most Jamaican species probably originate from tropical North America, with just a few from South America entering via the Lesser Antilles?

11 Are most Jamaican species derived from the arid lowland forest of Central America, with some from the lowland forest edge, but only a few from montane forest and almost none from lowland rain forest? What proportion of the montane species on Jamaica are derived from montane forest on the mainland, and what from the arid lowlands of Jamaica?

12 Have the lowlands of the Lesser Antilles been colonised mainly from the lowlands of South America, and the highlands mainly from the Greater Antilles?

13 Do the different islands of the West Indies have a sufficient number of species in common, and sufficient differences from those outside this area, to justify speaking of a West Indian fauna or flora?

14   Has the continental island of Tobago got many more species than the oceanic island of Grenada?

15   Are there species which are widespread in the West Indies and also reach small islands just off the coast of Mexico, Central or South America, but are not on the mainland itself?

16   Are there families in which many more species have colonised the West Indies from outside than are resident on any one island? Do you then get geographical replacement on different islands by species with broadly similar morphology and ecology, but with important minor differences? Are there any groups in which such geographical replacement occurs in northeast Puerto Rico compared with the rest of Puerto Rico?

ADAPTIVE RADIATION

The reader can readily discover further relevant questions from my text. Two more are of general importance. In the land birds, there has been virtually no adaptive radiation within the West Indies, though on Hispaniola the two species of todies and the two of endemic warblers represent a first step. Instead, as is usual in oceanic archipelagoes elsewhere, each ecological niche is filled by a different colonist from the mainland. The Galapagos finches and Hawaiian sicklebills are quite exceptional in this respect.

Has there been an adaptive radiation within the West Indies in any other group of land organisms? Evidently so in the *Anolis* lizards, in which a few original colonists have diverged into species of different morphology filling a diversity of arboreal and to a lesser extent terrestrial niches. The explanation is perhaps that these lizards spread much more infrequently from one island to another than do land birds, so it may have been possible for some of the colonists to become adapted to what, for *Anolis*, are unusual niches, without this being prevented by the arrival of a more efficient occupant of such a niche on the mainland. If, however, one of the Jamaican land birds had started evolving in a new direction for its genus, the chances are that, in the ecological niche in question, it would have met competition from a species in a different genus which had already colonised Jamaica from the mainland, and any effective move in that direction would have been prevented. That such evolution did take place in Darwin's finches is presumably because, owing to the unusual degree of isolation of the Galapagos, other species were not present to restrain or prevent it.

The final question is whether for other land organisms, as suggested for birds, the island might be 'ecologically full'. The fauna and flora of Jamaica, like those of other oceanic islands, are 'disharmonic' or 'unbalanced', a useful term meaning that certain orders or families of animals or plants which form a prominent part of the mainland fauna or flora are absent or poorly represented. Jamaica, for instance, has no true freshwater fish, a group which find it particularly difficult to cross seas, and excluding bats, also has only one unintroduced land mammal, the rodent *Geocapromys brownii*.

Such gaps have often led biologists to assume that there are corresponding ecological gaps, but this does not necessarily follow. While a family or order which fills a particular ecological niche on the mainland may be absent on the island, its place may be taken, perhaps unrecognised, by some other species in a different group altogether. Forest trees from the mainland with large seeds may not have been able to colonise Jamaica, but Jamaica's humid montane forest has a closed canopy, and though it presumably has fewer species of trees than the highland forest of the mainland, it does not follow that any further species of trees could fit in there. The air-borne and bird-borne transport of tree seeds have probably been effective. Similar considerations surely apply to land insects.

You may, if you will, picture the Lady Jamaica seated in splendid isolation on her limestone throne, gratefully receiving one beetle in a thousand years. A truer picture, I suggest, is that she is subject to a continuing bombardment by spores, seeds, and land insects, and that these invasions are expelled by her highly selected native sons with their broad shields. This is speculative, but on present evidence I see no reason why my new model of an island should not hold for land plants and land insects as much as for land birds, and I would welcome critical evidence on this point if it was available.

There are, of course, ecological gaps on Jamaica in some groups. In particular there is no native predatory mammal, and no native reptile filled this niche effectively, as shown by the rapid increase of the mongoose *Herpestes auropunctatus* when it was introduced quite late in the 19th century. The Black Rat *Rattus rattus* had spread rapidly some two centuries earlier. But most biologists, when they speak of an island being 'ecologically full', have not, I think, been considering those groups of animals which could on no account get there on their own. The important biological point, and the one which they have argued in particular for the land birds, is that dispersal is rare and that many further colonists of types similar to those already present would have settled on Jamaica if, by chance, they had made the journey; that there is plenty of 'ecological room' for them there. It is this view which I think mistaken, and I would guess that it is similarly mistaken for at least many groups of land plants and small land organisms. The reader can, on present evidence, argue that the Mongoose, rapidly filling the role of a predatory mammal in the absence of a native one, is merely a conspicuous example of a generally inconspicuous, but widespread, phenomenon of 'ecological room' on islands. But I do not believe it. Instead, I think that the larger mammals are the exception. The test will be, as suggested in this chapter, to examine critically the other land organisms and the land plants.

The generalisations with which island biogeography and the evolution of land organisms on islands have been concerned were discovered in birds; but birds depend on other types of organisms for their existence, and factors that were at one time thought to be of primary importance for birds, including the degree of isolation, probably really exert their influence on birds through their effects on other organisms on which the birds depend. The further analysis of the situation in land birds may now have to await critical information on other types of land organisms, especially perhaps the forest trees, and what the latter may reveal may well shed further light on evolutionary theory.

SUMMARY AND CONCLUSIONS

Virtually nothing has been published about the systematic or ecological relationship of land organisms (other than birds) on Jamaica in comparison with those of the rest of the West Indies and with those on the mainland of Central America. A series of questions is asked about these other organisms, and until these and other questions have been answered, it will be hard to make further progress in interpreting the facts for birds. The critical question is whether the findings for other land organisms are, or are not in parallel with those for land birds, and the most critical group for which answers are required is that of the forest trees.

There are 'ecological gaps' on Jamaica in groups of land organisms which cannot cross the sea, notably a predatory mammal. But when biologists have argued with me that the island is not 'ecologically full', notably in regard to land birds, they are referring to groups in which several species have successfully crossed from the mainland, and for these I consider that the evidence is that the island *is* ecologically full. The large mammals, witness the Mongoose, are a misleading exception because it is almost impossible for them to cross so wide a sea unaided. I think it likely that the plant species with air-borne and bird-borne seeds, and many families of small insects, resemble the birds in this respect, but research is needed to prove this. I would stress again that the faunal stability on which ecological 'fullness' depends holds good solely for natural habitats undisturbed by man, notably, on Jamaica, in the natural forests. The continuing changes in agricultural and forestry practice are doubtless producing new ecological vacancies in cultivated land all the time.

CHAPTER 14 · SOME OTHER ISLANDS

To compare the land birds of the West Indies with those of the other islands of the world would need a book in itself. My aim in this chapter is much narrower, to discuss the land birds of a few other islands which amplify or modify the story presented here for the West Indies. The selection is based on my own visiting and reading, and on relatively well known islands. Too little is known about most others for critical comparisons of ecology. In an earlier survey of this material (Lack 1969a), my figures referred to all land and freshwater species, but to conform with the treatment for the West Indies, I have here considered only birds in the families from pigeons to passerines inclusive, except where stated.

IRELAND

St Patrick explicitly banned snakes from Ireland, but the island's present state suggests that his prejudices extended to woodpeckers, nightingales and many other animals and plants. As shown in Table 34, only 67 per cent of the regular breeding land birds of Britain (England, Scotland and Wales) breed regularly in Ireland. For the

TABLE 34. *Status in Ireland of the 96 regularly breeding British land birds*

Irish status	Number of British species
Breed regularly	64
Breed occasionally	10
Do not breed, but recorded	13
Never recorded	9

Note Based on *The Status of Birds in Britain and Ireland* (British Ornithologists' Union 1971) and information in Appendix 23.

West Indies, as discussed in the previous chapter, it is not possible to compare the findings for birds with those for other land organisms, but this can be done for Ireland. The proportion of species of British breeding mammals which also breed in Ireland is 54 per cent, the figure being the same for bats, which can fly, as for the rest (from Van Den V. Brink (1967), including long-established but not recent introductions). For reptiles and amphibia combined the corresponding figure is 25 per cent, for myriapods 75 per cent, for molluscs 80 per cent (all from Praeger 1950), for the regular butterflies 53 per cent (South 1906, Ford 1945) and for the flowering plants 57 per cent (Praeger 1901, 1950). Hence the reduction found in birds is found, to a somewhat varying extent, in other land organisms, and indicates a general reduction in ecological diversity.

Yet one's first impression on travelling through Ireland is that it looks just like Britain, and one cannot conceive why so many species of birds should be absent. But general appearances can be deceptive. Ireland ranges through only $4°$ of latitude, compared with $11°$ for Britain, so has less extremes, and through its geographical position it has a higher rainfall, milder winter and cooler summer. It is a continental island, cut off from southern Britain at the end of the last glaciation, when the climate must have been subarctic, so that most of its present land organisms presumably reached it over the 80 km gap of sea in the south. (Southwestern Scotland is closer, and the land bridge continued for longer, but being in the colder north this would have been much less important.)

That the smaller number of breeding species than in Britain is not due to the sea gap is demonstrated in Table 34, which shows that as many as 10 of the 32 missing British breeding species have bred occasionally in Ireland, and so have evidently failed to become established through ecological deficiencies, while another 13 have been recorded on passage or as vagrants. That ecological restrictions are involved is also suggested by Table 35, the idea for which I got from Praeger (1901, cited by Turrill 1948), who found that, in flowering plants, almost all the species that are widespread in Britain also occur in Ireland, but of those with a more restricted British range only 60 per cent do so, and of the 'Germanic' species restricted to the dry eastern part of England, only 12 per cent do so. Similarly for the land birds, nearly all the species widespread in Britain also breed in Ireland, but of those with a more restricted British range less than half do so,

TABLE 35.   *Range in Britain of British breeding birds in relation to
Irish breeding birds*

British breeding range	Number of regular breeding species		Proportion of British species regular in Ireland
	Britain	Ireland	
Widespread			
Widespread	57	52 ⎫	
Widespread except southeast	4	4 ⎭	92%
Widespread except northern Scotland	9	4	44%
Northern			
Only northern England and Scotland	3	2 ⎫	
Only northern Scotland	6	2 ⎭	44%
Southern			
Only England and Wales	6	0 ⎫	
Only southern England	14	0 ⎭	0
Total	99	64	65%
Total resident throughout year	68	47	69%
Total summer visitors	31	17	55%

Note   Based on lists in Appendix 23, for all land birds in the families pigeons to passerines inclusive. Species which breed only occasionally in Britain are omitted; none of them breed in Ireland. No species breed in Ireland but not Britain.

and of the 20 confined in Britain to the east and south, none do so. Further, had difficulties of dispersal been important, one might have expected that migrants which regularly cross the sea would be well represented in Ireland; but, as shown by the last two lines in Table 35, they are proportionately less well represented there than in the British resident species.

In a few instances, the probable cause for the absence of a species from Ireland is known. For instance the Short-eared Owl *Asio flammeus* depends on voles of the genus *Microtus*, which are absent from Ireland. Again, the Redbacked Shrike *Lanius collurio* depends on warm dry summer weather for feeding on large moving insects. It has greatly declined in England with the recent run of wet summers (Durango 1950), so could hardly be expected to find enough food to raise young in the wet summers normally typical of Ireland. But in nearly all other instances, the possible factors involved are not known. If they are not known for the birds of Britain, which is perhaps the best-studied fauna in the world, it is hardly to be wondered that many distributions of West Indian land birds cannot yet be explained.

As already mentioned, at least 10 species of land birds have bred in Ireland without becoming established, and likewise many species breed occasionally in Britain without becoming established (B.O.U. 1971). From the faunistic viewpoint, this fact is more important than the number of species which wander to these islands as vagrants. Evidently birds rather often attempt to breed outside their normal range, but then fail through ecological deficiencies. Such occurrences have not been recorded in the West Indies, but while this might be due to a difference between tropical and north temperate regions, it seems more likely to be due to the far greater number of ornithologists in the British than the West Indian islands.

A few species have evolved broader ecological niches in Ireland. The Coal Tit *Parus ater* is relatively common in broadleaved woods and has evolved a somewhat broader bill than the British form (Lack 1971), perhaps linked with the absence from Ireland of two other tits of broadleaved woodland, the Marsh *P.palustris* and Willow *P.montanus*. Again, the Long-eared Owl *Asio otus* is widespread in Irish woods, where it eats many mice *Apodemus* (Fairley 1967), whereas in Britain it is local and depends mainly on *Microtus*; but in Britain the common predator on wood mice is the Tawny Owl *Strix aluco*, which is absent from Ireland. A full comparison of the ecology of British and Irish land birds would be rewarding.

THE CANARY ISLANDS

It is an extraordinary experience for the European birdwatcher to walk through the broadleaved forest on Tenerife. The woods seem typical and birds are plentiful, but he then finds that there are only 8 passerine species and two further land birds present; and there are only half that number in the pine forest above it. This is just another case of the drastic reduction in land birds on islands, but is striking because such familiar European species are involved.

In all, only 34 species of land birds breed in the Canary Islands, this being just over one quarter of the number, about 130, which breed on the mainland in Morocco (Etchécopar and Hüe 1967). Yet the sea crossing of 90 to 100 km is surely negligible, and in fact at least 41 of the missing Moroccan species have occurred on passage

TABLE 36. *Land organisms in the Canaries, Madeira and Azores*

	Canaries	Madeira	Azores
Distance from nearest mainland (km)	100	800	1400
Approximate area (sq. km)	7300	800	2400
Highest altitude (m)	2320	1860	3710
Number of species of			
Landbirds	**34**	**20**	**15**
Butterflies	26	11	5
Coleoptera (omitting synanthropic)	990	565	180
Orthoptera	96	40	26
Flowering plants	1531	c.690	c.610

Notes (i) The figures for distance and areas have been rounded off, as they are rather different in different works of reference.
(ii) The numbers of bird species are from Bannerman (1963–68), omitting introduced and probably introduced species. The numbers of flowering plants are from Good (1947); of butterflies from Rebel (1940), Baker (1891) and Guichard (1967), of Coleoptera from Uyttenboogaart (1946) and of Orthoptera from Chopard (1946). The bird lists are given in Appendices 25, 26 and 27.

or as vagrants in the Canary Islands (Appendix 24). Presumably, therefore, they are excluded by ecological factors.

Other land organisms vary in parallel with the birds, as shown by the comparison in Table 36 for the butterflies, Coleoptera, Orthoptera and flowering plants of the Canaries, and in addition Madeira and the Azores. This also shows that the Canary Islands, which are both the largest of the three groups and the nearest to the mainland, have the largest land fauna and flora. Madeira, though much smaller than the Azores, comes second, but it is much nearer to the mainland than are the Azores. Madeira has only 20 resident species of land birds, 15 per cent of the number in Morocco, but at least 39 of the missing Moroccan species have occurred there without breeding (Appendix 24), so difficulties of dispersal are presumably not involved.

The number of species of land birds on each of the main islands in the Canaries (Table 37) is more strongly correlated with altitude than area, the correlation probably being due to habitat diversity, since the four main habitats succeed each other in the vertical plane, as opposed to the horizontal, and habitat is undoubtedly one of the factors limiting the birds. The absence of many Moroccan species from the Canary Islands or Madeira is readily explicable through the absence on the islands of their typical habitats, desert on some,

TABLE 37. *Land birds of the main Canary Islands*

Islands arranged from east to west and distances apart	Area (sq km)	Altitude (m)	Habitat diversity	Number of species of		
				Land birds	Vascular plants	Butterflies
Lanzarote	870	670	1	18	370	9
10 km						
Fuerteventura	1730	810	1	19	350	10
80 km						
Gran Canaria	1530	1950	3	30	760	18
60 km						
Tenerife	2060	3710	4	31	1080	24
40 km						
Gomera	380	1480	1	26	540	20
60 km						
Hierro	280	1520	1	24	390	12
100 km						
La Palma	730	2420	2	28	580	20

Notes (i) Numbers of bird species are from Volsoe (1951, 1955), Bannerman (1963) and Hemmingsen (1963), and are listed in Appendix 25, the numbers of vascular plants are from Lems (1960) and of butterflies from Guichard (1967).

(ii) 'Habitat diversity' scores 1 each for the presence of the four main natural habitats, semi-desert, laurel forest, pine forest and the alpine zone.

(iii) The most isolated islands are Hierro and to the north La Palma, which both lie some 60 km from Gomera to the east, with none further west; and the next most isolated is Gran Canaria, 80 km from Fuerteventura and 60 km from Tenerife.

pine forest on others, for example. Once again, however, too little is known to explain most of the gaps in range. From Table 37, it can also be seen that the number of species of vascular plants and of butter-flies vary roughly in parallel with those of the land birds, showing that broad ecological differences are involved.

In general, the species that have colonised the Canary Islands from Morocco live in similar habitats in the two areas, but a few of them have broader habitats or ecological niches on the islands (Lack and Southern, 1949, for the Canaries, Buxton, 1960, for Madeira). The Blue Tit *Parus caeruleus* is of special interest, because it is the only member of its genus in the Canary Islands and there lives not only in broadleaved woodland, its normal habitat in Europe, but also in pine forest, to which the darker plumage and longer and thinner beak of the Canary Island form are adapted (Lack 1971). While this might be linked with the failure of the Coal Tit *P.ater* to reach the Canary Islands, it seems at least as likely, in view of the small area of these islands, that one form adapted to both broadleaved and pine forest might be able to displace two species, each adapted to only one of them.

A similar situation formerly existed in the sparrows of the Canary Islands. In Morocco, the Rock Sparrow *Petronia petronia* lives in the countryside and is replaced by a species of *Passer* in the towns. In the central and western Canary Islands and in Madeira, the Rock Sparrow was formerly the only species of sparrow present, and it lived both in the countryside and around houses. But since the mid-19th century, the Spanish Sparrow *Passer hispaniolensis* has gradually colonised the towns of the central and western Canary Islands, and recently of Madeira, and the Rock Sparrow is now confined to the countryside. The Spanish Sparrow spread slowly, and occasionally died out and then recolonised. Difficulties of dispersal from one island to another could hardly have been critical, and I suggest, instead, that there was not sufficient suitable habitat on the islands to allow both species to persist until the towns had grown to a certain size.

Only a few species are endemic to the Canary Islands, or to the Canaries with Madeira (Appendix 25), and most of them are merely well-marked island forms in continental superspecies. The most remarkable is the Blue Chaffinch *Fringilla teydea*, which presumably evolved from an invasion of the Canary Islands from the mainland by the Common Chaffinch *F.coelebs*, which at a later stage invaded again and stayed distinct. The Blue Chaffinch is limited to the pine forests of Gran Canaria and Tenerife. Elsewhere in its wide range the Common Chaffinch lives in both pine and broadleaved forest, but on these two islands it is restricted to broadleaved forest, presumably because it is excluded from the pines by the Blue Chaffinch. The latter has evolved the greyer upper parts, paler underparts and longer and thinner bill characteristic of passerine species which live in pine forest (Lack 1971). The westernmost island of the Canaries, La Palma, also has pine forest, but it is much less extensive than on Gran Canaria and Tenerife (Volsoe 1955, p. 124), and here the Blue Chaffinch is absent and the Common Chaffinch is resident in both broadleaved and pine forest. Further, as shown in Table 38, the La Palma chaffinch is intermediate in its appearance between the two species on the other islands. While its presence in the pine forest of La Palma might

TABLE 38.   *Differences in the Chaffinches* Fringilla *spp. of the Canary Islands*

	Common Chaffinch F.coelebs		Blue Chaffinch F.teydea
Island	Gran Canaria and Tenerife	La Palma	Gran Canaria and Tenerife
Habitat	broadleaved forest	broadleaved and pine forest	pine forest
Colour of underparts	rufous	pink chest and white abdomen	all white
Male winglength (mm)	83	87	94, 104
Male culmen (mm)	14.5	14.9	15.5, 18.3

Note Measurements are the middle positions between the extremes given by Volsoe (1955, p. 136). There are two subspecies of *F.teydea*, which differ greatly in size. There is a general tendency in tits *Parus*, nuthatches *Sitta* and some other forest birds for the species adapted to conifers to have paler underparts and proportionately longer and thinner beaks than their congeners adapted to broadleaved trees (Lack 1971). The Canary Island chaffinches follow these trends.

be attributed to failure of the Blue Chaffinch to reach this island, it seems far more likely that, with only a limited area of pine forest, one form adapted to both pine and broadleaved forest has excluded two forms, each specialised for one of them.

ISLANDS IN THE GULF OF GUINEA

Of the four islands in the Gulf of Guinea (see Table 39), the relatively large Fernando Po is a continental island cut off by sea at the end of the last glaciation, and the other three are oceanic. Fernando Po, 32 km offshore, has 35 non-passerine land birds and 95 passerine species, only about half the number on the mainland on Mount Cameroon (Eisentraut 1965, 1968, with full list for Fernando Po pers. comm.). Sao Tomé, half the size of Fernando Po and, like it, high enough to have cloud forest, has less than one quarter of the number of species of land birds on Fernando Po, which well illustrates the difference between a continental and an oceanic island. There is a further reduction on Principe, which is smaller and too low for cloud forest, and remote tiny Annobon has only 6 species (lists in Appendix 28). Hamilton and Armstrong (1965) showed that the number of

TABLE 39.   *Comparison of the islands in the Gulf of Guinea*

	Fernando Po	Principe	Sao Tomé	Annobon
Distance from African mainland (km)	32	220	280	340
Distance from next island to north (km)	—	220	146	180
Area (sq. km)	2000	126	1000	15
Altitude (m)	2850	948	2024	655
Number of plant species	826	276	556	115
Number of species of land birds	130	19	28	6

Note   Based on Eisentraut (1965, amplified pers. comm.) for Fernando Po, Amadon (1953) and Fry (1961) for the other islands, Exell (1944) and Carlquist (1965) for the plants.

species of birds on each of these islands is correlated with area, and to a smaller extent with distance offshore. More important, as shown in Table 39, it is at least partly correlated with the number of species of flowering plants, and hence presumably with ecological diversity.

Sao Tomé and Principe are only 146 km apart, but to fly from one to the other 'is like the crossing of a major zoogeographical boundary' (Snow 1950, pp. 582–3). The difference is more striking than the species lists in Appendix 28 might suggest, because some of the commonest species on both islands are their endemics, notably on Sao Tomé the warbler *Prinia molleri*, the sunbird *Nectarinia newtonii*, the white-eye *Speirops lugubris* and the weaver *Ploceus st thomae*, and on Principe the warbler-like *Horizorhinus dohrni*, the starling *Lamprotornis ornatus*, the sunbird *Nectarinia hartlaubii* and the weaver *Ploceus principes*. Equating geographically replacing species in the same superspecies, omitting human introductions, 20 of the 36 species on Sao Tomé are absent from Principe, and 16 of them are in different genera from any of Principe; while similarly 7 of the 20 on Principe are absent from Sao Tomé, 5 of them being in genera absent from Sao Tomé. In several cases, a bird family is represented on only one of the two islands. There are also strong resemblances, as well as differences, between the two islands, however, for they share endemic species of pigeon *Columba*, thrush *Turdus*, white-eye *Zosterops* and finch *Serinus*, and also, represented by different species, the peculiar white-eye genus *Speirops* (Zosteropidae).

This situation resembles that mentioned earlier for the Greater Antilles. Jamaica, Cuba and Hispaniola are roughly the same distance from each other as Principe is from Sao Tomé, and each of the Greater Antilles has some species which are in different genera or even families from those on the other islands, as well as many endemic species; but they also have other species or species-groups in common which are characteristic for the Greater Antilles. Whether such differences arose, in the Gulf of Guinea, and for that matter in the Greater Antilles, through the chance of which mainland species happened to arrive first, or whether there were already ecological differences between the islands favouring one mainland species rather than another, cannot be determined. In either case, however, the islands are sufficiently close to suggest that the differences must be maintained today by competitive exclusion if they are to persist, presumably because the bird species on each island have evolved into an interlocking ecological group which would make it hard for a species from another island to obtain a viable ecological niche. It is suggestive, in this context, that of the 276 species of flowering plants on Principe (Table 39), 33 per cent are not found on Sao Tomé, and even if endemic species in the same genus are equated, the proportion is 27 per cent; likewise 64 per cent of the species of flowering plants on Sao Tomé are not on Principe (derived from Exell 1944). Hence the difference between the avifaunas is matched in the floras, and the birds of the two islands could well be so different because the ecological conditions are different. It may be added that these islands have been colonised by both lowland and montane species from the mainland or from Fernando Po, the montane species including the endemic white-eye genus *Speirops*.

The family Zosteropidae are the most striking bird colonists of islands in the Indian and western Pacific Oceans, with good examples of double invasion by the same mainland species, and the independent evolution on different islands of large montane species sufficiently distinctive to be put in separate genera (Lack 1971). Sao Tomé and Principe each have two species of white-eye, a small and a large (with mean wing measurements on Sao Tomé of 55 mm and 74 mm respectively), whereas small and remote Annobon has only one intermediate species (wing 62 mm) (Moreau 1957). Presumably this is an instance in which, with the reduced ecological diversity of a very small and remote island, one generalised species has replaced two specialists. It recalls the even more striking situation in the white-eyes of the Caroline Islands in the Pacific. Here the two largest islands, Ponape and Palau, each have three species of white-eye, a small (wing c.55 mm), medium (wing c.63 mm) and large (wing 71–82 mm).

But the smaller intervening islands of Yap and Truk each have only two species, the small and the large, and remote Kusaie, far to the east, has only one, the medium species (summarised in Lack 1971). If, with more limited resources, two species exclude three, one would expect the medium-sized species to be the one to go out, while if resources are yet more limited, so that one generalised species excludes the other two, one would expect the successful bird to be the medium sized one (see p. 211), as it is. Such clear-cut instances involving closely related species are not found in West Indian land birds, but they are, of course, merely special cases of the general principle that, on oceanic islands fewer generalised species tend to exclude a greater number of specialists. That a generalised species might exclude a greater number of specialists was pointed out by MacArthur and Levins (1967) see p. 3), who analysed the conditions under which it might be expected to happen (though not with respect to islands).

THE TRISTAN GROUP

Among the most isolated islands in the world are those around Tristan da Cunha in the south Atlantic, 2800 km from South Africa and 3200 km from South America, whence the few land birds are derived (the prevailing winds being westerly). The Tristan archipelago has three resident species of land birds in two endemic genera, a thrush *Nesocichla* and two species of finch *Nesospiza* (also a different rail on two of the islands, one of which is now extinct). The larger of the two finches eats the seeds of the tree *Phylica arborea*, and the smaller the seeds of herbs. Gough Island, 350 km away, has (as well as a rail) only one species of land bird, another endemic finch *Rowettia goughensis*, which occurs in all the land habitats and also feeds below the high tide line. It eats grass seeds, berries and other fruits, adult diptera, moth larvae, spiders, amphipoda, vertebrate carrion, and food provided by visiting scientists (M.K. Swales pers. comm.). It would seem to be the ultimate 'all-purpose' land bird and evidently fills on Gough Island the feeding niches divided between the thrush and the two species of finch in the Tristan archipelago. Once again, therefore, a single species on a remote island replaces more specialised ones elsewhere.

It might be thought that Tristan da Cunha is so isolated that the small number of resident land birds must be the result of difficulties of dispersal, and that the islands cannot be 'ecologically full'. However,

in a stay of two years on Tristan, Elliott (1957) recorded 8 species
of shore, wading and waterbirds, as well as the swallow *Hirundo rustica*,
and in only three weeks on Gough Island his son C.. Elliott (pers.
comm.) recorded 6 species of wading and waterbirds. If these could
come, so can other land birds. Moreover, Tristan is only 135 sq. km in
area with only 38 species of angiosperm plants, and Gough only 100 sq.
km, with only 35 (Wace and Dickson 1965, modified by Wace pers.
comm.), so I cannot imagine what other species of land bird might be
able to survive there. These islands might well be 'ecologically full' so
far as land birds are concerned.

DISPERSAL ROUND NEW ZEALAND

As many as 10 passerine species introduced by man to New Zealand,
and one species that reached New Zealand by itself from Australia,
have within some 50 years established themselves also on the small
archipelagoes off New Zealand, 4 of them as far out as 1200 km and
another 8 as far out as 880 km from New Zealand (Williams 1953).
In the absence of comparable studies in other parts of the world, one
cannot assume that such rates of dispersal over the sea are abnormal;
but the high rates of establishment are abnormal, and are presumably
correlated with man having destroyed the natural vegetation of the
islands concerned, thereafter rendering them much more suitable
for introduced European species and much less suitable for native
New Zealand birds than before.

The self-introduced species concerned, the white-eye *Zosterops
lateralis*, earlier spread to New Zealand from Australia, some 1600 km
distant, and an Australian swallow *Hirundo neoxena* has done the same,
as have 8 species of water or marsh birds (Fleming 1962, Falla *et al.*
1966). Again, the rate of dispersal over the sea may not be unusual,
but the rate of establishment is, and is explicable through man's
great modifications of the natural habitats of New Zealand. For
instance, both the Australian passerine species concerned live in
open country, which would not have been present in New Zealand
before man cleared the forests.

Two of the wetland newcomers to New Zealand, the duck *Aythya
australis* and the avocet *Recurvirostra novaehollandiae*, flourished there
for a while, but then died out, presumably due to long-term interactions
with ecological factors. As another example of the same sequence of
events, the Reindeer *Rangifer tarandus* was introduced by man to

St Matthew Island in the Bering Sea because the island was thought suitable for it. So it was for a time, but after increasing and flourishing for just over 20 years, the Reindeer had eaten out the food supplies beyond the capacity of the plants to reproduce themselves, and then became extinct (Klein 1968). Such possibilities make it harder than it otherwise would be for an ecologist to assess whether a gap in range is due to an ecological deficiency, and illustrate the possible importance of long-term interactions as well as the difficulties of ecological guess-work.

ISLAND DUCKS

Ducks are not, of course, land birds, but those on remote islands present such clear examples of one generalised species excluding others that they may be briefly mentioned here. The West Indies have 5 resident species (Bond 1971), and most other archipelagoes have more, but certain extremely remote islands have only one, notably in the tropics the Hawaiian Islands, Laysan, Washington in the Line archipelago, and the Galapagos, and in the subantarctic, Kerguelen and South Georgia (Lack 1970). At least on some of these islands, the restriction to one species is not due to the failure of others to appear, for another 12 species, 8 in the genus *Anas*, have been recorded in the Hawaiian Islands, another 6 in the Line archipelago, and another one in the Galapagos.

These island species, always in the genus *Anas*, are derived from different mainland ancestors, those on Hawaii and Laysan from the Mallard *Anas platyrhynchos*, that in the Line archipelago (now extinct) from the Gadwall *Anas strepera*, that of the Galapagos from the Bahama Pintail *Anas bahamensis*, that of Kerguelen with the Crozets from the (Northern) Pintail *Anas acuta*, and that of South Georgia from the Chilean Pintail *Anas georgica*. These differences must, I think, be attributed to the chances of whichever species first colonised. Some of the mainland ancestors are large and others medium-large; but irrespective of this the island species is always of medium size. It also differs from its ancestor in apparently having a more generalised and varied diet, in the reduction of distinctive male plumage and of the female's recognition speculum, in its smaller clutch and in its pro-portionately larger eggs. Since all these features have been evolved independently by each of the species concerned, they are presumably

adapted to conditions on remote islands, where there is evidently
an ecological niche for only one medium-sized species of duck.

THE GALAPAGOS

The Galapagos are outstanding in that one original colonising finch
species has evolved into 13 species which occupy the various habitats
and many different feeding niches. The only other archipelago with a
comparable adaptive radiation is the Hawaiian group with its sicklebills Drepanididae, unless the miniature situation of the two finches
on Tristan be included; and it is significant that these three archipelagoes are the most isolated in the world. Adaptive radiations have also
occurred on the great islands of Madagascar, Australia, New Guinea
and South America, but more complex factors are involved there,
which it would not be relevant to discuss here.

That such adaptive radiations have occurred solely in the Galapagos and Hawaiian islands suggests that their isolation was so great
that the original colonists of Darwin's finches and the sicklebills had
sufficient time in which to evolve into full species with different ecological niches before further mainland species already adapted to such
niches appeared to displace them. In addition, however, it seems
likely that the ecological conditions on these two archipelagoes must
have been so peculiar that locally adapted birds, even when still
incompletely adapted, were able to exclude newcomers from outside.
The Galapagos also have 8 other land bird colonists, a dove, a cuckoo,
two owls, two tyrant flycatchers, a martin and the warbler *Dendroica
petechia*, of which only the last might be a potential competitor with
any of Darwin's finches.

Hamilton and Rubinoff (1963, 1964, 1967) concluded that the
major factor determining the number of species of Darwin's finches
resident on each Galapagos island is its isolation from other islands,
but that its altitude and the number of plant species present have some
influence. However, various of the finches have occurred sufficiently
often on islands outside their normal range to indicate that difficulties of
dispersal are not involved (Lack 1969b), and a new and much fuller
list of flowering plants has enabled Harris (1973) to show a strong
correlation between the number of species of land birds and of plants
on each island, suggesting that ecological diversity may be the key
factor for the birds, as shown in Appendix 29.

Much more important, the ecology of the finches is so simple that I have been able, in nearly all cases, to give reasons for the presence or absence of each species on each island (Lack 1969b), i.e. to replace a 'distant' by a 'close' view. Two factors are important, first the presence or absence of the particular habitats or particular foods of each species, and secondly a tendency on very small or remote islands for one species intermediate in size and shape of beak, and hence presumably in diet, to replace two species which coexist on larger and more central islands. This last tendency holds for the small species of *Geospiza* on Daphne, also for that on the Crossmans, for the small species of *Geospiza* on Culpepper and Wenman, for the large species of *Geospiza* on Hood, and for the species of *Camarhynchus* on both Chatham and Abingdon with Bindloe (reviewed in Lack 1971). Hence Darwin's finches provide further examples of the principle mentioned earlier in this chapter for the white-eyes, of a single generalised species replacing two specialised ones, though as yet, as in the white-eyes, the examples are based only on the size and shape of the beak. That such instances occur not only on very small, but also on remote, islands, is a further indication that ecological diversity is reduced on remote islands.

COCOS (COSTA RICA)

Cocos Island, just over 500 km southwest of Costa Rica and 700 km north of the Galapagos, and 26 sq. km in area, is the only place outside the Galapagos with one of Darwin's finches, namely the endemic *Pinaroloxias inornata*. This has an apparently wider range of feeding habits than any of the Galapagos species. Primarily insectivorous, it searches the leaves of both the canopy and the shrub layer, probes in crannies in bark, hangs head downward from twigs, turns over fallen leaves on the ground, even levers up small stones when searching scree on the beach, and inefficiently catches insects on the wing; and it also eats small seeds, fruits and nectar (Slud 1967). Hence it is another 'all-purpose' passerine. Only three other species of land birds breed on Cocos, a cuckoo, a tyrant flycatcher and the warbler *Dendroica petechia*. It would be easy to imagine that this well-forested island, though small, could not be 'ecologically full', and that its few land birds have been limited by difficulties of dispersal; but in a stay of only $9\frac{1}{2}$ weeks in spring, Slud (1967) observed another 18 passerine and 5 other species of land birds, so difficulties of dispersal cannot be great.

SUMMARY AND CONCLUSIONS

Many more species of land birds have reached Ireland, the Canary Islands, Madeira and Cocos than breed there. Dispersal is also not infrequent in Darwin's finches to islands in the Galapagos outside their normal range, and has occurred to distant surrounding islands on a dramatic scale in species introduced to New Zealand. Even remote Tristan da Cunha and Gough Island have visiting shore and water birds, and many more species of ducks visit the Hawaiian and Line archipelagoes than breed there, these extremely remote islands each supporting only one resident species of duck, presumably evolved through the chances of colonisation by different mainland species. Clearly, difficulties of dispersal are not critical in determining the numbers of resident species on remote islands.

In Ireland compared with Britain, in the Canary Islands compared with Madeira and the Azores, in the individual Canary Islands, in the islands in the Gulf of Guinea, and in the Galapagos, the number of resident species of land birds is correlated with the number of species of flowering plants, and in the first three of these examples also with the numbers of species of various groups of insects or other animals. Clearly, the reduced numbers of species of land organisms on islands, first described for birds, constitute a general trend. Indeed bird numbers probably depend on those of other organisms, ultimately on the plants, and hence on ecological diversity.

In Darwin's finches the presence or absence of each species on each Galapagos island can in almost every case be explained in ecological terms, the two critical factors being the distribution of the main habitats, and a tendency, on small or remote islands, for one generalised species to replace two or more specialised ones elsewhere, presumably by competitive exclusion. The latter tendency is also found in white-eyes *Zosterops*, and in relation to habitat in the tits, sparrows and chaffinches of the Canary Islands. On the extremely remote islands of Gough and Cocos, one passerine species has evolved exceptionally diverse feeding habits.

Most gaps in the Irish compared with the British avifauna cannot as yet be satisfactorily interpreted, through ignorance of ecological factors, so that even though British birds are probably better known ecologically than any other land animals in the world, it is no wonder that the ranges of the West Indian land birds cannot yet be explained in ecological terms. Probably many species breed outside their normal range at intervals, but can spread only if conditions change; the range of each species is dynamic, not static (Lack 1971). Examples of species which apparently colonise or are introduced to islands successfully, but later die out again, show that successful establishment may depend on long-term interactions, of which we may be ignorant or ill-informed.

Sao Tomé and Principe, 146 km apart in the Gulf of Guinea, have certain similarities as well as striking differences, in both their endemic and the other land birds, even at the generic and family levels (matched in the flowering plants), providing a parallel with the resemblances and differences in the avifauna of Jamaica, Hispaniola and Cuba, which are a similar distance apart. It is not possible to say whether the differences originated through the chances of which species colonised each island first, or through ecological differences already present between the islands which favoured one mainland species rather than another. But the differences are presumably maintained at the present time through competitive exclusion, each species being better adapted to the habitat conditions, including the combination of other land birds present, on its own island than elsewhere, and only on its own island having a viable ecological niche.

CHAPTER 15 · TROPICAL MOUNTAIN BIRDS

The birds of tropical mountains find a small place in this book because three recent workers, Vuilleumier (1970), Diamond (1972) and, following them, MacArthur (1972), have considered that the ranges of individual species and the numbers of species present on different peaks, are at least partly to be explained in terms of 'island effects' in the MacArthur/Wilson (1967) sense, a view which I do not wholly accept.

JAMAICA AND HONDURAS

On Jamaica, as shown in Table 4 (p. 41), there are in summer 53–54 species of land birds in arid lowland and midlevel wet forest, compared with only 42 in montane forest, a reduction of the total to 78 per cent, a much smaller reduction than for various mainland areas to be mentioned later, where montane forest often has only about 50 per cent of the number of species found in humid lowland forest. This difference is due partly to the broader habitats of Jamaican than mainland birds, and partly, perhaps, to the absence of rich lowland forest on Jamaica. On the much smaller island of Dominica (Appendix 4), we found 28 species in the lowland leeward forest, 25 in the midlevel rain forest and only 19 in the montane thicket, the last being about 75 per cent of the number in rain forest, again a much smaller reduction than those found on the mainland. On Dominica, the montane thicket is much more exposed than the rain forest, with lower and more stunted trees, and it might therefore be expected to support fewer species of birds.

These figures may be compared with those for Honduras in Table 7 (p. 48), derived from Monroe (1968). Here, the different types of lowland forest combined have 235 species, to which may be added 59 species on their edge, whereas the two types of montane forest combined have 111 species, a reduction to 38 per cent. As regards individual types of forest, the lowland rain forest (excluding edge birds) has 167 species, montane cloud forest 78 species, and montane pine-oak forest 55 species, reductions to 47 and 33 per cent respectively. (Lowland arid forest, excluding lowland pine and mangroves, has only 40 species, but probably nearly all of the 59 species of 'edge' birds should also be included, which would more than double the total, so it is hard to compare this habitat with the rest.) Lowland pine, a poor habitat, has only 22 species of land birds, which shows that a lowland forest does not necessarily have more species than a montane one, though nearly all of them do so.

THE EAST AFRICAN MOUNTAIN FORESTS

Moreau (1966) was the first to draw attention to the fact that the number of bird species in montane forest is smaller than in lowland tropical forest. His figures (pp. 286–7) for the birds in the families pigeons to passerines inclusive in two East African lowland forests average 115 species, and for five East African mountain forests 43 species, a reduction to 37 per cent. The trees in the montane forests are lower and less dense, and consist of fewer species than those in the lowland forests, so the smaller number of bird species might be related to ecological poverty.

Each of the East African mountains concerned is surrounded by dry lowland savanna, so is in a sense an island, but each has basically the same avifauna in the montane forest, which takes over at an altitude of about 1500 m above sea level, as it also does in similar forests in other parts of tropical Africa. However, while each of the East African montane forests in question is isolated, many are in sight of each other, and from the frequent lack of subspecific differentiation, and from actually seeing two of the montane species concerned in intervening country, Moreau concluded that there is movement of the montane forest birds between the isolated mountains. Further, nearly all of these montane forests were connected with each other by similar forest in the last glacial phase up to some 18,000 years ago, so they are, at best, 'continental islands', and Moreau concluded that isolation has not been an important factor in the biological situation.

A species present on some of these mountains may be absent on others, and then Moreau found that, in the absence of that species, a species elsewhere restricted to the lowlands may extend into montane forest and takes its place. This has happened to a flycatcher on Mount Cholo, a warbler and a barbet on Mount Hanang, a woodpecker, a thrush and a weaver-bird in the Mbulu highlands, and also, far outside East Africa, to a grass warbler and some other species on Mount Moco in Angola (details of species given in Lack 1971, pp. 143–5 from Moreau 1966). This kind of thing has been found on only a small proportion of the mountains concerned, and since the highland forest on Mount Moco is abnormally patchy, and that on Hanang is described as ragged, my interpretation is that the montane species in question have been excluded through competition with lowland species which expanded their altitudinal ranges under the unusual ecological conditions and not that the montane species were absent by chance, after which the lowland species could expand their niches. I have given a similar interpretation to the parallel situation in various island birds in this book.

LOWLAND AND MONTANE FOREST COMPARED

Everywhere in the tropics where the point has been tested, montane forest has considerably fewer species of birds than lowland humid forest. Everywhere, too, montane compared with lowland humid forest is colder and more exposed, has fewer species of trees, lower trees and fewer layers of trees in the canopy (Richards 1966). On Mount Maquiling in the Philippine Islands, for instance, sample plots of 0·25 ha. of dipterocarp forest at 450 m altitude, mid-mountain forest at 700 m and mossy forest at 1020 m had respectively 3, 2 and 1 storeys of canopy trees, the highest trees reached respectively 36, 22 and 13 m, and the number of species of woody plants over 2 m high was respectively 92, 70 and 21. Again, in the tropical, transitional and montane rain forests of the Belgian Congo, the volume of timber per hectare, which is a measure of productivity, was respectively 400–600, 300 and 200 m (cited by Richards 1966, pp. 333, 359). In the light of this, and much other evidence reviewed by Richards, it may be presumed that tropical montane forest is a much poorer environment than lowland rain forest, so it is reasonable to suppose that fewer ecological niches are available for birds.

Various of these montane forests include genera of trees, and also birds, characteristic of temperate regions. The forests of temperate regions have many fewer species of birds than the lowland forests of the tropics, so it is probable that some of the reasons for this also apply to the difference between lowland and montane tropical forest. MacArthur (1969) considered at length why there should be more species in the tropical than temperate forests.

COSTA RICA

In five sample areas of lowland forest in Costa Rica, all below an altitude of 150 m above sea level, the average number of species of birds was 60, whereas the average for a lower montane forest at 1950 m together with a montane oak forest at 2380 m was 29, a reduction to 48 per cent (Orians 1969). This is a similar decrease to some of those noted earlier in Honduras. (The small size of the total numbers of species arises because Orians studied only sample areas, and did not include all those in the habitats concerned in Costa Rica.)

Orians noted that montane forests, compared with lowland humid forest, are subject to stronger winds, that the trees have smaller leaves, that there are fewer arboreal reptiles and amphibia, smaller absolute numbers of insects and fewer nocturnal insects, while Janzen and Schoener (1968) noted a decline in the numbers of large insects. Arboreal reptiles and amphibia, nocturnal insects, often large, which conceal themselves on leaves or twigs by day, and other large insects, are captured particularly by birds which hunt by sitting quietly and looking around, then flying out to capture their prey while hovering alongside it. Birds which hunt in this way comprised 29 per cent of those at the five lowland sites but only 20 per cent of those at the two montane sites. Other groups found to be scarcer in montane than lowland forest were the terrestrial ground-gleaning ant-thrushes and tinamous, woodpeckers, and the species which feed by dropping from a perch to the ground; while Schoener (1971) noted a decline in large-beaked insectivorous birds, which is clearly linked with the decline in large insects already noted. Hence much of the decrease in the number of species at higher altitudes is due to the scarcity of birds which feed in particular ways. In addition, however, I would expect that more general factors would be involved as well, of the types considered by MacArthur (1969) in his comparison of the forests of temperate regions with those of the tropics, and that fewer species could be 'fitted in' in the poorer environment of montane forest.

Orians also compared tropical forests with those of temperate regions, and considered that various of the differences between lowland and montane forest already noted likewise help to explain the smaller numbers of species in the forests of temperate regions. He emphasised the big decline in temperate regions of the birds which hunt by watching for stationary prey, and also the absence of obligate fruit-eaters, since only in the tropics are fruits available throughout the year. Further, linked with the much higher proportion of large insects in the tropics than temperate regions (Schoener and Janzen 1970), large-beaked insectivorous birds are virtually confined to the tropics, the median size of culmen-length in tropical insectivorous species being 16 mm and in those of temperate latitudes only 11·8 mm (Schoener 1971).

BORNEO

In Sarawak, 188 species of pigeons to passerines were found in lowland mixed dipterocarp forest, but only 82, or rather less than half as many, in montane or moss forest (Fogden 1971). The mixed dipterocarp forest has three layers of canopy trees, the highest extending to over 60 m, and is extremely rich in tree species. The montane forest, which takes over at an altitude of 1100 to 1200 m, consists of only two layers of trees, the higher of which rarely exceed 15 m, and there is a much smaller number of tree species. Once again, therefore, the smaller number of bird species in montane than lowland forest is linked with an apparently poorer environment.

NEW GUINEA

On Mount Karimui in New Guinea, likewise, bird 'species diversity decreases with increasing altitude, and niche differences become correspondingly coarser' (Diamond 1972, p. 43). The broadening of niches with fewer species is an extremely important point, which has rarely been commented upon, and is exactly in line with what I postulate in this book for the land birds on oceanic islands compared with those of the mainland. Diamond attributed the decrease in the number of bird species at higher altitudes to three factors. First, the montane forest is more stunted than that lower down, which is in line with what has been said earlier in this chapter. Secondly, the higher up the mountain, the smaller the area occupied by the altitudinal zone concerned, which could well be important since there tend to be smaller numbers of species on smaller areas.

Thirdly, Diamond postulated an 'island effect' on the lines of the MacArthur/Wilson theory of island biogeography. Some of the typical mountain birds are absent without apparent ecological reason from some of the New Guinea mountains, especially the remoter and smaller ones, and this he attributed to random extinction, followed by relatively slow rates of recolonisation from other mountains. Where a particular species was absent, he found, like Moreau in East Africa, that another species had expanded its niche to fill the gap. I would therefore interpret such instances as due to the tendency, in ecologically poorer habitats, for a more generalized species to exclude in competition two more specialized ones. I have given many examples of this principle earlier in the book, and particularly might again refer here to the Chaffinch *Fringilla coelebs* on La Palma in the Canary Islands (p. 203), since there the absence of the second species is linked not with absence, but with a much smaller area of the habitat for which it is specialised. Similarly in New Guinea, the montane species in question are absent especially from the smaller or more remote mountains. Much further study of ecological factors is needed to check Diamond's idea; but whatever the explanation, the parallel with the situation on oceanic islands is close, and I consider that in both environments the critical factor is likely to be ecological impoverishment, and that on present evidence there is no need to invoke random extinction with slow recolonisation.

THE ANDEAN PARAMO

Similarly Vuilleumier (1970) interpreted the numbers of bird species in the paramo vegetation above the treeline on the various peaks in the northern Andes in terms of modified MacArthur/Wilson equations, finding a correlation with the area of paramo on each mountain and its distance from a presumed source area for recolonisation in the south. But while his figures fit this kind of explanation, search was not made for possible ecological factors which, when more is known, might in my view provide the key to the differences in question.

SUMMARY

Wherever the point has been studied in the tropics, montane forest
has fewer species of birds than humid lowland forest, but the difference
is much smaller on West Indian islands than on the mainland, linked
with the much broader habitats of the island birds than the mainland
birds. In general, tropical montane forest is ecologically poorer than
lowland rain forest, so it is likely that fewer bird species can be fitted in,
particularly because fewer species with broader niches tend to exclude
in competition a large number of more specialized feeders. In addition,
certain types of birds are scarce or absent in montane forest, notably
those which prey on large insects. More detailed studies have been
made of these differences than of the similar, but greater, differences
between island and mainland avifaunas, and they are valuable in
showing lines along which future research on island birds might be
carried out.

In both East Africa and New Guinea, there are unexplained gaps
in the ranges of various mountain birds, and where they are absent,
another species expands its niche to fill the gap. I have interpreted
the similar situation on oceanic islands as due to a tendency, when
conditions are poorer or areas of a particular habitat are smaller,
for one generalised species to exclude two more specialised ones,
and suggest that the same holds for these mountain birds. In general,
I conclude that the numbers of species of birds in tropical montane
forest are smaller than those in lowland rain forest for the same basic
reason as they are smaller on oceanic islands compared with the
mainland, but the latter differences are the greater.

CHAPTER 16 · CONCLUSION

Each chapter has its own conclusion and summary, so I will end with three general points, which repeat and emphasise some of the conclusions already reached.

THE COLONISATION OF JAMAICA

In the light of the facts and theories presented in earlier chapters, some idea can be given of how Jamaica was colonised by land birds, though this is inevitably speculation. Soon after the island first rose from the sea, it presumably supported mangroves and arid coastal scrub, the latter developing into arid lowland forest as the size of the island increased. At this point, it was presumably colonised by birds from Central America which lived there in arid lowland forest, though the more limited conditions on Jamaica doubtless meant that there were fewer species than on the mainland. This could have led eventually to a relatively stable avifauna, the length of time taken depending on whether the island continued to rise, on the frequency with which mainland species appeared, and on the chances of whether those best adapted to the habitat were among the first to appear. As the land rose, more humid conditions came to prevail inland, with the development of relatively rich lowland hill forest, followed by midlevel wet limestone forest, and finally montane forest, the mountains, as already mentioned, being colonised by trees adapted elsewhere to montane forest, whose seeds may or may not have been sometimes introduced by immigrant birds. However, these highland forests were colonised in part, and probably mainly, by birds already established in the arid lowland forest of Jamaica, which spread inland and upward, yet also by a few new immigrant montane species from Central America.

Some of the bird species which reached Jamaica from the mainland did not spread to other islands and remained unchanged, while others gave rise to endemic Jamaican species. The further spread of many of these species was probably checked by the presence of their ecological equivalents, not necessarily related, on other islands; but some Jamaican endemics have no ecological equivalent elsewhere, and their restriction to Jamaica is a puzzle. There are other species similarly confined to Hispaniola or Cuba, but we know far too little about their ecology, and about the general ecology of the islands, to speculate about their restriction. Other species which came to Jamaica from Central America spread, perhaps quickly, to other Greater Antilles, and doubtless Jamaica derived some of its species from colonists on Cuba or Hispaniola which originated in Central America. Probably, too, a few species reached Jamaica from South America via the Lesser Antilles. About a dozen of the endemic species are of unknown origin, but the great majority of Jamaican birds of known ancestry came from Central America.

The land birds of Jamaica, especially those in the highlands, have evolved many endemic forms, and they probably form a relatively stable group, each species with a broad ecological niche, among which it is hard for newcomers to establish themselves. I maintain that they presumably have broad niches because, with the reduced ecological diversity compared with the mainland, a smaller number of generalised species tend to exclude in competition a greater number of specialists. Whether the wintering parulid warblers form a partial (but only partial) exception to this because they are parulids (which have unusually narrow niches at all seasons), or because they are winter visitors, is not known.

The high rate of endemism in Jamaica might seem to accord ill with the view that land birds have frequently wandered to Jamaica; but many non-resident species still visit Jamaica every year, and endemism is high I suggest, not because the wandering of land birds from the mainland or other islands is a rarity, and gene flow minimal, but because selection is strong to suit peculiar habitats.

This view of the colonisation by land birds of an oceanic island is new, and will doubtless arouse opposition. I am afraid that, if it later comes to be accepted, it may still be accepted solely for Jamaica, as the special case of an oceanic island in a sea with coastal mainland composing three of its four sides; and that, in consequence, it may be thought unacceptable for remote archipelagoes such as those of the Pacific Ocean on which Ernst Mayr did his classic work, and which are far more isolated than the West Indies. I would guess, however, that my views for Jamaica hold here too, and in particular that the basic reason for the small numbers of species of land birds on these remote islands is their reduced ecological diversity, not the difficulty that land birds have had in reaching them. Consider, after all the birds that have reached Tristan da Cunha. But the 'close' view depends on facts, and I have no personal knowledge of those islands.

EVOLUTION ON ISLANDS

From the standpoint of the evolution of land organisms, islands are of three (or four) types: first continental islands cut off from the mainland in the Pleistocene; secondly oceanic islands and archipelagoes, which arose volcanically from the sea, usually in the Tertiary period, the evolutionary potential of those which are very remote being different from the rest; and thirdly, great islands, which have existed much longer than the volcanic and were probably connected with the main continents before they were separated from them by continental drift.

Most continental islands are close to the mainland, having been cut off by the rise in sea level as the ice melted at the end of the last glacial period, some ten to twelve thousands years ago. Ireland and Fernando Po were examples considered in the previous chapter. Both have considerably fewer species of land birds than the lands from which they were separated, and at least in the case of Ireland, this is linked with a parallel reduction in all the other types of land animals and with the land plants, hence with a general reduction in ecological diversity. Even so Fernando Po retains far more species than the oceanic island of Sao Tomé, which is half the size, and this might be linked with Fernando Po's richer forests, a point that requires study. Another continental island, Tobago is much smaller than nearby Trinidad (also continental), with less diverse habitats and a more uniform maritime climate, which probably helps to explain why it has only one-third of the number of species of land birds to be found on Trinidad. This number is, however, double that on the nearby oceanic island of Grenada, even though it is similar in size, altitude and climate. However, Tobago has a much richer humid forest, which may reasonably be attributed to its former land connection, whereas Grenada has a poor forest, derived from the Lesser Antilles to the north over the sea. Probably that is why Tobago has so many more resident species of land birds—the former land connection could hardly be critical for the dispersal of the birds themselves, for Grenada is only some 120 km from Tobago, and several Tobagan humming-birds have been recorded there as vagrants.

The West Indies provide an excellent example of the commonest type of oceanic archipelago, one arising from the sea in the Tertiary period as a group of disconnected islands which were never connected either with the mainland or with each other. The land plants and land animals arrived on the islands from over the sea, dispersed by air, birds, or perhaps less commonly, on objects drifting in the sea. Hence certain types of organisms which cannot disperse in this way, such as forest trees with large and heavy seeds, true freshwater fish, birds effectively flightless (tinamous) and large mammals are absent, which means that the fauna is 'disharmonic' or 'unbalanced'. While, however this means that the absence of such groups, notably predatory mammals, leaves ecological gaps, it does not at all follow that these ecological gaps were not filled by the many types of land organisms which did reach Jamaica. The evidence suggests to me that the groups which can disperse across the sea, and they are the vast majority, form a relatively stable fauna, each group with a relatively small number of species, each species with a relatively broad ecological niche and sufficiently interlocking with the others ('ecologically full') to exclude nearly all newcomers. But for this view there is, as yet, no proof.

Typically in these oceanic avifaunas, each ecological niche is filled by a different colonist from the mainland. As already mentioned the two most remote archipelagoes provide exceptions, with the adaptive radiations of Darwin's finches in the Galapagos and the sicklebills in Hawaii respectively. Since these are the most isolated of the archipelagoes, the key factor is presumably their isolation, but how it has worked is not really known, and I am no longer satisfied with the existing explanations. It is these islands which have on several occasions provided the stimulus for new theories of evolution and ecology, and I doubt if their role in this respect is yet finished.

Finally there are the 'great islands', such as Madagascar, Australia and South America. These constitute an evolutionary puzzle, and maybe they should not be put in a group together as if they had a common type of origin. South America is perhaps the most extraordinary of all, but it is only because South America and Australia are also called continents that they often escape consideration as islands. It is clear now that the evolutionary factors involved probably differ greatly from those on the oceanic islands discussed in this book. The islands are much older and almost certainly they were once connected by land to one or other of the main continents, and they have primitive mammals, ratite birds, other odd 'relicts' and some tremendous adaptive radiations among their mammals and land birds.

THE SIGNIFICANCE OF ISOLATION

Isolation, obviously, provides the key to this whole story—after all, that is how an island differs from an equivalent area of mainland. Further, there are quantitative relationships. For instance, the more isolated an island the smaller the number of species of land birds that it supports; while the adaptive radiations of Darwin's finches and the sicklebills have occurred only on the most isolated of all the oceanic archipelagoes. Again, the main islands of the Greater Antilles are much further apart from each other than are those of the Lesser Antilles from each other, yet it is only on the Greater Antilles that each island has many species of land birds found on no other island, some of them endemic and some from the mainland. Moreover, the same pheno-menon is shown on Sao Tomé and Principe in the Gulf of Guinea, which are a similar distance from each other as are those of the Greater Antilles. Isolation also helps in the development of endemism, since islands have many more endemics than equivalent areas of the main-land, and isolation of the West Indies has led to the unity of a West Indian avifauna.

Having said all this, however, it is clear that isolation as a factor affecting land birds must be largely secondary. Birds can, and many of them do, regularly cross seas of the distances involved. The smaller numbers of species on the remoter islands, and the other points just listed, cannot be attributed to difficulties of dispersal for birds. Under these circumstances, the simplest explanation is that isolation affects the birds because it affects the dispersal of the other land organisms on which they depend; but this cannot be seriously sustained in most cases. The spores of ferns, the aerial seeds of Compositae, the bird-borne fruits and seeds, the insects so light that they are kept aloft by breezes, these cannot be limited by difficulties of dispersal over the sea crossings involved, at least in the West Indies, and the same doubtless applies to many of even the larger other organisms.

Explanation must be looked for elsewhere. I have argued repeatedly in this book that the relatively small number of land bird species on very remote islands could be explained if one consequence of reduced ecological diversity is that a small number of generalised species exclude a greater number of specialists. As shown by many examples in Chapter 14, there is a general correlation on archipelagoes between island area, number of bird species and number of plant species. At least sometimes too there is correlation with isolation; while some of the remotest islands, notably in the Galapagos, the Tristan group and in the Gulf of Guinea, have an extremely reduced flora. So likewise do very small islands which are not remote, and here again, presumably linked with reduced ecological diversity, a generalised species may exclude two specialists (see for instance in the Galapagos p. 210)

This, of course, changes the problem to a question of why should remote islands have a reduced ecological diversity in their plants, especially if difficulties of dispersal over the sea are not the cause. One factor, I suggest, is the more uniform oceanic climate, and another may be that remote islands are almost invariably small. It will be recalled that Tobago, though a continental island formerly connected by land with the mainland, has only one third of the number of species of land birds of nearby Trinidad, the factor most likely to be involved being Tobago's reduced ecological diversity, probably linked with its more uniform maritime climate and much smaller size.

Other problems include the existence of a West Indian avifauna which might, I suggest, like that of a South American avifauna, be linked with the restricted range of a particular type of forest. Whereas, although the radiation of Darwin's finches might somehow be linked with a slow rate of colonisation by other mainland birds, I am, as already mentioned, unhappy about this and think that this particular problem should be re-opened.

Finally, there is the problem of insular endemism. As already mentioned, for their distance offshore the West Indies have an un- usually large number of species of land birds, which might suggest that dispersal from the mainland is easy, and at the same time an exceptionally high degree of endemism (70 per cent of species), which might suggest that dispersal is hard. The simplest way to dispose of this anomaly is to conclude that neither the number of resident species, nor the degree of endemism, are determined by difficulties of dispersal.

So far as endemism is concerned there would anyway be further great difficulties in considering geographical isolation as such to be the key factor. There is virtually no endemism in the water and wading birds in Jamaica, which may have been some of the first species to reach the island; and among the land birds endemism is low in the birds confined to arid lowland forest, but high among these confined to highland forest and those which live in both lowland and highland forest. In other words, endemism is high mainly in the birds which live in the peculiar forests of Jamaica, suggesting that it is linked with adaptations to ecological differences.

This also helps to explain the remarkable situation in West Indian hummingbirds, in which there are endemic species on separate islands although the wanderings of individuals of this group between the mainland and the West Indies, and within the West Indies, are frequent.

I hope I have said enough to show that the apparently simple problem of isolation in relation to the presence and evolution of land birds on remote islands is extremely complex and deserving of further study. The first stage must be a sound basis of facts, which I hope I have provided for the birds of Jamaica in this book. But we need similar studies of the birds of other groups of islands, and especially, similar studies of the land plants and other land animals of remote islands.

In ending, my thoughts inevitably go back to the start provided by P.H. Gosse, F.R.S. Many of the sound, but, frankly, rather dull traveller-naturalists of the 19th century have not received their due in histories of biology, and Gosse's sound work was put in undeserved eclipse by his extraordinary notions on evolution and also, I think, by the deservedly popular but distorted life 'Father and Son' written by his literary son, Edmund, who had earlier done full justice to his father in his two-volume official life. It is good to know that the Great House, Bluefields, where Gosse lived in Jamaica, is preserved. It is better still to know that there is now a University of international repute at Mona, with flourishing biology departments. I cannot think that it will be long before my questions in Chapter 13 are answered.

PART II
ECOLOGY AND SYSTEMATICS OF
JAMAICAN LAND BIRDS

INTRODUCTION

The aim of the second part of this book is to discuss in some detail the habitats, feeding habits and systematics of the Jamaican land birds (pigeons to passerines), to provide the documentation for the rest of the book. It is by no means a complete account of the biology of the species concerned, and in particular there is nothing on plumage or voice except where relevant to systematics, and nothing on breeding biology. Our knowledge of the habitats of each species is based on repeated visits to nearly every part of the island in both winter and summer, with regular timed counts in the main habitats, as summarised in Appendices 1 and 2. We obtained much information in addition to that in the counts, and this is included in the text where relevant. Our knowledge of feeding habits is based on observations made during the habitat counts and at other times, and is summarised for most species in the text, with special comparisons for those species which might be thought to compete with each other. We studied the smaller species more intensively than the larger. Our knowledge is incomplete as we did not collect birds or insects, though we identified the flowers and fruits taken that were accessible to us.

For the systematics, my wife and I examined the specimens of the Jamaican and other Greater Antillean species in the British Museum (Natural History) and compared them with specimens of related species on the American mainland. We reached our own conclusions, but found in fact that, for the passerines, we were in complete agreement with those of the contributors on these families to the successive volumes of Peters, including every case in which they differed from their predecessors, with the possible exception of one generic decision in swallows. As this last case was marginal, we have followed Peters in this respect also. With the volumes by Peters preceding those on the passerines, we were not always in full agreement, mainly because the standards for separating genera, and also insular species, have changed since his time; but in every case we found ourselves in agree-

231

ment with at least one worker subsequent to Peters, though not always the same one. We have made no innovations. We did not study subspecific variations except for deciding whether a form should be treated as a full species or as a subspecies of some other species. For the sequence of species, I have advocated elsewhere my support for Moreau's proposal for an alphabetical sequence of species within genera, genera within subfamilies, and so on (Moreau 1961, Lack 1968), but I do not consider this the proper place for such an innovation so have followed the sequence of species and genera in Peters. For the Tyrannidae, for which the volume of Peters concerned has not appeared at the time of writing, I have followed the nomenclature and sequence used by Bond (1971). For vernacular names, I have listed first that used by Bond (1971), followed in brackets by the name most often used by Jamaican ornithologists if different.

After the name of each species, I have added the Plate on which it is illustrated, and also the Figure with the map of its range where this is not set out in the section on the species concerned. A range map is given for every resident Jamaican species except for a few which are so widespread that they occur throughout the standard map, and for some of the endemic species confined to Jamaica; but a number of the latter are shown on maps which feature related species. Ranges within Jamaica are not mapped, because each species is widespread in the habitats mentioned in the text, hence its distribution can be seen with the help of Fig. 5 (p. 22), which shows the positions of the surviving natural forests on Jamaica (and its range in cultivated habitats is of little interest). In addition, however, the altitudinal range and natural habitat of each species are shown in a series of diagrams in Chapter 3.

PIGEONS AND DOVES COLUMBIDAE

Of the 66 breeding species of land birds on Jamaica, 10 are in the pigeon family. This attractive and varied group includes the Common Ground Dove, which is only a little larger than a sparrow, the 'beautiful Whitebelly' which "complains all day 'Rain-come-wet-me-through', the last (syllable) prolonged with such a melancholy fall" (Gosse 1847) and the Mountain Witch: 'no description can give an adequate notion of the lustrous radiance of this most lovely bird' (Gosse again).

We determined the habitats of the various species, but pigeons and doves seldom allow themselves to be seen feeding, and since we did not collect specimens, we found out little concerning how they might differ from each other in diet. We are indebted to Goodwin (1967 and in conversation) for his comments on the affinities of the Jamaican species.

Columba leucocephala **White-crowned Pigeon (Baldpate)**
(Plate 1, Fig. 25)

C.leucocephala is resident in lowland forest of all types, especially the less arid, and throughout the midlevel wet limestone forest, but is only a summer visitor to montane forest, up to an altitude of about 1500 m, where it arrives rather abruptly in late April. It is rare in wooded cultivation at all heights. We saw it feeding on fruits in trees, including those of *Bursera simaruba* in the lowlands and *Dipholis* sp. (*nigra* or *montana*) at midlevels. Gosse (1847) recorded it eating the seeds of the mangrove *Avicennia germinans*, and cultivated grain. He also recorded it taking fruits of *Citharexylum* sp., *Cordia collococca*, *Ficus* sp., *Guazuma ulmifolia*, *Metopium brownii* and *Nectandra antillana* and, among introduced species, those of *Artocarpus altilis*, and *Pimenta racemosa*. Paterson (1964) recorded it eating the fruits of *Sapium jamaicense*.

233

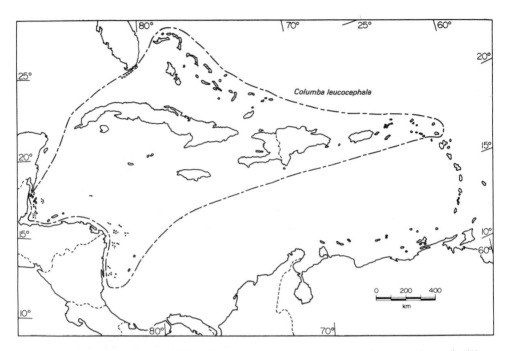

FIG. 25. *Range of the pigeon* Columba leucocephala, *a northern Antillean species which also extends to many islands off the mainland of Florida, Yucatan and Central America, but not to the mainland.*

C.leucocephala occurs throughout the Greater Antilles, also on the Bahamas, the Virgin Islands, Barbuda and Antigua, and on small islands off Florida and Central America, but has occurred only as a wanderer down the chain of the Lesser Antilles, as far as St Lucia, and also to the mainland of Florida. Most of the islands where it occurs are lowlying, but on Hispaniola, as on Jamaica, it has been recorded in the mountains.

As pointed out by Goodwin (1967), the nearest relative of *C.leucocephala* is the Red-necked Pigeon *C.squamosa*, which breeds on Cuba, Hispaniola, Puerto Rico, the Virgin Islands, the mountainous Lesser Antilles and a few islands off Venezuela, but not on Jamaica. These two species have many similarities in plumage, but differ strikingly in their head markings. They also have extremely similar songs, syllabised by Gosse (1847) for *C.leucocephala* as 'Sary-coat-blue', with a short second syllable and prolonged last, and both also have an extremely similar guttural rolled cooing note. To some extent they replace each other geographically (compare map, Fig. 7, p. 76), and where they coexist on Hispaniola, *C.leucocephala* tends to be in the lowlands and *C.squamosa* in the highlands, though with some overlap; but their possible separation here needs further study, as it also does on the Virgin Islands.

Two other species in the same superspecies are the Bare-eyed Pigeon *C.corensis*, which occurs in the arid lowlands of northern South America, including some of the islands off Venezuela, and the mainland species *C.picazuro*; but both of these lack the nuchal patch, and they are much more like each other than is either to *C.leucocephala* or *C.squamosa*. Where *C.squamosa* coexists with *C.corensis* on Curaçao and Bonaire, it tends to be at higher altitudes and *C.corensis* in the arid semi-desert (Voous 1957). On the available evidence it is not therefore

FIG. 26. *Range of the pigeon* Columba inornata, *closely related to a widespread Central American and Mexican species,* C.flavirostris.

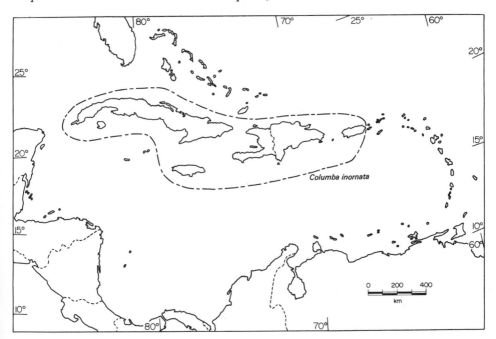

possible to say from what part of the mainland *C.leucocephala* was derived.

Columba inornata **Plain Pigeon (Blue Pigeon)** (Plate 1, Fig. 26)

This species was common in Jamaica up to the middle of the 19th century, but had greatly decreased before the end of the century (Scott 1891–3). Nowadays, there are only rare reports, the last published being in July and August 1963 (Jeffrey-Smith 1963). However, on 22 January 1971, I saw a large heavy *Columba* pigeon with dark wine-red underparts and no band on the tail fly through Hardwar Gap. I watched it for a long time, but only from below. However, the black band on the tail of *C.caribaea* is conspicuous from below, and it was a much darker pink than any *C.caribaea* which I saw. It was not *C.squamosa*, which I saw on many occasions elsewhere, and it could hardly have been anything except *C.inornata*, with which its size and colouring agreed, but I was not at all familiar with *C.caribaea* at the time, and did not otherwise see *C.inornata*. Gosse (1847) and March (1863–64) recorded *C.inornata* in both lowlands and mountains, mainly in open wooded country, not closed forest, which fits with descriptions from the other Greater Antilles, and it eats both fruits and seeds.

   C.inornata is confined to the Greater Antilles. As pointed out by Goodwin (1967), it is in the same superspecies as the Central American Red-billed Pigeon *C.flavirostris*, which it closely resembles in plumage, but is larger with a darker beak. In Honduras, the latter occurs in arid and fairly open country in both lowlands and highlands (Monroe 1968).

Columba caribaea **Ring-tailed Pigeon (Ringtail)** (Plate 1, Fig. 7, p. 76)

C.caribaea was long considered a delicacy, as noted by Gosse (1847) and Tom Cringle (Scott 1836), and its range has been reduced by hunting, but we found it common in the wet limestone forest of the Cockpit Country, the very wet forest of the John Crow Mountains and in the eastern part of the Blue Mountains; and it occurs sparsely through the rest of the Blue Mountains, locally up to an altitude of almost 2000 m. The lowest altitude at which we found it singing was at 150 m near Windsor, in the north of the Cockpit Country, in wet limestone forest of midlevel type. We saw none in lowland dry lime-

White-winged Dove
Zenaida asiatica

White-crowned
Pigeon
Columba leucocephala

Blue Pigeon
Columba inornata

Ring-tailed Pigeon
Columba caribaea

PLATE 1. *Pigeons and doves Columbidae, one-eighth natural size.*

stone forest. There are some in wooded cultivation a little below the present lower limit of forest in the Blue Mountains, but otherwise it is nearly restricted to wild forest. We once saw one in winter on Mount Diablo.

We saw *C.caribaea* feeding on the fruits of *Sapium jamaicense*, to get which it sometimes hung sideways or even upside down. Osburn (1859–60) and March (1863–64) noted that it differed from the other two Jamaican pigeons in eating solely fleshy fruits, correlated with which it has a weak gizzard, whereas the other two species also eat seeds. Osburn continued that it often seeks fruits at the end of branches and is an unusually good climber. He recorded it taking the fruits of *Cordia collococca*, March recorded it taking those of *Bumelia*, *Eugenia*, *Ficus*, *Laurus* species and other succulent fruits, while Gosse (1847) recorded it taking those of *Chrysophyllum oliviforme*, also mistletoe berries, and the fruits of the introduced *Ammona muricata*, *Cecropia peltata*, wild raspberries, the shoots of *Dioscorea rotundata* and palmetto thatch seeds.

The song, previously undescribed, consists of a group of similar coos, usually four or five, but occasionally between two and seven in a phrase. Each coo is rather long and complex, rising slightly in pitch and then falling again in the middle of the note. After a short interval the bird repeats the whole phrase. The song is thus very different from that of *C.leucocephala*.

C.caribaea is an endemic Jamaican species, which Goodwin rightly considered an island representative of the Band-tailed Pigeon *C.fasciata*, which breeds in the mountains of western North America, Central America and parts of South America. It particularly resembles in plumage the juvenile of *C.fasciata*, which lacks the white neck ring of the adult. It is also larger than *C.fasciata*, with a proportionately longer tail, and a prominent black tail band. *C.fasciata* resembles *C.caribaea* in its agility in climbing and hanging upside down when feeding, but its song seems different (Goodwin 1967). This superspecies is not otherwise represented in the Greater Antilles, where it is allopatric with *C.squamosa*. Since the latter has wandered to Jamaica (see p. 77), it is evidently prevented from becoming established there through competition with *C.caribaea*, even though the latter is not an exact ecological equivalent since, unlike *C.squamosa*, it does not normally occur in the lowlands.

Zenaida macroura **Mourning Dove** (Plate 2, Fig. 27)

We found this species throughout the year in small numbers near the south coast in dry lowland scrub forest, feeding in both dry and swampy grass fields, from the Hellshires in the east to a few miles west of Savanna-la-Mar in the west, and especially near Milk River and in the Black River swamp. There are no records for this species on Jamaica before the present century, so it might be a newcomer, but as it is scarce and local, it was perhaps overlooked in the past. It seems unlikely though, that Gosse, who lived within the area where it now occurs, would have missed it. (March (1863) recorded a 'Spanish Pea Dove', which looked like a cross between *Zenaida aurita* and *Leptotila jamaicensis*, which was conceivably *Z.macroura*, but presumably he knew this last species.) *Z.macroura* breeds in the other Greater Antilles and the Bahamas and is widespread in North and Central America. Its main diet in North America consists of seeds (Goodwin 1967).

FIG. 27. *Range of the dove* Zenaida macroura *in the West Indies. It is also widespread in North America, and many move south for the winter.*

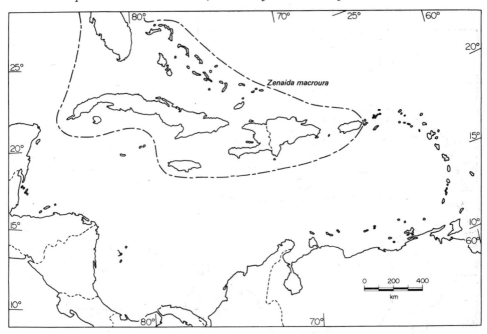

Zenaida aurita **Zenaida Dove** (**Pea Dove**) (Plate 2, Fig. 28)

Z.aurita breeds commonly in the less arid lowland dry limestone forests, including marsh forest, sea-level forest and also ruinate woodland where there are sufficient trees, but we saw only one in the arid natural forest of the Hellshires and Portland Ridge. It is also regular in small numbers in midlevel wet limestone forest, mainly but not exclusively near clearings, and a few breed in montane forest, chiefly around Hardwar Gap. It is commoner in wooded cultivation than in natural forest, and in cultivation extends to an altitude of at least 1500 m. We saw it feeding only on the ground, especially in short grass, mainly on seeds but at times on fallen fruits, including those of *Pithecellobium unguis-cati*. Gosse (1847) recorded it eating the seeds of *Jatropha curcas* and of various introduced grasses and fruits (?fallen), and Paterson (1964) recorded the fruits of *Sapium jamaicense*. *Z.aurita* breeds almost throughout the West Indies, and also on the offshore islands and in the coastal scrub of Yucatan.

Fig. 28. *Range of the dove* Zenaida aurita, *a typical West Indian species also on the coast and islands of Yucatan.*

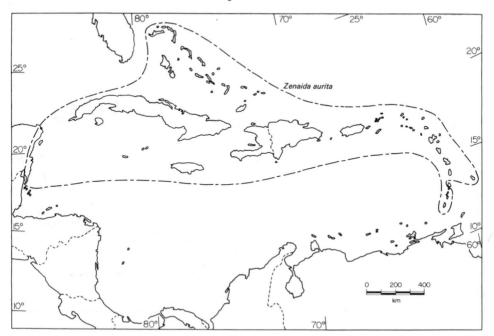

Zenaida asiatica **White-winged Dove** (Plate 1, Fig. 29)

Z.asiatica breeds in mangroves, strand woodland, the marsh forest of the Black River swamp and Morant Point, the dry limestone forest along the coast between Milk River and Alligator Pond, the ruinate wood- land round Mona and elsewhere in the southern lowlands, and in small numbers in the arid Hellshires. In early winter and again in July, but not in between, it was numerous in the ruinate arid scrub forest on Port Henderson Hill, owing to its fondness for the fruits of the dildo cactus *Stenocereus hystrix*, also noted by Gosse (1847). In winter it was also common in the citrus groves and adjoining midlevel wet limestone forest in Worthy Park, owing to its fondness for orange seeds, likewise noted by Gosse; we did not see it there in summer, but A. Cruz (1972 seen in MS.), reported it as common there in summer. In April and early May, but not later in the summer, several sang in the very wet midlevel limestone forest on both east and west sides of the John Crow Mountains, up to an altitude of 500 m, but we do

FIG. 29. *West Indian range of the dove* Zenaida asiatica, *also widespread on the mainland (where range not shown)*.

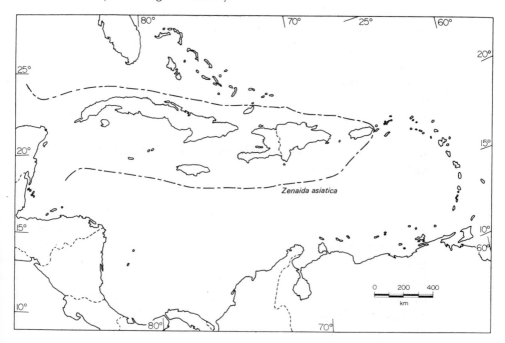

not know if they were breeding there. The wing of *Z.asiatica* is of similar length to that of *Z.aurita*, but its beak is longer, which presumably means that it differs from it in diet. Apart from cactus fruits, already noted, it eats mainly seeds on the ground. The only wild seeds recorded by Gosse were those of *Jatropha curcas*. Paterson (1964) recorded it eating the fruits of *Sapium jamaicense*.

Z.asiatica occurs in the other Greater Antilles and in southern North America, Central America and a small part of South America. In southern North America it is a summer visitor, but it is not known whether any of this population comes to Jamaica for the winter.

Columbina passerina **Common** (**Scaly-breasted**) **Ground Dove** (Plate 2)

C.passerina breeds in the marsh forest of the Black River swamp, and in all types of lowland dry limestone forest, both natural and ruinate, being commonest at their edges but occurring all through them. It also breeds locally in mangroves (in Kingston harbour), also sparsely and only at the edges of some parts of the midlevel wet limestone forest, but not in montane forest. However, it is found in wooded cultivation, especially on tracks, to the upper limit of cultivation in the mountains, and is common in this habitat up to about 600 m. It feeds on open ground, primarily on small seeds, and Gosse (1847) recorded the seeds of grasses, of *Argemone mexicana* and of *Jatropha curcas*. The species occurs throughout the West Indies (and is therefore not mapped), and on the mainland it ranges from the southern U.S.A. through Central America to much of northern South America.

Leptotila jamaicensis **White-bellied** (**or Caribbean**) **Dove** (**White-belly**) (Plate 2, Fig. 30)

L.jamaicensis is common in lowland dry limestone forest, including the arid Hellshires and Portland Ridge and the much less arid secondary forest above the Ferry River, and also in ruinate lowland forest, as around Mona, provided that there is enough tree-cover overhead. It is also numerous in midlevel wet limestone forest, notably on Mount Diablo and in the Cockpit Country, and a few were found singing in the very wet limestone forest of the John Crow Mountains and in montane forest up to nearly 2000 m in the Blue Mountains. It is absent from mangroves and true marsh forest with water below,

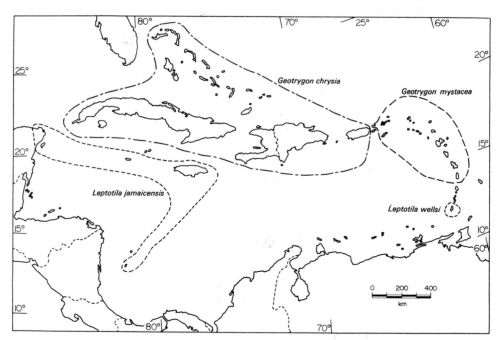

Fig. 30. *Allopatric range of the doves* Leptotila jamaicensis *and* L.wellsi, *showing also the ranges of* Geotrygon chrysia *and* G.mystacea, *which are in the same superspecies and also allopatric.*

presumably because it feeds on the ground, and is also absent from most wooded cultivation, presumably because the tree-cover overhead is insufficient. However, it is common in citrus orchards when the oranges have fallen, doubtless owing to its fondness for orange seeds noted by Gosse (1847), who also recorded it picking up the seeds of fallen cultivated fruits of other species. In its natural habitat, it feeds on seeds on the ground, under the forest canopy.

It has a unique range for a West Indian species, since, besides on Jamaica, it also occurs on the islands of Grand Cayman, St Andrew and some of those off the mainland of Yucatan (and Honduras), and also on part of the mainland of Yucatan. It has a narrower habitat on the mainland of Yucatan than on Jamaica, since it is restricted to lowland scrub forest, as it inevitably is on the other islands in its range.

As Goodwin (1967) wrote, and amplified in conversation, all the species of *Leptotila* are so similar in appearance that, had they been allopatric, they would probably have been considered to be sub-species of one, or at most two, species. Hence it is not possible to determine to which other mainland species *L.jamaicensis* might be most closely related. The song, the elaborate 'Rain-come-wet-me-through', of *L.jamaicensis* is strikingly beautiful when many sing from the same hillside, and is very different from that of all the other species, which so far as known have a song consisting of a single cooing note, including the only other West Indian species, *L.wellsi*, endemic to Grenada (Fig. 30). Since these two species are also far apart in range, I do not consider (*pace* Goodwin 1967) that they are in the same superspecies.

Geotrygon montana **Ruddy Quail-Dove (Partridge)** (Plate 2, Fig. 31)

G.montana breeds in small numbers in lowland dry limestone forest on Jamaica, one being heard singing in summer in each of the Hell-shires, Portland Ridge, Ferry River Forest and the riverine secondary

FIG. 31. *West Indian range of the dove* Geotrygon montana, *also widespread on Central and South American mainland (where range not shown).*

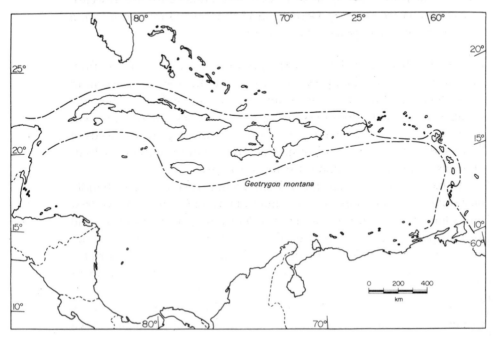

forest of Bog Walk gorge, but the only hilly area near the coast where we found it breeding fairly commonly was the tall riverine forest of Fern Gully in the north, which is too humid to be called arid lowland forest. It also breeds fairly commonly in midlevel wet limestone forest, on Mount Diablo, in the Cockpit Country, at Dolphin Head and in the John Crow Mountains, and a little less commonly in montane forest, up to an altitude of at least 1500 m. It moves into montane forest during May and June, some apparently arriving even in late June, but only a few stay for the winter there. It is at least as common in winter as in summer in wet midlevel forest and in Fern Gully. Many others descend in winter to the less arid forests of the lowlands, notably in the woods above the Ferry River and in coastal woodland in the west between Negril and Green Island. At all times of year it is almost confined to forest, but at different times we saw four in wooded cultivation, two at midlevels and two in the mountains. It feeds on the forest floor in dark woods, usually among leaf litter and often, in the mountains, in dry stream beds. Gosse (1847) recorded it eating the seeds of *Jatropha curcas* and of cultivated mangoes, also fallen pimento fruit and slugs. Goodwin (1967) noted, for its range in general, that it eats seeds, fallen fruits, slugs and other invertebrates.

G.montana occurs on nearly all of the Greater and Lesser Antilles with humid forest, which is its main habitat, though on such islands it is also regularly heard singing, and presumably breeds, in semi-arid lowland forest. It does not occur on the lowlying islands. It is widespread in Central and South America. In Honduras, it occurs in lowland rain forest and lower montane forest (Monroe 1968), so it has a broader habitat on Jamaica and other West Indian islands than on the mainland.

Geotrygon versicolor **Crested Quail-Dove (Mountain Witch)**
(Plate 2, Fig. 32)

This bird glows with a purple iridescence on the floor of dark forest. It is common in montane forest and fairly common in the midlevel wet limestone forest of the John Crow Mountains, Mount Diablo and the Cockpit Country, in the last down to an altitude of 100 m near Windsor in the north (in forest of midlevel, not lowland, type). We did not see it in midlevel forest on Dolphin Head, and it is also absent from lowland, dry limestone and riverine forest, and from

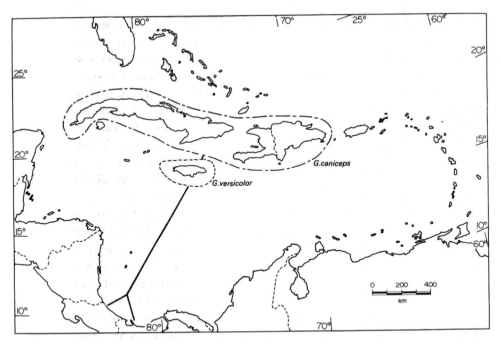

FIG. 32. *Ranges of two doves in the same superspecies*, Geotrygon versicolor (*Jamaica*) *and* G.caniceps (*Cuba, Hispaniola*), *with a line to the range of their probable mainland ancestor.*

wooded cultivation at all heights. Gosse concluded that its song and secretive habits are responsible for its local name of Mountain Witch. The song is two-syllabled, with one, which may be either the first or the second syllable, much louder and more prolonged than the other; the pitch is higher than in the monosyllabic song of the Ruddy Quail-Dove *G.montana*. *G.versicolor* feeds off the ground among leaf litter in deep shade, evidently on seeds and fallen fruits. It is fond of forest tracks, where it is readily (and illegally) caught by local people in a drop-trap baited with a red berry.

The species is endemic to Jamaica, and very distinctive, as it is the only species of *Geotrygon* with a crest (for which reason Peters put it in a genus of its own, but this is not justified). It is replaced in montane forest in Hispaniola and in humid lowland forest in Cuba by *G. caniceps* (Fig. 32). The latter does not have a crest, but resembles *G.versicolor* both in lacking the head markings characteristic of all the other species of *Geotrygon*, and in possessing a chestnut underwing.

Zenaida Dove
Zenaida aurita

Common Ground
Dove
Columbina passerina

Ruddy Quail
Dove
Geotrygon montana

Mourning Dove
Zenaida macroura

White-bellied Dove
Leptotila jamaicensis

Mountain Witch
Geotrygon versicolor

PLATE 2. *Pigeons and doves Columbidae, one-eighth natural size.*

Hence although they look rather unlike each other, there is no serious doubt that these two Antillean species are in the same superspecies.

Goodwin (1967) noted that, in size and most plumage characters, *G.versicolor* and *G.caniceps* closely resemble the Buff-fronted Quail-Dove *G.costaricensis*, which occurs in montane forest from Costa Rica to Panama, and also *G.lawrencii*, the Purplish-backed Quail-Dove, which occurs further south and may be con-specific; but these two latter species lack the chestnut underwing. On the other hand the Olive-backed Quail-Dove *G.veraguensis*, a smaller species found in lowland rain forest in part of Costa Rica, Panama and northwestern South America, does have the chestnut underwing; but in all other features the two Antillean species are closer to *G.costaricensis*, which is therefore assumed to be their nearest mainland relative. *G.costaricensis* also resembles them in living in montane forest. The only species of *Geotrygon* in montane forest in Honduras, *G.linearis*, is quite unlike *G.versicolor* and *G.caniceps*, so does not come in question here.

COMPETITION BETWEEN JAMAICAN COLUMBIDAE

It has been suggested that some of the congeneric pigeons and doves on Jamaica are segregated from each other by habitat, but this is not true. While, for instance, *Columba leucocephala* breeds in lowland forest, from which *C.caribaea* is absent, both these species breed in midlevel forest and the lower parts of montane forest. Similarly *Geotrygon montana* breeds at a lower altitude than *G.versicolor*, but both breed in midlevel and montane forest. These two latter species differ in habitat to a greater extent in winter, when *G.montana* is scarce in montane forest where *G.versicolor* is common, and is fairly common in lowland forest, from which *G.versicolor* is absent; but they occur together in midlevel forest. Again, the three species of *Zenaida*, though they have partly different habitats, are sometimes found in the same lowland scrub forest.

We scarcely studied the feeding of the Columbidae, but a few differences may be noted. *Columba caribaea* feeds on fruits, but *C. leucocephala* and *C.inornata* on both fruits and seeds. *Zenaida aurita* and *Z.macroura* feed solely on the ground, but the longer beaked *Z. asiatica* also in trees, and eats cactus fruits, which we did not see the other two species eating. *Geotrygon versicolor* is much larger than *G.montana* (see Table 1), which suggests that there might be a difference in their preferred foods. More cannot be said from our observations, and the information on foods given by Gosse (1847) is too incomplete to say how, or indeed whether, the Jamaican species are segregated in their feeding. Certainly they are not segregated effectively by habitat.

VAGRANTS AND DOUBTFUL SPECIES

Gosse (1847) wrote that "woodmen speak of a Blue Partridge and a Red-necked Dove". The latter is the pigeon *Columba squamosa*, and hunters also told Scott (1891–3) that it sometimes occurred on Jamaica, a statement confirmed by a specimen in the Institute of Jamaica collected on Portland Point in September 1953. Not breeding on Jamaica, this species evidently wanders there at times, presumably from Cuba or Hispaniola, where it is resident. As already mentioned, it appears to be excluded from Jamaica through competition with *C.caribaea* (see Fig. 7, p. 76).

Since Gosse's woodmen were right about the Red-necked Pigeon, they might also have been right about the 'Blue Partridge.' The word 'partridge' implies a ground pigeon ('the partridge' in Jamaica being *Geotrygon montana*). Gosse (1849) named this bird *Zenaida plumbea*. His colour plate was from a picture in the Institute of Jamaica attributed to Dr. Robinson, a keen naturalist who died in 1768 and left many illustrations of Jamaican birds and flowers. As shown by Steward (1969), however, this particular picture was signed by A. Mackey, a clergyman, and since a number of Robinson's own attributions are doubtful, including, for instance, his 'White Potoo', the illustration cannot be taken as certain evidence that a blue dove occurred wild in Jamaica. D. Goodwin (pers. comm.) said that the picture, if of an existing species, is of the Blue Ground Dove *Claravis pretiosa* of Central and South America, with which it agrees in general colouring, dark wing-band and dark outer tail feathers, though it lacks the pale head and the smaller dark markings on the wing. Osburn (1859) wrote to Gosse that he had not yet found the Blue Dove, which he was told was only in the east of Jamaica. The latter statement, if correct, would explain why Gosse never saw it. However March (1863), after discussing the two resident species of *Geotrygon* wrote: 'The Blue Dove is another ground pigeon, with the form of the Pea Dove [*i.e. Zenaida aurita*] and the habits of the White Belly [*i.e. Leptotila jamaicensis*]. The body is blue, the neck and head grey [a description which does not altogether tally with Gosse's picture, but nearly fits for *C.pretiosa*]. It builds in low shrubs, generally in clumps of *Tillandsia*, or on the ground.' None of the other early naturalists in Jamaica mention such a bird. Hence it seems best to consider it as a very doubtful former breeding record of either *Claravis pretiosa* or a species near to it, and to exclude it from the analysis in this book. It was square-bracketed by Peters.

Domestic pigeons *Columba livia* are kept by many people in Jamaica, but they keep extremely close to their dovecotes and do not, as in Europe, feed regularly in fields. March (1863) noted that, in his day, feral individuals of the Barbary Dove *Streptopelia 'risoria'* (a domestic form of *S.roseogrisea*) fed in the fields and salinas, but we saw none. Finally the Blue-headed Quail-Dove *Starnoenas cyanocephala*, an endemic Cuban species was recorded for Jamaica by the 18th century naturalists, but Gosse (1847) rejected this, and said this species was often imported as a cagebird.

COLUMBIDAE OF NEARBY LANDS

Hispaniola, like Jamaica, has 10 resident species of pigeons and doves, Cuba one more. The three islands have 7 species in common, namely *C.leucocephala*, *C.inornata*, *Z.macroura*, *Z.aurita*, *Z.asiatica*, *C.passerina* and *G.montana*, while an eighth species on Jamaica, *G.versicolor*, is replaced by a member of the same superspecies, *G.caniceps*, on the other two islands. The other two islands have *C.squamosa* instead of *C.caribaea*, as already discussed. They also have a third species of *Geotrygon*, the Key West Quail Dove *G.chrysia*, which lives in dry lowland forest, and might be an ecological replacement of Jamaica's *Leptotila jamaicensis*, which they lack; geographical replacement through competitive exclusion can occur between species in different genera (Lack 1971). Finally, Cuba has another quail dove, *Starnoenas cyanocephala*, in lowland forest. Hence, except for this last species, the ecological situation among the members of the pigeon family on Jamaica, Cuba and Hispaniola is very similar.

Grand Cayman has only mangroves and lowland dry limestone forest, in which live the same five species that are common in lowland forest on Jamaica, namely *C.leucocephala*, *Z.aurita*, *Z.asiatica*, *C.passerina* and *L.jamaicensis*. It has no other Columbidae.

Honduras has 18 species of Columbidae. Of the 8 species in the arid lowlands, 4 occur on Jamaica, namely *Z.asiatica*, *C.passerina* and (solely on offshore islands in Honduras) *C.leucocephala* and *L.jamaicensis*, while another of them, *C.flavirostris*, is the mainland representative of *C.inornata* on Jamaica. One further species of the arid lowlands on the mainland, in Yucatan but not Honduras, namely *Z.aurita*, is present on Jamaica. In contrast, of the 7 species confined to lowland rain forest in Honduras, none are on Jamaica, which is in line with what is found in other families of birds, as discussed in Part 1. However, one species on Jamaica, *G.montana*, is found in Honduras in lowland rain forest and also in the lower part of the cloud forest. Finally, of the two species restricted to montane forest in Honduras, *C.fasciata* is represented by the related *C.caribaea* on Jamaica, but *G.linearis* is not represented, the montane Jamaican *Geotrygon* probably being derived from a montane species in Costa Rica. Hence Jamaica has been colonised mainly by Columbidae which on the mainland live in the arid lowlands, and also by some which there live in montane forest, but not by any confined to lowland rain forest.

PARROTS PSITTACIDAE

Jamaica has two species of *Amazona* parrots, whereas each of the other Greater Antilles has only one. There is also a parakeet, an introduced parrotlet and probably, until the first part of the 19th century, there was one wild species of macaw.

Ara sp. **Macaw**

No wild macaw has been seen in Jamaica for over a century, the last records being by a man who told Osburn (1859) that he had seen them four of five times in the previous 25 years, always flying at a height. Three possible wild species have been described from Jamaica in the past, but the evidence is confused and contradictory (Gosse 1847, Clark 1905, Rothschild 1905, 1907, Greenway 1967.)

On faunistic grounds, the most likely macaw to have lived wild in Jamaica is a small red species close to the Scarlet Macaw *Ara macao*. Not only is this species common in Central America, but a smaller red species closely related to it, *A.tricolor*, occurred wild in Cuba until the middle of the 19th century, and specimens of it, the last collected in 1864, exist. Further, a specimen was collected near Lucea in north western Jamaica in the year 1765. A description of the stuffed bird was left by Dr. Robinson (see p. 73), and it seems to have been broadly similar to *A.tricolor*, the chief differences being a yellow, not red, forehead and some yellow, instead of blue, in the mainly red tail. These are the sort of differences to be expected in an island form, and the bird was illustrated and named *Ara gossei* by Rothschild (1905, 1907). The specimen has disappeared, but the existence of such a bird in Jamaica has been accepted by almost every 19th and 20th century writer, including Greenway (1958). Yet neither Sloane (1725) nor Browne (1789), who listed all the wild and captive members of the parrot family on Jamaica, noted it as wild in their day, and nor has any later observer recorded it. Indeed, Browne explicitly stated that the Red Macaw of Edwards, *i.e. Ara macao*, is not native to Jamaica, and he would presumably have included '*A.gossei*' under the Red

Macaw had it existed. One vanished specimen is not enough on which to base a Jamaican species, and it might have been an escape from captivity or a vagrant, possibly of the Cuban or the extinct Hispaniolan Macaw. I therefore reject the evidence for it as a wild resident species on Jamaica.

Browne (1789) saw one or two of the Blue Macaw of Edwards, *i.e.* the Blue-and-Yellow Macaw *Ara ararauna*, wild in St Anne's parish, but stated that they were rare, occurring in unfrequented parts inland, those seen about gentlemen's houses having been introduced from the mainland. Again Gosse (1847) reported that about the year 1842, the Rev. Mr. Coward saw two macaws in flight in the parish of St Elizabeth and he (Mr. Coward) was told by others that the species was blue and yellow. Likewise March (1863–64) was told by a resident in the mountains of St James that he saw three blue and yellow macaws there, evidently in 1836. Hence a few blue and yellow macaws were formerly wild or feral on Jamaica, but one may suspect that all, not just those near 'gentlemen's houses', were derived from introduced individuals. This seems the accepted view, for no later writer has claimed *A.ararauna* for the Jamaican list. (Sloane (1725) described what must have been a captive bird, as it talked well.) Hence this species shall also be rejected as a native resident on Jamaica.

Finally, a small green macaw has been noted by four observers. First, Sloane (1725) wrote that 'the small Macaws' 'are very common in the woods, and are eaten as Pigeons, but when young, are tamed, and kept as Parrots'. Later writers, including Greenway (1958), seem wrongly to have assumed that this bird was the red macaw already mentioned, but Sloane referred it to a species described by Marcgrave and included in Willughby's 'Ornithology' (English edition, 1678, p. 112). Willughby wrote of 'The other Maracana of Marggrav,' as 'of the shape of a Maccaw, but, about the bigness of a Parrot', green almost all over, including the head, but red under the wings and tail. The bird to which he referred was undoubtedly the South American Chestnut-fronted Macaw *Ara severa* (Salvadori 1891), and Sloane could hardly have referred the Jamaican bird to this species unless, at the least, it had been small and mainly green. Secondly, Browne (1789) included a small, green, long-tailed parrot among the native Jamaican birds, and as he listed the parakeet, and both wild *Amazona* parrots separately, it was presumably a small green macaw, but he gave no further details.

Thirdly, the reliable Mr. Hill, in a letter to Gosse (1847), ascertained that 'Macaws are occasionally, if not constantly, denizens of our mountain forests...in the central mountains westward of the island' and every description makes them 'to be the *Ara militaris*, the Great Green [or Military] Macaw of Mexico'. Hill did not see this bird, but was told that it was mainly green, with a red head, blue primaries, the tail red and blue above and orange-yellow underneath, as were the wings, on the basis of which Rothschild (1905, 1907) named it *Ara erythrocephala*. Fourthly, March (1863–64) remembered, from before the time that he became interested in birds, the remains of a macaw collected in the mountains of St James in 1834. The body was missing, but the head and neck were bright green, the forehead and chin red, the wings blue and green and the tail blue and red. This was presumably the same species again, and the description fits *A. militaris* better than Hill's, in that only the forehead, not the whole head, was red. (Since Hill referred the bird to *A.militaris*, Rothschild was wrong to illustrate it with a wholly red head.)

I can find no support for Clark's (1905) statement that the juveniles of Cuban *A.tricolor*, and by inference of '*A.gossei*', were green, so the Jamaican macaw was evidently in a different superspecies from that on Cuba, a situation similar to that in the parakeets discussed in the next section.

In view of this evidence, I think there is no reasonable doubt that a single wild species of macaw, small and mainly green, existed formerly on Jamaica. Presumably it was derived from one of the three green macaws in Central America, *A.severa*, *A.militaris* or the Great Green Macaw *A.ambigua*, with mean male wing lengths of 241, 386 and 405 mm respectively. On grounds of size, the largest species, *A.ambigua*, can presumably be ruled out, especially as it lives in lowland rain forest, from which extremely few species have colonised Jamaica (see Chapter 7). *A.severa* is the only one of the three which could be called small, but it does not extend further north than Panama, and has a chestnut-brown, not a red, forehead (Salvadori 1891), and so it also can be excluded. *A.militaris* on the other hand, occurs in Mexico and has a red forehead, as the Jamaican species was said to have had. Admittedly it is large, but the endemic Cuban *A.tricolor* has a much shorter wing than its mainland relative *A.macao* (282 *cf.* 394 mm), and if the Jamaican bird were derived from *A.militaris* with a similar reduction in size, its wing would have been only 275–280 mm in length. The latter might have been considered small, at least in comparison with the other species available to Sloane, the Blue-and-Yellow *A.ararauna* (male wing length 382 mm). Probably, therefore, the small green macaw in Jamaica was an endemic species derived from *A.militaris*, but this cannot be considered certain.

Aratinga nana **Jamaican Parakeet** (**Olive-throated Parakeet,** in Bond) (Plate 3, Fig. 12, p. 102)

This species is commonest in midlevel wet limestone forest and in wooded cultivation at midlevels and in the northern lowlands. In the southern lowlands, it is fairly common in the less arid parts of the secondary woodland and wooded cultivation, and intermittently visits the arid natural forest of the Hellshires and Portland Ridge for particular fruits, but it is generally absent from ruinate woodland. Although commonest at midlevels, it is absent from the very wet John Crow Mountains and also from montane forest, though we occasionally saw it in wooded cultivation in the Blue Mountains. We saw it feeding on the fruits or seeds of *Bursera simaruba*, *Guazuma ulmifolia*, *Lantana camara* and *Fagara martinicensis*, and on the flowers of an introduced *Erythrina*. Other natural fruits or seeds recorded by Gosse (1847) were those of *Citharexylum caudatum*, *Ficus* sp. and *Metopium brownii*, also cultivated bananas, guava and pimento.

Peters (1937) treated the Jamaican bird as an endemic species, but it is sufficiently close to the Central American *A.astec* for Marien

TABLE 40. *Measurements (in mm) of Greater Antillean parakeets and their nearest mainland relatives*

| | | mean length (in mm) of males | |
		wing	culmen
One subgenus			
Aratinga astec	Mexico, Central America	137	18.4
Aratinga nana	Jamaica	140	21.6
Another subgenus			
Aratinga holochlora holochlora	Mexico, Central America	168	24.9
Aratinga chloroptera chloroptera	Hispaniola	177	26.6
Aratinga euops	Cuba	142	19.9

Note Measurements from Ridgway. There is no overlap in culmen-length for individuals of *A.astec* (16 males and 9 females, 16.5–20 mm) and *A.nana* (5 males and 5 females, 21–22.5) in Ridgway's measurements.

Jamaican
Parakeet
Aratinga nana

Black-billed Parrot
Amazona agilis

Yellow-billed Parrot
Amazona collaria

Jabbering Crow
Corvus jamaicensis

PLATE 3. *Parrots Psittacidae and crow Corvidae, one-eighth natural size.*

and Koopman (1955) and Bond (1956) to have regarded them as conspecific (the name *A.nana* having priority). However, the rather darker Jamaican bird does not overlap in beak measurements with the mainland form (see footnote to Table 40). This is a border line case, for which I made a rule to follow Peters, and the latter has anyway been followed in this respect by both Eisenmann (1955) and Monroe (1968), Monroe noting that, in Honduras, *A.astec* occurs in lowland rain forest, monsoon (vega) forest and open wooded cultivation, both humid and arid. When the Jamaican bird is treated as a separate species, it is best called the Jamaican Parakeet, leaving the name Olive-throated Parakeet for *A.astec*.

The endemic parakeets *Aratinga euops* of Cuba and *A.chloroptera* of Hispaniola, formerly Mona and perhaps also Puerto Rico, are in a different subgenus from *A.nana* and *A.astec* (Marien and Koopman 1955). The several mainland species in this subgenus replace each other geographically. Bond (1963) linked the Cuban and Hispaniolan birds with *A.finschi*, but they seem as similar to *A.holochlora*, which is the nearest species geographically to Cuba. *A.holochlora* occurs in Mexico and most of Central America, where it lives in cloud and pine-oak forest (Monroe 1968). In the Greater Antilles, *A.nana* on the one hand, and *A.euops* with *A.chloroptera* on the other hand, occupy similar habitats and replace each other geographically, presumably through competitive exclusion; but their respective mainland relatives both live in Honduras, where they are segregated by habitat, in lowland and montane forest respectively.

Amazona collaria **Yellow-billed Parrot** (Plate 3, Fig. 33)

This, the more widespread of the two Jamaican parrots, is typically a bird of midlevel wet limestone forest, being common in the Cockpit Country, on Mount Diablo and in the John Crow Mountains, and we saw some in wooded cultivation near these forests. Birds regularly fly from the John Crow Mountains over Cornpuss Gap into the eastern end of the Blue Mountains, but they are only occasional visitors to the rest of the montane forest. We saw only one much further west, near Morce's Gap, and others have occasionally seen them in this area. This species is also an occasional visitor to wooded cultivation in the higher parts of the southern lowlands. For instance a small flock, which included an escaped captive, intermittently visited the University

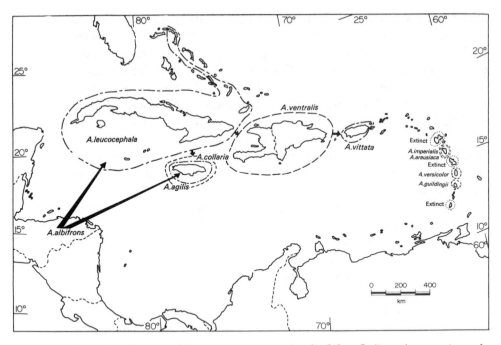

FIG. 33. *Ranges of* Amazona *parrots in the West Indies. Arrows show the probable origin of the two Jamaican species from* A.albifrons *of the mainland and of other Great Antillean species. The Lesser Antillean species are of separate origin.*

campus and elsewhere in Mona in 1969 and 1971. *A.collaria* feeds on fruits and seeds near the tops of trees. In Mona, we saw the birds taking seeds from the pods of the introduced *Spathodea campanulata* and from *Melia azedarach* in a garden, and Gosse (1847) noted that it feeds on pimento and orange seeds and on the kernels of the cashew nut *Anacardium occidentale*.

Amazona agilis **Black-billed Parrot** (Plate 3, Fig. 33)

A.agilis is as abundant as *A.collaria* in the midlevel forests of the Cockpit Country and Mount Diablo, but we saw it nowhere else. Scott (1891–3) stated that it was common in Portland Parish at the eastern end of Jamaica, but no modern ornithologist has seen it in the John Crow Mountains, and since this is one of the least disturbed areas in the island, and *A.collaria* is common there, it seems unlikely that *A.agilis* would have died out in the present century. Yet, although Scott could hardly have been mistaken, it is not now possible to decide whether he was correct. *A.agilis*, like *A.collaria*, feeds high up in forest trees, but though we often saw it close to *A.collaria*, and even resting in the same tree during rain, we did not see the two species feeding together; but this is not very meaningful since we rarely saw them feeding at all. *A.agilis* is a little smaller than *A.collaria* (see Table 41), with a much thinner beak (mean depth at base 24 mm, *cf.* 27.5 mm in *A.collaria*) which suggests that the two species might be segregated by diet. Gosse (1847) recorded *A.agilis* eating bananas and pimento seeds, but the natural foods of both species are almost unknown. It would be interesting to know how Jamaica supports two species but Cuba, Hispaniola and Puerto Rico only one.

RELATIONSHIPS OF GREATER ANTILLEAN AMAZONA PARROTS (FIG. 33)

The Hispaniolan Parrot *A.ventralis* and the Cuban Parrot *Amazona leucocephala* (which is also on the Caymans and some of the Bahamas) are in the same superspecies as the Jamaican *A.collaria*, but have wider habitats, as they occur in both arid lowlands and wet highlands. Bond (1963) rightly related them to the White-fronted Parrot *A.albifrons*, which occurs in Central America, mainly in lowland arid areas but also in monsoon forest (Monroe 1968). The second Jamaican species, *A.agilis*, is also in the same species-group. The features summarised in Table 41 suggest that *A.albifrons* spread from the mainland to Cuba, where it gave rise to *A.leucocephala*, and that the latter spread to Jamaica, where it gave rise to *A.collaria*; and that independently, *A.albifrons* spread from the mainland to Jamaica, where it gave rise to *A.agilis*. The critical points in this assessment (Table 41) are that *A.agilis* agrees with mainland *A.albifrons* and differs from the other species in having a relatively shallow beak, red on the forewing and no pink on chin or abdomen, while *A.collaria* is more like Cuban *A.leucocephala* than mainland *A.albifrons* in its deeper beak, absence of red on forewing, and presence of reddish on the chin; and these three species have a white forehead, unlike *A.agilis*. It is also reasonable to infer that Cuban *A.leucocephala* (or possibly Jamaican *A.collaria*) later spread to Hispaniola to give rise to *A.ventralis* and that the latter in turn gave rise to the smaller *A.vittata* on Puerto Rico.

TABLE 41.   *Features of Greater Antillean* Amazona *parrots and their presumed mainland ancestor*

	Species: Range:	A.albifrons Mexico, Central America	A.agilis Jamaica	A.collaria Jamaica	A.leucocephala Cuba, Bahamas, Caymans	A.ventralis Hispaniola
Red forewing		present	present	absent	absent	absent
White forehead		large	absent	small	large	small
Chin and nearby		green	green	pink	red	green
Pink feathers on green abdomen		absent	absent	absent	present	present
Mean wing-length (males, mm)		178,167	171	184	192	191
Mean beak-depth (both sexes, mm)		24.5	24	27.5	29	25.4

Notes   (i) Mean wing-lengths are from Ridgway, the two figures for *A.albifrons* referring to the subspecies *A.a.albifrons* and the smaller *A.a.nana* respectively. Mean beak-depths, for both sexes combined, are based on respectively 8, 4, 5, 9 and 4 specimens in the British Museum (Natural History) measured by myself.
(ii) Features restricted to one species are the black beak of *A.agilis* (yellow in rest), wholly green head of *A.agilis* (blue or bluish-grey crown and nape in rest), and red on sides of head in *A.albifrons* (but no others).
(iii) Puerto Rican *A.vittata* is generally smaller (male wing 103 mm) than the rest, and the body and head are wholly green except for a thin red band above the beak; it also has much less red on the tail than the other species.

[*Forpus passerinus* **Guiana Parrotlet**]

This South American species was introduced to Jamaica in 1918 (Bond 1956). It is now widespread in wooded cultivation from sea level to an altitude of about 500 m, and also occurs in the ruinate woodland of Port Henderson Hill and around Mona, and the secondary forest above the Ferry River. Unlike the few other species introduced to Jamaica, it occurs to some extent in natural forest, since it is regular but scarce in the arid Hellshires, and it also flies into the midlevel forest round Worthy Park if disturbed when feeding in the adjoining pastures. We saw it eating the fruits or seeds of *Ficus maxima* and *Lantana camara,* and C. and A. Kepler (pers. comm.) saw it eating the fleshy fruits of *Cereus* cacti.

CUCKOOS CUCULIDAE

Jamaica has five species of non-parasitic cuckoos, four of them in the New World subfamily Neomorphinae and one ani (Crotophaginae). The two largest species are in genera endemic to the Greater Antilles and are among the grand cuckoos of the world.

Coccyzus americanus **Yellow-billed Cuckoo** (Plate 4)

This species is regular on spring passage through Jamaica, and some stay for the summer. We saw it in April and May in the lowland dry limestone forest, natural and ruinate, of Port Henderson Hill, the Hellshires, Ferry River, Long Mountain (Mona) and near Milk River, but all these birds later disappeared, so were evidently transients. However, one in marsh forest beside the Black River on 30 June was probably breeding. Scott (1891–3) noted that Mr. Taylor had taken its eggs, and Field (1894), who also recorded a nest, wrote that at Port Henderson it far outnumbers *C.minor*, though it is not clear whether he meant as a breeding bird. Perhaps the number staying to breed on Jamaica differs in different years. In 1971, May and June were exceptionally dry and the trees of the arid lowland woods were not in full leaf even when we left in mid-July, so possibly individuals, which would have bred if the normal May rains had come, moved away and it is suggestive that our one late summer record was in marsh forest.

C.americanus breeds on the other Greater Antilles, on some of the Bahamas and some of the northern Lesser Antilles, but its breeding range on the smaller islands is uncertain owing to the number of birds that pass through on passage (and a map has therefore not been drawn). It breeds in North America south to Mexico. In Florida and Mexico, where *C.minor* really is a 'mangrove cuckoo', the two species are segregated by habitat, in mangroves and arid scrub forest respectiveley. But this does not hold in the Greater Antilles, where both occur

Old Man Bird
Hyetornis pluvialis

Mangrove Cuckoo
Coccyzus minor

Yellow-billed Cuckoo
Coccyzus americanus

Old Woman Bird
Saurothera vetula

Smooth-billed Ani
Crotophaga ani

PLATE 4.   *Cuckoos Cuculidae, one-eighth natural size.*

primarily in arid lowland scrub forest, and how they might be separated ecologically is not known.

Coccyzus minor **Mangrove Cuckoo** (Plate 4)

The vernacular name of *C.minor* is not justified on Jamaica, where we had only one record in mangroves, on the edge in winter. This species is fairly common in the less arid lowland limestone woods; for instance, in the secondary, riverine and ruinate woods round Mona and the Ferry River, and also at Green Island in the west, and is present in smaller numbers in the arid forest on Portland Ridge and Port Henderson Hill. It is scarce in wooded cultivation. In summer, we did not meet it above an altitude of 200 m, but in winter A. W. Diamond recorded it at Irish Town at 600 m, and Robert Sutton informed us that it occasionally occurs during winter droughts at a similar altitude in woodland near Mandeville. It searches for food by hopping slowly through the branches of the trees, usually about half-way between the low canopy and the ground, repeatedly stopping to peer around; but we did not see it take anything. Since it is chased away from their nests by small birds, including the hummingbird *Mellisuga minima*, its diet probably includes eggs or nestlings. Gosse (1847) recorded it taking soft insects and large spiders.

The species occupies all of the standard map including the Lesser Antilles where, unlike on Jamaica, it extends in small numbers into humid forest. It is widespread in Central and South America, in parts of which it is confined to mangroves, for instance in Honduras (Monroe 1968), Surinam (Haverschmidt 1968) and Trinidad (Herklots 1961), whereas elsewhere it is also in arid woodland, for instance in Mexico (Friedmann *et al.* 1950) and Panama (Wetmore 1968).

Hyetornis pluvialis **Chestnut-bellied Cuckoo** (**Old Man Bird**) (Plate 4, Fig. 34)

The magnificent 'Old Man Bird', with its white 'beard' and bass voice, occurs chiefly in midlevel wet limestone and montane forest, between altitudes of 400 and 1500 m, mainly in open woodland and wooded cultivation rather than dense forest. A very few occur in the southern lowlands, notably a pair which stayed for the whole year at 60 m above sea level in the rich secondary woodland above the Ferry

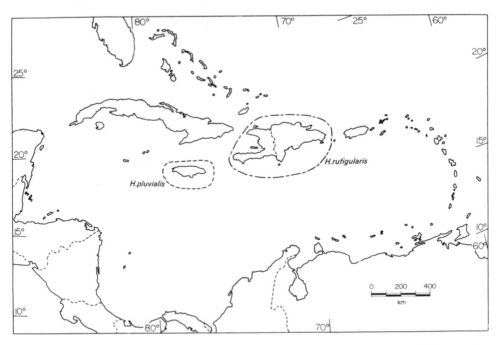

Fig. 34. *Range of the endemic Greater Antillean cuckoo genus* Hyetornis.

River. We did not see *H.pluvialis* feeding, but it hunts in a similar way to the other neomorphine cuckoos on Jamaica. Hill (in Gosse 1847) recorded it as taking insects. Salmon (1966) saw it fly out and catch a flying mantis, but this is probably unusual. It is an endemic Jamaican species closely related to a smaller congener, with a longer beak and more uniform colouring, on Hispaniola. Peters put these two species in the mainland genus *Piaya*, but except in their large size (larger than *Piaya*), they seem about as similar to the much smaller *Coccyzus*, and are sufficiently distinct from either to justify the separate genus *Hyetornis*. While all three genera probably had a common ancestor, *Hyetornis* is too distinctive to determine to what mainland form it is most closely related.

Saurothera vetula **Jamaican Lizard Cuckoo (Old Woman Bird)** (Plate 4, Fig. 35)

The 'Old Woman Bird' is smaller than the 'Old Man Bird', with

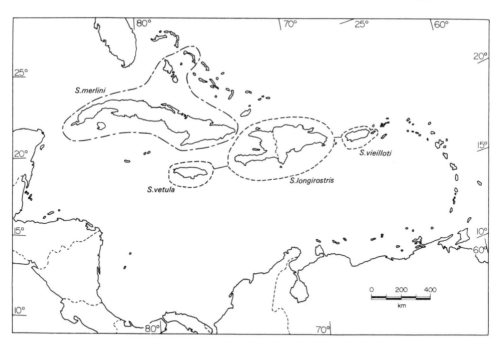

FIG. 35. *Range of the Greater Antillean endemic cuckoo genus* Saurothera, *of which the Jamaican* S.vetula, *the Hispaniolan* S.longirostris *and the Puerto Rican* S.vieilloti *are very similar.*

a much longer dagger-shaped beak and a higher and more prolonged cackle. It is commonest in lowland dry limestone forest, both the arid natural forest of Portland Ridge and the ruinate, riverine and secondary woodland around Mona and the Ferry River, and is also regular in the lower parts of the midlevel wet limestone forest, notably on Mount Diablo. In summer, but not winter, we saw a few in the very wet limestone forest of the John Crow Mountains, and also two pairs at an altitude of about 1200m, the one in montane forest in the Blue Mountains above Silver Hill Gap, and the other in wooded cultivation on Guava Ridge. This species, like *C.minor*, moves slowly through the branches, well below the canopy and some 3 to 4 m above the ground, stopping to peer in many directions, and at times twisting its neck right round to do so, but we did not see it feed. Gosse (1847) recorded it taking large caterpillars, large adult insects such as locusts, and small lizards.

S.vetula is endemic to Jamaica and the genus is endemic to the

TABLE 42.   *Variations in size of Greater Antillean cuckoos*
(Neamorphinae)

Species	Island	Mean length (in mm) for males of wing	culmen
Hyetornis pluvialis	Jamaica	182	35.9
Hyetornis rufigularis	Hispaniola	166	36.5
Saurothera vetula	Jamaica	126	45.4
Saurothera longirostris	Hispaniola	140	47.7
Saurothera vieilloti	Puerto Rico	132	45.3
Saurothera merlini merlini	Cuba	174	52.6
Saurothera merlini bahamensis	Bahamas	155	51.7
Coccyzus minor	all	133	27.5
Coccyzus americanus	widespread	138	25.7

Note Measurements are from Ridgway. Those of *C.minor* are of the Jamaican race and those of *C.americanus* are of the southern race.

Greater Antilles, with three further species *longirostris, vieilloti* and *merlini* on, respectively, Hispaniola, Puerto Rico and Cuba, the last also on some of the Bahamas (Fig. 35). As shown in Table 42, these four species differ greatly from each other in wing-length and length of beak, the Jamaican being the smallest and the Cuban the largest. It is tempting to suppose that the Cuban species evolved its large size owing to the absence on that island of *Hyetornis,* but *Hyetornis* is also absent from Puerto Rico, where the *Saurothera* species is almost as small as on Jamaica. The possible reasons for these size differences would make an interesting ecological study. When both size and colour are considered, the species nearest to the Jamaican is that on Hispaniola, and the next nearest that on Puerto Rico. Indeed, Peters treated all three as subspecies of *S.vetula,* but they are sufficiently distinct to be regarded as full species, as by Bond (1971), though they are nearer to each other than are any of them to the Cuban-Bahaman species. This endemic Antillean genus is closest in appearance to *Coccyzus,* less close to *Hyetornis* or *Piaya,* and the beak is longer than in any of these others.

Crotophaga ani **Smooth-billed Ani** (Plate 4)

This species, widespread throughout the West Indies, occurs abundantly in only one natural habitat in Jamaica, the open parts of the Black

River freshwater swamp, and it is also present, but very scarce, in mangroves. It is found chiefly in cultivated land with grass and scattered trees, especially in the lowlands, but extends up to the limit of cultivation in the mountains. It feeds mainly on insects on the ground but we saw one take a large grasshopper in flight, and another ate the small fruits of the creeper *Trichostigma octandrum*. Gosse (1847) wrote that it eats mainly insects when they are settled, including caterpillars, grasshoppers, beetles, moths and the external parasites of cattle, but occasionally takes insects such as dragonflies or lepidoptera in flight, also anole lizards and the fruits of *Citharexylum caudatum* and *Cissus sicyoides*. Pearson (1964) saw one take a nestling ground dove *Columbina passerina*. *C.ani* is also common in northern South America, but very local in Central America, chiefly, on offshore islands (Monroe 1968), and only recently became established in Florida. Hence it probably reached Jamaica from the south via the Lesser Antilles, possibly only after man started to clear the forests for cultivation.

DISCUSSION OF CUCKOOS

Of the five Jamaican cuckoos, *C.ani* is separated ecologically from the rest by habitat and by feeding mainly on the ground. *H.pluvialis* and *S.vetula* are partly separated by habitat, in the mountains and lowlands respectively, but with a big overlap at midlevels; the difference in the shape of their beaks suggests that they may be segregated by diet, but we have no evidence for this. Of the three species which breed in lowland forest, *S.vetula* has a much longer beak than the two species of *Coccyzus*, so may be separated from them by its food; but whether and how *C.minor* and *C.americanus* might be segregated is not known.

A similar five species, except that *H.pluvialis* and *S.vetula* are represented by congeners, occur in Hispaniola, and four of them do so on Cuba and Puerto Rico, where *Hyetornis* is absent, as already mentioned. Eight species of Cuculidae are resident in Honduras, including *C. minor* and *C.ani*, and a species of *Piaya* perhaps fills a niche similar to that of the Jamaican *Hyetornis* and *Saurothera*. The other species are parasitic or ground-living, with another ani (Monroe 1968).

NIGHT BIRDS: TYTONIDAE, STRIGIDAE, NYCTIBIIDAE, CAPRIMULGIDAE

We did not study the ecology of the species which feed at night, of which Jamaica has four, while a fifth is extinct.

Tyto alba **Barn Owl** (Tytonidae) (Plate 5)

We saw *T.alba* from sea level up to an altitude of about 500 m, and others have seen it in the Blue Mountains. It hunts in open wooded country, farmland and towns, and its main food at the present time probably consists of introduced rats, though we also found some bird bones in pellets in a cave in Worthy Park. This cosmopolitan species is widespread in the West Indies.

Pseudoscops grammicus **Jamaican Owl** (Strigidae) (Plate 5)

This genus is endemic to Jamaica. *P.grammicus* is regular in lowland and midlevel forest, but we did not see it, and had no reports of it, from montane forest. We heard it in woodland and wooded cultivation at the edge of Kingston and Mona, and also in wild forest in the Cockpit Country. In addition A. W. Diamond saw it in the Dolphin Head forest, C. and A. Kepler (pers. comm.) in Fern Gully, and R.W. Smith (1971) in the John Crow Mountains. It differs from *T.alba* both in habitat, since it lives in woodland rather than open country, and in taking smaller prey, Gosse (1847) recording mice and beetles. Its asymmetrical external ears and its ear tufts suggest that it is close to the genus *Asio*, but it is much smaller than the two mainland species in this genus, the Stygian Owl *A.stygius* and Short-eared Owl *A.flammeus* (mean male wing-lengths 305 and 313 mm respectively—from Ridgway) and it also differs from them in colour, so is probably not closely related. Its nearest ancestor is unknown, and an endemic genus seems justified.

GREATER ANTILLEAN OWLS

T.alba is also on Cuba and Hispaniola, but not Puerto Rico. In the family Strigidae, Hispaniola has endemic subspecies of three mainland species, *A.stygius*, *A.flammeus* and the Burrowing Owl *Speotyto cunicularia*. Cuba also has three species, a subspecies of *A.stygius* and two endemic species, the very small *Glaucidium siju* and the small *Otus lawrencii*, the latter usually put in an endemic genus *Gymnoglaux*. Puerto Rico has an endemic subspecies of *A.flammeus* and the small *Otus nudipes*, which is so similar to the Cuban *O.lawrencii* that it has sometimes been put with it in the genus *Gymnoglaux* (or *Gymnasio*). However, the only important features separating these two latter species from *Otus* are the absence of ear-tufts and the bare or partly bare tarsus, and I agree with Bond (1956) that they should be in *Otus*.

Hence the owls of the four main Greater Antilles are different. The absence from Cuba of the Short-eared and Burrowing Owls is not due to their failure to reach it, for individuals of both species have wandered there from the mainland (Bond 1956); perhaps suitable habitats are lacking on Cuba. In forest, Jamaica has only a medium-sized species (wing length 213 mm), Puerto Rico only a small species (wing length 148 mm), Hispaniola only a large species (wing length 305 mm), and Cuba a large, a small and a very small species (wing lengths respectively 305, 163 and 91 mm)—measurements from Ridgway. The possible ecological reasons for these differences would make a rewarding study. It is also interesting that the smallish woodland owl on Jamaica is derived from *Asio*, that on Cuba and Puerto Rico from *Otus*.

Nyctibius griseus **Common Potoo** (Nyctibiidae) (Plate 5, Fig. 36)

Thanks to Robert Sutton, we saw this species in midlevel woodland near Mandeville, and it is also in ruinate lowland woodland around Kingston (*per* I. Goodbody, R.W. Smith). It feeds by flying out from a perch to catch large crepuscular insects, notably beetles, on the wing. The species is also on Hispaniola but not elsewhere in the West Indies, though it is widespread in both arid and humid lowlands in Central and South America. Honduras has this and another congeneric species (Monroe 1968).

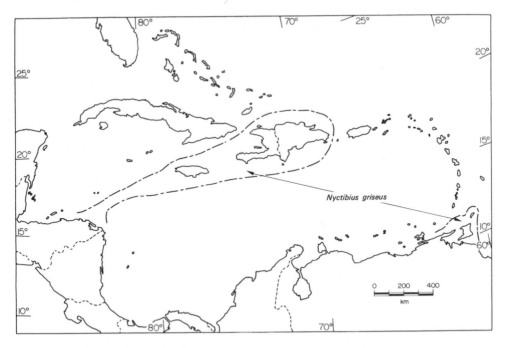

F<small>IG</small>. 36. *West Indian range of the potoo* Nyctibius griseus, *also widespread on the mainland (where range not shown).*

Chordeiles gundlachii (**Common or West Indies Nighthawk**) (**Piramidig**) (Camprimulgidae) (Plate 5, Fig. 37)

This species is a common summer visitor in the dry lowlands from the beaches to an altitude of about 200 m, and we occasionally saw it hunting at middle altitudes up to about 600 m, but do not know whether it breeds there. It usually hunts fairly high in the air, but at times low over open ground. Eisenmann (1962) concluded, from the evidence of skins, songs and sympatric breeding on the southern Florida Keys, that *C.gundlachii* is a separate species from the North American *C.minor*, a view accepted here, though Bond (1971) retained *gundlachii* as a subspecies of *C.minor* and Mayr and Short (1970) reserved judgment.

Siphonorhis americanus **Jamaican Pauraque** (Caprimulgidae)

This extinct species was last collected in 1859. It occurred formerly

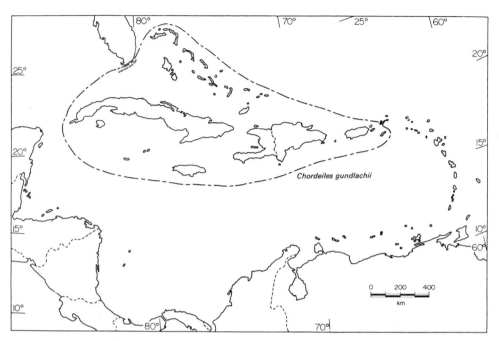

Fɪɢ. 37. *Breeding range of the nighthawk* Chordeiles gundlachii, *a summer visitor to the Greater Antilles and Bahamas (often treated as a subspecies of* Chordeiles minor*).*

in lowland woodland, and its relatively short wings and tail suggest that it hunted among trees, not in the open. Its extinction is credited to the introduction of the mongoose, though its Hispaniolan relative survives. The latter, *S.brewsteri*, lives in arid scrub forest and is much smaller (mean wing length 117 mm *cf.* 138 in *S.americanus*—Ridgway). Peters (1940) treated them as conspecific, but they are so different in size that I have followed Bond and others in regarding them as separate species.

Siphonorhis is an endemic Antillean genus characterised by a strong broad bill, long bare tarsi and a strongly rounded tail. It is generally agreed (*e.g.* Wetmore and Swales 1931) that its nearest mainland relative is the pauraque *Nyctidromus albicollis*, but the latter is so much larger (mean wing length 155 mm), and differs so much in colouring, that it is best treated as belonging to a separate monotypic genus. *N.albicollis*, found in Central and northern South America, occurs in semi-open, especially humid but also arid, forest (Monroe 1968).

Barn Owl
Tyto alba

Jamaican Owl
Pseudoscops grammicus

Common Potoo
Nyctibius griseus

Common Nighthawk
(flying)
Chordeiles gundlachii

Common Nighthawk
(sitting)

PLATE 5. *Night birds : Tytonidae, Strigidae, Nyctibiidae and Caprimulgidae, one-eighth natural size.*

GREATER ANTILLEAN NIGHTJARS

Cuba and Hispaniola have a further species of nightjar, *Caprimulgus cubanensis*, which is endemic to them and which Wetmore and Swales (1931) considered to be close to Chuck-Will's-Widow *C.carolinensis* of the mainland. Hispaniola also has an endemic species of *Siphonorhis*, already mentioned. Puerto Rico has neither of these, but has an endemic species, *Caprimulgus noctitherus*, close to the mainland Whip-poor-Will *C.vociferus* (Wetmore 1962, Mayr and Short 1970; Bond (1971) keeping it as a subspecies of *C.vociferus*). In Honduras, *C.vociferus* breeds in cloud and pine-oak forest (Monroe 1968). Hence the nightjars provide another instance in which the main islands of the Greater Antilles have been colonised by different mainland species, Jamaica by *Nyctidromus*, which has also spread to Hispaniola; Cuba by *C.carolinensis*, which has also spread to Hispaniola; and Puerto Rico by *C.vociferus*. Honduras has five resident species of nightjars including *Nyctidromus albicollis* and *Caprimulgus vociferus*.

SWIFTS APODIDAE

Streptoprocne zonaris **Collared (or Cloud) Swift** (Plate 9, Fig. 38)

S.zonaris breeds, so far as known, solely in the Blue Mountains in the east of Jamaica. Its nest has not been found, but R.W. Smith showed us one area, and we later saw two more, where this Swift descends to inaccessible inland cliffs with waterfalls, such as provide its breeding sites on the mainland. It feeds commonly in the east of Jamaica, but regularly also, though less commonly, in the western hills, where we have seen it throughout the day from dawn onward. Its powerful

FIG. 38. *West Indian range of the swift* Streptoprocne zonaris, *also widespread on the mainland (where range not shown).*

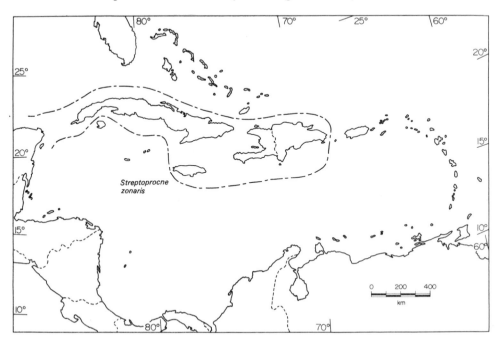

flight enables it to range quickly over the island. In addition, we regularly saw parties ascending with screams high into the air at dusk from Kingston, in just the way that the Common Swift *A.apus* does in England (Lack 1956), and presumably for the same purpose, to spend the night on the wing, since by then it was too dark for them to have found roosting places in the mountains. Those seen at dawn in the west had perhaps spent the night on the wing. *S.zonaris* usually feeds in groups fairly high in the air, usually above the trees of montane forest, but it descends in large numbers to the lowlands when there is rain in the mountains, and also appears regularly over Kingston at at dusk.

In the West Indies, *S.zonaris* is resident solely on Jamaica, Cuba and Hispaniola, but it also breeds in Mexico, Central and northern South America. I earlier suggested that the genus *Streptoprocne* should be merged in *Cypseloides*, because the genera are closely related and the Great Dusky Swift *senex* is intermediate between them (Lack 1956); but this procedure has not found general favour (which means that *senex* has to be in the genus *Aërornis*).

Cypseloides niger **Black Swift** (Plate 9, Fig. 39)

C.niger is a common summer visitor on Jamaica. Bond (1971) recorded one sight record for the winter, but in 1970–71 we saw none between mid-October and early April. It breeds, so far as known, solely in the Blue Mountains, and usually feeds within ten miles of them. Like *S.zonaris*, it feeds in the air in groups over montane forest, and descends to the lowlands when it rains in the mountains, but it differs to an important extent in its feeding. First, it is much smaller (see Table 1). This need not mean that it is adapted to take smaller insects, but perhaps means that it has less rapid flight, so ranges less far, and that it has a greater ability to manoeuvre, so can feed rather closer to vegetation. Secondly, it is rare in western Jamaica. This is perhaps linked with its less rapid flight, and since we did not see night ascents, it may be restricted to the vicinity of its breeding areas in the east at dusk. Thirdly, unlike *S.zonaris* it regularly descends to lowlying coastal areas to feed for the first hour or two after dawn. These three differences might well be sufficient to segregate the two species in summer, but further field observations are needed to prove this. In winter, as already mentioned, *C.niger* departs, presumably because airborne

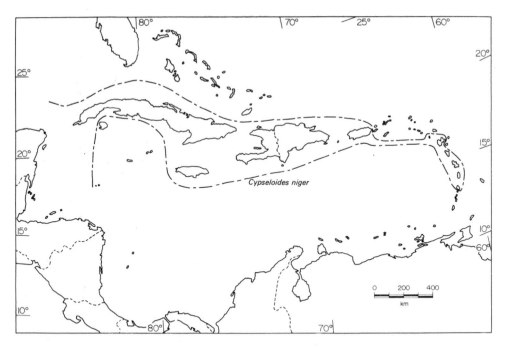

FIG. 39. *West Indian range of the swift* Cypseloides niger, *a summer visitor, also widespread on the mainland (where range not shown).*

insects are so much scarcer and less diverse in winter than in summer that the two species could not be sufficiently segregated to coexist. *C.niger* is widespread as a summer visitor in the mountains of the rest of the West Indies, and also breeds in the mountains in North and Central America.

Tachornis phoenicobia **Antillean Palm Swift** (Plate 9, Fig. 40)

T.phoenicobia breeds solely in the lowlands, among the dead fronds of palms, especially those of the thatch palm *Sabal jamaicensis*, and we also found it using exotic palms in Kingston Botanic Garden. At one time it is said to have bred on buildings in Spanish Town (March 1863–4), which seems unlikely. In the first part of the day, it feeds in the lowlands near its nest or roosts in a palm, but as the day warms up, it often ascends into the hills or the lower parts of the mountains, and is regular in sunny weather up to an altitude of about 1200 m. Although it sometimes feeds fairly high above the ground, it often does

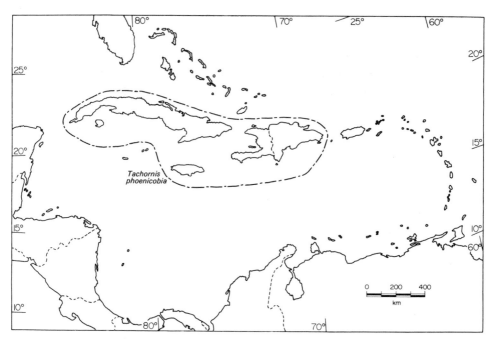

FIG. 40. *Range of the endemic Greater Antillean swift* Tachornis phoeni-cobia.

so low over, or even between, the trees, and sometimes close to the ground on forest tracks. It is much smaller, and much more agile at twisting and turning, than the two large swifts *S.zonaris* and *C.niger*, and in feeding close to the vegetation it taps a different source of insects from them. Whether it also takes smaller insects than they do is not known. In its way of flight and feeding, it recalls the Lesser Antillean Swift *Chaetura martinica*, which is separated in its feeding from *Cypseloides niger* by similar means in the Lesser Antilles.

Tachornis phoenicobia is a monotypic genus endemic to the Greater Antilles, which I formerly merged with the South American palm swifts of the genus *Reinarda* (Lack 1956). Brooke (1970) agreed with this, although he retained as separate genera all the other genera of swifts that I merged. However, having now seen *Reinarda squamata* in the field in Trinidad, I consider it so different that it should be placed in a separate genus, and I greatly doubt whether *Reinarda* is the nearest relation of *Tachornis*. That both of them nest in palms does not necessarily mean close relationship, for the Old World Palm

Swift *Cypsiurus parvus* also nests in palms, and is certainly not a close relative. Perhaps the resemblances in flight and feeding between *Tachornis* and *Chaetura martinica*, already noted, are due to convergence, but on present evidence I would not rule out *Chaetura* being the genus from which *Tachornis* evolved.

GREATER ANTILLEAN SWIFTS

The three species of swifts on Jamaica are also on Cuba and Hispaniola, but only *C.niger* is regular on Puerto Rico, to which both the others have wandered (Kepler 1971, 1972). Honduras has seven breeding species, including *S.zonaris*, which is found in both arid and humid country up to an altitude of 1400 m, and *C.niger*, which is rare but presumed to breed in the mountains (Monroe 1968).

HUMMINGBIRDS TROCHILIDAE

Three species of hummingbirds breed on Jamaica. They show a high degree of endemism, since one species is in a monotypic endemic genus, another is an endemic species of a mainland genus, and the third is a species shared only with Hispaniola and is in a genus confined to the Greater Antilles.

Anthracothorax mango **Jamaican Mango** (Plate 6, Fig. 9, p. 91)

A.mango, endemic to Jamaica, is common in open woodland near the coast, including the beaches and strand woodland, the marsh forest of the Black River, sea level forest at Morant Point, especially on the edges and where partly cleared by man, the partly cleared arid forest on Port Henderson Hill at the edge of the Hellshires, and less commonly in mangroves. It is also regular in small numbers in other types of lowland dry limestone forest, mainly at the edges and in more open parts, and is regular though scarce at natural edges of the midlevel wet forest in both the Cockpit Country and the John Crow Mountains. In cultivation, it is common in the lowlands especially in gardens, and at midlevels especially in banana plantations; but it is rare in the mountains, though we saw it periodically near Hardwar Gap.

In natural habitats in the lowlands it is largely but not entirely separated from the other fairly large hummingbird *Trochilus polytmus*, because it frequents the open parts which *T.polytmus* avoids, and avoids the closed parts; but the two species are not infrequently seen near each other, perhaps more often now than in the past because man has partly cleared so much of the woodland near the coast. In the sea level forest at Morant Point, for instance, *A.mango* is largely in the partly cleared areas, and *T.polytmus* in the thicker parts. In cultivated habitats in the lowlands, especially in gardens with many flowers, they are often seen together, but this is an artificial situation.

The main flowers visited for nectar by *A.mango* are summarised in Table 43, and there is a full list in Appendix 7. Those of cacti predominate, especially of the prickly-pear *Opuntia spinosissima*, which is much scarcer than the tall dildo-cactus *Stenocereus hystrix* in the same areas. *A.mango* is the only Jamaican hummingbird to feed to any extent on cactus flowers, but this might be because it is the only one that is common in open arid lowlying areas where cacti are abundant. The other flowers recorded were also taken by other species (see Appendix 7).

Out of 80 feeding records, 20 were of small insects, a higher proportion than we recorded for the other two species of hummingbirds, but this is at least partly because it hunts for insects in open places where it is readily seen, whereas the other two usually hunt for insects under cover. It takes most insects when hovering, and our records included ten in the air, four entangled in cobwebs, two off leaves, one off a bough and one off a vertical bank. Twice, also, we saw a perched bird extend its tongue to take an insect off vegetation. We saw one insert its beak into a fruit of the cactus *Stenocereus hystrix* previously opened by some other bird. Popular introduced flowers include agave, banana, coffee, *Calliandra, Erythrina, Leonotis nepetifolia, Spathodea companulata* and *Syzygium jambos*, on all of which we also saw *Trochilus polytmus*.

This endemic Jamaican species belongs to the mainland genus *Anthracothorax*. It is larger and much darker than its congeners on Hispaniola and Puerto Rico, and also than the sole Central American species, the Green-breasted Mango *A.prevostii*, which is here tentatively assumed to be its nearest mainland relative.

Trochilus polytmus **Streamertail (Doctor Bird)** (Plate 6, Fig. 10. p. 93)

T.polytmus, endemic to Jamaica, is said to be called the 'Doctor' because the male's long tail streamers recall the tail-coats formerly worn by doctors. This 'gem of Jamaican ornithology' (Gosse 1847) is very scarce in mangroves, strand woodland and the arid forest of the Hellshires and Portland Ridge, but is fairly common in the thicker woods near sealevel, notably the marsh forest at Morant Point. It is fairly common in the richer woods (riverine and secondary) of the southern lowland hills, and is abundant in midlevel and montane forest, where it was the commonest bird in our counts. In forest, we usually saw it from the edges, because on narrow trails it was much

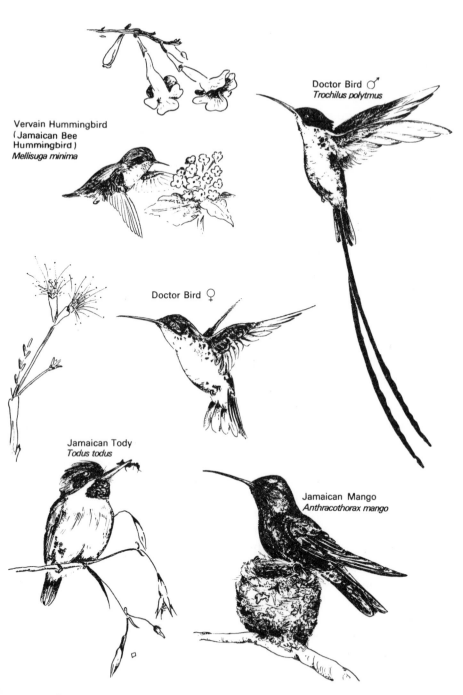

Vervain Hummingbird
(Jamaican Bee
Hummingbird)
Mellisuga minima

Doctor Bird ♂
Trochilus polytmus

Doctor Bird ♀

Jamaican Tody
Todus todus

Jamaican Mango
Anthracothorax mango

PLATE 6. *Hummingbirds Trochilidae and tody Todidae, half natural size.*

more often heard than seen in the canopy above us. It is abundant in wooded cultivation at all altitudes, and was second in numbers only to the Bananaquit *Coereba flaveola* in our counts in highland cultivation.

Nectar is taken from a huge variety of flowers, indeed it may be one of the main pollinators of wild flowers on Jamaica. It visits them at all heights from about 5 cm to over 20 m above the ground. The commonest species taken are set out in Table 43 and a full list of identified species is in Appendix 7, but we noted many individuals feeding from flowers of forest trees which we could not collect to identify. It does not overlap to any important extent with *A.mango* in the species of flowers taken, but this is probably due, at least largely, to their difference in habitat already noted, though the popularity of *Opuntia* flowers with *A.mango* and their avoidance by *T.polytmus* may be related to the plant species concerned. The small *Mellisuga minima* visits the small, but not the large, flowers visited by *T.polytmus*. As shown in Appendix 7, nearly all the larger flowers visited by *T.polytmus* are also visited by at least one of the other two nectar-feeders, the Bananaquit *Coereba flaveola* and Orangequit *Euneornis campestris*, so it is not segregated from other species by its selection of wild flowers. Its preference for the montane *Besleria lutea* may be noted.

Apart from the native *Besleria lutea*, the plants on which we saw *T.polytmus* feeding most often were introduced species, notably the trees of *Erythrina*, *Eucalyptus*, *Pittosporum undulatum* and *Spathodea campanulata*; also *Calliandra*, *Hedychium coronarium*, *Hibiscus*, *Rubus* spp. and *Syzygium jambos*. The *Erythrina* and *Spathodea* trees attract especially males, together with large numbers of Bananaquits *Coereba flaveola*.

Some of the introduced garden flowers have too long corolla tubes for the beak of *T.polytmus*, but the latter takes nectar from them when *C.flaveola* has already pierced the base of the flower for the same purpose. *T.polytmus* searches carefully for the holes pierced in this way. On one occasion on Guava Ridge, for instance, there was a steep bank with many flowers of the red hibiscus *Malvaviscus arboreus* and, in much greater abundance, the larger and more prominent purple flowers of the introduced *Saritaea magnifica*. A male *T.polytmus* repeatedly fed from the hibiscus, then from one of the *Saritaea*, after which it searched repeatedly among the latter, but tried to feed from only a few of them, always inserting its beak at the base, and did not touch most of them. Inspection showed that a small proportion of these flowers had been pierced at the base by *C.flaveola*, and it was presumably only from these

TABLE 43. *Wild flowers most frequently visited by the hummingbirds*

| Type of flower | Number of visits (each individual recorded only once) | | |
	Anthracothorax mango	Trochilus polytmus	Mellisuga minima
Midlevel bromeliads			
(*Hohenbergia* spp.)	2	13	1
Montane bromeliads	—	9	2
Cacti	23	1	—
Bauhinia divaricata	—	7	1
melastomes	—	21	1
Vaccinium meridionale	—	9	2
Urechites lutea	—	11	—
Asclepias curassavica	—	8	1
Cordia spp.	3	6	1
Lantana camara	—	8	8
Tabebuia riparia	3	—	—
Tecoma stans	—	12	—
Besleria lutea	—	29	—
Columnea hirsuta	—	5	—
Goldfussia glomerata	—	8	—
Psychotria spp.	—	12	—
Feeds on identified wild flowers	34	214	27
Feeds on insects	20	56	4

Notes (i) The totals for identified flowers are larger than the numbers in the tables, as flowers uncommonly visited are not listed. The totals for all wild flowers are larger still, as many were not identified. For full lists, see Appendix 7 where the species taken by the other two nectar-eaters, the Bananaquit *Coereba flaveola* and Orangequit *Euneornis campestris* are also shown.
(ii) Feeds on introduced species, including many garden flowers and exotic trees, are excluded. Hummingbirds are more numerous there than on wild flowers.
(iii) The number of feeds on insects is badly underestimated for both *Trochilus polytmus* and *Mellisuga minima*.

that *T.polytmus* fed, though we could not ascertain this, as those it actually fed on were inaccessible. In large garden flowers elsewhere, however, we could check that *T.polytmus* fed from these individuals which *C.flaveola* had already pierced, and not on intact ones. This method of feeding does not, of course· pollinate the flowers. We saw it used only on introduced species with large flowers.

We twice saw *T.polytmus* insert its beak into holes in eucalyptus trunks made by the Yellow-bellied Sapsucker *Sphyrapicus varius*, and twice it inserted its beak into fruits of *Pithecellobium unguis-cati* opened by some other bird. It often hovers to feed on small insects, especially in the air, but also off leaves, branches or cobwebs. We greatly under-estimated the proportion of feeds on insects in our records, because it usually feeds in this way inconspicuously under the canopy. It takes insects at any height from 3 cm to at least 20 m, usually above 1 m above the ground. Occasionally, it flies out from the forest to take an insect in the air at the edge, or above a trail. We saw more females than males taking insects, but did not measure this point.

Trochilus polytmus is a Jamaican endemic genus and species. It is replaced on Cuba and Hispaniola by species in the mainland genus *Chlorostilbon*, but though it shows some resemblances to the latter, it is highly distinctive, justifying its generic separation, and I doubt if it is closely related.

Mellisuga minima **Vervain Hummingbird (Jamaican Bee Hummingbird)** (Plate 6, Fig. 8, p. 90)

M.minima is the smallest bird in the world except for its Cuban congener. It is present in every type of forest, and in wooded cultivation, from sea level to the top of Blue Mountain. It greatly prefers open to closed forest, and we found it the commonest species of hummingbird both in the sealevel forest at Morant Point and, at the other extreme in altitude, in the sclerophyll forest on exposed slopes of the Blue Mountains. It is the least uncommon species in the arid forest of the Hellshires and Portland Ridge, but here all hummingbirds are scarce. Relatively few *M.minima* were seen on our counts in tall closed forest at midlevels or in the mountains, but this is partly because it is often in the tops of the trees, where it is so small that it is hard to see except when it has been heard in song.

It regularly feeds from the smaller species of flowers visited by *A.mango* and *T.polytmus* (see Table 43 and Appendix 7), so is not separated from them by its nectar diet, though they visit many larger flowers which it does not. In gardens, it feeds mainly on flowers with a small corolla, including two species hardly ever visited by *T.polytmus*, namely *Cuphea ignea* and *Holmskioldia sanguinea*.

It commonly feeds on insects when hovering in flight, especially seeking them under the canopy, and our few records on counts are a gross under-estimate. For instance, we often saw it feeding on insects during our watches at nests, which were not included in the feeding counts. Since it is the second smallest bird in the world, and its Cuban relative has not been studied, it may be added that three adults netted by A. W. Diamond weighed respectively 2.1, 2.1 and 2.2 grams, that our weights for two newly laid eggs in one clutch were 0.365 and 0.375 g (17 per cent of the body-weight) and that two young on the day that each hatched, but after each had had at least one meal, weighed respectively 0.325 and 0.320 g. Despite the small size of the bird, incubation and nestling periods are relatively long, as in other hummingbirds, incubation of the second egg at three different nests taking 16 or 17 days, and the nestling periods of 7 young averaging 21 days (19–22 days) (*cf.* Lack 1968 for other species).

M.minima also occurs on Hispaniola, and there is one other species in the genus the smaller *M.helenae*, on Cuba. Peters put the latter in the mainland genus *Calypte*, but Bond removed it to *Mellisuga*, adding that *Mellisuga* is close to *Calypte*, and might be derived from it.

As already noted, the three Jamaican hummingbirds are not separated from each other by the wild flowers which they visit. *M.minima* is so much smaller than the other two species that it may well take smaller insects than they do, though we have no evidence on this point. The other two are separated primarily by habitat, as already noted. The species of hummingbird on the other islands of the West Indies have been reviewed in Chapter 6. Honduras has 37 species (Monroe 1968), over twelve times as many as Jamaica.

TODIES TODIDAE

Todus todus **Jamaican Tody** (**Robin Redbreast**) (Plate 6, Fig. 41)

This tiny bird, with its emerald upper parts and ruby gorget and beak, deserves the name 'gem' as much as the hummingbird *T.polytmus*. *T.todus* is abundant in all types of natural forest, from mangroves and arid lowland woods to montane forest, and it was the commonest species on our counts in the rich secondary woodland above the Ferry River. It is scarce in wooded cultivation, however, especially in the lowlands. When seeking for food, it perches on a twig well below the

FIG. 41. *Range of the endemic Greater Antillean genus* Todus. *Note two species on Hispaniola.*

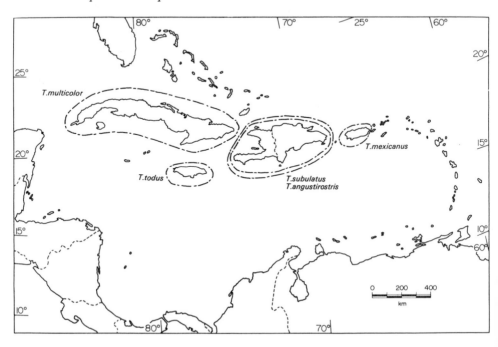

286

canopy, usually between 1 and 5 metres, but sometimes up to 15 metres, from the ground, with beak pointed upward, and periodically flies out to take a relatively large insect, usually from the underside of a leaf, occasionally from the upper side, and occasionally from the air. It then flies back to a different perch.

The family Todidae, endemic to the Greater Antilles, is considered close to the motmots Momotidae, a tropical North American family (Mayr 1948). The single genus, *Todus*, has five species, one on each of Jamaica, Cuba and Puerto Rico and two on Hispaniola. In a full study of these species, A. Kepler (1972) suggested that the two on Hispaniola originated there at a time when it consisted of two islands. On Hispaniola she found the Broad-billed Tody *T.subulatus* from sea level up to about 1700 m, including in arid woodland, and the Narrow-billed Tody *T.angustirostris* above 1700 m, mainly in wet montane forest, but with extensive overlap in altitude in the southwest of the Dominican Republic, where they are segregated from each other by many aspects of feeding. They also show character displacement in beak-width, which averages 4·3 to 4·4 mm in the species on Jamaica, Cuba and Puerto Rico, but 5·4 mm in *T.subulatus* and only 3·9 mm in *T.angustirostris*.

WOODPECKERS PICIDAE

Centurus radiolatus **Jamaican Woodpecker** (Plate 14, Fig.14, p. 104)

C.radiolatus, an endemic, is the only woodpecker resident on Jamaica. It is present in all types of woodland with mature trees, from mangroves and lowland arid forest to high montane forest, probably being commonest at midlevels, as around Worthy Park. It is absent where mature trees have been removed, as in much of the lowland ruinate woodland, but is present in wooded cultivation where there are larger trees. It feeds mainly by excavating for insects in trunks, branches, large twigs, and even the aerial roots of mangroves, from a few centimetres above the ground to the tops of tall trees. We also saw it eating a small number of wild fruits, listed in Appendix 6.

I have here followed Selander and Giller (1963), not Peters or Goodwin (1968), in keeping the genus *Centurus* separate from *Melanerpes*, the species of *Centurus* being separated by their black and white barring on the upper parts from those of the unbarred *Melanerpes* (*sens. strict.*).

As shown by Selander and Giller (1963), Jamaican *C.radiolatus*, with its narrow barring, is closest to the Golden-fronted Woodpecker *C.aurifrons*, which is widespread in Central America and Mexico and just reaches the United States. In Honduras, it occurs in semi-open situations in the arid lowlands and in monsoon forest (Monroe 1968). It is replaced in most of southeastern United State, by the closely related Red-bellied Woodpecker *C.carolinus*, which they considered to be the nearest mainland relative of the woodpecker *C.superciliaris* found on Cuba, Grand Cayman and some of the Bahamas; these two species have broader bars. Hence, while the Cuban and Jamaican species may be regarded as members of the same superspecies, they appear to be derived from different mainland species, which is reasonable in view of the ranges on the mainland of the species concerned. Hispaniola has yet another different species in this group, with similar patterning, but with black bars on a yellow instead of a white background and also a red rump. Further, the male has a much longer beak than the female and feeds differently. Formerly in a separate genus *Chryserpes*, Selander and Giller (1963) later merged it in *Centurus*, and Goodwin (1968) similarly merged it in *Melanerpes*. Its mainland ancestor is not known.

Puerto Rico has an endemic species in the closely related genus *Melanerpes*, *M.portoricensis*, which Bond thought close to the Redheaded Woodpecker *M.erythrocephalus* of the eastern and central United States; but it seems equally as like the Acorn Woodpecker *M.formicivorus*, which occurs in western United States, part of Mexico, and much of Central America, mainly in montane pine oak forest (Monroe 1968). The Puerto Rico bird is darker than these mainland species, and there is a similar but even darker species, clearly derived from it, on Guadeloupe.

Jamaica and Puerto Rico each have only one species of woodpecker. Hispaniola has two, the second being an unusually large piculet in an endemic genus. Grand Cayman, though small and lowlying, likewise has two species of woodpeckers, the Cuban *C.superciliaris* and the North American Yellow-shafted Flicker *Colaptes auratus*, which is also on Cuba. Cuba has three further species, another endemic flicker (Short 1965), the large North American Ivory-billed Woodpecker *Campephilus principalis*, and a medium sized endemic genus and species *Xiphidiopicus percussus*, so distinctive that its mainland ancestor is not certain. A green woodpecker, presumably this last species, has been reported from Jamaica in winter (see p.77).

COTINGAS COTINGIDAE

Platypsaris niger **Jamaican Becard** (**Mountain Judy,** the male; and **Mountain Dick,** the female) (Plate 8)

The sexes are reversed in the vernacular names, perhaps because the brown female, with a rufous head, looks brighter than the black male, and both sexes sing. *P.niger* is endemic and rather scarce. It is seen most often at the edges and in open parts of tall midlevel forest, and is also regular in closed montane forest, mainly in the lower parts of the mountains, and in wooded cultivation at midlevels where there are groups of tall trees. It hangs its huge nest from the end branch of a tall tree, usually in the open or above the canopy. We did not see it in the southern lowlands in summer, but saw it occasionally in winter in the secondary woodland above the Ferry River. It hunts by moving slowly through the twigs and branches below the canopy, usually between 8 and 10 m above the ground, but we have records of it between 1 and 20 m up. It perches, looks around, and eventually flies to another perch a few metres further on. We rarely saw it take food, presumably because it is searching for large but scarce insects. Five times we saw it fly a short way from its perch to take an insect, sometimes by hovering, twice taking a large caterpillar off a leaf. Once it took an insect from a leaf when perched, and three times it took fruit (unidentified).

This endemic Jamaican species is the sole representative in the West Indies of the primarily South American family Contingidae, but the genus *Platypsaris* extends further north than any other in the family, one species just reaching the United States. *Platypsaris* consists of five allopatric species, which show a mosaic distribution of their main colour patterns, notably in whether or not they have dark plumage, a reddish throat in the male, or a rufous head in the female. *P.niger* is larger and darker than the four mainland species, and cannot be related more closely to one of them than to any other, but all form one superspecies. It is convenient to retain the genus *Platypsaris* and not, as sometimes proposed, to merge it with the rather dissimilar group of species of *Pachyrhamphus* (*sens.strict.*) (D. W. Snow, pers.comm.). The main Central American species is the Rose-throated Becard *Platypsaris aglaiae*, which in Honduras lives in lowland arid and monsoon forest (Monroe 1968), so its Jamaican relative has a broader habitat.

D. W. Snow (pers.comm.) collected all published feeding records for the species of *Platypsaris*. Of 17 analysed stomach contents, 7 included only insects, 4 insects and fruit, and 6 only fruit, but the last were from one source, doubtless birds collected at one time, whereas the 7 containing only insects were from 5 different sources. Hence the main food appears to be insects, supplemented by fruit. In feeding on insects, it is described as peering about, then darting out to pick an insect off a leaf or twig, or occasionally in the air. These findings fit with the little we saw of the feeding of the Jamaican species.

TYRANT FLYCATCHERS TYRANNIDAE

Tyrant flycatchers are, next to pigeons, the family of land birds with most breeding species in Jamaica, and the 8 species comprise nearly one quarter of the breeding passerines. Their feeding methods are summarised in Table 44.

Tyrannus dominicensis **Grey Kingbird** (**Petchary**) (Plate 7, Fig. 42)

T.dominicensis is a summer visitor to Jamaica arriving at the end of

Fig. 42. *West Indian breeding range of the kingbird* Tyrannus dominicensis, *a summer visitor in the north of its range. Breeding range in northern South America (Venezuela) not shown.*

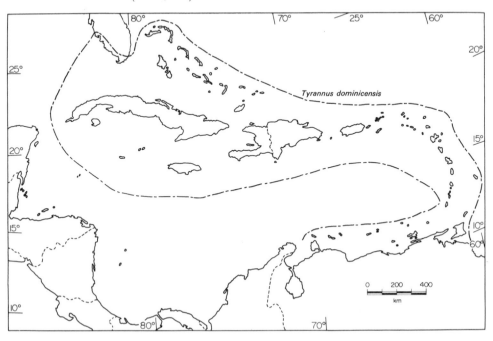

PLATE 7. *Tyrant flycatchers Tyrannidae, one-quarter natural size.*

March and leaving in early October. Its natural habitat, where it is common, is lowlying open woodland, notably the marsh forest alongside the Black River and the sea-level forest at Morant Point, where it is found chiefly near cleared areas. It is scarce in open parts of the arid Hellshires and rare by the sea, but locally a few are present in mangroves. We did not see any in the more or less closed forest on the lowland hills, at midlevels or in the mountains. It is abundant in open wooded cultivation throughout the lowlands, and is widespread, but much less numerous, in wooded cultivation at midlevels and in the mountains.

T.dominicensis typically hunts from a perch between 6 and 15 m above the ground and most commonly about 10 m up, in an isolated tree, from which it flies out horizontally, often for 30 m or more, to take large insects in the air. Twice we saw one fly out some 30 m to take a large insect off the surface of water into which it had fallen, once on the sea and once on a lagoon, and once we saw one take an insect off vegetation 0·3 m above the ground; but almost always it catches its prey in mid-air, and it is prepared to fly a long way for it. This habit largely separates it in its feeding from the related *T.caudifasciatus*, which feeds mainly by flying down from a perch to take insects off vegetation or the ground. Correlated with this difference, A.W. Diamond pointed out to me that the primaries of *T.dominicensis*, but not those of *T.caudifasciatus*, are heavily emarginated and notched, presumably an anti-stalling adaptation to increase its power of manoeuvre in the air when close to its prey.

T.dominicensis ranges from the extreme south of the United States throughout the West Indies to part of northern South America. In the eastern and southern West Indies, it is resident throughout the year. In Florida, it is restricted to coastal woodland, so has a narrower habitat than on Jamaica. Our short visit to Dominica suggested that there, in the absence of *T.caudifasciatus*, it might take a higher proportion of its prey off vegetation or the ground than on Jamaica, but this needs checking. We also saw it take insects off the surface of rivers. *T.dominicensis* belongs to the subgroup of grey kingbirds, which includes two other West Indian species (discussed next), and the Eastern Kingbird *T.tyrannus* of North America (Smith 1966).

TABLE 44.   *Differences in feeding of Jamaican Tyrannidae*

Species	Mean length of culmen (in mm)	Number of observed feeds	Percentage of observed feeds					
			on insects by sallying				on insects	
			in air	off leaf	off ground vegation	off water	reached from perch	on fruit
Tyrannus dominicensis	26	small	c.95	×	—	×	—	—
Tyrannus caudifasciatus	25	85	19	34	33	—	4	11
Myiarchus stolidus	19	131	26	60	1	—	4	9
Myiarchus barbirostris	16	146	35	58	5	—	1	2
Myiarchus validus	22	34	9	44	3	—	—	44
Contopus caribaeus	13	161	96	4	—	—	—	—
Elaenia fallax	10	98	2	65	—	—	6	27
Myiopagis cotta	10	33	15	75	—	—	7	4

Note   Culmen measurements from Ridgway. The proportion of feeds on fruits recorded for *M.validus* is misleadingly high, as it is conspicuous when feeding on fruits, inconspicuous when feeding on insects.

×   less than 0.5%

—   (not recorded).

Tyrannus caudifasciatus **Loggerhead Kingbird (Loggerhead)** (Plate 7, Fig. 43)

T.caudifasciatus, which is a little smaller than *T.dominicensis,* is resident throughout the year. It differs from *T.dominicensis* partly in habitat, since the latter hunts in extremely open woodland from an isolated tree, whereas *T.caudifasciatus* is common in the more open parts of typical lowland and midlevel forest and usually hunts from a tree beside an opening, and at times occurs in closed woodland, perching on the top of the canopy. It is very scarce in montane forest, occurring mainly at the edges but occasionally in the canopy. It is widespread in wooded cultivation at all heights, but prefers thicker and less open parts than *T.dominicensis.*

   When hunting, it may perch at any height from 0.3 to 18 m above the ground, half of our records being between 3 and 6 m up. The main prey consists of large insects, and we occasionally saw one take a lizard and once a centipede. As can be seen from Table 44, it rarely takes an insect from the air. When it does so, it does not usually fly far from

FIG. 43. *Range of the kingbird* Tyrannus caudifasciatus.

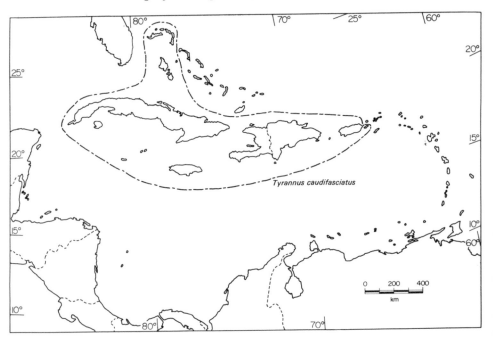

its perch, and almost all our records of this type occurred between January and March, before *T.dominicensis* had arrived. We found it taking insects off leaves especially between October and December, often within 1 m of the ground, but as often about 6 m up, sometimes by hovering, sometimes by snatching in passing flight and sometimes by alighting and then reaching out from its perch. It takes a little fruit (see Appendix 6), by hovering, snatching in passing flight, or perching and reaching.

T.caudifasciatus is confined to the Greater Antilles and Bahamas. A third and larger grey kingbird, *T.cubensis*, is found in pine forest in Cuba and a few of the Bahamas. The relationships of these three species to each other and to *T.tyrannus* are not clear.

Myiarchus stolidus **Stolid Flycatcher** (Plate 8, Fig. 44)

There are three species of crested flycatchers in the genus *Myiarchus*

FIG. 44. *Range of the flycatcher* Myiarchus stolidus *species or superspecies, and also of* M.nugator, *which replaces it on St Vincent and Grenada and is in a different superspecies.*

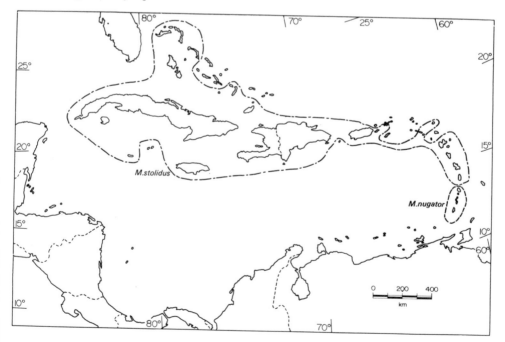

on Jamaica, of which *M.stolidus* is the middle-sized one. It is widespread in all types of lowland forest, notably the arid Hellshires and Portland Ridge, and is also found in ruinate woodland and mangroves. It occurs all through the lowland forests, not mainly at the edges, like *T.caudifasciatus*, but in wet midlevel forest it is very scarce and is there seen almost entirely at the edges. It is absent from the mountains, and also from wooded cultivation at all altitudes.

M.stolidus hunts from an inconspicuous perch in any part of a tree within the forest, from a few cms to 13 m above the ground, half our records being between 3 and 9 m up. Its most usual method is to fly a short way from its perch to take an insect off a leaf or twig, usually by snatching it in passing flight or by hovering beside it. It takes some insects from the air, but usually flies only a short way to do so, sometimes in the open, but often so close to leaves that it is hard to know whether it is taking from the leaves or in the air nearby. Exceptionally one bird took the numerous mosquitoes settled on a film of water over wet mud in a mangrove swamp in the early morning. Some fruit is eaten, mainly *Bursera simaruba* (See Appendix 6).

According to Lanyon (1967), *M.stolidus* is confined to Jamaica and Hispaniola, with three related species in the same superspecies, one on Cuba, the Bahamas and Grand Cayman, the second on Puerto Rico and the Virgin Islands, and the third on the Lesser Antilles south to St Lucia; but Bond (1971), who is followed here, treated them as subspecies of *M.stolidus*. The nearest mainland relative of *M.stolidus* is not known, and though Lanyon postulated that it arrived from Central America first on Jamaica and spread out from there, I do not see why it should not have started on one of the other islands. There is much subspecific variation in size in the Lesser Antilles, where the form on St Lucia is about as large as the largest Jamaican species *M.validus* and feeds rather similarly to it (Diamond 1973).

Myiarchus barbirostris **Dusky-capped Flycatcher (Little Tom Fool)** (Plate 8)

Bond's English name of Dusky-capped Flycatcher will have to be changed, as this is used for the related Central American species *M.tuberculifer* (Eisenmann 1955), from which this endemic Jamaican bird is now separated. *M.barbirostris* is smaller than *M.stolidus* in overall size and length of beak, but has as wide a beak. In the lowlands,

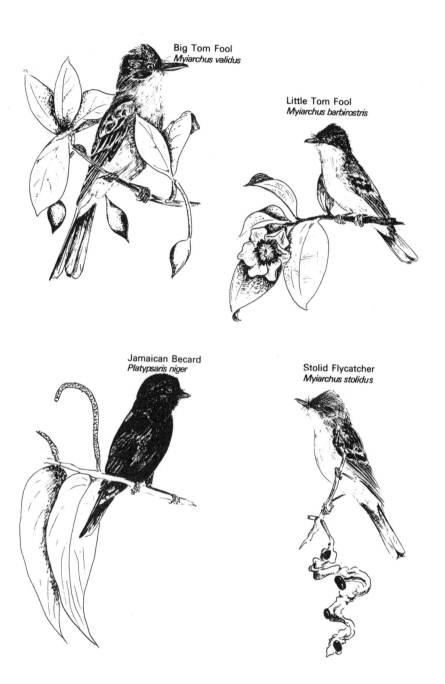

Big Tom Fool
Myiarchus validus

Little Tom Fool
Myiarchus barbirostris

Jamaican Becard
Platypsaris niger

Stolid Flycatcher
Myiarchus stolidus

PLATE 8. *Tyrant flycatchers Tyrannidae and becard Cotingidae, one-quarter natural size.*

it breeds in mangroves, the denser parts of sealevel forest, and especially the secondary woods of the lowland hills, as above the Ferry River, but it is virtually absent from the arid forest of the Hellshires and Portland Ridge, and from ruinate lowland woodland, and hence from the main habitat of *M.stolidus*. It breeds regularly in midlevel forest, not just at the edges like *M.stolidus*, but is somewhat less common there than in the secondary woodland of the lowland forest. It is regular but scarce in montane forest, usually where it is fairly open. Its distribution is much the same in winter, but it is scarcer in sealevel forest and very scarce in montane forest. It is absent from wooded cultivation and gardens.

As summarised in Table 44, *M.barbirostris* usually flies from a perch to take insects off vegetation, but it takes them rather more often from the air than *M.stolidus*, and its relatively broad beak also suggests that it may be more of an aerial flycatcher. Compared with *M.stolidus*, it not infrequently takes two or three insects, not just one, in the course of a single short flight, and it finds an insect more frequently, both points suggesting that, in general, it takes smaller and more plentiful insects. It usually perches between 3 and 9 m above the ground, but we saw it between 1 and 18 m up. From *M.stolidus* it is largely but not entirely separated by habitat, and perhaps also by taking smaller insects.

M.barbirostris is an endemic Jamaican species close to the Central American *M.tuberculifer*, which in Honduras occurs mainly in open lowland forest, but ranges up to montane pine-oak (Monroe 1968). There is no similar species elsewhere in the West Indies.

Myiarchus validus **Rufous-tailed Flycatcher** (**Big Tom Fool**) (Plate 8)

M.validus, another endemic species, is larger than the two other Jamaican species of *Myiarchus*, being almost as large as *T.caudifasciatus*. A few breed in the arid lowland forest of the Hellshires and Portland Ridge, including at its edge in mangroves (where we found nests of all three species of *Myiarchus* within a few metres of each other). It is rather commoner in the secondary woodland above the Ferry River, also along the river margin itself, and we also saw it in the sealevel forest at Negril, but not otherwise in the lowlands. It is the commonest species of *Myiarchus* in midlevel forest and in the tall riverine forest of Fern Gully, in the north, and is regular, but uncommon, in montane forest. In wooded cultivation, it is absent from the lowlands, but regular at both midlevels and in the mountains.

As shown in Table 44, *M.validus* feeds in the same type of way as the other two species of *Myiarchus*, by flying out from a perch, but compared with them it takes a much higher proportion of its prey off leaves or twigs, and we only once saw one make a series of aerial sallies. Further, it finds a food item on leaves or twigs much less often than the other two species, which suggests that it hunts for larger and scarcer prey. Indeed we often watched one for several minutes or longer without it once feeding. Nearly always, *M.validus* perches inconspicuously in thick vegetation in a dim light well below the closed canopy, and it then works steadily through, with periodic changes of perch. This separates it from the similar-sized kingbird *T.caudifasciatus*, which as already noted perches on the wood-edge and takes nearly all of its prey in the open. *M.validus* usually takes insects, but one brought a small lizard to the nest. It eats much more fruit than the other species of *Myiarchus*, taking it from a perch or by hovering, but the high proportion of records in Table 44 is misleading, as it eats fruits conspicuously, but insects inconspicuously. It especially takes *Bursera simaruba*.

M.validus is another Jamaican endemic species and no other West Indian bird is comparable with it, save perhaps the unusually large subspecies of *M.stolidus* on St Lucia (Diamond 1973).

Contopus caribaeus **Greater Antillean Pewee** (Plate 7, Fig. 45)

C.caribaeus breeds especially in midlevel forest and is regular, but less common, in montane forest. In addition, one or two pairs remained for the summer in the secondary woodland of the lowland hills above the Ferry River, but we saw no others in the lowlands at this season. In winter, it is regular in some lowland woods, notably above the Ferry River, and we even saw one in mangroves, so there is a small seasonal movement in altitude; but a few remain in montane forest for the winter.

C.caribaeus catches almost all its food in the air, and its prey consists of very small insects. It usually perches beside an opening below the canopy, in closed, and hence rather dark, forest, anywhere from close to the ground up to 18 m up. Three-quarters of our records were at between 2 and 9 m up, but birds perched high up tend to be overlooked, so probably more fed higher up than our records suggest. Occasionally

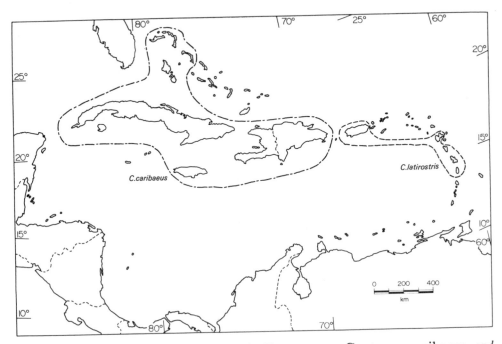

Fig. 45. *Ranges of the two Antillean pewees,* Contopus caribaeus *and* C.latirostris.

it uses a more open perch at the forest edge. Usually it makes an outward flight of only a few metres, and moves on to a different perch.
Rarely it takes an insect from a leaf, but not from the ground, though
it sometimes takes them a few cms up. Two birds followed us along
forest trails for the insects that we disturbed, and caught them in the air
close to our ankles.

The only possible competitor of *C.caribaeus* in Jamaica is *M.barbiros-
tris,* which also catches small insects on the wing, but chiefly in more
open places than *C.caribaeus,* for instance above a road, and as already
noted it takes most of its food off leaves. The Eastern Pewee *Contopus
virens,* of which we saw four transients in Jamaica, feeds rather differently, flying almost vertically upwards, not out horizontally, and it then
usually returns to the same perch.

C.caribaeus is found on Jamaica, Cuba, some of the Bahamas and
Hispaniola, but is replaced on Puerto Rico and some of the Lesser
Antilles south to St Lucia by the similar *C.latirostris.* The Central and
South American Tropical Pewee *C.cinereus,* which I saw in Trinidad,

looks very similar and is presumed here to be their nearest mainland relative. When the genus *Contopus* was subdivided, all three were at one time put in the genus *Blacicus* (Oberholser 1899).

Elaenia fallax **Greater Antillean Elaenia** (Plate 7, Fig. 46)

E.fallax is mainly a summer visitor to Jamaica, arriving near the end of April, and thereafter it is one of the commonest species in montane forest. It also breeds sparsely in the very wet limestone forest high up in the John Crow Mountains, and we saw an extremely small number elsewhere in wet limestone forest. In winter nearly all of them depart, but we saw a few in montane and midlevel forest, in the Blue Mountains, Cinchona Gardens, Guava Ridge, the John Crow Mountains, the Cockpit Country and Worthy Park.

Like the species of *Myiarchus*, which are much larger, *E.fallax* obtains nearly all its insect food by flying out from a perch to take it off a leaf or twig. Most of our recorded feeds were at between 3 and 9 m

FIG. 46. *Breeding range of the flycatcher* Elaenia fallax (*main winter range not known*).

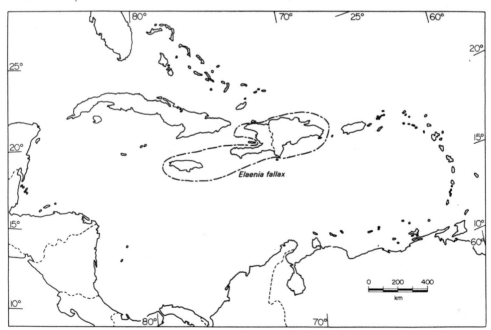

above the ground, some below 1 m up, but it also feeds high in the canopy in closed forest, where it is inconspicuous, so the proportion of high records in Table 44 is misleadingly small. Occasionally a bird reaches for an insect from its perch, and one took one from the air. The rest of its diet consists of small fruits, of which it takes a higher proportion than any other Jamaican flycatcher. The recorded species are set out in Appendix 6, those of the myrtle *Myrica cerifera* being the favourite, which we otherwise saw taken by only one other species. Fruits are sometimes taken by the bird when perched, but more often by hovering at the outside of the tree, by which means it obtains fruits at the end of small twigs, out of reach of the many frugivorous species which take fruits only from a perch. The solitaire *Myadestes genibarbis* also takes many fruits by hovering, but it hovers chiefly inside a rather open tree, and takes mainly melastomes, not *Myrica*.

E.fallax is a species confined for breeding to Jamaica and Hispaniola, the Jamaican subspecies being much the larger of the two. Where most of them spend the winter is not known, but presumably in South America. *E.fallax* has no obvious close relatives, and in particular it does not seem close to the Caribbean Elaenia *E.martinica*, which occurs in the Lesser Antilles and various other islands. Although it replaces *E.martinica* geographically (See Fig 24, p. 152), the two species are not in potential competition, as *E.fallax* breeds solely in the mountains and *E.martinica* mainly in the arid lowlands.

Myiopagis cotta **Yellow-crowned Elaenia** (Plate 7)

M.cotta is a widespread but scarce endemic but it is so inconspicuous that it might be more common than our counts suggest. It is commonest in wet midlevel forest, but is also regular in lowland arid forest, including the most arid parts of the Hellshires, and is present but scarce in montane forest, chiefly in the lower parts.

It feeds on insects in a similar manner to *E.fallax*, by flying out from a perch and taking them in flight from off leaves or twigs, and it also takes a few by reaching from its perch, or in the air. In contrast to *E.fallax*, however, it almost never eats fruits (see Table 44). About half our feeding records were at between 4.5 and 7.5 m above the ground, with almost as many above as below these limits; it feeds close to the ground much less often than *E.fallax*. From the latter it is separated mainly by habitat, but the two species coexist in the higher parts of midlevel and the lower parts of montane forest. We do not know enough to say whether they differ to an important extent in their insect diet. In winter, *E.fallax* is too scarce to be a potential competitor of *M.cotta*.

M.cotta, an endemic Jamaican species, is closely related to the Greenish Elaenia *Myiopagis viridicata* of Central America, with which it has sometimes been treated as conspecific. No species of *Myiopagis* occurs elsewhere in the West Indies.

DISCUSSION OF TYRANNIDAE

Feeding observations carried out for ten months in the course of a general survey of Jamaican forest birds are not enough on which to base firm conclusions. Nevertheless, we saw enough to show that at least most of the eight Jamaican species of tyrant flycatchers are separated from each other ecologically, particularly if a big difference in size is accepted as a segregating factor, without a test that it is linked with size of prey. The three large species are separated from each other by where they take their prey, *T.dominicensis* in the air in open country with trees, *T.caudifasciatus* mainly off the ground or off leaves at the forest edge, and *M.validus* mainly off leaves and twigs well below the canopy in closed forest. The middle-sized species of *Myiarchus*, *M.stolidus*, differs from its larger and smaller congeners in that its main habitat is in arid lowland forest, where the others are found almost entirely at the edges, while it is very scarce and mainly at the edges in wet midlevel forest, and absent from montane forest, where the other two are regular. However, there is a small overlap in habitat. *M.barbirostris* appears to take smaller and more numerous prey than *M.stolidus*, but this needs checking. It certainly takes smaller prey than *M.validus*. The small *C.caribaeus* differs from the other species in feeding almost entirely on small flying insects under the canopy in closed forest. The two elaenias feed like the species of *Myiarchus*, by taking insects off leaves, but they are so much smaller that they presumably take smaller prey than the *Myiarchus* species. From each other the two elaenias differ largely in altitudinal range, with only a small overlap, and in addition *E.fallax* is primarily a summer visitor, whereas *M.cotta* stays throughout the year, and *E.fallax* eats much fruit, *M.cotta* hardly any. It looks, therefore, as if all eight species are separated ecologically from each other.

The other Greater Antilles lack three of the eight Jamaican species, namely *Myiarchus barbirostris*, *M.validus*, and *Myiopagis cotta*.As already mentioned, *M.barbirostris* and *M.cotta* are closely related to Central American species, and since they have made the relatively long sea crossing from the mainland to Jamaica, it is absurd to suppose that they could not also have reached Cuba or Hispaniola from Jamaica. Presumably they are unable to survive on these neighbouring islands, but why this might be so is not known, and they are not replaced by similar-looking species which might there fill their respective niches. Cuba has a species of kingbird absent from Jamaica, but it lives in pines which do not grow wild on Jamaica. In Honduras, there are 40 resident species of Tyrannidae, in 29 genera. The three close relatives of Jamaican species present in Honduras, namely *Myiarchus tuberculifer*, *Contopus cinereus* and *Myiopagus viridicata*, all there occur in mangroves, lowland arid forest and vega (Monroe 1938).

SWALLOWS AND MARTINS
HIRUNDINIDAE

"Jamaica; a sight of the hirundines of that hot and distant land would be a great entertainment to me" (Gilbert White, 1789).

Kalochelidon euchrysea **Golden Swallow** (Plate 9, Fig. 47)

This bird, "whose plumage reflects the radiance of the hummingbirds" (Gosse 1847), is a brilliant iridescent green all over the upper parts

FIG. 47. *Breeding range of the swallow* Kalochelidon euchrysea *and of the related* Callichelidon cyaneoviridis. *The latter has a wider range in winter.*

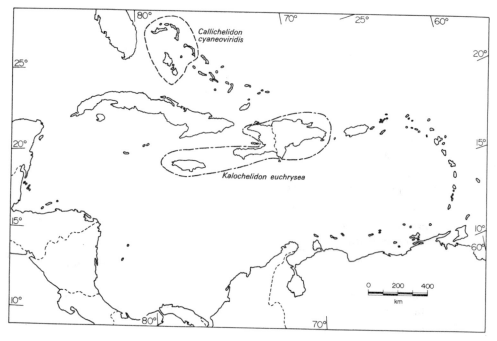

and the purest of whites below. It was common in the Blue Mountains and on the northern side of the midlevel wet limestone hills until about a century ago, but is now, for unknown reasons, reduced to an extremely small number in the Cockpit Country. Osburn (1859–60) saw many in the central highlands of Jamaica, and the bird was still so common on the southern slopes of the Blue Mountains in 1879 and 1880 that Edward Newton then collected 11 specimens, now in the zoology museum at Cambridge University. It seems to have been absent from the south side of the island at midlevels, for Gosse never saw it alive, but described it from a specimen sent to him after his departure by Mr. Hill. It was this bird that gave rise to the famous entry in Gosse's diary: "E. delivered of son. Received green swallow from Jamaica." (E. Gosse, 1890, who added "Two ephemeral vitalities indeed ... The one stands for ever behind a pane of glass in the Natural History Museum at South Kensington; the other, whom the green swallow will doubtless survive, is he who now puts together these deciduous pages.")

According to Bond (1956), *K.euchrysea* was still in the Blue Mountains in 1950, but we did not see any there. (A few seen one winter day which we at first thought might be this species turned out to be Tree Swallows *Tachycineta bicolor*, an occasional visitor to Jamaica from North America.) We eventually saw one in summer near Barbecue Bottom in the Cockpit Country with Robert Sutton, who in the following summer (1972) saw a pair in the same place; and wintering birds have been seen at the lower limit of the Cockpit Country at Windsor in recent years, as reported in several numbers of the Gosse Bulletin. On Hispaniola, *K.euchrysea* likewise breeds in the highlands and may come lower in winter. On Hispaniola it nests in holes in trees (Wetmore and Swales 1931), but the sole breeding records for Jamaica are in holes in a cave or building (Osburn 1859–60, March 1863).

The Hispaniolan race is much duller than the Jamaican, and the species is confined to these two islands. It is put in a monotypic genus, *Kalochelidon*, in Peters and by Bond, but this is a borderline decision, since it is agreed that it is close to the mainland genus *Tachycineta*, and seems no more distinctive than the former genus *Iridoprocne*, now merged in *Tachycineta* in Peters. I would have merged *Kalochelidon* except that it seems wisest to follow the nomenclature in Peters unless later research has shown it to be actually wrong. Bond (1963) considered *K.euchrysea* nearest to the Tree Swallow *T.(Iridoprocne) bicolor*, but

Caribbean Martin
Progne dominicensis

Black Swift
Cypseloides niger

Antillean Palm Swift
Tachornis phoenicobia

Golden Swallow
Kalochelidon euchrysea

Cave Swallow
Petrochelidon fulva

Collared Swift
Streptoprocne zonaris

PLATE 9. *Swifts Apodidae, swallows and martins Hirundinidae, one-quarter natural size.*

in size, in most proportions and in green colouring it looks more like the Violet-Green Swallow *T.thalassina*, which lives in montane forest in western U.S.A. and Mexico, and which Wetmore and Swales (1931) showed a resemblance in its habitat to that of *K.euchrysea*. The endemic Bahaman swallow *Callichelidon cyaneoviridis* is another related species in a monotypic genus which might likewise be merged in *Tachycineta*.

Progne dominicensis **Caribbean Martin** (Plate 9, Fig. 48)

This is a scarce summer resident, mainly near the coast, where it breeds in holes in trees made by woodpeckers, also in holes in rocks (Gosse 1847) or buildings (R.W. Smith pers. comm.). We saw two in mid-January in the Black River swamp, where others have seen it in winter, and Gosse also noted that a few stay for the winter. It feeds higher in

FIG. 48. *Breeding range of the martin* Progne dominicensis, *which is almost entirely a summer visitor to the Antilles. There is a further race (range not shown) in western Mexico.*

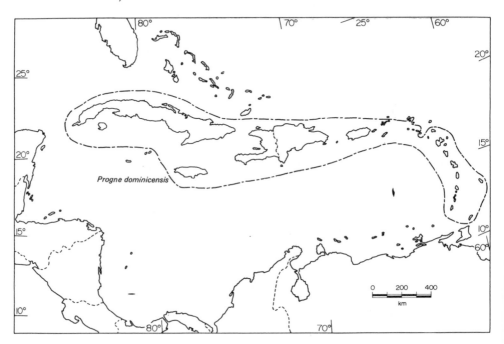

the air than the smaller Cave Swallow *Petrochelidon fulva*, hunting chiefly in the lowlands, sometimes at midlevels, but we did not find it in the mountains, nor breeding at midlevels. Formerly classified as a subspecies of the North American Purple Martin *Progne subis*, it is now (Mayr and Short 1970) considered a distinct species, with, oddly, another race in the western mountains of Mexico. They put *P.chalybea* of Mexico, Central and South America in the same superspecies.

Petrochelidon fulva **Cave Swallow** (Plate 9, Fig. 49)

P.fulva is a common resident in the lowlands and fairly common at midlevels, nesting in limestone cliffs and caves, and sometimes under bridges or in buildings. We occasionally saw it feeding in the Blue Mountains, but did not find it breeding there. Usually it feeds fairly low over the ground or over forest trees, and sometimes just skims

Fɪɢ. 49. *Range of the swallow* Petrochelidon fulva, *which has additional races (ranges not shown) in Mexico and Texas (and perhaps parts of South America).*

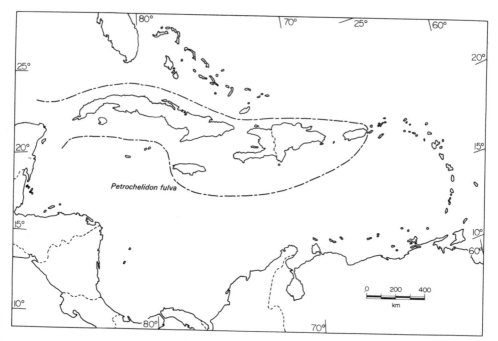

the tree tops or the ground, but at other times feeds moderately high up. *P.fulva* also breeds in the other Greater Antilles, in Mexico, and a small part of the United States.

When we saw *K.euchrysea* in the Cockpit Country, it was feeding in company with *P.fulva* in a similar way. The past records make it clear, however, that the two species were separated, with a small overlap, by altitudinal range, *K.euchrysea* in the Blue Mountains and the highest parts of the midlevel limestone hills, primarily on their northern side, and *P.fulva* lower than this.

Three species of hirundines breed in Honduras, including one species of *Tachycineta* and one of *Progne*.

MOCKINGBIRDS MIMIDAE

Mimus polyglottos **Northern Mockingbird (Nightingale)** (Plate 10, Fig. 50)

M.polyglottos is common in only one natural habitat, strand woodland, where it is one of the two abundant species, the other being the Banana-quit *C.flaveola*. A few occur in mangroves. In other lowland forest it is found only at the edges and in clearings, but there it is abundant, in habitats varying from the extremely arid Port Henderson Hill

Fig. 50. *Ranges in the West Indies of the two mockingbirds* Mimus poly-glottos *and* M.gilvus, *sometimes treated as a single species.* (*Mainland ranges not shown.*)

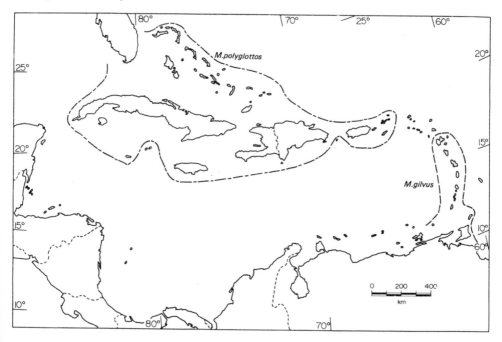

to the fairly rich secondary woodland of the lowland hills. It is also numerous in lowland wooded cultivation, especially where there are scattered trees and grass. At midlevels, it is absent from forest, but is regular in wooded cultivation and in pastures adjoining woods, and in the mountains it is very scarce, solely in wooded cultivation. Although now one of the commonest birds on Jamaica, it was presumably scarce and local before the advent of man.

It feeds mainly in short grass, where it often holds out its wings briefly when hunting. We saw one pick up a grasshopper, another a large green caterpillar, and a third took a caterpillar off a trunk 2 m above the ground. It regularly eats fruits (See Appendix 6). In the Botanic Garden it sometimes feeds in the large red flowers of the introduced *Spathodea campanulata* until its breast becomes heavily rouged by the pollen.

M.polyglottos (*sens. strict.*) is found throughout the Greater Antilles, Bahamas and much of the United States, but is absent from Central America, so probably colonised Jamaica from the north (unless *M. polyglottos* was in Central America in the last glacial period). Mayr and Short (1970) have treated it as conspecific with the Central and South American *M.gilvus* but it is *M.polyglottos* (*sens. strict.*) that is in the Greater Antilles.

Mimus gundlachii **Bahama Mockingbird** (Plate 10, Fig. 19, p. 118)

M.gundlachii is almost restricted to continuous woodland in the extremely arid natural forest of the Hellshire Hills and Portland Ridge, in both of which it is abundant. It is not found in clearings. We also saw three in arid lowland forest a few miles from Portland Ridge, two by the Milk River and Alligator Pond, and one inland at the edge of the Braziletto Mountains. It is one of the few Jamaican land birds with a very restricted habitat. *M.polyglottos*, which is absent from natural lowland forest as already mentioned, but present in clearings and at the edge, is thus sharply segregated by habitat from the larger *M.gundlachii*, with a very narrow zone of overlap at the forest edge. The only place where we often saw both near each other was on the man-modified Port Henderson Hill, an outlier of the Hellshire Hills where the larger trees have been removed by charcoal-burners, and here *M.gundlachii* is in the thicker and *M.polyglottos* is in the more open parts. *M.gundlachii* hunts in a similar way to *M.polyglottos*, but we did not see it take animal food (nor open its wings when hunting). The recorded fruits are set out in Appendix 6.

M.gundlachii is otherwise found solely on the Bahamas and some cays off the north coast of Cuba. In the absence of white on wings and tail it resembles *M. (p.) gilvus*, especially the large-billed form *magnirostris* on St. Andrew, but this could be due to parallel evolution, and its distribution suggests that it may have evolved in the north from a form like *M.p.polyglottos*.

THRUSHES TURDIDAE

Myadestes genibarbis **Rufous-throated Solitaire** (Plate 10, Fig. 13, p. 103)

Ian Fleming, creator of the other James Bond, was so moved by the song of the Jamaican solitaire that he wrote a special article on it. This almost unbelievably strange and beautiful noise, unique except for the songs of other solitaires, is the characteristic sound of the mountains of Jamaica in summer. It consists of sustained clear liquid notes, some with the character of musical glasses, others trilled, uttered over a very wide range of frequencies, often at harmonic intervals of several tones, and sometimes the bird even appears to sing two sustained notes simultaneously.

M.genibarbis breeds primarily in montane forest, where many do not arrive until June. A few more stay for the summer in the highest parts of the midlevel forest, in the Cockpit Country, Mount Diablo and the John Crow Mountains. In winter, many remain in montane forest, where their song is replaced by a call like a policeman's whistle; but many others move down to become abundant throughout the midlevel forests, and a few move lower, to Fern Gully and elsewhere near the north coast, and to secondary woodland in the hills of the southern lowlands, as above the Ferry River, in the Bog Walk and Cane River gorges and around Mona. Wintering birds move out of the lowlands in late March, but many remain in midlevel forest until late May when all except a few in the highest parts disappear.

M.genibarbis eats many fruits (see Appendix 6), especially those of melastomes, for which it either reaches from a perch or hovers in the air, by the latter means obtaining individual fruits inaccessible to a perched bird. The relatively broad beak with surrounding bristles recalls that of a flycatcher, but it is so secretive that we rarely saw it take animal food. We had five records, and A.W. Diamond another, of a bird flying out from a perch to take an insect off a leaf between 4 and 6 m above the ground, and we twice saw one take an insect from a leaf

Rufous-throated Solitaire
Myadestes genibarbis

Hopping Dick
Turdus aurantius

Glasseye
Turdus jamaicensis

Northern Mockingbird
Mimus polyglottos

Bahama Mockingbird
Mimus gundlachii

PLATE 10.   *Thrushes Turdidae and mockingbirds Mimidae,
one-quarter natural size.*

when perched. We twice, and A.W. Diamond once, saw one fly out to take an insect from the air, and we had one similar record on Dominica. We twice, and A.W. Diamond 15 times in the second half of August, saw one drop from a perch to pick up something off the ground. We cannot generalise from these few observations, but it may be noted that leaf-snatching is the least conspicuous of the three feeding methods recorded, so might be the commonest, and also that feeding on insects was conceivably reduced in the abnormally dry summer of 1971.

M.genibarbis, found on Jamaica, Hispaniola and four of the Lesser Antilles (see p. 102), is the only solitaire with any rufous colouring. Of the Central American species, it resembles in its blue-grey upper and under parts the Slate-coloured Solitaire *M.unicolor* and the allopatric Black-faced Solitaire *M.ralloides melanops*; and like the latter, but unlike *M.unicolor*, it has some black below the eye, while like *M.unicolor* but unlike *M.ralloides* it has some white in the tail. Presumably, these three species are closely related. Cuba has a different, dull brown species, which looks closely related to a different mainland species, *M.obscurus*, so is evidently of separate origin. While the Cuban and Jamaican species replace each other geographically, their putative ancestors live alongside each other and are at least partly separated by *M.unicolor* in cloud forest and lower montane forest and *M.obscurus* in montane pine-oak (Monroe 1968).

Turdus aurantius **White-chinned Thrush (Hopping Dick)** (Plate 10, Fig. 16, p. 110)

The name 'White-chinned Thrush' is muddling because the white chin is much smaller than the white throat of the other Jamaican thrush, *T.jamaicensis*. *T.aurantius*, endemic to Jamaica, breeds commonly in midlevel and montane forest, also in small numbers down to sea level on the north and west coasts, and in the hills of the southern lowlands. We even saw one in summer by a spring near sea level at Milk River, but otherwise none in the arid southern lowland forest. In winter, a small number move down to the secondary woodland, including ruinate woodland, of the southern lowland hills, but not into arid lowland forest.

T.aurantius feeds mainly on the ground, where it hops about like an American Robin *T.migratorius* or European Blackbird *T.merula*, which it also resembles in size and proportions. We made too few feeding records for generalisations. On five occasions we saw one take an earthworm, once a larva and once a snail; it also tosses leaves aside in leaf-litter and we once saw it searching in cowdung. It hunts regularly on the roads through the mountains, and takes fallen crumbs at picnic sites. It also eats a little fruit (see Appendix 6, including note (iii)), but the figure of 41 per cent of our observations is misleadingly high because we saw so little of it taking animal food. Miss Salmon (pers. comm.) recorded slugs, a small lizard and a mouse; Foster (1964) recorded a tree toad almost as large as the bird, and Black (1966) a fledgling *Vireo altiloquus* and probably a fledgling Bananaquit *C.flaveola*.

T.aurantius is an endemic Jamaican species presumably related to the other North and Central American thrushes which feed mainly on the ground, but its nearest relatives are not known, and I do not find the various possible relationships for it suggested by other authors convincing. It is not at all close to the other Jamaican species, *T.jamaicensis*, nor do I think it close to the widespread Greater Antillean thrush *T.plumbeus*.

Turdus jamaicensis **White-eyed Thrush (Glass-eye)** (Plate 10, Fig. 16, p. 110)

T.jamaicensis breeds commonly in montane forest, in wet midlevel forest down to its lowest limit at 100 m above sea level at Windsor, and in the tall riverine forest of Fern Gully. It is also regular in wooded cultivation in the mountains and at midlevels. We did not find it breeding in lowland forest, but a small number descend for the winter to the southern lowland valleys, for instance by the Ferry River, Mona and in the Cane River gorge.

T.jamaicensis, endemic to Jamaica, is a short-tailed thrush, in proportions rather like the European Song Thrush *T.philomelos*. Unlike *T.aurantius*, it is commonly caught in mist-nets extending from the ground to 2 m up (*per* A.W. Diamond), but it is secretive, and we did not find out why it should so often fly at this height. Its different proportions and stance, and its shorter beak, suggest that it seeks animal prey in different ways from *T.aurantius*, but we did not discover what these might be. We saw it feeding on the ground much less often than *T.aurantius*, usually under thick canopy on or near narrow tracks through closed montane forest, and rarely on roads or in other more open places. One was shifting leaf litter, two took earthworms, one an insect, but the rest were disturbed before we could see what they were doing. It eats fruits throughout the year, and we saw it doing so about half as often again as *T.aurantius*. The identified species are set out in Appendix 6, but we often saw it high in trees eating fruits that we could not identify. Like *T.aurantius*, and unlike *M.genibarbis*, it usually takes fruits when perched, and removes pieces out of them with its beak.

As pointed out by Bond, in its general colouring and white throat *T.jamaicensis* is close to the South American *T.albicollis* (*sens. strict.*). It is less similar to the Central American *T.*(*albicollis*) *assimilis*, which Monroe (1968) treated as a full species, and which lives in lowland rain forest, monsoon forest and cloud forest in Honduras. It is not related to the other West Indian thrushes, which have been discussed in Chapter 7.

BUNTINGS EMBERIZIDAE

Ammodramus savannarum **Grasshopper Sparrow** (Plate 11, Fig. 51)

The natural habitat of *A.savannarum* on Jamaica is lowland grassy marshland, but nowadays it occurs mainly in grass pastures and at the grassy edges of sugarcane fields, in both lowlands and at midlevels, where it feeds on seeds on the gound. On the Caribbean islands, it breeds solely on Jamaica, Hispaniola, Puerto Rico, Curacao and

Fig. 51. *West Indian range of the sparrow (bunting)* Ammodramus savannarum. (*Mainland range not shown but includes parts of Central and South America.*)

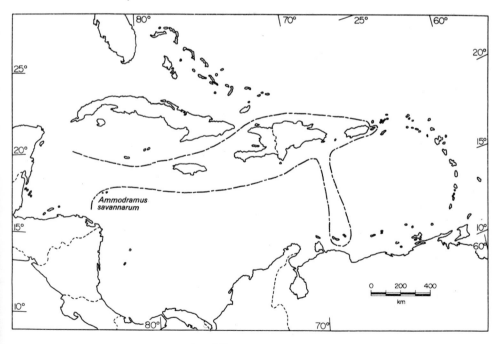

Bonaire (see Fig. 1, p. 16) and is also found in parts of mainland North, Central and South America.

Tiaris olivacea **Yellow-faced Grassquit** (Plate 11, Fig. 52)

T.olivacea breeds throughout the most arid, barren and open parts of the Hellshire forest; but in other types of lowland forest, including the richer parts of the Hellshires, and also in midlevel forest, it occurs almost entirely in man-made grassy rides and clearings, commonly in the lowlands and fairly commonly at midlevels. It is absent from montane forest. In cultivated grassland with scattered bushes or trees, it is regular in the lowlands and at midlevels, but rare in the mountains.

We did not study its feeding, but of 24 recorded items, nearly three-quarters were grass seeds, including those of *Chloris barbata*, *Paspalum fimbriatum*, *Echinochloa colonum*, *Panicum maximum* and *Andropogon pertusus*. It normally takes a seed directly off the seed-head on the living plant, by stretching up from the ground for it, or by taking a

Fɪɢ. 52. *Range in the West Indies of the grassquit* Tiaris olivacea. (*Mainland range not shown.*)

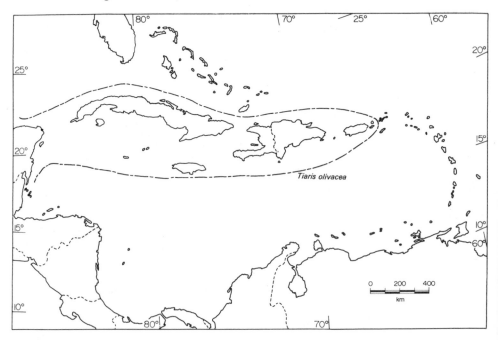

flutter-jump from the ground, gripping the seed-head and pulling it down, or by perching on a small bush or other slight elevation on the ground beside the grass concerned and stretching out from there. We occasionally saw it take the seeds of other herbs from a seed-head, once it ate a seed on the ground and once an unidentified fruit. *T.olivacea* is found in the Greater Antilles, also in Mexico, Central and northern South America.

Tiaris bicolor **Black-faced Grassquit** (Plate 11, Fig. 53)

The natural habitat of *T.bicolor* is open woodland and the wood-edge at all altitudes, except that it is absent from the arid open forest of the Hellshires and Portland Ridge where *T.olivacea* occurs, and also from mangroves. It occurs alongside *T.olivacea* in man-modified grassy rides through the higher lowland woods and midlevel forest, but is not, like *T.olivacea*, confined to grassy areas. Pulliam (1969)

FIG. 53. *Range of the grassquits* Tiaris bicolor *and* T.canora. (*Range of T.bicolor in South America not shown.*)

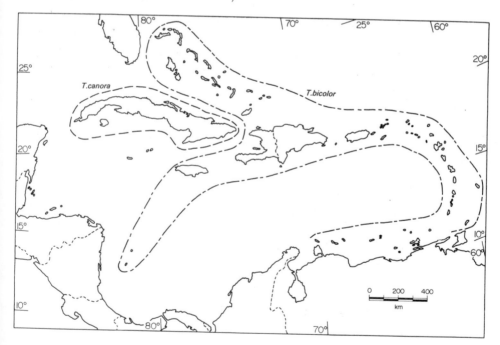

found that whereas *T.olivacea* takes most of its food above the ground, but less that 1 m up, *T.bicolor* feeds mainly on the ground or above a height of one metre. Our few feeding records confirm this. Of 53 items taken, 55 per cent were seeds, usually the fallen seeds of grasses or trees on the ground. We rarely saw a bird reach up for a grasshead like *T.olivacea* does, but sometimes it fed in trees. Just over one quarter of our records were of fruits, nearly always in the lowlands, and especially those of *Pithecellobium unguis-cati* (see Appendix 6).

T.bicolor occurs throughout the West Indies except Cuba, where it is replaced by an endemic congener, *T.canora*, and on the Caymans, where neither occurs, but where *T.olivacea* is present. It is also found in part of northern South America and some of its offshore islands.

Loxipasser anoxanthus **Yellow-shouldered Grassquit** (**Yellow-shouldered Finch**) (Plate 11)

Loxipasser anoxanthus is a Jamaican endemic genus and species, with no equivalent on any other island. In the shape of its beak, mainly black male plumage and chestnut under tail coverts, it resembles the endemic Antillean genus *Loxigilla*, from which it may have evolved. Neither vernacular name is good, because the bird is not a grassquit, nor is it in the finch family Fringillidae; in view of its possible relationship to *Loxigilla*, it might perhaps better be called the Yellow-shouldered Bullfinch. On Jamaica, it is regular in all types of natural forest except mangroves and strand woodland, being equally at home in extremely arid lowland and wet montane forest. It is commonest in the rich secondary woodland near the Ferry River.

Just over half of our 80 feeding observations were on fruits, including those of *Fagara martinicensis* and *Alchornea latifolia*, which are also popular with other species (see Appendix 6 for full list). One-fifth of its feeds were on seeds, especially of natural and introduced Compositae herbs (*Vernonia* and *Bidens* spp. *etc.*), of low bushes such as *Chamissao altissima* and of certain trees, mainly introduced, including acacias. We only once saw one take a grass seed, of *Panicum maximum*. Fifteen per cent of the feeds were on native flowers of a variety of tree species, eight per cent on leaves, one took fern spores and one an insect.

Black-faced
Grassquit
Tiaris bicolor

Yellow-faced
Grassquit
Tiaris olivacae

Yellow-shouldered
Finch
Loxipasser anoxanthus

Grasshopper Sparrow
Ammodramus savannarum

Greater Antillean
Bullfinch
Loxigilla violacea

PLATE 11.   *Buntings Emberizidae, half natural size.*

Loxigilla violacea **Greater Antillean Bullfinch** (Plate 11)

L.violacea, endemic to Jamaica, is fairly common in every type of forest except mangroves and the ruinate arid Port Henderson Hill, and is about equally common in lowland, midlevel and montane forest. It is also regular in wooded cultivation at midlevels and in the mountains, but not in the southern lowlands. Out of 119 recorded feeds, four-fifths were on fruits, especially those of *Trichostigma octandrum*, *Fagara martinicensis*, *Bursera simaruba*, *Alchornea latifolia* and *Dunalia arborescens*, all of which are popular with other species (see Appendix 6). We were therefore puzzled to know how, if at all, it might be separated in diet from other fruit-eating species, especially the tanager *Spindalis zena*, in which, likewise, four-fifths of the diet consists of fruit, mainly of the same species as those recorded for *L.violacea*. We did not appreciate when in Jamaica that the extremely strong beak of *L.violacea*, with which it nipped the mist-netters severely, is adapted for crushing, like that of the Hawfinch *Coccothraustes*, so it presumably visits fruits primarily for their seeds. This is doubtless why, though it often feeds on the same species of fruits as the tanager, even on the same day, we did not see these two species feeding in the same tree, suggesting that they seek fruits at a different stage of ripeness. We also saw *L.violacea* eating various seeds of native species, including those of herbs such as *Cassia ligustrina* and *Sida acuta*, of shrubs such as *Desmanthus virgatus*, *Lantana camara* and *Dunalia arborescens*, and of the low tree *Bauhinia divaricata*. We recorded only one species of seed in common with those taken by *L.anoxanthus*, namely that of *Chamissoa altissima*, and in particular did not see it eating the seeds of Compositae or acacias; but we had too few records to determine whether it overlaps with this species. It rarely eats flowers.

    L.violacea is so much larger than *L.anoxanthus* (see Table 1) that it is reasonable to suppose that the two are segregated in diet. Character displacement is probably involved, because on Jamaica, where *L. anoxanthus* is also present, *L.violacea* is larger than on the other islands in its range, where *L.anoxanthus* is absent (mean wing-lengths and culmen-lengths 83 and 15.8 mm on Jamaica, 75 and 14.7 mm on Hispaniola, and 78 and 15.5 mm on the Bahamas—from Ridgway). Possibly in opposition to this view, *L.anoxanthus* is also absent from Puerto Rico, which has a different species of *Loxigilla*, *L.portoricensis*, larger than *L.violacea* (wing 90 and culmen 16.5 mm).

Loxigilla is an endemic West Indian genus of uncertain affinities, found in one of three geographically replacing species on all the main islands except Cuba, where it is replaced by an unrelated large-beaked species in the monotypic endemic genus *Melopyrrha*, which Bond considered was derived from the mainland genus *Sporophila*.

TANAGERS THRAUPIDAE

Spindalis zena **Stripe-headed Tanager** (Plate 12, Fig. 54)

S.zena is common in montane forest, nearly as common in midlevel forest, and regular in lowland woods in the north and west. In summer, in the south, in the dry lowlands, however, we found it only in two places, both near water, the Cane River Gorge and Milk River, though in winter it is also regular in the secondary woodland above the Ferry River and elsewhere.

Out of 116 feeding observations, just over four-fifths were on fruits, of a diversity of species, and as shown in Appendix 6, all those that we

FIG. 54. *Range of the tanagers* Spindalis zena *and* Tangara cucullata.

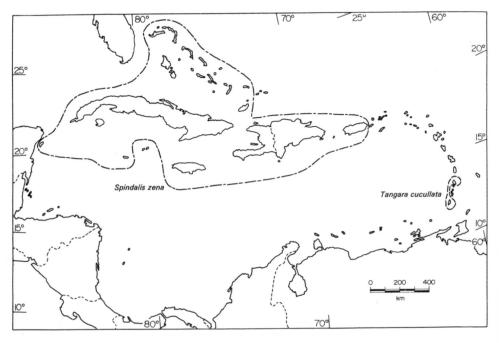

recorded it taking more than once we also recorded for other frugivorous species. The 9 records of *Ficus perforata* were in only two trees, and other bird species eat other species of *Ficus*. As already mentioned the apparent big overlap in diet with *Loxigilla violacea* is perhaps because the tanager eats the fruits, the bullfinch the seeds. The only other species which eats mainly fruits, the euphonia *Euphonia jamaica*, is separated because it specialises on mistletoes, which *S.zena* does not take. More puzzling is *S.zena*'s extensive overlap in fruit diet with the many species which take mainly animal prey but which also take an important proportion of fruit (see Table 10). Each of these species is separated from the others and from *S.zena* by its invertebrate prey, but how *S.zena* might be separated from them, if it is, is not known. Our other feeding records for *S.zena* included 6 per cent on leaves, between October and December, and 12 per cent on flowers, between October and mid-March, while two birds ate buds and one an acacia seed.

Spindalis zena, a monotypic genus, not close to any other tanager, is found in the Greater Antilles, Bahamas, and also Cozumel off Yucatan. On Grand Cayman and some other islands, unlike Jamaica, it is common in arid lowland forest.

Euphonia jamaica **Jamaican Euphonia** (Plate 12, Fig. 55)

E.jamaica, a species endemic to Jamaica, is common in all types of forest and wooded cultivation from sea level to the mountains, being most numerous in the richer secondary woods of the lowland hills. Like other euphonias, it specialises on mistletoe berries, Loranthaceae, which no other Jamaican species takes to an appreciable extent. These and the other fruits that we recorded for it are set out in Appendix 6. All the other fruits were also taken by other species (those of *Guazuma ulmifolia* by the parakeet *Aratinga nana* and the ani *Crotophaga ani* which, being large birds, are omitted from the table). If introduced fruits are omitted, 70 per cent of our records for *E.jamaica* were on fruits, 8 per cent on flowers, 13 per cent on buds, 7 per cent on green leaves, and one fed on a caterpillar.

E.jamaica was until recently placed in the monotypic genus *Pyrrhuphonia* owing to its unusually shaped beak, but in Peters and elsewhere is now rightly merged in *Euphonia*. It does not seem particularly close to any other species in this genus. On Hispaniola, Puerto Rico

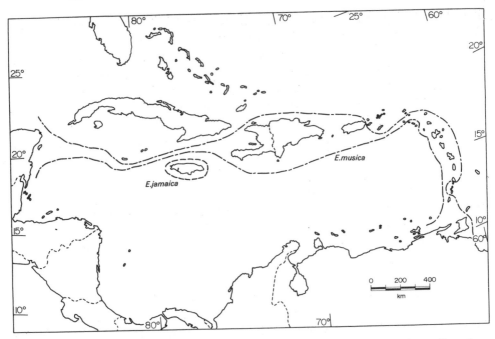

Fig. 55. *Range of the euphonia* Euphonia jamaica, *endemic to Jamaica, and of separate origin from the extremely widespread* E.musica *(mainland range not shown).*

and many of the Lesser Antilles, there is a different species, *E.musica*, which is also in Central and northern South America.

Euneornis campestris **Orangequit** (Plate 12)

This species, endemic to Jamaica, formerly placed with the Bananaquit *Coereba flaveola* in the family Coerebidae, is tentatively placed in the Thraupidae in Peters. Its moderately long and thin decurved beak is not typical for a tanager, but the beak is often much modified in island birds.

    E.campestris is common in wet midlevel forest, fairly common in montane forest, and present but scarce in the richer secondary woodland of the southern lowland hills, where it becomes commoner in winter. It is widespread in wooded cultivation, especially at midlevels.

    Out of 252 feeding observations, 65 per cent were on nectar and 29 per cent on fruits, but when the many records for introduced flowers

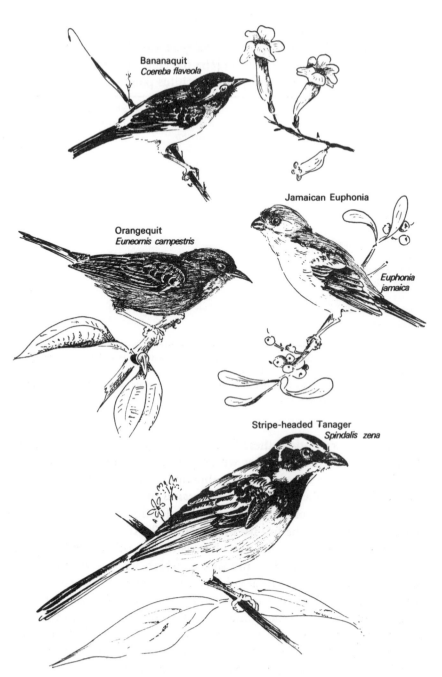

Bananaquit
Coereba flaveola

Jamaican Euphonia

Euphonia jamaica

Orangequit
Euneornis campestris

Stripe-headed Tanager
Spindalis zena

PLATE 12.   *Tanagers Thraupidae and Bananaquit Coereba, half natural size.*

TABLE 45. *Main flowers visited by the two 'honey-creepers'*
Euneornis campestris *and* Coereba flaveola, *showing the overlap
with the hummingbird* Trochilus polytmus

Flowers visited	Number of visits recorded for		
	Euneornis campestris	*Coereba flaveola*	*Trochilus polytmus*
Midlevel bromeliads	1	—	13
Montane bromeliads	4	—	9
Piperaceae	3	—	—
Cecropia peltata	4	2	2
Bauhinia divaricata	6	9	7
Melastomataceae	8	4	21
Vaccinium meridionale	4	5	9
Cordia spp.	7	7	6
Tabebuia riparia	—	9	—
Tecoma stans	—	3	12
Besleria lutea	2	—	29
Goldfussia glomerata	—	1	8
Psychotria spp.	2	2	12

Notes (i) Based on full lists in Appendix 7. Compare also with the records for the three species of hummingbirds in Table 43 (p. 253).

(ii) *Tabebuia riparia*, here recorded solely for *Coereba flaveola*, was also recorded for the hummingbird *Anthracothorax mango* (see Table 43).

and fruits are excluded, these figures are 49 per cent on flowers and 41 per cent on fruits, together with 4 per cent (in summer) on insects and 6 per cent (in winter) on sap, obtained by probing the holes made by the Yellow-bellied Sapsucker *Sphyrapicus varius*. The native flowers in which we most often saw *E.campestris* feeding are summarised in Table 45, based on the full list in Appendix 7. All the species which it frequently visits for nectar are also visited by other nectar-feeding species (though it was the only species which we saw eating the inflorescences of the Piperaceae). Likewise as shown in Appendix 6, all the wild fruits which it eats most often are eaten by various other frugivorous species. Hence while it is separated in diet from the other regular nectar-feeders by the large amount of fruit which it takes, and from the other regular fruit-eaters by the large amount of nectar which it takes, we did not record any type of food which it eats commonly and other species do not. In comparison with any other particular species, it differs in at least half of its main diet, but whether it thereby avoids competition for food with other species seems doubtful.

Euneornis is a monotypic genus endemic to Jamaica, and there is no other bird like it in the West Indies. Cuba has only one species of tanager *S.zena*, but Hispaniola has five, *S.zena*, *Euphonia musica* and two endemic genera, one of which has two allopatric species; their ecology has not been studied.

NEW WORLD WARBLERS PARULIDAE
(including COEREBA)

Dendroica petechia **Yellow Warbler** (Plate 13)

In winter, *D.petechia* is nearly confined to mangroves, where it is much the commonest passerine species. It is also regular in the narrow belt of strand woodland, and occasional in dry limestone forest close to the shore or mangroves. In summer, it becomes a little less scarce in dry limestone forest near the coast, and is common in the marsh forest of the Black River swamp and the trees bordering rivers in the southern lowlands, including the Sweet and Ferry rivers, up to at least 8 km inland, moving there after nearly all the North American wintering warblers have departed.

Over three-quarters of our feeding observations were of insects gleaned off leaves, but occasionally it takes one off the ground or in the air and eats a small fruit or probes in a flower. Its feeding is analysed in comparison with that of the wintering warblers in Chapter 12.

D.petechia is found almost throughout the West Indies, also in North, Central and northwestern South America. In Central and South America, as on Jamaica, it lives mainly in mangroves, and to some extent in dry coastal scrub.

Dendroica pharetra **Arrow-headed Warbler** (Plate 13, Fig. 23, p. 147)

D.pharetra, endemic to Jamaica, is common in montane forest and also breeds regularly in midlevel wet limestone forest, where it probably becomes commoner in winter. In winter, we also saw it regularly in the tall riverine forest of Fern Gully and the rich secondary woodland above the Ferry River, but though we saw one in the latter area in July, and A. W. Diamond saw one in sealevel forest near Negril in July, we had no evidence that they breed there. It is absent from arid lowland forest and ruinate woodland. Hence it is separated completely by habitat from *D.petechia*, with a large gap between them, namely the arid lowlands, where neither occurs.

334

D.pharetra feeds almost entirely by gleaning insects off thick ever-green leaves of native forest trees, usually fairly high above the ground, both in and below the canopy. Its feeding is compared with that of the wintering warblers in Chapter 12.

D.pharetra is an endemic Jamaican species which is probably close to the recently discovered *D.angelae* of the high montane forest on Puerto Rico (Kepler and Parkes 1972). It has no obvious relatives on the American mainland. The other species of parulid warblers resident in the West Indies have been discussed in Chapter 12.

Coereba flaveola **Bananaquit** (Plate 12, Fig. 15, p. 106)

Until recently *C.flaveola* was, with *Euneornis campestris* already discussed, put in the family of honeycreepers Coerebidae, but the latter has now been broken up because it is considered to be polyphyletic, and *C. flaveola* is tentatively placed in the Parulidae in Peters. We occasionally mistook it briefly for a parulid in the field.

C.flaveola is one of the commonest, and perhaps the commonest, land bird on Jamaica, and is found in all types of natural and man-modified forest and woodland from sea level to the top of Blue Moun-tain. In natural forest, we usually found it the commonest bird on our counts in winter, although outnumbered by the vireo *V.altiloquus* in summer; while in wooded cultivation it was usually the commonest bird at all seasons, being particularly abundant where a favourite tree was in flower, notably the introduced eucalyptus on Guava Ridge and the introduced *Pittosporum undulatum* on the trail from Cinchona through the montane forest to Morce's Gap. It was also abundant when a favourite fruit, that of the dildo cactus *Stenocereus hystrix*, was ripe on Port Henderson Hill, where this plant is unnaturally plentiful owing to the clearance of many trees by man.

Of 438 individuals seen feeding, 74 per cent took nectar, 11 per cent fruits and 14 per cent insects. These figures need serious qualification, however, because three-quarters of the birds seen taking nectar were on introduced flowering trees, nearly all the fruits were of one species of cactus in one area, and the bird is inconspicuous when feeding on insects. If all introduced flowers and fruits are excluded, the figures (based on 187 feeding records) are 46 per cent on flowers, 24 per cent on fruit and 29 per cent on insects. In addition, we saw one probing for sap in a hole in a eucalyptus trunk made by a wintering Yellow-bellied Sapsucker *Sphyrapicus varius,* and one eating small buds.

When feeding on nectar, *C.flaveola* probes from the front into small flowers, but often nips through the base to get at the nectaries of large flowers. The latter method is used on many introduced garden flowers and also on the native *Centrosema pubescens* and *Tecoma stans.* As already noted, the resulting holes are often used by the hummingbird *Trochilus polytmus.* The native flowers visited are set out in Appendix 7 and the common ones are summarised in Table 45, which shows the big overlap in diet with the other nectar-feeding species, already mentioned.

Out of 45 individuals seen eating fruits, one was at midlevels and all the rest in the arid lowlands, over four-fifths of them on the dildo cactus *Stenocereus hystrix,* into the fruits of which *C.flaveola* inserts its beak and extracts the juice as if feeding on nectar. These fruits are commonly taken by only one other species, the White-winged Dove *Zenaida asiatica.* Since the only area that we watched regularly where *Stenocereus hystrix* is abundant was Port Henderson Hill, the number of feeding records for *C.flaveola* on fruit depended closely on how often we happened to make counts in this area in summer and autumn when the fruits are ripe. As this was rather often, our overall figure of 24 per cent of feeding records on fruit is misleadingly high.

Most insect food is gleaned off leaves in trees, often in the canopy, and in the lowlands usually between 7 and 9 m above the ground; a little is taken off twigs, and we saw two birds fly out to take an insect on the wing. Nearly all the insects were very small, like those taken by the leaf-gleaning warblers, but we occasionally saw one with a caterpillar rather longer than its beak. At least twice we saw one remove from twigs what appeared to be ants, but it was hard to be sure; this behaviour might well be commoner than our records suggest. We saw more insects taken in summer than winter, probably because the species breeds mainly in summer and needs them for its young, and perhaps also because the wintering leaf-gleaning warblers are then absent. As it is inconspicuous when feeding on insects, we almost certainly underestimated the proportion doing so.

Nearly half of our recorded observations on native foods were on nectar, but as shown in Table 45 and Appendix 7, it is not segregated from the other nectar-feeding birds by the flowers which it visits. Further, its fondness for the fruits of *Cereus* cacti is too local to be of significance in ecological isolation. Presumably, therefore, it is segregated ecologically from other species, if at all, by its insect diet. In summer, it is the only regular gleaner for small insects off leaves in arid lowland forest, and the only common one in midlevel forest, but the two native warblers are leaf gleaners in mangroves and montane forest respectively. Whether it competes for insects in winter with the North American warblers is not known, but it takes far more nectar than they do.

C.flaveola is on all of the West Indies except Cuba, which is the sole West Indian station of the Red-legged Honeycreeper *Cyanerpes cyaneus*. These two species coexist on the Central and South American mainland. On Trinidad, they are segregated because *C.flaveola* feeds to a much greater extent on nectar, and finds most of its insect prey on the underside of leaves, whereas *C.cyaneus* feeds to a much greater extent on fruits, and takes insects chiefly from twigs and the upper side of leaves (Snow and Snow 1971). It is therefore hard to imagine that the two species could be sufficiently similar in ecology in the West Indies to exclude each other geographically, yet their respective ranges (Fig. 15, p. 106) hardly permit any other explanation.

VIREOS VIREONIDAE

Vireo modestus **Jamaican White-eyed Vireo (Sewi-sewi)** (Plate 13, Fig. 18, p. 113)

V.modestus is the smallest of the three vireos on Jamaica. It is common in all types of forest except mangroves, ranging from sea level to the

TABLE 46.   *Differences in feeding of Jamaican Vireos*

	V.modestus	*V.osburni*	*V.altiloquus*
Mean culmen length (mm)	8.9	13	16.3
Number of observations	125	48	91
Percentage of feeds—			
on fruit	14	2	55
on insects			
off leaves	42	73	43
off dead leaves	6	8	—
off twigs	28	19	1
off other vegetation	6	—	1
from air	2	—	—
Number of times birds seen hunting for insects at observed heights	82	41	36
Percentage of records—			
Height (in m)			
0—1	11	12	0
1—2	17	7	0
2—3	15	15	3
3—6	18	32	17
6—9	24	27	42
9—12	15	7	25
12—15	0	0	14
over 15	0	0	0

Note   The number of feeding observations includes all records for each individual, except that one in a fruiting tree was scored only once, irrespective of the number of fruits that it ate. The number of observed heights was one per bird, that at which it was first seen hunting for insects, and heights to which it subsequently moved are excluded.

mountains and from extremely arid to extremely humid forest. It is probably most numerous in the arid lowland forest of the Hellshires and Portland Ridge, and indeed is one of the three commonest species present there. It is normally absent from wooded cultivation at all altitudes.

Differences in the feeding of the three vireos are set out in Table 46. *V.modestus* hunts by hopping from twig to twig, especially in creepers and thick bushes, but also in the crowns of the trees, particularly in the relatively low canopy of arid limestone forest and some types of montane forest. It searches to an almost equal extent at all heights from 0.5 to 12 m above the ground, finding most of its insect prey on leaves, but a higher proportion on twigs than do the other two vireos, or the leaf-gleaning warblers. It obtains food items much less frequently than do the warblers, probably because it seeks larger prey than they do, and the larger insects tend to be the less numerous. We often saw it with a relatively large insect larva in its beak, and sometimes, unlike the warblers, it takes a significant time to extract a prey item from a twig, bud or leaf. It takes only a small amount of fruit (see Appendix 6), and when in a fruiting tree, it usually takes only one or two fruits before moving on.

V.modestus is in the same species-group as the North American White-eyed Vireo *V.griseus* and the Central American Mangrove Vireo *V.pallens*, and the ranges of the five other geographically-replacing species in this group in the West Indies are shown with that of *V.modestus* in Fig. 18. The systematic relationships of West Indian forms to each other and to *V.pallens* are uncertain, and Hamilton (1958) and Bond and Blake (in Peters) came to different conclusions, so it is best to treat each as a separate species until the situation has been clarified. They are of similar size, but the culmen is smaller than the usual 12.0–12.6 mm, in the Puerto Rican (11.4 mm) and Hispaniolan (9.5 mm) species, and especially in the Jamaican *V.modestus* (8.9 mm), which also has a thinner beak than the rest. The small beak of *V. modestus* might be due to character displacement, since unlike the other West Indian species, it coexists with another ·and larger species, *V.osburni*, in the same species-group.

The nearest mainland relative, *V.pallens*, lives in mangroves and arid lowland scrub forest (Monroe 1968, Land 1970), so *V.modestus*, which extends into montane forest, has a wider habitat. It also has a wider range of feeding stations since the species in the *V.griseus* group

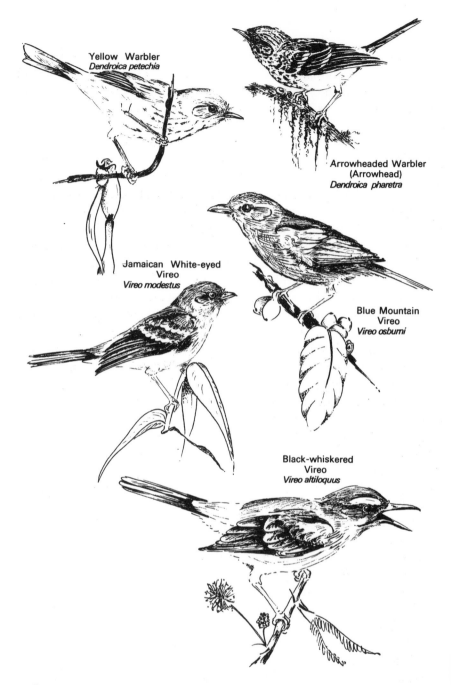

Yellow Warbler
Dendroica petechia

Arrowheaded Warbler
(Arrowhead)
Dendroica pharetra

Jamaican White-eyed
Vireo
Vireo modestus

Blue Mountain
Vireo
Vireo osburni

Black-whiskered
Vireo
Vireo altiloquus

PLATE 13. *New World warblers Parulidae and vireos Vireonidae, half natural size.*

typically feed in the bushes of the under-storey (Hamilton 1962), but *V.modestus* also feeds in the canopy.

Vireo osburni **Blue Mountain Vireo** (Plate 13, Fig. 18, p. 113)

V.osburni, endemic to Jamaica, is scarce but regular in montant forest, and also in the wet limestone forest of Mount Diablo and the Cockpit Country, down to the lowest limit of the latter at Windsor, 100 m above sea level, but it is absent from arid lowland forest and from cultivation. It is larger than *V.modestus* and hunts in a similar way, but finds food less frequently, which suggests that it takes larger, and hence scarcer, insects. This is also suggested by its proportionately deeper beak (6 mm *cf.* 4 mm in *V.modestus*). Hamilton (1962) described the beak as 'shrike-like', but we never saw it feeding like a shrike. Its beak is so distinctive that it was at one time put in a separate genus *Laletes,* but it is generally agreed to belong to the *V.griseus* section of the genus *Vireo,* even though it lacks the characteristic white eye-ring and wingbars. It presumably evolved from an earlier invasion of Jamaica by *V.griseus/pallens* stock than that which gave rise to *V.modestus.*

Vireo altiloquus, **Black-whiskered Vireo (John Chewit)** (Plate 13, Fig. 56)

V.altiloquus, unlike the other two Jamaican vireos, is a summer visitor, arriving in March and leaving in September. In summer, it is the commonest passerine species in most of the lowland and midlevel forest, and is fairly common in the lower parts of the montane forest, but uncommon higher up. It is present but scarce in mangroves and ruinate lowland woodland and fairly common in wooded cultivation. It is larger than the other two species and is separated from them in feeding, since its animal food consists almost entirely of large caterpillars and other insects taken from the leaves of the canopy, and it also eats many fruits (for identified species see Appendix 6). In European passerine birds such as tits *Parus*, the small species feed higher in the trees than the larger (Lack 1971). In contrast, the large *V.altiloquus* feeds in the canopy and the members of the small *V.griseus* group mainly in bushes and creepers, perhaps because the twigs of the canopy tend to be larger than those of the bushes and creepers frequented by the *V.griseus* group. A similar difference holds for the representatives of these two species in North America (Hamilton 1962).

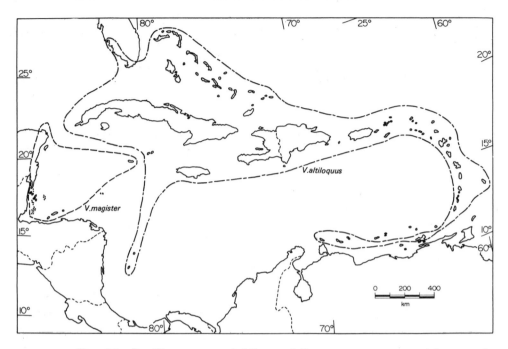

Fig. 56. *Breeding range of* Vireo altiloquus, *a summer visitor to the West Indies, and of* V.magister, *which is in the same superspecies (both are in the red-eyed vireo* V.olivaceus *group).*

V.altiloquus breeds on nearly all the West Indian islands, and just reaches Florida, where it breeds in mangroves. It is replaced on Grand Cayman by the related *V.magister*, which also breeds on the Caribbean coasts of Mexico, British Honduras and Honduras, mainly on offshore islands, in mangroves and littoral scrub forest, and in places in arid lowland forest a little way inland. Hence *V.altiloquus* has a broader habitat. Both species belong to the same group as the Red-eyed Vireo *V.olivaceus* of North America (Hamilton 1958). It is curious that except for Jamaica, in each of the Greater Antilles and the Bahamas there are only two species of vireo; Jamaica has three, and how a further species is fitted in there, but not elsewhere, is as puzzling as in the *Amazona* parrots, *Myiarchus* flycatchers and elaenias already discussed.

ORIOLES, BLACKBIRDS AND GRACKLES
ICTERIDAE

Icterus leucopteryx **Jamaican Oriole** (**Aunt Katie**) (Plate 14, Fig. 11, p. 100)

'Jamaican Oriole' is a misleading name for this species, as it also occurs on St Andrew and, until recently, Grand Cayman, where it seems now to be extinct. *I.leucopteryx* is regular in all types of forest and wooded cultivation on Jamaica except mangroves, where it is rare. Our feeding observations are summarised in Table 47. Over two thirds of the feeds were on insects obtained from bark, nearly one fifth on

TABLE 47. *Differences in feeding of two Jamaican Icterids (introduced flowers and fruits omitted)*

	Icterus leucopteryx	*Nesopsar nigerrimus*
Number of observations	88	82
Percentage of observed feeds		
Insects taken from:		
under bark	69	5
bromeliad	3	46
Phyllogonium moss	0	18
tree fern	0	15
Usnea lichen	0	5
other sources	1	8
Wild fruits	16	0
Wild flowers	10	2

Notes   (i) The number of feeding records on flowers by *I.leucopteryx* would have been doubled if those on introduced *Erythrina* and banana had been included; one bird visited a hummingbird feeder, one took fruit of the introduced *Pittosporum*; the only other natural source was one insect from under a leaf.

(ii) The other natural sources used by *N.nigerrimus* were one on a palm frond, one climbing up a vertical roadside bank, on which it found a lizard's egg, one probing in a crack in bark, and three on dead twigs (but without trying to remove the bark). Three of the four records of this species pulling off bark were in Cinchona Gardens on 14th April, the other on Blue Mountain three months later.

343

fruits, and one tenth on flowers, but the true proportion feeding on insects may have been higher, because we became so used to seeing the birds feeding in this way that we may sometimes have omitted to record it. Gosse (1847) was wrong to say that it eats mainly fruit, though its fondness for bananas has led to it being called 'banana bird'.

It searches persistently for insects, stripping off bark in its beak from trunks, thick and thin branches, and even narrow twigs, usually at a height of between 3 and 16 m above the ground, but occasionally down to 0.3 m above the ground. Sometimes it probes in rotting wood. On three occasions we saw it tearing into the leaves of bromeliads, but this is too rare to be important. It tends to ignore the observer when searching for insects, but is timid if watched when feeding on fruits. The wild fruits recorded are set out in Appendix 6. We rarely saw it feed in wild flowers, but occasionally it probes the large red flowers of the introduced *Erythrina*, which is a favourite with the few wintering Baltimore Orioles *Icterus galbula* from the United States. The main method of feeding, by tearing off bark, seems unique in the genus *Icterus*. It also has the thickest beak of any species in the genus, though it is nearly as thick in various other island forms mentioned later.

According to Beecher (1950), the nearest relative of *I.leucopteryx* is the Mexican and Central American Flame-headed Oriole *I.pustulatus*, and our examination of skins supports his view that this is the species with the most similar colour pattern. *I.leucopteryx* differs in lacking red, and in being a duller yellow, also in having a thicker and stronger beak, but in all these respects it is close to the form *I.pustulatus graysonii*, of the Tres Marias islands off western Mexico, which suggests parallel adaptation to island life. In Honduras, *I.pustulatus* occurs in arid forest, chiefly in the lowlands (Monroe 1968). Since *I.leucopteryx* occurs not only in arid but also in humid forest, it has a wider habitat than its presumed mainland ancestor.

A different species of oriole, *I.dominicensis*, lives on Cuba, Hispaniola and Puerto Rico, and this is closely related to a different Central American species *I.prosthemelas*, often treated as conspecific, which lives in lowland rain forest (Monroe 1968) and eats mainly nectar (Beecher 1950). Although it has a much thinner beak than *I.leucopteryx*, the two species replace each other on different islands in the Greater Antilles (see Fig. 11, p. 100), presumably through competitive exclu-

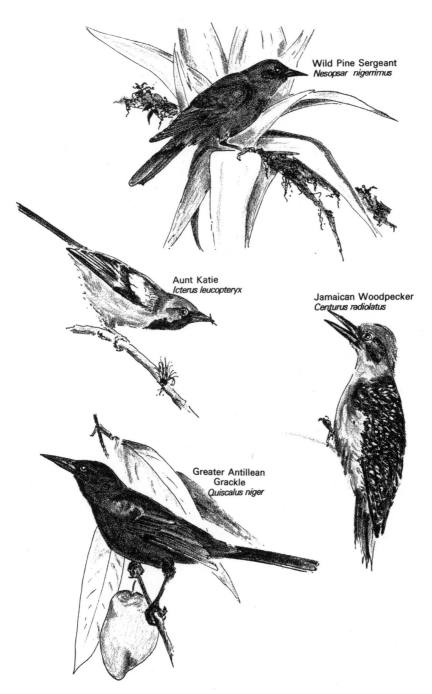

Wild Pine Sergeant
Nesopsar nigerrimus

Aunt Katie
Icterus leucopteryx

Jamaican Woodpecker
Centurus radiolatus

Greater Antillean
Grackle
Quiscalus niger

PLATE 14. *Oriole, blackbird and grackle Icteridae, and woodpecker Picidae, one-quarter natural size.*

sion, although their putative ancestors in Central America are separated by habitat, in humid and arid forest respectively. Beecher (1950)
put them in different subgenera of *Icterus*, *I.pustulatus* in the thicker-
beaked *Icterus* (*sens. strict*), which eat mainly fruit, and *I.prosthemelas*
in the thinner-beaked *Bananivorus*, which eat mainly nectar. The
Puerto Rico form of *I.dominicensis* eats mainly insects and has a thicker
beak than the Hispaniola form (Wetmore 1927), which makes it easier
to understand how two species as different as *I.pustulatus* and *I.prostheme-
las* might become potential competitors in the simplified condition on
islands.

Nesopsar nigerrimus **Jamaican Blackbird (Wild Pine Sergeant)** (Plate 14)

The vernacular name refers to the fact that this species obtains most
of its food from wild pines (bromeliads). *N.nigerrimus*, endemic to
Jamaica, is regular, but not numerous, throughout the wetter parts of
the montane forest, wherever the trees have many epiphytic small
bromeliads or *Phyllogonium* moss, but it is usually absent from the
sclerophyll forest on exposed slopes, where the main epiphyte is the
lichen *Usnea*. The species is also regular in the higher parts of the John
Crow Mountains and the highest parts of the Cockpit Country,
but not lower down at midlevels. However, a very few move to a
somewhat lower altitude in winter, and we saw one at only 210 m
above sea level in the wet northeast of the island.

N.nigerrimus searches for feeding places by short flights from tree
to tree or branch to branch, and then climbing up trunks or along
branches. It readily alights on and walks up vertical trunks. Of the
feeding records summarised in Table 47, just under half were in the
small bromeliads typical of wet montane forest, the bird probing into
the base from above or below, or tearing off the basal leaves. It does
not normally tackle the much larger and tougher bromeliads common
in wet midlevel forest. The only other important sources of food were
insects in epiphytic *Phyllogonium* moss and in very small ferns on
branches, and also in tree-fern fonds. The birds usually feed at between
3 and 12 m above the ground, occasionally up to 18 m. The information
in Table 47, though based on a fairly small number of observations,
shows that the two Jamaican forest icterids are almost completely
separated from each other in feeding. Just 3 times out of 86, we saw
I.leucopteryx tearing into bromeliads, and just 4 times out of 82 (3 on

one day), we saw *N.nigerrimus* stripping bark like *I.leucopteryx*. Hence the potentiality for competition between the species is there. In addition of course, *I.leucopteryx* has a much wider habitat than *N. nigerrimus*.

Nesopsar is an endemic Jamaican genus, considered to be near the American blackbirds *Agelaius* by Bond. It also has similarities with *Icterus*, but with no other icterid genus. Conceivably it evolved from their common ancestor, for as shown in Table 48 it has marked similarities with, and marked differences from, both *Agelaius* and *Icterus*.

TABLE 48. *Comparison of Nesopsar with typical Agelaius and typical Icterus*

Feature	*Nesopsar*	*Agelaius*	*Icterus*
Size, proportions, beak-shape	similar	similar	similar
Male plumage	black	black with bright shoulder	yellow, with black on head and wings
Female plumage	like male	duller than male	duller than male
Habitat	forest	marshes	forest
Altitude	montane	lowland	lowland and montane
Main feeding station	trees	ground	trees
Main food	insects	insects and seeds	insects and nectar or fruit
Feeds	solitarily	in flocks	solitarily except in flowering or fruiting trees
Breeds	solitarily	in loose colonies	solitarily
Song	wheezing	wheezing	musical
Nest	bulky cup	bulky cup	small, neat, slung

Note The Greater Antillean species of both *Agelaius* and *Icterus* are rather more similar than mainland ones to *Nesopsar*, but are still so different from it that they could hardly be ancestral. Thus *Agelaius humeralis* (Cuba, Hispaniola) and the closely related *A.xanthomus* (Puerto Rico) are partly arboreal, nesting and sometimes feeding in trees near the water, *A.xanthomus* is insectivorous and even probes in lowland bromeliads (C. Kepler pers. comm.), in which *A.xanthomus* may nest (Bond). Again, *I.dominicensis*, is blacker than most species in the genus, and the Puerto Rico form and *I.leucopteryx* are more insectivorous than most other species.

Quiscalus niger Greater Antillean Grackle (Kling-Kling) (Plate 14, Fig. 57)

Q.niger is common in only one natural habitat on Jamaica, the big sedge marsh, with marsh woodland, of the Black River swamp; locally it is also common in mangroves. It visits the sea-level forest of Morant

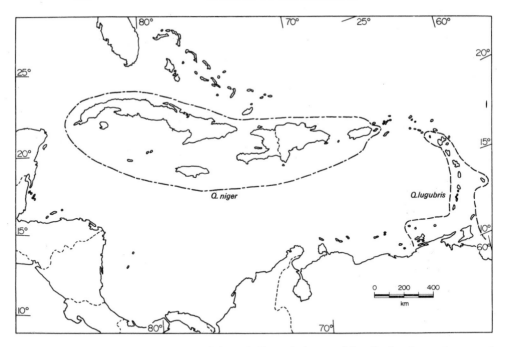

FIG. 57. *Range in the West Indies of the grackles* Quiscalus niger *and* Q.lugubris, *the latter also on the mainland (where range not shown).*

Point and elsewhere for the fruits of *Bursera simaruba* when they are ripe, but does not reside there. It is common in most of the wooded cultivation and grassland of the lowlands, including coconut plantations, but is scarce round Kingston. It is scarce and local in wooded cultivation and grassland at midlevels and is absent from the mountains. We saw it seeking food in grass and in low trees, and several times saw one take a lizard. According to Gosse (1847), it eats mainly insects, including many larvae, extracted from the roots of the grass with its relatively long beak.

Q.niger, is restricted to the Greater Antilles. On Grand Cayman, we found it abundant in mangroves. Probably its closest relative is *Q.lugubris*, which occurs in the Lesser Antilles and northern South America, so that *Q.niger* may have reached Jamaica from the south. Other species in the same group are the very local *Q.nicaraguensis* in Nicaragua and probably the Common Grackle *Q.quiscula* of North America (Yang and Selander 1968).

ICTERIDS OF THE OTHER GREATER ANTILLES

Hispaniola has the oriole *I.dominicensis*, the blackbird *A.humeralis* and the grackle *Q.niger*. Cuba has the same three species, also two North and Central American species, the Red-winged Blackbird *A.phoeniceus* in lowland marshland, and the Common Meadowlark *Sturnella magna* in dry grassland (in Central America in montane grassland), and finally the endemic *Dives atroviolaceus,* which, except in being smaller, is close to the Melodious Blackbird *D.dives* of Central America, where it lives in open woodland. Puerto Rico, like Hispaniola, has *I.dominicensis* and *Q.niger,* also the endemic *Agelaius xanthomus,* a close relative of *A.humeralis.*

CROWS CORVIDAE

Corvus jamaicensis **Jabbering Crow** (Plate 3, Fig. 58)

C.jamaicensis, endemic to Jamaica, is common in undisturbed midlevel wet limestone forest, as in the Cockpit Country and the John Crow Mountains, and is not uncommon in disturbed forest at this level, as round Worthy Park. We did not see it in either the lowlands or the mountains. On four occasions we saw one or more individuals feeding high in forest trees on large fruits, which we did not identify. In Worthy

FIG. 58. *Ranges of three Antillean species of crow* Corvus. *A fourth species,* C.palmarum, *inhabits Cuba and Hispaniola.*

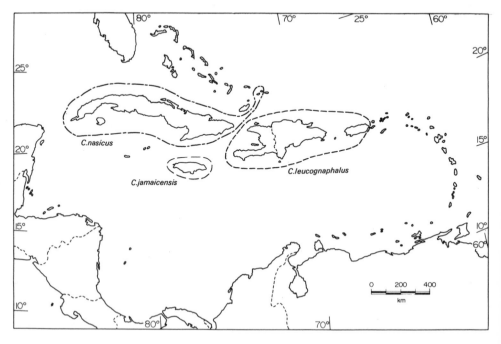

Park one was carrying an orange and another a frog. Gosse (1847) recorded it eating various cultivated fruits.

C.jamaicensis (wing 238 mm) is clearly in the genus *Corvus*, but Johnston (1961) could not determine its nearest relatives, and thought it rather uncrowlike, with unique morphology and voice. The latter, from which the bird gets is vernacular name, is a wavering semi-musical jabbering, described to Gosse (1847) as "like half a dozen Welshmen quarrelling".

Johnston (1961) considered that the larger *C.nasicus* (wing 285 mm), on Cuba and a few of the Bahamas, is closely related to the Common Crow *C.brachyrhynchos* (wing 304 mm) of North America, while *C.leucognaphalus*, on Hispaniola and formerly on Puerto Rico (wing 298 and 309 mm respectively) is derived from the North American White-necked Raven *C.cryptoleucus* (wing 356 mm). *C.leucognaphalus* agrees with *C.cryptoleucus* and differs from *C.nasicus* and *C.brachyrhynchos* in its concealed white on the hind neck, relatively high-pitched call and general habits (Wetmore and Swales 1931). I therefore accept Johnston's view, whereas Bond (1956) and Mayr and Short (1970) considered that *C.leucognaphalus* is closest to *C.nasicus* and *C.brachyrhynchos*. On Johnston's view, the crows provide another example of congeneric species which replace each other on different islands in the Greater Antilles, but are derived from different mainland species. In addition, another species of *Corvus*, *C.palmarum*, is found on Cuba and Hispaniola, but it is smaller (wing 233 and 261 mm respectively) with a narrower beak than its congeners, and is derived from the Fish Crow *C.ossifragus* of North America (Johnston 1961). On this view, all three crows on Cuba and Hispaniola are smaller than their nearest mainland relatives.

APPENDICES

APPENDICES

INTRODUCTION

The following section presents the data which is discussed in Parts I and II. All the original data collected for the book are now lodged at the Edward Grey Institute, Department of Zoology, University of Oxford.

APPENDIX 1

Summarised summer counts of the numbers of individual land birds (omitting aerial feeders and nocturnal birds) seen or heard per 10 hours in the main habitats on Jamaica.

	LOWLAND						
	1 Mangroves	2 Strand woodland	3 Sea level forest	4 Marsh forest	5 Arid limestone (natural)	6 Very arid ruinate	7 Arid ruinate in hills
Columba leucocephala			68	65	3		
Columba caribaea							
Zenaida macroura				30			
Zenaida aurita			8	15			20
Zenaida asiatica	67	80	64	90	40	27	160
Columbina passerina	53	173	20	90	114	63	80
Leptotila jamaicensis			28		93		
Geotrygon montana					3		
Geotrygon versicolor							
Aratinga nana			8				
Amazona collaria							
Amazona agilis							
Coccyzus americanus				5	2		
Coccyzus minor			4	5	8		
Hyetornis pluvialis							
Saurothera vetula					5		
Crotophaga ani	7	40	24	150			
Anthracothorax mango	22		44	115	11	33	
Trochilus polytmus			24	15	2		20
Mellisuga minima	20		60	5	51	17	40
Todus todus	5		4		45		60
Centurus radiolatus	31		80	100	50		
Platypsaris niger							
Tyrannus dominicensis	7		72	75	14	30	20
Tyrannus caudifasciatus	18		40	45	14		40
Myiarchus stolidus	5		32	25	43	27	
Myiarchus barbirostris	9		4	25	22		
Myiarchus validus	X				14		
Contopus caribaeus							
Elaenia fallax							
Myiopagis cotta					8		
Mimus polyglottos	13	427	28	10	3	103	20
Mimus gundlachii					118	13	
Myadestes genibarbis							
Turdus aurantius			20				
Turdus jamaicensis							
Tiaris olivacea	2		28	5	16		20

Botanic Garden	8 Fairly rich secondary in hills	9 Southern riverine	10 Northern riverine	11 Wet limestone forest	Wooded cultivation	12 Very wet limestone forest	13 Hardwar forest	Morce's Gap trail	Wooded cultivation
	67	16	96	63		9	17	40	
				11		51		8	
40	23	12	24	11			1		
10		32				7			
110	60	92	56	12					
	60	28	32	51	8	2		X	
			80	16		36	4	8	
				14		20	18	28	8
	70		24	160					
				80		55			
		10							
	X			3	X	7	1		
	10			7		X	2		15
50		26		3					
	7	6		4	X		X		
180	57	70	120	94	135	217	182	156	83
30	53	16		17	X	51	2	32	38
	107	46	8	35	120	27	35	32	8
	73	20	64	71	75	80	15	68	8
			48	6		13	4	4	
180		22	8	18		4			15
20	33	32	40	22	23	9			15
	30	8		4					
	70	22		7	15	15	6		
	20	4	8	21	45	5	2		15
	7			14	23	9	8	X	
				1		2	39	124	
	7	4	24	14	8	2	5	16	
230	3	72		6					
				18	60	42	151	288	98
	7	2	80	32	90	62	23	36	23
			112	75	45	69	26	104	30
90	63	42		55					

APPENDIX 1 (*cont.*)

	1 Mangroves	2 Strand woodland	3 Sea level forest	4 Marsh forest	5 Arid limestone (natural)	6 Very arid ruinate	7 Arid ruinate in hills
			LOWLAND				
Tiaris bicolor	4		20	10	6	57	
Loxipasser anoxanthus			20		35	7	40
Loxigilla violacea			24	10	27		40
Spindalis zena							
Euphonia jamaica	X		32	15	8		20
Euneornis campestris			12				
Dendroica petechia	285	240	36	135	19	13	
Dendroica pharetra			X				
Coereba flaveola	31	133	68	90	78	293	60
Vireo modestus	X		36	10	102	93	100
Vireo osburni							
Vireo altiloquus	53		228	160	150	30	80
Icterus leucopteryx	2		44	35	18	27	60
Nesopsar nigerrimus							
Quiscalus niger	25		4	10	X		
Corvus jamaicensis							
Forpus passerinus				40	32	23	
Sturnus vulgaris							
Sicalis flaveola							
Hours counted	$5\frac{1}{2}$	$\frac{3}{4}$	$2\frac{1}{2}$	2	$6\frac{1}{4}$	3	$\frac{1}{2}$
Total birds seen or heard per *hour*	66	109	118	139	116	116	88

Notes   (i) Numbers of forest types derived from Table 2, p. 23.

(ii) X indicates less than 0.5 birds seen and heard per 10 hours.

(iii) Botanic garden and wooded cultivation have been included although not natural forest.

	LOWLAND			MIDLEVEL			MONTANE		
Botanic Garden	8 Fairly rich secondary in hills	9 Southern riverine	10 Northern riverine	11 Wet limestone forest	Wooded cultivation	12 Very wet limestone forest	13 Hardwar forest	Morce's Gap trail	Wooded cultivation
100	3	6		26	8	11	12		8
	23	72	24	31	53	4	9	12	38
	30	44	40	34	30	18	29	52	30
				18		20	28	32	38
60	43	50	8	21	15	5	6	8	15
10	17	4	112	40	120	67	22	12	60
		40							
				10	23	24	10	52	8
240	63	110	88	49	68	100	72	100	83
	130	84	128	100	53	53	65	148	90
				16	8	13	6		
100	190	174	136	111	210	156	55	32	83
10	17	26	8	27	38	11	14	4	8
				2		X	5	12	
110									
				34		38			
30	63	40							
110		2			8				
100					8				
1	3	5	$1\frac{1}{4}$	16	$1\frac{1}{3}$	$5\frac{1}{2}$	13	$2\frac{1}{2}$	$1\frac{1}{3}$
181	142	123	137	147	128	132	87	141	81

APPENDIX 2

Summarised winter counts of the number of individual land birds (omitting aerial feeders, nocturnal birds and, except in the total, wintering passerines) seen (only) per 10 hours in the main habitats on Jamaica

	LOWLAND						
	1 Mangroves	2 Strand woodland	3 Sea level forest	5 Arid limestone (natural)	6 Very arid ruinate	7 Arid ruinate in hills	Botanic Garden
Columba leucocephala	2		25	9		2	
Columba caribaea							
Zenaida aurita	8		1			17	21
Zenaida asiatica		10	8	X	11	7	10
Columbina passerina		50	9	9	73	14	57
Leptotila jamaicensis	1		3	22	1	4	
Geotrygon montana				X			
Geotrygon versicolor							
Aratinga nana			3	7			
Amazona collaria							5
Amazona agilis							
Amazona sp.							
Coccyzus minor			3	2	1	7	2
Hyetornis pluvialis							
Saurothera vetula				2		1	
Crotophaga ani	2		15				19
Anthracothorax mango	4	10	16	3	38	1	5
Trochilus polytmus	1	5	19	5	1	33	55
Mellisuga minima	2		43	5	3	7	30
Todus todus	6			5		17	
Centurus radiolatus	3		18	4		X	2
Platypsaris niger							
Tyrannus caudifasciatus	10		51	8	6	14	18
Myiarchus stolidus	11		4	17	12		
Myiarchus barbirostris	1		13				
Myiarchus validus			4	4			
Contopus caribaeus							
Elaenia fallax							
Myiopagis cotta			1				
Mimus polyglottos	7	110	36	2	59	28	143
Mimus gundlachii	1			35	13		
Myadestes genibarbis						1	
Turdus aurantius			X			5	
Turdus jamaicensis						2	
Tiaris olivacea	2		10	2	X	6	38
Tiaris bicolor			5		25	26	22

	LOWLAND			MIDLEVEL			MONTANE		
8 Fairly rich secondary in hills	9 Southern riverine	10 Northern riverine	11 Wet limestone forest	Wooded culti-vation	12 Very wet limestone forest	13 Hardwar Forest inside	edge	Morce's Gap trail	Wooded culti-vation
10	4	5	5	9	6				
			1		18		X	2	1
2	10		9		2		1		
	24		15		6				X
7	46	19	10	1	2				2
10	10	5	11	1	2				
2		31	2	3	2			1	
			2		2	3	1	4	
17	10	5	29						
	1		6		61				
			2						
			15						
1	4								2
2			3	3	6	X	X		
1	2		1		2				
	13		6	8	8				X
X	4		5	5	12		X		85
21	33	38	66	61	65	45	64	121	8
2	7	5	2	3	6	1	X	12	11
42	23	19	14	23	20	5	6	16	8
20	11	7	24	5	11	1	3	7	
2			4	4	3	1	1	1	17
16	28	14	26	20	15		2	1	
7	7		8						1
9	9		10	6	2		1		2
11	2		5	3		X			2
9		2	12	11	2	1	3	1	4
			2		4	1		3	X
2	2	2	3	4	4	X	1		
2	34		4		4				
1	1	5	4	9	8	5	2	9	10
11	6	28	21	35	26	6	18	6	23
4	13	X	13	1	Q	7	4	22	10
19	33		17	15			X		1
1	13	2	8	6	2	2	15	1	27

APPENDIX 2 (*cont.*)

LOWLAND

	1 Mangroves	2 Strand woodland	3 Sea level forest	5 Arid limestone (natural)	6 Very arid ruinate	7 Arid ruinate in hills	Botanic Garden
Loxipasser anoxanthus			10	7	2	6	7
Loxigilla violacea	2		19	23		7	2
Spindalis zena							
Euphonia jamaica	3		9	8		2	28
Euneornis campestris						5	20
Dendroica petechia	58	40	3		2		
Dendroica pharetra							
Coereba flaveola	24	190	70	35	103	54	158
Vireo modestus	1		10	35	24	12	
Vireo osburni							
Icterus leucopteryx	X		9	5	3	7	8
Nesopsar nigerrimus							
Quiscalus niger	8		19	X			16
Corvus jamaicensis							
Winter visitors	137	55	152	52	14	85	96
Forpus passerinus				3	24		7
Sturnus vulgaris							87
Sicalis flaveola						4	39
Hours counted (winter)	9	2	8	22	21	10	10
Birds seen (only) per hour (winter)	30	47	58	30	42	37	89
Hours counted (summer)	5½	¾	5⅔	3¾	3	5	1½
Birds seen (only) per hour (summer)	25	73	98	52	85	45	109

Notes   (i) Numbers of forest types derived from Table 2, p. 23.

(ii) X indicates less than 0.5 birds seen (only) per 10 hours.

(iii) *64 birds were seen in Worthy Park area per hour in 15½ hours; 83 were seen in the Cockpit Country per hour in 8½ hours.

(iv) Botanic Garden and Wooded cultivation have been included although not natural forest.

(v) The discrepancies between the totals in the last lines of Appendices 1 and 2 are because in winter (13 October–31 March) a bird was recorded only when seen, while in summer (from 1 May) a bird was recorded when seen *or* heard. During April a bird was recorded if seen as well as heard, so the figures were added to the summer totals of birds seen only (in Appendix 2).

	LOWLAND			MIDLEVEL		13 Hardwar Forest		MONTANE	
8 Fairly rich secondary in hills	9 Southern riverine	10 Northern riverine	11 Wet limestone forest	Wooded cultivation	12 Very wet limestone forest	inside	edge	Morce's Gap trail	Wooded cultivation
7	23		8	9	2	1	5	4	7
23	13	12	15	6	15	13	13	8	14
3	1	19	22	16	17	13	21	25	34
17	33	5	8	11	6	5	X	1	9
8	8	14	33	78	72	7	11	36	37
	(4)								
8		5	10	5	8	21	16	10	4
22	70	16	24	31	22	12	37	67	75
19	15	12	16	5		5	8	12	14
			4			1	6	4	X
12	16	9	10	11	20	1	3	1	6
					2	4	4	1	
			8		22				1
95	212	45	44	116	58	34	41	18	55
28	19		9						
	6		5	6					
	4			1					
20	26	4¼	31	8	6½	29½	30	14	25
47	78	32	58	54	56	19	29	39	52
6½	7½	1¼	24*	1⅓	5½	22¼	Not counted	8	3
58	58	32	64 ⎱ 83 ⎰ *	54	38	32	Not counted	38	42

APPENDIX 3

Birds of lowland forest (omitting aerial and nocturnal feeders) in southern Jamaica

	1 Man-groves	2 Strand woodland	3 Sea-level forest	4 Marsh forest	5 Arid limestone (natural)	7 Arid ruinate in hills	8 Fairly rich secondary in hills	9 Southern riverine
Columba leucocephala	w	—	R	X	R	w	R	R
Zenaida macroura	—	—	—	X	r	—	—	—
Zenaida aurita	(e)	—	R	X	—	R	R	R
Zenaida asiatica	S	R	R	X	R	R	—	R
Columbina passerina	S	R	R	X	R	R	(E)	R
Leptotila jamaicensis	(e)	—	R	—	R	R	R	R
Geotrygon montana	—	—	—	—	S	—	W	r
Aratinga nana	---	—	R	—	W	—	R	W
Amazona collaria	—	—	—	—	—	—	—	w
Coccyzus americanus	—	—	(s)	X	(s)	(s)	—	(s)
Coccyzus minor	(e)	—	R	X	R	R	R	R
Hyetornis pluvialis	—	—	—	—	—	—	sW	—
Saurothera vetula	—	—	—	—	R	r	R	r
Crotophaga ani	R	R	(E)	X	(E)	(E)	(E)	R
Anthracothorax mango	R	R	R	X	R	r	r	r
Trochilus polytmus	w	W	R	X	r	R	R	R
Mellisuga minima	R	—	R	X	R	R	R	R
Todus todus	R	—	r	—	R	R	R	R
Centurus radiolatus	R	—	R	X	R	r	R	R
Platypsaris niger	—	—	—	—	—	—	w	—
Tyrannus dominicensis	S	—	S	X	S	S	R	S
Tyrannus caudifasciatus	R	—	R	X	R	R	R	R
Myiarchus stolidus	R	—	R	X	R	W	R	R
Myiarchus barbirostris	R	—	R	X	S	—	R	R
Myiarchus validus	s	—	r	—	R	—	R	R
Contopus caribaeus	(e)	—	—	—	—	—	sW	—
Myiopagis cotta	—	—	w	—	S	—	R	R
Mimus polyglottos	R	R	R	X	(E)	R	(E)	R
Mimus gundlachii	(e)	—	—	—	R	—	—	—
Myadestes genibarbis	—	—	—	—	—	w	W	w
Turdus aurantius	—	—	(w)	—	—	W	R	sW
Turdus jamaicensis	—	—	—	—	—	w	W	W
Tiaris olivacea	(e)	—	R	X	R	(E)	(E)	(E)
Tiaris bicolor	(e)	—	R	X	r	R	(e)	R
Loxipasser anoxanthus	—	—	R	—	R	R	R	R
Loxigilla violacea	(e)	—	R	X	R	R	R	R
Spindalis zena	—	—	—	—	—	—	w	w
Euphonia jamaica	W	—	R	X	R	R	R	R
Euneornis campestris	—	—	(w)	—	—	w	R	R

APPENDIX 3 (*cont.*)

	1 Man- groves	2 Strand woodland	3 Sea- level forest	4 Marsh forest	5 Arid limestone (natural)	7 Arid ruinate in hills	8 Fairly rich secon- dary in hills	9 Southern riverine
Dendroica petechia	R	R	R	—	r	—	—	s
Dendroica pharetra	—	—	—	—	—	—	W	—
Coereba flaveola	R	R	R	X	R	R	R	R
Vireo modestus	(e)	—	R	X	R	R	R	R
Vireo altiloquus	S	S	S	X	S	S	S	S
Icterus leucopteryx	(e)	—	R	X	R	R	R	R
Quiscalus niger	R	—	R	X	—	—	—	(E)
Total (Summer)	16(+1)	8	27(+2)	26	26(+4)	19(+3)	25(+3)	27(+5)
Total (Winter)	13(+2)	8	25(+3)	—	22(+4)	19(+7)	30(+3)	28(+6)

Notes   (i) The numbers above the forest types are derived from Table 2, p. 23.

(ii) R = resident, S = in summer, W = in winter, (E) = at edge, r, s, w, e mean the same but rare. (S) = rare or migrant only.

(iii) So many species were seen at the edge of mangroves near scrub forest that it was difficult to know which to include.

(iv) Only a few counts were made in strand woodland, so the totals are probably incomplete.

(v) Marsh forest was counted only once, in summer, so 'X' is used meaning present, instead of 'R'.

(vi) For Sea-level forest, '(*w*)' (italic) means seen in the west but not in the south, and the birds concerned are omitted from the total.

(vii) Similar habitats in northern Jamaica have rather more species.

(viii) The totals cannot be compared directly with those in Table 4, p. 41, because 3 swifts, 2 swallows, 2 owls, a potoo and 2 nightjars have been omitted since we did not have full records for the nocturnal species and did not always note when the aerial feeders were overhead.

APPENDIX 4

Part 1. Summarised counts of birds seen per 10 hours on Dominica, 1–3 June 1971 and 2–15 June 1972

	Leeward below 230 m semi-arid $6\frac{1}{2}$	Windward below 100 m evergreen $4\frac{1}{4}$	Rain forest mainly 250–700 m inside $10\frac{1}{2}$	Rain forest mainly 250–700 m from road $3\frac{1}{4}$	Montane thicket 800–1000 m 9
Hours counted:					
pigeon *Columba squamosa*	8	7	29	59	23
dove *Zenaida aurita*	58	7	—	—	—
dove *Columbina passerina*	29	(E)	—	—	—
dove *Geotrygon montana*	14	—	14	3	2
cuckoo *Coccyzus minor*	9	—	X	3	—
ani *Crotophaga ani*	8	(E)	—	—	—
swift *Chaetura martinica*	6	—	7	69	—
swift *Cypseloides niger*	9	7	5	48	16
hummingbird *Cyanophaia bicolor*	—	—	10	8	34
hummingbird *Eulampis jugularis*	2	5	16	24	28
hummingbird *Sericotes holosericeus*	14	33	—	13	—
hummingbird *Orthorhyncus cristatus*	28	28	—	3	(E)
flycatcher *Tyrannus dominicensis*	17	21	2	27	—
flycatcher *Myiarchus stolidus*	2	2	—	8	—
flycatcher *Contopus latirostris*	3	—	1	11	2
flycatcher *Elaenia martinica*	40	85	3	56	89
martin *Progne dominicensis*	6	2	—	—	8
wren *Troglodytes aedon*	9	28	33	6	24
mockingbird *Mimus gilvus*	23	—	—	—	—
thrasher *Allenia fusca*	35	66	9	115	30
thrasher *Margarops fuscatus*	—	—	59	43	2
thrasher *Cinclocerthia ruficauda*	11	35	33	99	29
solitaire *Myadestes genibarbis*	—	—	66	80	106
thrush *Cichlherminia lherminieri*	—	—	24	53	18
thrush *Turdus plumbeus*	48	—	—	—	—
finch *Tiaris bicolor*	79	35	—	29	10
finch *Loxigilla noctis*	123	146	75	104	56
finch *Saltator albicollis*	77	75	—	19	4
euphonia *Euphonia musica*	—	—	1	3	—
warbler *Dendroica petechia*	123	33	—	—	—
warbler *Dendroica plumbea*	12	12	12	13	20
bananaquit *Coereba flaveola*	86	146	62	101	100
vireo *Vireo altiloquus*	71	93	40	88	26
grackle *Quiscalus lugubris*	26	(E)	—	—	—

Note The following species are omitted: the dove *Geotrygon mystacea* (not seen), the parrots *Amazona arausiaca* and *Amazona imperialis* (seen in and confined to rain forest), the barn owl, *Tyto alba* (not seen), and the kingfisher *Ceryle torquata* (seen by a lowland river). Full details are deposited at the Edward Grey Institute, Oxford.

(E) = at edge

X = less than 0.5 birds seen per 10 hours

APPENDIX 4

Part 2. Summary of habitats of resident species on Dominica in June

A. LOWLAND AND HIGHLAND FOREST: 20 species		C. SOLELY HIGHLAND: 6 species	
L.W.R.M. (14)	**L.W.R. (4)**	**R.M. (3)**	**R. (3)**
pigeon *C.squamosa*	cuckoo *C.minor*	hummingbird *C.bicolor*	parrot *A.arausiaca*
dove *G.montana*	swift *C.martinica*	solitaire *M.genibarbis*	parrot *A.imperialis*
swift *C.niger*	kingfisher *C.torquata*	thrush *C. lherminieri*	euphonia *E.musica*
hummingbird *E.jugularis*	flycatcher *M.stolidus*		
flycatcher *C.latirostris*			
flycatcher *E.martinica*			
wren *T.aedon*	**L.W.M. (1)**		
thrasher *C.ruficauda*	martin *P.dominicensis*		
thrasher *A.fusca*			
bullfinch *L.noctis*			
saltator *S.albicollis*	**W.R.M. (1)**		
warbler *D.plumbea*	thrasher *M.fuscatus*		
bananaquit *C.flaveola*			
vireo *V.altiloquus*			

B. SOLELY LOWLAND: 9 species		D. OTHERS: 4 species	
L.W. (4) (also edge of R)	**L.W. (1)** (not also edge of R)	Solely cultivated grassy lowlands (2): ani *C.ani* and grackle *Q.lugubris*	
hummingbird *S.holosericeus*	dove *Z.aurita*	Not seen by us (2): dove *G.mystacea* (probably both lowlands and highlands, as it is on other Lesser Antilles) and barn owl *T.alba* (certainly highlands (Lawrence 1878) and probably lowlands, as it is on other Lesser Antilles).	
hummingbird *O.cristatus*			
▾ flycatcher *T.dominicensis*	**L. (4)**		
grassquit *T.bicolor*	dove *C.passerina*		
	mockingbird *M.gilvus*		
	thrush *T.plumbeus*		
	warbler *D.petechia*		

Notes   (i) L = lowland leeward, W = lowland windward, R = rain forest, M = montane thicket.
(ii) Both swifts feed regularly, but probably do not breed, in the lowlands.
(iii) Four species recorded in both L and R were not seen by us in W, but presumably occur there, namely *G.montana, C.latirostris, C.minor* and *C.torquata* (and we did not, though Drs. Kepler and Zusi (pers. comm.) did, see the last species in the highlands).
(iv) Our counts refer solely to the wet month of June. There are probably seasonal movements. For instance in autumn the Keplers (pers. comm.) reported the thrush *Turdus plumbeus* in humid forest, where we did not find it.

APPENDIX 5
Basis for the figures in Table 6

The basis of these figures is the set of tabulations by Monroe (1968, pp. 391–399), but his aim was to give the main habitat of each species, whereas in testing for overlap in habitat, it is necessary to include each species under all the habitats in which it is regular, even if it is commoner in one than others. For this and other reasons, I modified Monroe's habitat lists as follows, in the light of what he wrote in his main text, and he kindly checked (*in litt.*) what I had done.

p. 391: add to tabulated list *Tityra semifasciata* (which he omitted from all lists) and *Camptostoma imberbe* (from the second tabulation on p. 396) and remove *Tolmomyias sulphurescens* and *Hylophilus decurtatus*, here classified under rain forest and deciduous forest.

p. 392, second tabulation: add *Cyanocorax yncas* (which he omitted altogether), *Xiphorhynchus erythropygius* and *Tanagra elegantissima* (both of which he placed in the third tabulation on p. 395), and remove *Turdus assimilis*, here classified under rain forest, deciduous forest and cloud forest.

p. 392, third tabulation: remove *Hylocharis eliciae*, *Amazilia candida*, *Todirostrum sylvia*, *Oncostoma cinereigulare*, *Pipromorpha oleaginea*, *Amblycercus holosericeus*, *Tanagra lauta* and *Habia fuscicauda*, all here classified under rain forest and deciduous forest. (*Pionus senilis* might have been removed for the same reason, but is borderline, so is retained here.)

p. 394, lines 5–6: remove *Arremonops chloronotus*, here classified under rain forest and deciduous forest.

p. 394, first tabulation: remove *Columba cayennensis* and *Aratinga astec*, here classified under rain forest and deciduous forest.

p. 394, second tabulation: add *Pachyrhamphus polychopterus* (which he omitted altogether) and remove *Picumnus olivaceus*, here classified under rain forest and deciduous forest.

p. 395: transfer *Elaenia frantzii* from first to third tabulation, transfer *Tilmatura dupontii* and *Icterus wagleri* from second to first tabulation, transfer *Strix fulvescens*, *Dendrocolaptes picumnus*, *Cyanolyca pumilo*, *Aphelocoma unicolor*, *Vireo leucophrys*, *Myioborus miniatus* and *Piranga leucoptera* from third to first tabulation.

From third tabulation on p. 395, transfer *Xiphorhynchus erythropygius* to second tabulation on p. 392, and *Tanagra elegantissima* to a group on its own in lowland rain, vega, cloud and pine-oak forest, and to the third tabulation on p. 395 add *Eugenes fulgens* from first tabulation on p. 397.

p. 396, second tabulation: add three species omitted from all tabulations, *Amazona ochrocephala* (which Monroe referred to in his text below), *Todirostrum cinereum* (with asterisk) and *Tanagra affinis* (with asterisk). Remove *Camptostoma imberbe* to tabulation p. 391. Add asterisk (meaning in deciduous forest) to *Myiarchus nuttingi*, *Thyothorus pleurostictus*, *Polioptila albiloris* and *Icterus pectoralis*.

p. 397, top line: add to high steppe and savanna species *Empidonax albigularis* (omitted entirely from Monroe's lists), remove *Speotyto cunicularia* (based on one record), and transfer *Cistothorus platensis* and *Sturnella magna* to species occurring in both low and high pine (actually in grassland in pine areas).

p. 397, first tabulation: add *Icterus chrysater* (also in low pine). Transfer *Eugenes fulgens* to third tabulation p. 395. Transfer *Pachyrhamphus major*, *Mitrephanes phaeocercus*, *Myadestes obscurus*, *Catharus aurantiirostris*, and *Vermivora superciliosa* to first tabulation p. 395. Monroe reserved the latter tabulation for species equally common in both cloud forest and high pine-oak forest, but for my analysis I need to include all species that are regular in both, even if much commoner in one of them.

Note that a number of species in the first tabulation on p. 397 are also included in the second (which is continued on p. 398), and that the following species are common to both low and high pine forest: *Amazilia cyanocephala*, *Melanerpes formicivorus*, *Sialia sialis*, *Dendroica graciae*, *Piranga flava*, *Aimophila rufescens*, *Spizella passerina*, *Spinus notatus* and *Loxia curvirostra*; also *Icterus chrysater*,

APPENDIX 5 (*cont.*)

listed by Monroe solely for low pine. Further, *Piculus rubiginosus* was listed earlier for species widespread in arid and humid lowlands p. 391. This leaves only *Pyrocephalus rubinus* in the list of species restricted to low pine forest.

p. 398, second tabulation: note that *Columbigallina passerina* was included in the second tabulation on p. 396, and is here classified as in low arid and low pine, and that *Cistothorus platensis* and *Sturnella magna*, listed earlier under high savanna species (top p. 397), are here classified as in low and high pine.

Five of the species listed for the offshore islands on p. 399 are confined to them, namely *Columba leucocephala, Leptotila jamaicensis, Amazona xantholora, Centurus pygmaeus* and *Vireo magister,* and are here classified as such; but the others are in one of the lists already discussed, including *Crotophaga ani*, described in Monroe's book as restricted to the islands but recently also found on the mainland (Monroe pers. comm.).

I made one further change on the basis, not of Monroe's text, but of what is found elsewhere, in Central America. *Coereba flaveola* is rare in Honduras and recorded for the edge of lowland rain forest, but elsewhere in Central America it is recorded not only at the edge of rain forest but also in second growth; so I have transferred it from the rain forest birds in the second column on p. 394 to the edge birds on p. 391 (even though Monroe used this latter category for birds equally at home in both arid and humid forest-edge).

APPENDIX 6

Numbers of individuals of Jamaican birds seen feeding on wild fruits

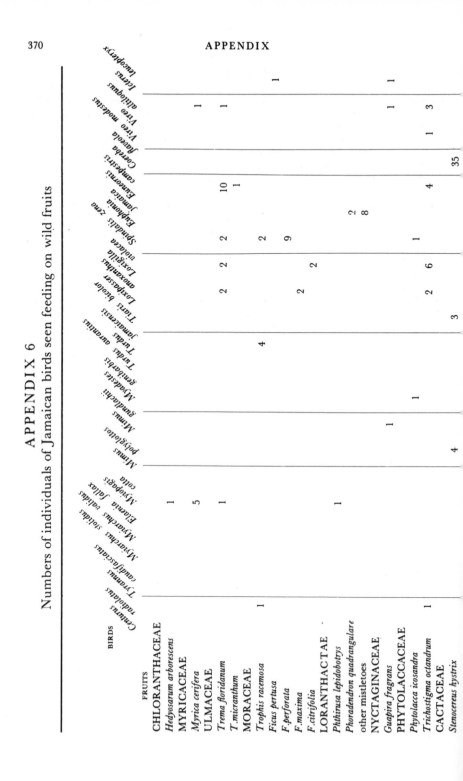

FRUITS	Centurus radiolatus	Tyrannus caudifasciatus	Myiarchus stolidus	Myiarchus validus	Elaenia fallax	Myiopagis cotta	Mimus polyglottos	Mimus gundlachii	Myadestes genibarbis	Turdus aurantius	Turdus jamaicensis	Turdis bicolor	Loxipasser anoxanthus	Loxigilla violacea	Spindalis zena	Euphonia jamaica	Euneornis campestris	Coereba	Vireo modestus	Vireo altiloquus	Icterus leucopteryx
CHLORANTHACEAE																					
Hedyosarum arborescens			1																		
MYRICACEAE																					
Myrica cerifera				5																	
ULMACEAE																					
Trema floridanum			1										2	2	2		10		1	1	
T. micranthum																	1				
MORACEAE																					
Trophis racemosa	1									4			2	2	2						
Ficus pertusa																					
F. perforata															9						
F. maxima													2	2							
F. citrifolia																					
LORANTHACEAE																					
Phthirusa lepidobotrys						1															
Phoradendron quadrangulare																2					
other mistletoes																8					
NYCTAGINACEAE																					
Guapira fragrans							1	1													
PHYTOLACCACEAE									1						1						
Phytolacca icosandra									1						1						
Trichostigma octandrum										2				6			4	1	1		1
CACTACEAE																					
Stenocereus hystrix							4					3						35	3	1	1

LAURACEAE												
Nectandra antillana		2			6			3		4		1
CANELLACEAE										1		
Canella winterana									1			
MENISPERMACEAE												
Cissampelos pareira	1										1	
GUTTIFERAE												
Clusia flava											2	
PAPAVERACEAE												
Boconia frutescens						2				2	2	3
CAPPARACEAE												
Capparis ferruginea												
MIMOSACEAE												
Pithecellobium unguis-cati			6	1		9	2	1	10	2	2	
RUTACEAE	2	2	1		4		11	6		11	1	1
Fagara martinicensis		3	1		4			3			1	
F.elephantiasis												1
BURSERACEAE	2	8	6	5	4	1	2	8	2		2	
Bursera simaruba											4	1
MELIACEAE						1						
Trichilia hirta				1				1				
T.moschata								1				1
EUPHORBIACEAE				2			1					
Croton eluteria							1					
Adelia ricinella							27					
Alchornea latifolia		3					4		8	8	1	9
ANACARDIACEAE		1						1		1		
Comocladia pinnatifolia							2					
C.velutina				1			3		1			
Metopium brownii												
SAPINDACEAE												
Allophylus cominia												
Cupania glabra				1	2			2	3		1	
AQUIFOLIACEAE											5	
Ilex macfadyenii		1										

APPENDIX 6 (cont.)

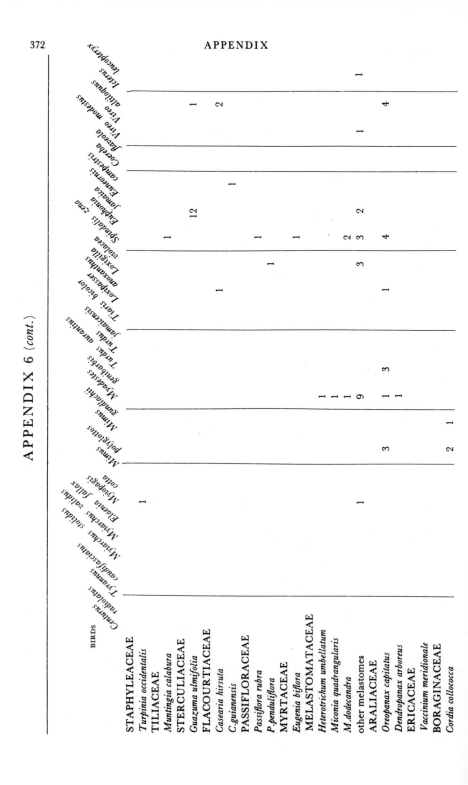

BIRDS	Centurus radiolatus	Tyrannus caudifasciatus	Myiarchus stolidus	Myiarchus barbirostris	Elaenia fallax	Myiopagis cotta	Mimus polyglottos	Mimus gundlachii	M. badioides	Myadestes genibarbis	Turdus aurantius	Turdus jamaicensis	Tiaris bicolor	Loxipasser anoxanthus	Loxigilla violacea	Spindalis zena	Euphonia jamaica	Euneornis campestris	Coereba flaveola	Vireo modestus	Vireo altiloquus	Icterus leucopteryx
STAPHYLEACEAE																						
Turpinia occidentalis					1																	
TILIACEAE																						
Muntingia calabura																						
STERCULIACEAE																						
Guazuma ulmifolia															1	12	1	1		1	2	
FLACOURTIACEAE														1								
Casearia hirsuta														1								
C. guianensis																						
PASSIFLORACEAE															1			1				
Passiflora rubra															1			1				
P. penduliflora																1						
MYRTACEAE																1						
Eugenia biflora																1						
MELASTOMATACEAE									1									2				
Heterotrichum umbellatum									1													
Miconia quadrangularis									1													
M. dodecandra									1							2		3				
other melastomes			1					3	9	3					3	3	2					1
ARALIACEAE								1	1						1	4		4			4	
Oreopanax capitatus								1	1						1						4	
Dendropanax arboreus									3													
ERICACEAE																						
Vaccinium meridionale																						
BORAGINACEAE							2	3								1						
Cordia collococca							2	3								1						

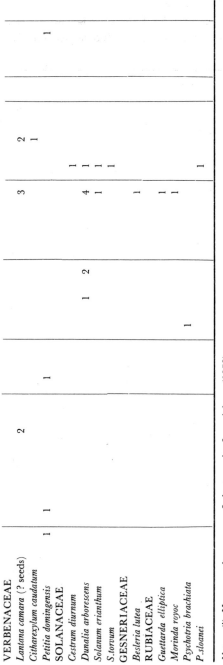

VERBENACEAE
Lantana camara (? seeds)
Citharexylum caudatum
Petitia domingensis
SOLANACEAE
Cestrum diurnum
Dunalia arborescens
Solanum erianthum
S.torvum
GESNERIACEAE
Besleria lutea
RUBIACEAE
Guettarda elliptica
Morinda royoc
Psychotria brachiata
P.sloanei

Notes (i) Names and sequence of plant species from Adams (1972)

(ii) The numbers are the total of individual birds seen feeding, irrespective of how many fruits each ate while we were watching. The number of fruits taken is very incomplete, first because we did not identify by any means all of the fruits seen taken, and secondly because we did not make special observations on fruiting trees, but simply recorded the bird species present as we walked past—the one exception being some trees of *Pithecellobium unguis-cati* which, being near the University, we could watch on several days.

(iii) The following records were received from Miss L. Salmon (from which have been excluded those already listed in Table 11 for the species concerned): *Chlorophora tinctoria* (Moraceae) by *L.violacea*; Loranthaceae by *L.violacea* and *L.anoxanthus*; *Nectandra antillana* by *C.radiolatus*, *M.polyglottos*, *T.aurantius* and *V.altiloquus*; *Guaiacum officinale* (Zygophyllaceae) by *M.polyglottos*; *Picrasma excelsa* (Simaroubaceae) by *C.radiolatus*, *T.caudifasciatus*, *V.altiloquus*, *S.zena* and *L.anoxanthus*; *Bursera simaruba* by *T.aurantius* and *E.campestris*; *Eugenia* sp. by *E.campestris*, *S.zena*, and *L.anoxanthus*; *Bumelia salicifolia* (Sapotaceae) by *C.radiolatus*, *T.aurantius*, *S.zena*, and *L.anoxanthus*; *Duranta repens* (Verbenaceae) by *S.zena*; and *Citharexylum* sp. by *C.radiolatus* and *M.polyglottos*.

(iv) Paterson (1964) recorded the following taking *Sapium jamaicense*: *Tyrannus dominicensis*, *T.caudifasciatus*, *Mimus polyglottos*, *V.altiloquus* and *I.leucopteryx*.

(v) Fruits eaten by species in the families Columbidae, Psittacidae, Cuculidae, and Todidae are recorded in Part 2 under the species concerned.

(vi) The fruits of cultivated and other introduced trees were omitted but those of one introduced species, *Pittosporum undulatum*, found on mountain trails, were so popular that it may be noted that they were taken by *Elaenia fallax*, *Myadestes genibarbis*, *Turdus jamaicensis*, *Loxigilla violacea* and *Icterus leucopteryx*.

APPENDIX 7

Number of observed feeds on wild flowers by Jamaican nectar-eating birds. Single feeds by *Trochilus polytmus* are recorded separately at the end

	Hummingbirds			Bananaquit	Orangequit
FLOWER	*Anthracothorax mango*	*Trochilus polytmus*	*Mellisuga minima*	*Coereba flaveola*	*Euneornis campestris*
BROMELIACEAE					
midlevel *Hohenbergia* spp.	2	14	1		1
montane bromeliads		8	2		4
STRELITZIACEAE					
Heliconia swartziana		2			
MARANTACEAE					
Thalia geniculata					1
PIPERACEAE					
Piper aduncum					1
Piper hispidum					1
Pothomorpha umbellata					1
MORACEAE					
Cecropia peltata		2		2	4
CACTACEAE					
Opuntia spinosissima	15	1			
Opuntia dillenii	3				
Stenocereus hystrix	5		1		
MARCGRAVIACEAE					
Marcgravia brownei		2			
CAESALPINIACEAE					
Bauhinia divaricata		7	1	9	6
Cassia emarginata				1	
MIMOSACEAE					
Calliandra pilosa			1		
Acacia sp.			1		
PAPILIONACEAE					
Crotolaria falcata		1	1		
Canavalia maritima	2	1		2	
Centrosema plumieri		2			
Centrosema pubescens				1	
SIMAROUBACEAE					
Picrasma excelsa				1	4
POLYGALACEAE					
Securidaca brownei			1	1	
EUPHORBIACEAE					
Croton linearis			1		
Euphorbia punicea				1	
Pedilanthus tithymaloides		2			
COMBRETACEAE					
Laguncularia racemosa			1		

APPENDIX 7 *(cont.)*

FLOWER	Hummingbirds			Bananaquit	Orangequit
	Anthracothorax mango	*Trochilus polytmus*	*Mellisuga minima*	*Coereba flaveola*	*Euneornis campestris*
MELASTOMATACEAE					
Meriania leucantha		10			2
Miconia quadrangularis		4	1	1	
Miconia dodecandra				1	
Blakea trinervia					3
montane melastomes					
(unidentified)		7		2	3
ARALIACEAE					
Oreopanax capitatus				2	
Schefflera sp.		2			1
Dendropanax arboreus					1
CLETHRACEAE					
Clethra occidentalis		2			
ERICACEAE					
Vaccinium meridionale		9	2	5	4
APOCYNACEAE					
Urechites lutea		11			
ASCLEPIADACEAE					
Asclepias curassavica		8	1		
BORAGINACEAE					
Cordia sebestena	3	2			
Cordia gerescanthus		3		3	7
Cordia globosa			1		
Cordia sp.		1		4	
Bourreria baccata			1		
Bourreria venosa			1	1	
VERBENACEAE					
Lantana camara		8	8		
LABIATAE					
Plectranthus blumei			1		
SOLANACEAE					
Dunalia arborescens		8	1	4	6
BIGNONIACEAE					
Tabebuia riparia	3			9	
Tecoma stans		12		3	
GESNERIACEAE					
Besleria lutea		29			2
Columnea hirsuta		5			
ACANTHACEAE					
Goldfussia glomerata		8		1	
RUBIACEAE					
Morinda royoc			2		
Cephaelis elata		4	1		
Psychotria corymbosa		10		2	
Psychotria brachiata					2
Psychotria pubescens		2			

APPENDIX 7 (*cont.*)

Single records for *Trochilus polytmus* only:

Family	Species
Bromeliaceae	*Hohenbergia penduliflora*
	Guzmania monostachia
	Tillandsia sp.
Cannaceae	*Canna sylvestris*
Caesalpiniaceae	*Caesalpinia decapetala*
	Caesalpinia sp.
Papilionaceae	*Crotolaria verrucosa*
	Gliricidia sepium
	Canavalia altipendula
	Mucuna sloanei
Malvaceae	*Malvaviscus arboreus*
Passifloraceae	*Passiflora lancifolia*
Araliaceae	*Dendropanax pendulus*
Plumbaginaceae	*Plumbago scandens*
Verbenaceae	*Stachytarpheta mutabilis*
Acanthaceae	*Barleria cristata*
	Pachystachys coccinea
Rubiaceae	*Hamelia cuprea*
Campanulaceae	*Lobelia martagon*

Notes (i) Each individual bird was recorded once only, however many flowers of the species concerned it visited.

(ii) A great variety of introduced plants were visited, not listed here, including garden flowers such as hibiscus, and especially flowering trees such as *Calliandra, Erythrina, Eucalyptus, Pittosporum* and *Spathodea*.

(iii) The total number of feeds recorded on native flowers was 34 for *A.mango* (and another 6 unidentified), 215 (and at least another 45 unidentified) for *T.polytmus*, and 27 (one more unidentified) for *M.minima*.

(iv) The total of midlevel bromeliads recorded for *T.polytmus* includes the single feeds on identified species at the start of the second part of the table.

APPENDIX 8
Ranges of Jamaican land birds on the mainland

A. *Same species as on Jamaica*

	Range on American mainland			
	North	Mexico	Central (South to Panama)	South
pigeon *Columba leucocephala*	X		X	
dove *Zenaida macroura*	X	X	X	
dove *Zenaida aurita*		X		
dove *Zenaida asiatica*	X	X	X	X
dove *Columbina passerina*	X	X	X	X
dove *Leptotila jamaicensis*		X		
dove *Geotrygon montana*		X	X	X
cuckoo *Coccyzus americanus*	X	X		
cuckoo *Coccyzus minor*	X	X	X	X
ani *Crotophaga ani*	X		X	X
owl *Tyto alba*	X	X	X	X
potoo *Nyctibius griseus*		X	X	X
swift *Streptoprocne zonaris*		X	X	X
swift *Cypseloides niger*	X	X	X	
flycatcher *Tyrannus dominicensis*	X			X
martin *Progne dominicensis*		X		
martin *Petrochelidon fulva*	X	X		(?)
mockingbird *Mimus polyglottos*	X	X	(x)	(x)
sparrow *Ammodramus savannarum*	X	X	X	X
finch *Tiaris olivacea*		X	X	X
finch *Tiaris bicolor*				X
warbler *Dendroica petechia*	X	X	X	X
bananaquit *Coereba flaveola*		X	X	X
vireo *Vireo altiloquus*	X			
tanager *Spindalis zena*		X		
Total	15	20	15	14

APPENDIX 8 (*cont.*)

B. *Mainland species extremely closely related to Jamaican species*

	Closely related mainland species	Range on American mainland			
		North	Mexico	Central (South to Panama)	South
pigeons and doves					
Columba inornata	*C.flavirostris*		X	X	
Columba caribaea	*C.fasciata*	X	X	X	X
Geotrygon versicolor	*G.costaricensis*			X	
parrots					
Amazona collaria, A.agilis	*A.albifrons*		X	X	
Aratinga nana	*A.astec*		X	X	
nightjars					
Siphonorhis americanus	*Nyctidromus albicollis*	X	X	X	X
Chordeiles gundlachii	*C.minor*	X	X		
woodpecker					
Centurus radiolatus	*C.aurifrons*	X	X	X	
becard					
Platypsaris niger	*Platypsaris* superspecies	X	X	X	X
flycatchers					
Myiarchus barbirostris	*M.tuberculifer*	X	X	X	X
Contopus caribaeus	*C.cinereus*		X	X	X
Myiopagis cotta	*M.viridicata*		X	X	X
thrushes					
Myadestes genibarbis	*M.unicolor*		X	X	
Turdus jamaicensis	*T.albicollis*		(X)	X	X
vireos					
Vireo modestus, V.osburni	*V.griseus, V.pallens*	X	X	X	
V.altiloquus	*V.magister*		X	X	
icterids					
Icterus leucopteryx	*I.pustulatus*		X	X	
Quiscalus niger	*Q.lugubris*				X
	Q.nicaraguensis			X	
Total		7	15	17	8

APPENDIX 8 (cont.)

C. *Jamaican species with no close mainland representative*
Comment

cuckoo *Hyetornis pluvialis*	near *Piaya* or *Coccyzus*
cuckoo *Saurothera vetula*	near *Coccyzus* (mainly North American)
owl *Pseudoscops grammicus*	near *Asio*
swift *Tachornis phoenicobia*	probably not near *Reinarda* (South American) (see Part 2)
hummingbird *Anthracothorax mango*	near Central or South American congeners (*A.prevostii*—only one in C.America)
hummingbird *Trochilus polytmus*	
hummingbird *Mellisuga minima*	perhaps near *Calypte* (North American)
tody *Todus todus*	near motmots Momotidae (tropical North American)
flycatcher *Tyrannus caudifasciatus*	in 'grey kingbird' group (see Part 2)
flycatcher *Myiarchus stolidus*	
flycatcher *Myiarchus validus*	
flycatcher *Elaenia fallax*	summer visitor (? from South America)
swallow *Kalochelidon euchrysea*	near to *Tachycineta* (*sens.lat.*)
mockingbird *Mimus gundlachii*	near to *M.polyglottos/gilvus*
thrush *Turdus aurantius*	
finch *Loxipasser anoxanthus*	near *Loxigilla*
finch *Loxigilla violacea*	endemic West Indian genus
tanager *Euphonia jamaica*	not close to *E.musica* of rest of Antilles
orangequit *Euneornis campestris*	perhaps a tanager Thraupinae
warbler *Dendroica pharetra*	nearly all *Dendroica* spp. are North American
icterid *Nesopsar nigerrimus*	near *Icterus* and *Agelaius*
crow *Corvus jamaicensis*	not far from North American congeners

Notes   (i) The question-mark for *Petrochelidon fulva* in South America is because the *ruficollaris* group in South America is not certainly in *P.fulva* (Mayr & Short 1970). The brackets for *Mimus polyglottos* in Central and South America are because here it belongs to the *M.gilvus* group, which many workers treat as a full species, though Mayr and Short treat it as a subspecies.

(ii) In two instances in Part B, the parrots *Amazona* and *Vireo*, two Jamaican species, are thought to have the same closest relative on the mainland. In two other instances, in the genera *Tyrannus* and *Mimus* respectively, an endemic Jamaican species is thought to be most closely related to an Antillean and mainland species in Part A. For *V.modestus* (with *V.osburni*), I have cited two mainland species in the same species group.

(iii) While *Turdus jamaicensis* is close to the mainland species *T.albicollis*, it is less close to the form *assimilis* of Mexico and northern Central America, often treated as a full species, than to *T.albicollis* (*sens.strict.*) further south. Here the presence of *T.albicollis* in Mexico is put in brackets in the table, and this species is not scored for Mexico in the text.

(iv) The parauque *Nyctidromus albicollis* was included with diffidence, but it is the only mainland parauque.

APPENDIX 9
Land birds of the Lesser Antilles

	Range on 6 main islands	Lowlands or highlands	Endemic to Lesser Antilles	Present on Greater Antilles	Present on mainland north-central	Present on mainland south	Probably entered Lesser Antilles from
pigeons Columbidae							
Columba leucocephala	—	L	—	+	(isles)	—	NW
Columba squamosa	all	LH	—	+	—	(isles)	S
Zenaida auriculata	L,V,Gr.	L	—	—	—	+	S
Zenaida aurita	Gu,D,M,L,Gr	L	—	+	+	+	NW
Columbina passerina	all	L	—	+	+	(+)	?
Leptotila wellsi	Gr	L	+	—	—	+	S
Geotrygon montana	all	LH	—	+	+	—	?
Geotrygon mystacea	Gu, D,M,L	LH	—	PR	—	—	NW
parrots Psittacidae							
Amazona imperialis	D	H	+	—	—	—	?
Amazona guildingii	V	H	+	—	—	—	?
Amazona versicolor	L	H	+	—	—	—	?
Amazona arausiaca	D	H	+	—	—	—	?
cuckoos Cuculidae							
Coccyzus minor	all	LH	—	+	+	+	?
Crotophaga ani	all	L	—	+	+	+	S
owls Strigiformes							
Tyto alba	D,V,Gr	LH	—	+	+	+	?
Speotyto cunicularia	—	L	—	+	+	+	?

nightjars Caprimulgidae							
Caprimulgus rufus	L	L	−	−	−	+	S
Caprimulgus cayennensis	M	L	−	−	−	+	S
Swifts Apodidae							
Chaetura cinereiventris	Gr	H	−	−	−	+	S
Chaetura martinica	Gu to V	H	+	−	−	(+)	S
Chaetura brachyura	V	L	−	−	−	+	S
Cypseloides niger	Gu to V	H	−	+	+	−	NW
hummingbirds Trochilidae							
Glaucis hirsuta	Gr	H	−	−	−	+	S_
Cyanophaia bicolor	D,M	H	+	−	−	−	?
Eulampis jugularis	Gu to V	H	+	PR	−	−	?
Sericotes holosericeus	all	L	−	PR	−	−	?
Orthorhyncus cristatus	all	LH	−	−	−	−	?
kingfishers Alcedinidae							
Ceryle torquata	Gu,D,M	LH	−	−	+	+	?
woodpeckers Picidae							
Melanerpes herminieri	Gu	H	+	(+)	(+)	−	NW
flycatchers Tyrannidae							
Tyrannus melancholicus	Gr	L	−	−	−	+	S
Tyrannus dominicensis	all	L	+	+	+	+	S
Myiarchus nugator	V,Gr	LH	−	+	(+)	(+)	NW?
Myiarchus stolidus	Gu,D,M,L	LH	−	PR	−	(+)	?
Contopus latirostris	Gu,D,M,L	LH	−	−	+	+	S
Empidonax euleri	Gr	H	−	PR	−	+	?
Elaenia flavogaster	V,Gr	L	−	−	+	+	S
Elaenia martinica	all	LH	−	+	(isles)	(isles)	W?

APPENDIX 9 (*cont.*)

	Range on 6 main islands	Lowlands or highlands	Endemic to Lesser Antilles	Present on Greater Antilles	Present on mainland north-central	Present on mainland south	Probably entered Lesser Antilles from
martins Hirundinidae							
Progne dominicensis	all	LH	—	+	+	—	NW
wrens Troglodytidae							
Troglodytes aedon	all	LH	—	—	+	+	S
mockingbirds, thrashers Mimidae							
Mimus gilvus	all	L	—	—	+	+	S
Allenia fusca	all	LH	+ +	—	—	—	NW?
Margarops fuscatus	Gu to V	LH	—	+	—	(isles)	NW?
Cinclocerthia ruficauda	Gu to V	LH	+ +	+	—	—	NW?
Ramphocinclus brachyurus	M,L	L	+ +	—	—	—	NW?
thrushes Turdidae							
Myadestes genibarbis	D,M,L,V,	H	—	+	(+)	—	NW
Cichlherminia lherminieri	Gu,D,L	H	+ +	—	—	—	?
Turdus plumbeus	D	L	—	+	—	—	NW
Turdus fumigatus	V,Gr	H	—	—	—	+	S
Turdus nudigenis	M,L,V,Gr	L	—	—	—	+	S
buntings Emberizidae							
Volatinia jacarina	Gr	L	—	—	—	+	S
Sporophila nigricollis	Gr	L	—	—	—	+	S
Tiaris bicolor	all	L	—	+	—	+	S
Loxigilla portoricensis	—	H	—	PR	—	—	?

	Islands	Habitat					Entry
Loxigilla noctis	all	LH	+	+	+	—	?
Melanospiza richardsoni	L	LH	++	—	—	+	?
Saltator albicollis	Gu,D,M,L	L	—	+	+	+	S
tanagers Thraupidae							
Euphonia musica	all	H	+	+	+	+	?
Tangara cucullata	V,Gr	LH	+	—	—	—	S
warblers Parulidae							
Dendroica petechia	Gu,D,M,L	L	—	+	+	+	?
Dendroica plumbea	Gu,D	LH	+	—	—	—	NW
Dendroica adelaidae	L	LH	—	PR	(+)	—	NW
Catharopeza bishopi	V	H	++	—	—	—	NW?
Leucopeza semperi	L	H	++	—	—	—	?
Coereba flaveola	all	LH	—	+	+	+	S
vireos Vireonidae							
Vireo altiloquus	all	LH	—	+	+	+	S
icterids Icteridae							
Icterus laudabilis	L	LH	+	(+)	(+)	—	NW
Icterus bonana	M	LH	+	(+)	(+)	—	NW
Icterus oberi	Montserrat	LH	+	(+)	(+)	—	NW
Quiscalus lugubris	all	L	—	(+)	(+)	+	S
Molothrus bonariensis	M,L,V,Gr	L	—	PR	—	+	S

Notes (i) In 1st column, the 6 main islands are arranged from north to south (left to right), Gu Guadeloupe, D Dominica. M Martinique, L St Lucia, V St Vincent and Gr Grenada. — indicates bird occurs or did occur on smaller islands.

(ii) In 2nd column, L stands for lowlands, usually semi-arid, and H for highlands, mainly rain forest and montane thicket. Only the main habitat is given, which in a few species differs on different islands.

(iii) In 3rd column, ++ means an endemic genus and + an endemic species.

(iv) In 4th, 5th and 6th columns, (+) means member of same superspecies but not same species.

(v) The species recorded in 4th column as present in Greater Antilles are endemic to West Indies if not recorded on mainland in 5th or 6th column. Those labelled PR are solely in Lesser Antilles, Virgins and Puerto Rico or islands off latter.

(vi) In 7th column, probable way of entry is assessed from present range and is not very reliable, though more so in some cases than others.

APPENDIX 10

Main West Indies islands, arranged broadly from north to south and west to east, with number of species of land birds (pigeons to passerines)

Island	Area (sq. km)	Altitude (m)	Distance from mainland (km)	Nearest island (km)	Number of resident species of land birds
BAHAMAS					
Grand Bahama	2000	low	100	25	35
Great Abaco	1100	low	250	25	36
Andros	4200	low	200	40	34
New Providence	150	low	250	40	32
Eleuthera	420	low	350	25	28
Cat I.	410	120	450	25	17
Watlings I.	160	low	550	75	17
Long I.	340	low	500	40	19
Acklins I.	310	low	650	60	20
Mayaguana	250	low	750	60	18
Caicos	190	low	900	60	19
Great Inagua	1450	low	800	60	24
GREATER ANTILLES					
Cuba	114,000	2000	200	90	68
Isle of Pines	3000	310	400	50	51
Grand Cayman	180	low	500	300	28
Little Cayman	24	low	600	100	17
Cayman Brac	33	low	600	120	19
Jamaica	11,400	2260	650	150	66
Hispaniola	80,000	3200	600	90	73
Gonave	660	700	700	20	42
Mona	50	low	700	60	12
Puerto Rico	9000	1350	800	120	55
Vieques	130	300	850	15	32
Culebra	28	200	900	30	17
VIRGIN ISLANDS					
St Thomas	70	470	850	4	22
St John	49	390	850	4	21
Tortola	54	540	850	40	16
Anegada	34	low	850	40	12
St Croix	210	360	800	60	20

APPENDIX 10 (*cont.*)

Island	Area (sq. km)	Altitude (m)	Distance from mainland (km)	Nearest island (km)	Number of resident species of land birds
LESSER ANTILLES					
Anguilla	90	low	850	7	11
St Martin	85	410	800	7	13
St Bartholemew	25	300	800	20	12
Saba	12	860	750	25	18
St Eustatius	21	600	750	15	18
St Kitts	180	1140	750	3	21
Nevis	130	1100	700	3	19
Barbuda	160	low	800	45	20
Antigua	280	400	700	60	20
Montserrat	100	910	650	35	22
Guadeloupe	1500	1500	600	40	34
Desirade	27	280	600	5	19
Marie Galante	24	low	600	35	14
Dominica	800	1450	550	40	39
Martinique	1100	1340	450	30	38
St Lucia	600	960	350	30	42
St Vincent	350	1240	300	40	35
Barbados	430	340	400	250	16
Bequia	19	low	300	10	19
Carriacou	34	300	200	25	21
Grenada	310	840	150	100	35
CONTINENTAL					
Tobago	300	580	150	35	70
Trinidad	4800	940	15	35	205

Note Prepared by Peter Lack from standard geographical gazeteers and based on Bond (1956, 1971).

APPENDIX 11
Land birds of the Bahamas (pigeons to passerines) and their ranges elsewhere

ENDEMIC: 3
hummingbird *Calliphlox evelynae*
swallow *Callichelidon cyaneoviridis*
warbler *Geothlypis rostrata*

SOLELY ANTILLEAN: 17
dove *Geotrygon chrysia*
parrot *Amazona leucocephala*
cuckoo *Saurothera merlini*
nightjar *Chordeiles gundlachii*
hummingbird *Chlorostilbon ricordii*
woodpecker *Centurus superciliaris*
flycatcher *Tyrannus cubensis*
flycatcher *Tyrannus caudifasciatus*
flycatcher *Myiarchus stolidus*
flycatcher *Contopus caribaeus*
mockingbird *Mimus gundlachii*
bullfinch *Loxigilla violacea*
thrush *Turdus plumbeus*
warbler *Dendroica pityophila*
vireo *Vireo crassirostris*
oriole *Icterus dominicensis*
crow *Corvus nasicus*

SOLELY ANTILLEAN AND OFFSHORE ISLES: 3
pigeon *Columba leucocephala*
thrasher *Margarops fuscatus*
tanager *Spindalis zena*

ANTILLEAN AND MAINLAND: 16
(mainland includes North America
    unless stated)
dove *Zenaida macroura*
dove *Zenaida aurita* (not North America)
dove *Columbina passerina*
cuckoo *Coccyzus minor*
cuckoo *Coccyzus americanus*
ani *Crotophaga ani*
barn owl *Tyto alba*
owl *Speotyto cunicularia*
flycatcher *Tyrannus dominicensis*
mockingbird *Mimus polyglottos*
grassquit *Tiaris bicolor* (not North America)
warbler *Dendroica petechia*
warbler *Dendroica pinus*
bananaquit *Coereba flaveola* (not North America)
vireo *Vireo altiloquus* (just in Florida)
icterid *Agelaius phoeniceus*

SOLELY NORTH AMERICA: 4
woodpecker *Dendrocopos villosus*
nuthatch *Sitta pusilla*
gnatcatcher *Polioptila caerulea*
warbler *Dendroica dominica*

Notes   (i) The endemic warbler *Geothlypis rostrata* is derived from a North American species *G.trichas*, so could be added as a fifth North American species.
(ii) The Chuck-will's-widow *Caprimulgus carolinensis*, another North American species, bred in the Bahamas in 1970 (Peterson 1972), but I have not included it in the above list in case it should be only irregular.

APPENDIX 12
Land birds of Swan Island and their ranges elsewhere

pigeon *Columba leucocephala*	Antilles and offshore islands
cuckoo *Coccyzus minor*	Antilles and mainland
ani *Crotophaga ani*	Antilles and mainland
warbler *Dendroica vitellina*	endemic to Swan and Caymans

Note Specimens of the west Cuban race of the thrush *Turdus plumbeus* were collected on one visit to Swan Island, but the species has never otherwise been seen there, and this is not enough on which to classify it as a resident.

APPENDIX 13
Land birds of Old Providence and St Andrew and their ranges elsewhere

SPECIES COMMON TO BOTH ISLANDS	RANGES ELSEWHERE
pigeon *Columba leucocephala*	Antilles and offshore islands
dove *Zenaida asiatica*	Antilles and mainland
cuckoo *Coccyzus minor*	Antilles and mainland
ani *Crotophaga ani*	Antilles and mainland
hummingbird *Anthracothorax prevostii*	mainland
flycatcher *Elaenia martinica*	Antilles and offshore islands
grassquit *Tiaris bicolor*	Antilles and mainland
warbler *Dendroica petechia*	Antilles and mainland
bananaquit *Coereba flaveola*	Antilles and mainland
vireo *Vireo altiloquus*	Antilles and mainland

ONLY ON OLD PROVIDENCE	RANGES ELSEWHERE
vireo *Vireo crassirostris*	Antillean

ONLY ON ST ANDREW	RANGES ELSEWHERE
dove *Leptotila jamaicensis*	Antilles and mainland
mockingbird *Mimus gilvus*	Antilles and mainland
vireo *Vireo caribaeus*	endemic, closest relative not known, but in *V.griseus* group
oriole *Icterus leucopteryx*	Antillean

APPENDIX 14
Land birds of Aruba, Curacao and Bonaire and their ranges elsewhere

SOLELY ANTILLES AND OFFSHORE ISLANDS: 3
pigeon *Columba squamosa*
flycatcher *Elaenia martinica*
thrasher *Margarops fuscatus*

ANTILLES AND MAINLAND: 13
dove *Zenaida auriculata*
dove *Columbina passerina*
barn owl *Tyto alba*
owl *Speotyto cunicularia*
nightjar *Caprimulgus cayennensis*
flycatcher *Tyrannus dominicensis*
mockingbird *Mimus gilvus*
bunting *Ammodramus savannarum*
bunting *Zonotrichia capensis*
grassquit *Tiaris bicolor*
warbler *Dendroica petechia*
bananaquit *Coereba flaveola*
vireo *Vireo altiloquus* (mainland solely Florida)

SOLELY SOUTH AMERICAN: 11
pigeon *Columba corensis*
dove *Leptotila verreauxi*
parrot *Amazona barbadensis*
parakeet *Aratinga pertinax*
ani *Crotophaga sulcirostris*
hummingbird *Chlorostilbon mellisugus*
hummingbird *Chrysolampis mosquitus*
flycatcher *Myiarchus tyrannulus*
flycatcher *Sublegatus modestus*
oriole *Icterus nigrogularis*
oriole *Icterus icterus*

Notes   (i) Based on Voous (1957).
(ii) Since the vireo *Vireo altiloquus* is on the mainland solely in Florida, from the zoogeographical viewpoint of these islands it might have been scored as solely on Antilles and offshore islands.
(iii) A few of the species recorded for the Antilles and the mainland have a very restricted distribution in the Antilles.

APPENDIX 15
Land birds of Grenada and their ranges elsewhere

ENDEMIC: 1

dove *Leptotila wellsi* (from South America)

SOLELY ANTILLES: 6

hummingbird *Sericotes holosericeus*
hummingbird *Orthorhyncus cristatus*
flycatcher *Myiarchus nugator* (from South America)
thrasher *Allenia fusca*
bullfinch *Loxigilla noctis*
tanager *Tangara cucullata* (from South America)

SOLELY ANTILLES AND OFFSHORE ISLANDS: 2

pigeon *Columba squamosa*
flycatcher *Elaenia martinica*

ANTILLES AND MAINLAND: 20
(in both South and Central America unless specified)

dove *Zenaida auriculata* (South America)
dove *Zenaida aurita* (Mexico)
dove *Columbina passerina*
dove *Geotrygon montana*
cuckoo *Coccyzus minor*
ani *Crotophaga ani*
barn owl *Tyto alba*
flycatcher *Tyrannus dominicensis* (South and North America)
flycatcher *Elaenia flavogaster*
martin *Progne dominicensis* (Mexico)
wren *Troglodytes aedon*
mockingbird *Mimus gilvus*
thrush *Turdus nudigenis* (South America)
thrush *Turdus fumigatus* (South America)
grassquit *Tiaris bicolor* (South America)
tanager *Euphonia musica*
bananaquit *Coereba flaveola*
vireo *Vireo altiloquus* (North America)
cowbird *Molothrus bonariensis* (South America)
grackle *Quiscalus lugubris* (South America)

APPENDIX 15 *(cont.)*

SOUTH AMERICA: 6

swift *Chaetura cinereiventris*
hummingbird *Glaucis hirsuta*
flycatcher *Tyrannus melancholicus*
flycatcher *Empidonax euleri*
bunting *Sporophila nigricollis*
bunting *Volatinia jacarina*

Notes (i) Of the species on the Antilles and the mainland, the dove *Z.aurita* and the martin *P.dominicensis* are on the mainland solely in Mexico, and the vireo *V.altiloquus* solely in Florida, so these should be included in the Antillean element on Grenada.

(ii) The endemic dove *L.wellsi* is close to the South American *L.verreauxi* (see p. 393) while the flycatcher *M.nugator* (Lanyon 1967) and the tanager *T.cucullata* (Bond 1963), which are endemic to Grenada with St Vincent, are close to South American species, so these three should be included in the South American element on Grenada.

(iii) Six of the twenty species found both in the Antilles and on the mainland are found on the mainland only in South America, so can be included in the South American element on Grenada. This especially applies to the dove *Zenaida auriculata,* the thrushes *Turdus nudigenis* and *T.fumigatus* and the cowbird *Molothrus bonariensis,* which are restricted to the southern Lesser Antilles or have recently been spreading north.

APPENDIX 16
Land birds of Tobago and their ranges elsewhere

MAINLAND AND LESSER ANTILLES (omitting those
restricted to Grenada and St Vincent): 13

dove *Zenaida auriculata*
ani *Crotophaga ani*
barn owl *Tyto alba*
nightjar *Caprimulgus cayennensis* (only Martinique)
flycatcher *Tyrannus dominicensis*
martin *Progne dominicensis* (not South America)
wren *Troglodytes aedon*
mockingbird *Mimus gilvus*
thrush *Turdus nudigenis*
grassquit *Tiaris bicolor*
bananaquit *Coereba flaveola*
cowbird *Molothrus bonariensis*
grackle *Quiscalus lugubris*

MAINLAND AND GRENADA AND/OR ST VINCENT: 7

swift *Chaetura cinereiventris* (Grenada)
swift *Chaetura brachyura* (St Vincent)
hummingbird *Glaucis hirsuta* (Grenada)
flycatcher *Tyrannus melancholicus* (Grenada)
flycatcher *Elaenia flavogaster* (Grenada, St Vincent)
bunting *Sporophila nigricollis* (Grenada)
bunting *Volatinia jacarina* (Grenada)

APPENDIX 16 *(cont.)*

IN FAMILIES SOLELY ON MAINLAND (number of species in brackets) : 50

doves Columbidae (4)
parrots Psittacidae (1)
owls Strigidae (1)
potoos Nyctibiidae (1) (also in Greater Antilles)
hummingbirds Trochilidae (5)
trogons Trogonidae (1)
kingfishers Alcedinidae (1)
motmots Momotidae (1)
jacamars Galbulidae (1)
woodpeckers Picidae (3)
wood-hewers Dendrocolaptidae (3)
ovenbirds Furnariidae (2)
ant-thrushes Formicariidae (3)
cotingas Cotingidae (1)
manakins Pipridae (1)
flycatchers Tyrannidae (7)
wrens Troglodytidae (1)
thrushes Turdidae (2)
buntings Emberizidae (3)
tanagers (and honeycreepers) Thraupidae (4)
vireos Vireonidae (2)
icterids Icteridae (2)

Notes   (i) Based on Bond (1970), modifying Herklots (1961).
(ii) The species common to Tobago and Grenada are all those in the first two sections except the nightjar *C.cayennensis* in the first and the swift *C.brachyura* in the second, making 18 species in all. In addition, the endemic Grenadian dove *Leptotila wellsi* is, I consider, in the same super-species as the South American *L.verreauxi*, found on Tobago (see p. 159), and the flycatcher *Myiarchus nugator,* endemic to Grenada with St Vincent, is extremely closely related to the South American *M.tyrannulus*, found on Tobago (Lanyon 1967).
(iii) One species on the mainland and in the Antilles, the martin *Progne dominicensis*, is 'Antillean' so far as Tobago is concerned, since it is on the mainland solely in Mexico.
(iv) The typically South American families present on Tobago but absent from the Lesser Antilles are the Nyctibiidae, Trogonidae, Galbulidae, Dendrocolaptidae, Furnariidae, Formicariidae, Cotingidae and Pipridae.

APPENDIX 17
Numbers of Parulid warblers seen in Jamaica in winter per 10 hours of slow walking in different habitats

| | NATURAL FOREST | | | | GARDENS, PARKLAND | | |
	Mangroves	Lowland	Midlevel	Montane	Lowland	Midlevel	Montane
Yellow	62	1					
Arrow-headed		2	11	18		5	10
Black-and-White	24	22	12	12	16	13	10
Swainson's		2	x	2			
Worm-eating		2	2	1	1	4	1
Tennessee		1		1	1		1
Parula	3	17	5	x	10		1
Magnolia		5	x	x	5	3	(x)
Cape May		5			16	1	4
Black-throated Blue		10	13	6	4	25	14
Myrtle		(x)		(x)	7		x
Black-throated Green		3	2	1	3		7
Yellow-throated					2		3
Prairie	5	19	4	x	4	10	3
Palm	5	3	x	(x)	3	3	1
Ovenbird	6	7	2	2	3	3	2
Northern Waterthrush	35	2			5	(x)	
Louisiana Waterthrush		(x)		1	(x)	10	x
Common Yellowthroat	6	14	3	3	7	15	3
American Redstart	29	17	7	1	3	28	1
Total warblers per 10 hours	174	131	61	49	90	121	60
Total passerines per 10 hours	230	396	392	180	676	401	319
No. of hours counted (to nearest hour)	9	86	30	65	10	8	40

Notes (i) x means recorded, but fewer than 0.5 birds seen per 10 hours.

(ii) (x) means seen in the habitat concerned, but only outside the counts.

(iii) Individual bird totals are rounded off to whole birds.

APPENDIX 18

Numbers of Parulid warblers seen in Jamaica in winter per 10 hours counting in different types of lowland dry limestone forest

	3 Sea-level forest	5 Arid limestone (natural)	6 Very arid ruinate	7 Arid ruinate in hills	8 Fairly rich secondary in hills	9 Southern riverine
Yellow	8	—	2	—	—	—
Arrow-headed	—	—	—	—	8	—
Black-and-White	22	14	3	25	16	35
Swainson's	3	—	—	3	1	2
Worm-eating	5	1	—	2	3	1
Tennessee	—	—	—	—	—	3
Parula	19	4	1	19	22	22
Magnolia	6	—	—	9	4	9
Cape May	6	1	—	10	4	4
Black-throated Blue	19	1	—	2	17	14
Myrtle	—	—	—	1	—	—
Black-throated Green	—	1	—	9	2	5
Prairie	29	11	4	30	7	22
Palm	3	—	1	12	—	1
Ovenbird	2	9	2	12	4	6
Northern Waterthrush	—	—	—	2	—	8
Common Yellowthroat	27	—	2	19	2	31
American Redstart	29	6	—	9	14	30
Total warblers per 10 hours	179	49	16	163	103	196
Total passerines per 10 hours	552	234	264	389	300	599
Number of hours counted (to nearest hour)	11	20	21	17	20	18

Notes (i) Sea-level forest was counted at Morant Point and Negril (part liable to flooding, part much cut over).

(ii) Arid limestone (natural) forest was counted in the Hellshire Hills and on Portland Ridge.

(iii) Very arid ruinate, heavily cut over, was counted on the extremely arid Port Henderson Hill on the edge of the Hellshires.

(iv) Arid ruinate forest in hills was counted on Long Mountain, alongside the University campus at Mona.

(v) Fairly rich secondary forest in hills was counted in a valley up from the Ferry (or Fresh) River.

(vi) Southern riverine forest was counted along the Ferry River and in Mona wood alongside Mona reservoir.

(vii) Individuals of each species seen per 10 hours are rounded off to the nearest whole number; the totals are also rounded off to the numbers of passerines counted per 10 hours, hence the discrepancies.

APPENDIX 19

Comments on counting methods used for Parulid warblers in Appendices 17, 18 and 20

Counts were made on slow walks through the various habitats, and the observer stopped to record feeding when this was seen. The speed of walking was roughly 0.8 km per hour, but uniformity was not attempted, and the speed varied somewhat with the number of birds seen feeding and other conditions. All birds seen, but not those only heard, were recorded. Such counts are much superior to a simple record of 'common', 'rare', etc., but we found no satisfactory way of relating them to the density of birds per unit area, in which connection the following difficulties may be noted.

First, warblers are seen much more readily soon after dawn than later in the day, for which reason all our counts were made in the first part of the morning. But the decline in warbler activity later in the day is much greater in some habitats, notably arid lowland forest, than others, notably montane forest, and greater on some days than others. Secondly, in the Jamaican forests, counts are usually possible only along tracks, since otherwise the observer has to watch his feet or cut his way, and many slopes are too steep to walk on. But some tracks are much wider than others, and while wide tracks help the observer to see birds in the canopy, narrow tracks often help him to see those on the ground. Further, in some forests, tracks are found only at the edge, where birds of the edge become more frequent but from where it is hard to see birds on the forest floor. In addition, a quick walk reveals more of the shy ground-feeding species, which on a slow walk usually see the observer a long way off and slip away unnoticed before he reaches them. The counts summarised in Appendix 20 show that two ground-feeding species (Swainson's and Ovenbird) are seen more often on quick than slow walks, and the herb-feeding Common Yellow-throat occurs most often at the edge, whereas the tree-feeding species (all the rest) are about equally common on all three types of count. Similar differences are revealed by a comparison of birds seen and birds caught in mist-nets stretching from the ground to a height of 2 m, as shown in Appendix 21. In the areas compared, a much higher proportion of the ground-feeding and low-feeding species was netted than seen, and a higher proportion of the tree-feeding species was seen than netted. This is crudely shown by the totals in the last lines of the note to Table 21, and the difference is particularly marked in the ground-feeding Swainson's and Ovenbird, the low-feeding Worm-eating Warbler and, in the opposite direction, in the tree-feeding Parula, Yellow-throated and Prairie Warblers.

The number of birds seen per unit time may also be affected by the number of participating observers, since on slow walks through montane forest near Hardwar Gap with one, two, three or four observers, the average number of warblers seen per hour was respectively 5.6, 4.1, 6.4 and 6.9, but these differences are not statistically significant. In thick forest, two observers a few feet apart often see different individual birds, partly because each tends to watch in a somewhat different direction and partly because, even looking in the same direction, each has a somewhat different view through the cover.

Further, there are differences, occasionally large, in the number of warblers seen on different days in the same place, between the same times and by the same observers. Much the biggest difference was observed in the Ferry forest, where the same three observers counted from 08.00 until 10.30 hours along the same narrow road on 15 and 27 January, on the 15th seeing 24 parulids and 44 other passerine species and on the 27th 48 parulids and 17 other passerine species. The 27th was windy, which may have depressed the activity of the other passerine species, but we cannot suggest why warblers were so much more conspicuous on that day. For these and various less important reasons, great caution is needed in interpreting the quantitative differences observed.

APPENDIX 20

Variations in numbers of Parulid warblers seen under different conditions near Hardwar Gap, Jamaica

	Number of birds per 10 hrs.		
	Slow walks through forest	Quick walks through forest	Fairly slow walks along road-side edges of forest
Arrow-headed	21	18	19
Black-and-White	13	11	12
Swainson's	3	6	0
Worm-eating	1	1	1
Black-throated Blue	7	7	8
Ovenbird	2	6	1
Common Yellowthroat	x	2	11
American Redstart	1	0	2
Total warblers	50	53	61
Total passerines	138	120	265
Number of hours counted (to nearest hour)	32	9	12

Notes (i) The counts were in montane forest at around 1200 m above sea level. The warblers selected are the commonest in the Hardwar area. x means present, but less than 0.5 counted per 10 hours. Slow walks were made at about 0.8 km per hour and quick walks about four times as fast. The difference between the two ground-feeding species (Swainson's and Ovenbird) and the tree-feeders (all the rest except Common Yellowthroat) on slow and quick walks respectively is statistically significant ($X^2 = 10.98$, P < 01).

(ii) The total warblers is higher than summation of the figures for each species suggest, because the uncommon and rare species are omitted from the details of the table.

APPENDIX 21
Comparison of Parulid warblers seen and mist-netted in the same or similar areas on Jamaica

| | Percentage of those recorded | | | | | |
| | Lowland riverine | | Midlevel | | Montane | |
	seen	caught	seen	caught	seen	caught
Yellow	—	—	—	—	—	—
Arrow-headed	—	—	8	21	28	18
Black-and-White	21	10	21	18	16	10
Swainson's	1	5	—	2	—	5
Worm-eating	(x)	7	—	11	1	15
Tennessee	2	2	—	—	1	—
Parula	10	5	4	2	2	—
Magnolia	4	2	—	—	1	—
Cape May	2	—	12	10	—	—
Black-throated Blue	7	7	25	11	17	21
Myrtle	—	—	—	—	—	—
Black-throated Green	4	1	7	6	8	8
Yellow-throated	—	—	5	1	2	—
Prairie	14	3	9	4	1	—
Palm	—	—	1	3	3	—
Ovenbird	3	12	3	7	1	8
Northern Waterthrush	5	7	—	—	—	—
Louisiana Waterthrush	—	—	—	—	3	—
Common Yellowthroat	15	33	3	1	12	10
American Redstart	12	5	2	2	3	5
Total warblers recorded	248	136	126	90	138	39

Notes (i) The lowland riverine and secondary forest, near Mona reservoir at 150 m above sea level, has been somewhat disturbed by cutting; it includes a stream and many mimosaceous trees.

(ii) The midlevel trapping area was in a wild garden with adjoining woodland and cultivation at Irish Town at 600 m above sea level, and the nearest equivalent habitat where counts were made was Guava Ridge (which has many more conifers) at 1200 m above sea level.

(iii) The montane trapping was at the Institute of Jamaica's field station at Green Hills, a wild and overgrown garden adjoining montane forest, and the counts were made through gardens and forest on the adjoining road and at Hardwar Gap, at around 1100–1200 m above sea level.

(iv) (x) means seen outside the counts.

If the figures for lowland riverine, midlevel and montane forest are summed as they stand, then the totals for the 6 ground- or low-feeding species are 47 seen and 123 netted, and those for the 11 tree-feeding species are 248 seen and 172 netted.

APPENDIX 22

The absence of foraging parties on Jamaica

Foraging parties of insectivorous birds of diverse species are characteristic of both tropical forest and north temperate woodland, and Parulid warblers join such parties in both winter and summer quarters (*e.g.* Eaton 1953, Morse 1970). In a typical party, the flock moves steadily through the forest, each individual keeping one to a few metres from its nearest neighbours, maintaining contact by calls, and feeding in its specific fashion. In Jamaica, we saw no foraging parties, whether of Parulids or of resident insectivorous species.

Instead, there are what we came to call 'collections'. When we stopped to observe a bird feeding, we often saw an individual of another species a few metres away, though rarely so close as two metres. In the collection there might be up to five or six, rarely up to eight birds, with not more than two of the same species, feeding in an area of perhaps 40 metres square. Both ground-feeding and arboreal Parulids are frequent members of such collections, and they may associate with virtually any of the resident forest birds, passerines, woodpeckers, or doves. The main noticeable differences from a foraging party were the small number of individuals involved, their wide spacing, the absence of regular contact calls and the fact that the birds do not travel together through the forest; instead, each stays near where first seen for several minutes and then gradually drifts away, apparently independently of the others.

At first we thought that such collections might be apparent, not real, due to the fact that when we saw a bird, we usually stopped to look for a feed, and we thought that in forest, more birds are perhaps seen if an observer stands still than if he walks. But this latter observation proved to be wrong, and on random stops in the forest we often saw no birds. We then wondered if they could be the result of a purely random distribution, but the groups are too definite and too frequent for this. At the same time, we should not exaggerate their frequency, for we saw the species concerned more often singly than in collections. We recorded most such collections where both Parulids and resident birds are scarce, in very arid lowland forest and in montane forest, but this was almost certainly because such collections are most readily noticed where birds are scarce. Where birds are more numerous, a group of a few widely spaced individuals does not attract attention. We have, of course, excluded from consideration here the instances in which several birds feed at a common food source, such as a fruiting tree or a swarm of insects. In 'collections', each bird feeds on its own, often in a different way from the rest, and while most of the birds involved are insectivorous, they sometimes include a seed-eater or fruit-eater.

Two questions are raised. The first is the function, if any, of these small loose collections of birds of different species; for this, I cannot suggest an answer. The second is why foraging parties are absent from Jamaica, and this is the more strange since such parties, with Parulids, occur on others of the Greater Antilles, including Cuba (Eaton 1953), Hispaniola and Puerto Rico (C. and A. Kepler in prep.). There are no avian predators on passerine birds in the Jamaican forests, whereas accipitrine hawks are present on Cuba, Hispaniola and Puerto Rico. But although this fits with the suggestion (Lack 1954) that an advantage of feeding in mixed flocks is that several birds are more likely than one to notice an approaching predator, I am reluctant to believe that this is the main factor responsible for the absence of such flocks on Jamaica. Observations are needed from more islands, especially those without predators on small birds.

APPENDIX 23

Breeding status in Ireland of regularly breeding British land birds.
R = resident (or partial migrant), S = summer visitor

A. SPECIES WHICH BREED REGULARLY IN IRELAND

(i) Widespread in Britain: 52 species

Stock Dove	*Columba oenas*	R
Woodpigeon	*C.palumbus*	R
Collared Dove	*Streptopelia decaocto*	R
Cuckoo	*Cuculus canorus*	S
Barn Owl	*Tyto alba*	R
Long-eared Owl	*Asio otus*	R
Nightjar	*Caprimulgus europaeus*	S
Swift	*Apus apus*	S
Kingfisher	*Alcedo atthis*	R
Skylark	*Alauda arvensis*	R
Sand Martin	*Riparia riparia*	S
Swallow	*Hirundo rustica*	S
House Martin	*Delichon urbica*	S
Grey Wagtail	*Motacilla cinerea*	R
Pied Wagtail	*M.alba*	R
Meadow Pipit	*Anthus pratensis*	R
Wren	*Troglodytes troglodytes*	R
Dunnock	*Prunella modularis*	R
Robin	*Erithacus rubecula*	R
Whinchat	*Saxicola rubetra*	S
Stonechat	*S.torquata*	R
Wheatear	*Oenanthe oenanthe*	S
Blackbird	*Turdus merula*	R
Song Thrush	*T.philomelos*	R
Mistle Thrush	*T.viscivorus*	R
Sedge Warbler	*Acrocephalus schoenobaenus*	S
Blackcap	*Sylvia atricapilla*	S
Whitethroat	*S.communis*	S
Willow Warbler	*Phylloscopus trochilus*	S
Goldcrest	*Regulus regulus*	R
Spotted Flycatcher	*Muscicapa striata*	S
Long-tailed Tit	*Aegithalos caudatus*	R
Coal Tit	*Parus ater*	R
Great Tit	*P.major*	R
Blue Tit	*P.caeruleus*	R
Treecreeper	*Certhia familiaris*	R
Corn Bunting	*Emberiza calandra*	R
Yellowhammer	*E.citrinella*	R
Reed Bunting	*E.schoeniclus*	R
Chaffinch	*Fringilla coelebs*	R
Greenfinch	*Carduelis chloris*	R
Goldfinch	*C.carduelis*	R
Redpoll	*C.flammea*	R
Linnet	*C.cannabina*	R

APPENDIX 23 (cont.)

Bullfinch	Pyrrhula pyrrhula	R
House Sparrow	Passer domesticus	R
Tree Sparrow	P.montanus	R
Starling	Sturnus vulgaris	R
Jay	Garrulus glandarius	R
Magpie	Pica pica	R
Jackdaw	Corvus monedula	R
Rook	C.frugilegus	R

(ii) Widespread in Britain except southeast England (where in most cases no suitable habitats):
4 species

Rock Pipit	Anthus spinoletta	R
Dipper	Cinclus cinclus	R
Ring Ouzel	Turdus torquatus	S
Raven	Corvus corax	R

(iii) Widespread in Britain except northern Scotland: 4 species

Grasshopper Warbler	Locustella naevia	S
Garden Warbler	Sylvia borin	S
Chiffchaff	Phylloscopus collybita	S
Chough	Pyrrhocorax pyrrhocorax	R

(iv) Regular in Scotland and northern England, but not further south: 2 species

Siskin	Carduelis spinus	R
Twite	C.flavirostris	R

(v) Regular in Britain only in northern Scotland: 2 species

Rock Dove	Columba livia	R
Hooded Crow	Corvus cornix	R

B. SPECIES WHICH HAVE BRED ONLY OCCASIONALLY IN IRELAND

(i) Widespread in Britain: 2 species

Redstart	Phoenicurus phoenicurus	S
Wood Warbler	Phylloscopus sibilatrix	S

(iii) Widespread in Britain except northern Scotland: 3 species

Yellow Wagtail	Motacilla flava	S
Hawfinch	Coccothraustes coccothraustes	R
Carrion Crow	Corvus corone	R

(iv) Regular in Scotland and northern England, but not further south: 1 species

Short-eared Owl	Asio flammeus	R

(vi) Regular in England and Wales but not Scotland: 1 species

Turtle Dove	Streptopelia turtur	S

(vii) Regular only in southern England: 3 species

Woodlark	Lullula arborea	R
Reed Warbler	Acrocephalus scirpaceus	S
Common Crossbill	Loxia c.curvirostra	R

APPENDIX 23 (*cont.*)

C. SPECIES RECORDED, BUT NOT BREEDING, IN IRELAND

(i) Widespread in Britain: 2 species

Great Spotted Woodpecker	*Dendrocopos major*	R
Tree Pipit	*Anthus trivialis*	S

(iii) Widespread in Britain except northern Scotland: 1 species

Pied Flycatcher	*Ficedula hypoleuca*	S

(vi) Regular in England and Wales, but not Scotland: 3 species

Little Owl	*Athene noctua*	R
Green Woodpecker	*Picus viridis*	R
Lesser Whitethroat	*Sylvia curruca*	S

(vii) Regular only in southern England: 7 species

Wryneck	*Jynx torquilla*	S
Red-backed Shrike	*Lanius collurio*	S
Nightingale	*Luscinia megarhynchos*	S
Black Redstart	*Phoenicurus ochruros*	R
Dartford Warbler	*Sylvia undata*	R
Firecrest	*Regulus ignicapillus*	S
Cirl Bunting	*Emberiza cirlus*	R

D. BIRDS WHICH BREED IN BRITAIN AND HAVE NEVER BEEN RECORDED IN IRELAND: 9 species

Tawny Owl	*Strix aluco*
Lesser Spotted Woodpecker	*Dendrocopos minor*
Savi's Warbler	*Locustella luscinioides*
Marsh Warbler	*Acrocephalus palustris*
Bearded Tit	*Panurus biarmicus*
Marsh Tit	*Parus palustris*
Willow Tit	*Parus montanus*
Crested Tit	*Parus cristatus*
Nuthatch	*Sitta europaea*

Note Sequence and nomenclature are those of *The Status of Birds in Britain and Ireland* (British Ornithologists Union 1971), except that it is convenient in comparing Ireland with Britain to treat the Scottish Crossbill *Loxia* (*pityopsittacus* or *curvirostra*) (it is not settled of which species it is a race) as a separate species from *L.curvirostra* which breeds in England, and the Hooded Crow *Corvus cornix* as a separate species from the Carrion Crow *C.corone*. Both decisions are borderline from the taxonomic viewpoint.

APPENDIX 24

Species which breed in Morocco but not in the Canary Islands or Madeira, but which have occurred on passage in either or both of these groups. (C has occurred in Canaries, M in Madeira, S on Salvages if not otherwise in Canaries)

Cuckoos		Chats	
Clamator glandarius	CM	*Erythropygia galactotes*	M
Cuculus canorus	CM	*Luscinia megarhynchos*	CM
		Phoenicurus ochruros	CM
Owls		*P.phoenicurus*	CM
Otus scops	CM	*Saxicola torquata*	CM
Strix aluco	C	*Oenanthe oenanthe*	CM
		O.deserti	CM
Nightjars		*O.hispanica*	C
Caprimulgus ruficollis	M		
C.europaeus	SM	Warblers	
		Acrocephalus scirpaceus	CM
Swifts		*A.arundinaceus*	CM
Apus melba	CM	*Hippolais polyglotta*	CM
A.apus	CM	*H.pallida*	C
		Sylvia hortensis	M
Kingfisher		*S.communis*	CM
Alcedo atthis	CM		
		Flycatchers	
Bee-eaters		*Muscicapa hypoleuca*	CM
Merops apiaster	CM	*Muscicapa striata*	CM
M.persicus.	C		
		Bunting	
Roller		*Emberiza striolata*	C
Coracias garrulus	CM		
		Finches	
Wryneck		*Carduelis chloris*	CM
Jynx torquilla	CM	*Loxia curvirostra*	M
		Coccothraustes coccothraustes	M
Larks			
Melanocorypha calandra	CM	Sparrow	
Alauda arvensis	CM	*Passer domesticus*	M
Martins		Starling	
Riparia riparia	CM	*Sturnus unicolor*	C
Hirundo rustica	CM		
H.rupestris	C	Oriole	
Delichon urbica	CM	*Oriolus oriolus*	CM
Wagtails		Crow	
Motacilla flava	CM	*Corvus monedula*	CM
M.alba	CM		
Shrike			
Lanius senator	CM		

Note Based on Bannerman (1963, 1965).

APPENDIX 25

Breeding birds of the Canary Islands. The islands on which each species breeds or has bred are listed by their initial letters from east to west as follows: Lanzarote (L), Fuerteventura (F), Gran Canaria (GC), Tenerife (T), Gomera (Go), Hierro (H), and Palma (P); but if a species occurs on all 7 it is listed as 'all'. *indicates an endemic species, but if followed by (+ M) it also occurs on Madeira, or (A) it also occurs on the Azores

Rock Dove	*Columba livia*	all
Laurel Pigeon	**C.junoniae*	Go, P
Long-toed Pigeon	**C.trocaz* (+ M)	GC, T, Go, H, P
Turtle Dove	*Streptopelia turtur*	all
Barn Owl	*Tyto alba*	L, F, GC, T, (Go?), P
Long-eared Owl	*Asio otus*	GC, T, (Go?), H, P
Plain Swift	**Apus unicolor* (+ M)	F, GC, T, Go, H, P
Pallid Swift	*A.pallidus*	all (Go? H?)
Hoopoe	*Upupa epops*	all
Great Spotted Woodpecker	*Dendrocopos major*	GC, T
Lesser Short-toed Lark	*Calandrella rufescens*	L, F, GC, T
Grey Wagtail	*Motacilla cinerea*	GC, T, Go, P
Berthelot's Pipit	**Anthus berthelotii* (+ M)	all
Great Grey Shrike	*Lanius excubitor*	L, F, GC, T, P
Robin	*Erithacus rubecula*	GC, T, Go, H, P
Canarian Chat	**Saxicola dacotiae*	L, F
Blackbird	*Turdus merula*	GC, T, Go, H, P
Blackcap	*Sylvia atricapilla*	GC, T, Go, H, P
Sardinian Warbler	*S.melanocephala*	all
Spectacled Warbler	*S.conspicillata*	all
Chiffchaff	*Phylloscopus collybita*	L, GC, T, Go, H, P
Firecrest	*Regulus ignicapillus*	T, Go, H, P
Blue Tit	*Parus caeruleus*	all
Corn Bunting	*Emberiza calandra*	all
Common Chaffinch	*Fringilla coelebs*	GC, T, Go, H, P
Blue Chaffinch	**F.teydea*	GC, T
Canary	**Serinus canaria* (+M, A)	GC, T, Go, H, P
Goldfinch	*Carduelis carduelis*	F, GC, T, Go, H, P
Linnet	*C.cannabina*	all
Trumpeter Bullfinch	*Rhodopechys githaginea*	L, F, GC, T
Spanish Sparrow	*Passer hispaniolensis*	all
Rock Sparrow	*Petronia petronia*	GC, T, Go, H, P
Chough	*Pyrrhocorax pyrrhocorax*	P
Raven	*Corvus corax*	all

Note Status is based on Bannerman (1963, 1965), the latter work including a supplement for the Canaries, and nomenclature is based on Vaurie (1959, 1965). *Apus pallidus* has not been found breeding on Gomera or Hierro, but is otherwise so widespread that it presumably does so. No other doubtful records have been included. One other species suspected of breeding is the Scops Owl *Otus scops* (on Lanzarote).

APPENDIX 26

Breeding birds of Madeira (with Porto Santo). *indicates an endemic
species (all shared with Canaries, one also with Azores)

Rock Dove	*Columba livia*
Wood Pigeon	*Columba palumbus*
Long-toed Pigeon	*Columba trocaz*
Barn Owl	*Tyto alba*
Plain Swift	*Apus unicolor*
Pallid Swift	*Apus pallidus*
Hoopoe	*Upupa epops*
Berthelot's Pipit	*Anthus berthelotii*
Grey Wagtail	*Motacilla cinerea*
Robin	*Erithacus rubecula*
Blackbird	*Turdus merula*
Blackcap	*Sylvia atricapilla*
Spectacled Warbler	*Sylvia conspicillata*
Firecrest	*Regulus ignicapillus*
Chaffinch	*Fringilla coelebs*
Canary	*Serinus canaria*
Goldfinch	*Carduelis carduelis*
Linnet	*Carduelis cannabina*
Spanish Sparrow	*Passer hispaniolensis*
Rock Sparrow	*Petronia petronia*

Note Based on Bannerman (1965). The Turtle Dove *Streptopelia turtur* has bred occasionally
and the Greenfinch *Carduelis chloris* is suspected of breeding. The only Madeiran species which
does not breed in the Canaries is the Wood Pigeon *C.palumbus*, now extinct in Madeira.

APPENDIX 27
Breeding birds of the Azores

Rock Dove	*Columba livia*
Wood Pigeon	*C.palumbus*
Long-eared Owl	*Asio otus*
Woodpecker	*Dendrocopos minor* (probably)
Grey Wagtail	*Motacilla cinerea*
Robin	*Erithacus rubecula*
Blackbird	*Turdus merula*
Blackcap	*Sylvia atricapilla*
Goldcrest	*Regulus regulus*
Chaffinch	*Fringilla coelebs*
Canary	*Serinus canaria*
Greenfinch	*Carduelis chloris*
Goldfinch	*C.carduelis*
Bullfinch	*Pyrrhula pyrrhula*
(House Sparrow)	(*Passer domesticus*, introduced)
Starling	*Sturnus vulgaris*

Note Based on Bannerman (1966).

The woodpecker was seen by several people but was never collected; the description fits *Dendrocopos minor*. The sparrow *Passer domesticus* was introduced in 1960. The Goldfinch *C.carduelis* and Greenfinch *C.chloris* colonised only in the latter half of the nineteenth century, and are often thought to have been introduced. The Canary *Serinus canaria* and Starling *Sturnus vulgaris* have also been thought to be introduced, but without positive evidence; this is not impossible even for the Canary, though it has been long-established in the Azores, since it has always been so popular as a cagebird.

APPENDIX 28

Resident land birds of oceanic islands in the Gulf of Guinea. *endemic species, **endemic genus on island concerned, but if P, T, or A is added, they are shared between Principe, Sao Tome or Annobon respectively. (introd. = introduced; ext. = extinct)

	Species	Principe	Sao Tome	Annobon
pigeon	*Columba thomensis	—	+	—
pigeon	*Columba malherbii PTA	+	+	+
pigeon	Aplopelia larvata	+	+	+
pigeon	Streptopelia senegalensis	introd.	+	
pigeon	Treron calva	+	—	—
pigeon	*Treron s. thomae	—	+	—
parrot	Psittacus erithacus	+	—	—
parrot	(Agapornis pullaria)	introd. ?ext.	+ (?introd.)	—
cuckoo	Chrysococcyx cupreus	+	+	+
owl	Tyto alba	—	+	—
owl	Otus scops	—	+	+
swift	Apus affinis	+	+	—
swift	Cypsiurus parvus	+	+	—
swift	*Chaetura thomensis	—	+	—
kingfisher	Alcedo leucogaster	+	+	—
kingfisher	Halcyon malimbica	+	(error?)	—
martin	(Riparia cincta)	(+ ? resident)	—	—
drongo	Dicrurus adsimilis	+	—	—
oriole	*Oriolus crassirostris	—	+	—
thrush	*Turdus olivaceofuscus PT	+	+	—
warbler	*Prinia molleri	—	+	—
warbler	**Amaurocichla bocagei	—	+	—
flycatcher	Terpsiphone rufiventris	—	—	+
flycatcher	*Terpsiphone atrochalybeia	—	+	—
flycatcher?	**Horizorhinus dohrni	+	—	—
shrike	*Lanius newtoni	—	+	—
starling	Lamprotornis splendidus	(doubtful)	—	—
starling	Lamprotornis ornatus	+	—	—
starling	Onychognathus fulgidus	—	+	—
sunbird	*Nectarinia thomensis	—	+	—
sunbird	*Nectarinia newtonii	—	+	—
sunbird	*Nectarinia hartlaubii	+	—	—
sunbird	Nectarinia olivacea	+	—	—
white-eye	*Speirops leucophoea	+	—	—
white-eye	*Speirops lugubris	—	+	—
white-eye	*Zosterops griseovirescens	—	—	+
white-eye	*Zosterops ficedulina PT	+	+	—
weaver	*Ploceus principes	+	—	—
weaver	*Ploceus s. thomae	—	+	—
weaver	*Ploceus grandis	—	+	—
weaver	(Ploceus cucullatus)	—	?introd.	—

APPENDIX 28 (*cont.*)

	Species	Principe	Sao Tome	Annobon
weaver	(*Euplectes aureus*)	—	?introd.	—
weaver	(*Euplectes hordeacea*)	—	?introd.	—
weaver	(*Quelea erythrops*)	?introd. ?ext.	?introd.	—
estrildine	(*Estrilaa astrild*)	?introd. ?ext.	?introd.	
estrildine	*Lonchura cucullata*	+	+	—
estrildine	(*Uraeginthus angolensis*)	—	introd.	—
estrildine	(*Nigrita bicolor*)	introd.	—	—
viduine	(*Vidua macroura*)	—	?introd.	—
finch	**Serinus rufobrunneus* PT	+	+	—
finch	(*Serinus mozambicus*)	—	?introd.	—
finch?	***Neospiza concolor*	—	+	—

Note   Based on Amadon (1953), Snow (1950) and Fry (1961).

APPENDIX 29

Numbers of species of land birds and land plants in the Galapagos

Island	Number of species of		
	breeding land birds (if extinct, added in brackets)	flowering plants	ferns
Albermarle	19(+ 1)	244	59
Narborough	17(+ 1)	90	7
James	19	185	40
Jervis	12(+ 1)	68	1
Duncan	13(+ 2)	89	11
Indefatigable	18(+ 1)	306	71
Barrington	11(+ 1)	60	2
Chatham	16(+ 1)	221	31
Hood	7(+ 1?)	96	1
Charles	16(+ 1)	227	23
Tower	8	40	0
Bindloe	13	45	4
Abingdon	15	85	16
Wenman	6(+ 1?)	21	1
Culpepper	7	10	0

Notes   (i) Based on Harris (1973). For the land birds, I have included all those which he considers almost certainly breed now and probably breed now. In brackets I have added some of those once resident but now extinct, but have added a question mark for *G.fortis* for Hood and *G.fuliginosa* for Wenman, as I consider the evidence for past breeding there inadequate. I have excluded those probably once resident (labelled E by Harris), now not present, as I think the evidence for former breeding inadequate, and also probable stragglers (labelled X). I have also excluded the one hawk, included by Harris, to conform with treatment throughout this book.

(ii) The plant number in Harris's and my table are from Wiggins & Porter (1971). Harris also included altitude, area, distance to next island and distance to next high island, but these have been reproduced so often that there is no need to include them here.

REFERENCES

Adams C.D. 1972. Flowering Plants of Jamaica. (University of the West Indies, Jamaica.)

Agar N. 1966. House Sparrow. Gosse Bird Club Broadsheet 7:22.

Amadon D. 1953. Avian Systematics and evolution in the Gulf of Guinea. Bull. Am. Mus. nat. Hist. 100 (3):399–451.

Asprey G.F. & Robbins R.G. 1953. The vegetation of Jamaica. Ecol. Monogr. 23:359–412.

Austin O.L. 1963. On the American status of *Tiaris canora* and *Carduelis carduelis*. Auk. 80:73-74.

Baker G.T. 1891. Notes on the Lepidoptera collected in Madeira by the late T. Vernon Wollaston. Trans. R. ent. Soc. Lond: 197–221.

Bangs O. & Kennard F.H. 1920. A list of the birds of Jamaica, *in* The Handbook of Jamaica, 1920.

Bannerman D.A. 1963. A History of the Birds of the Canary Islands and of the Salvages. (Edinburgh and London.)

Bannerman D.A. & Bannerman W.M. 1965. A History of the Birds of Madeira, the Desertas and the Porto Santo Islands. (Edinburgh and London.)

Bannerman D.A. & Bannerman W.M. 1966. A History of the Birds of the Azores (Edinburgh and London.)

Bannerman D.A. & Bannerman W.M. 1968. A History of the Birds of the Cape Verde Islands. (Edinburgh and London.)

Beard J.S. 1944. The natural vegetation of the Island of Tobago, British West Indies. Ecol. Monogr. 14:135–163.

Beard J.S. 1949. The natural vegetation of the Windward and Leeward Islands. Oxf. For. Mem. 21.

Beecher W.J. 1950. Convergent evolution in the American orioles. Wilson Bull. 62:51–86.

Bent A.C. 1939. Life histories of North American woodpeckers. Bull. U.S. natn. Mus. 174.

Black C.V. 1966. White-chinned Thrush. Gosse Bird Club Broadsheet 7:20.

Bond J. 1928. On the birds of Dominica, St Lucia, St Vincent and Barbados. B.W.I. Proc. Acad. nat. Sci. Philad. 80:523–545.

Bond J. 1936. Birds of the West Indies. (Acad. nat. Sci. Philad.)

Bond J. 1948. Origin of the bird fauna of the West Indies. Wilson Bull. 60:207–229.

Bond J. 1950. Some remarks on West Indian Icteridae. Wilson Bull. 62:216–217.

Bond J. 1951. Notes on Jamaican birds. Nat. Hist. Notes Jamaica 47:219–220.

Bond J. 1956. Check-List of Birds of the West Indies. (Acad. nat. Sci. Philad.)

Bond J. 1963. Derivation of the Antillean avifauna. Proc. Acad. nat. Sci. Philad. 115 No. 4:79–98.

Bond J. 1966. Eleventh supplement to the Check-List of Birds of the West Indies (1956), p. 5. (Acad. nat. Sci. Philad.)

Bond J. 1970. Native and Winter Resident Birds of Tobago. (Acad. nat. Sci. Philad.)

Bond J. 1971. Birds of the West Indies. 2nd. ed. (London.)

Bowinan R.I. 1961. Morphological differentiation and adaptation in the Galapagos finches. Univ. Calif. Publs. Zool. 58.

British Ornithologists' Union. 1971. The Status of Birds in Britain and Ireland. ed. D.W. Snow. (Oxford.)

Brooke R.K. 1970. Taxonomic and evolutionary notes on the subfamilies, tribes, genera and subgenera of the Swifts (Aves: Apodidae). Durban Mus. Novit. 9:13–24.

Browne P. 1789. The Civil and Natural History of Jamaica, p. 472. (London.)

Browning M.R. 1964. Third United States record of the Black-faced Grassquit (*Tiaris bicolor*) Auk 81:233.

Buxton E.J.M. 1960. Winter notes from Madeira. Ibis 102:127–129.

Carlquist S. 1965. Island Life. (New York.)

Carlquist S. 1966. The biota of long-distance dispersal. I. Principles of dispersal and evolution. Q. Rev. Biol. 41:247–270.

Chopard L. 1946. Les orthopteroides des iles atlantides. Mem. Soc. Biogeogr. 8:199–208.

Clark A.H. 1905a. The Greater Antillean macaws. Auk 22:345–348.

Clark A.H. 1905b. Birds of the southern Lesser Antilles. Proc. Boston Soc. nat. Hist. 32:203–312.

Cory C.B. 1890. The Birds of the Bahama Islands (esp. p. 109). (Boston, Mass.)

Crowell K. 1961. The effects of reduced competition in birds. Proc. natn. Acad. Sci. U.S.A. 47:240–243.

Crowell K.L. 1962. Reduced interspecific competition among the birds of Bermuda. Ecology 43:75–88.

Crowell K.L. 1968. Competition between two West Indian flycatchers *Elaenia*. Auk 85:265–286.

Cruz A. 1972. MS for 'Birds of the Lluidas Vale (Worthy Park) Region, Jamaica.' Q.J.l. Fla. Acad. Sci. 35(1).

Danforth S.T. 1934. The birds of Antigua. Auk 51:350–364.

Danforth S.T. 1935. Supplementary account of the birds of the Virgin Islands, including Culebra and adjacent islets pertaining to Puerto Rico, with notes on their food habits. J. Agric. Univ. P. Rico 19:439–472.

Danforth S.T. 1936. The birds of St Kitts and Nevis. Trop. Agric. Trin. 13:213–217.

Danforth S.T. 1939. The birds of Guadeloupe and adjacent islands. J.Agric., Univ. P. Rico 23: 9–46.

Darlington P.J. 1957. Zoogeography. (New York.)

Diamond A.W. 1973. Habitats and feeding stations of St Lucia forest birds. Ibis 115:313–329.

Diamond J.M. 1969. Avifaunal equilibria and species turnover rates on the Channel Islands of California. Proc. natn. Acad. Sci. U.S.A. 64:57–63.

Diamond J.M. 1970. Ecological consequences of island colonization by Southwest Pacific birds. 1. Types of niche shifts. Proc. natn. Acad. Sci. U.S.A. 67:529–536.

Diamond J.M. 1971. Comparison of faunal equilibrium turnover rates on a tropical island and a temperate island. Proc. natn. Acad. Sci. U.S.A. 68:2742–2745.

Diamond J.M. 1972. Avifauna of the Eastern Highlands of New Guinea. Publ. Nuttall Orn. Club no. 1. (Cambridge, Mass.)

Durango S.M. 1950. The influence of climate on distribution and breeding success of the Red-backed Shrike. Fauna Flora, Upps. 45:49–78.

Eaton S.W. 1953. Wood warblers wintering in Cuba. Wilson Bull. 65:169–174.

Eisenmann E. 1955. The species of middle American birds. Trans. Linn. Soc. N.Y. 7:1–128.

Eisenmann E. 1962. Notes on Nighthawks of the genus *Chordeiles* in southern Middle America with a description of a new race of *Chordeiles minor* breeding in Panama. Am. Mus. Novit. 2094.

Eisentraut M. 1965. Rassenbildung bei säugetieren und Vögeln auf der Insel Fernando Po. Zool. Anz. 174:37–53.

Eisentraut M. 1968. Beitrag zur Vogelfauna von Fernando Po und Westkamerun. Bonn. zool. Beitr. 19:49–68.

Elliott H.F.I. 1957. A contribution to the ornithology of the Tristan da Cunha group. Ibis 99: 545–586.

Etchécopar R.D. & Hüe F. (transl. P.A.D. Hollom) 1967. The Birds of North Africa. (Edinburgh and London.)

Exell A.W. 1944. Catalogue of the Vascular Plants of S. Tomé. (Brit. Mus. (Nat. Hist.) London.)

Fairley J.S. 1967. Food of Long-eared Owls in north-east Ireland. Br. Birds 60:130–135.

Falla R.A., Sibson R.B. & Turbott E.G. 1966. A Field Guide to the Birds of New Zealand. (London.)

Ficken R.W. & M.S., & Morse D.H. 1968. Competition and character displacement in two sympatric pine-dwelling warblers (*Dendroica*, Parulidae). Evolution 22:307–314.

Field G.W. 1894. Notes on the birds of Port Henderson, Jamaica, West Indies. Auk 11:117–127.

Fleming C.A. 1962. History of the New Zealand land bird fauna. Notornis 9:270–274.

Fogden M.P.I. 1971. Some aspects of the ecology of bird populations in Sarawak. D.Phil. thesis, Univ. Oxford.

Ford E.B. 1945. Butterflies. (London.)

Foster S. 1964. White-chinned Thrush. Gosse Bird Club Broadsheet 3:18.

Foster W.L. & Tate J. 1966. The activities and coactions of animals at sapsucker trees. Living Bird 5:87–113.

Friedmann H., Griscom L. & Moore R.T. 1950. Distributional Checklist of the Birds of Mexico, Part 1. Pacific Coast Avifauna. no. 29. (Berkeley, California.)

Fry C.H. 1961. Notes on the birds of Annobon and other islands in the Gulf of Guinea. Ibis 103a:267–276.

Good R. 1947. The Geography of the Flowering Plants, p. 133. (London.)

Goodwin D. 1967. Pigeons and Doves of the World. (Brit. Mus. (Nat. Hist.) London.)

Goodwin D. 1968. Notes on woodpeckers (Picidae). Bull. Brit. Mus. (Nat. Hist.) (Zool.) 17(1): 1–44.

Gosse Bird Club. Broadsheets nos. 1–17 (1963–1971).

Gosse E. 1890. The Life of Philip Henry Gosse F.R.S. (esp. p. 223.) (London.)

Gosse P.H. 1847. The Birds of Jamaica. (London.)

Gosse P.H. 1849. Illustrations of the Birds of Jamaica. (London.)

Gosse P.H. 1851. A Naturalist's Sojourn in Jamaica. (London.)

Grant P.R. 1968. Bill size, body size and the ecological adaptations of bird species to competitive situations on islands. Syst. Zool. 17:319–333.

Grayce R.L. 1957. Range extensions in Puerto Rico. Auk. 74:106.

Greenway J.C. 1967. Extinct and Vanishing Birds of the World. 2nd rev. ed., pp. 314–320. (New York.)

Griscom L. 1950. Distribution and origin of the birds of Mexico. Bull. Mus. comp. Zool. Harv. 103:341–382.

Guichard K.M. 1967. Butterflies of the Canary Islands. Entomologist 100:293–299.

Guth R.W. 1971. New bird records from Guadeloupe and its dependencies. Auk 88:180–182.

Hamilton T.H. 1958. Adaptive variation in the genus *Vireo*. Wilson Bull. 70:307–346.

Hamilton T.H. 1962. Species relationships and adaptations for sympatry in the avian genus *Vireo*. Condor 64:40–68.

Hamilton T.H. & Armstrong N.E. 1965. Environmental determination of insular variation in bird species abundance in the Gulf of Guinea. Nature, Lond. 207:148–151.

Hamilton T.H., Barth R.H. & Rubinoff I. 1964. The environmental control of insular variation in bird species abundance. Proc. natn. Acad. Sci. U.S.A. 52:132–140.

Hamilton T.H. & Rubinoff I. 1963. Isolation, endemism and multiplication of species in the Darwin finches. Evolution 17:388–403.

Hamilton T.H. & Rubinoff I. 1964. On models predicting abundance of species and endemics for the Darwin Finches in the Galapagos Archipelago. Evolution 18:339–342.

Hamilton T.H. & Rubinoff I. 1967. On predicting insular variation in endemism and sympatry for the Darwin finches in the Galapagos Archipelago. Am. Nat. 101:161–172.

Harris M.P. 1973. The Galapagos avifauna. Condor 75:265–278.

Hart H.T. 1964. Plain Pigeon. Gosse Bird Club Broadsheet 2:19.

Harty A.H. 1951. Observations on our nightingale. Nat. Hist. Notes Jamaica 50:38, 42.

Harvey J.M. 1968. Inca Dove. Gosse Bird Club Broadsheet 10:15.

Haverschmidt F. 1968. Birds of Surinam. (Edinburgh and London.)

Hemmingsen A.M. 1963. Birds on Hierro and the relation of number of species, and of specific abundances and body weights, to island area. Vidensk. Meddr dansk. naturh. Foren. 125:207–236.

Herklots G.A.C. 1961. The Birds of Trinidad and Tobago. (London.)

Holmes R.T. & Pitelka F.A. 1968. Food overlap among coexisting sandpipers on northern Alaskan tundra. Syst. Zool. 17:305–318.

Howell T.R. 1969. Avian distribution in Central America. Auk 86:293–326.

Hutchinson G.E. 1959. Homage to Santa Rosalia, or Why are there so many kinds of animals? Am. Nat. 93:145–159.

Janzen D.H. & Schoener T.W. 1968. Differences in insect abundance and diversity between wetter and drier sites during a tropical dry season. Ecology 49:96–110.

Jeffrey-Smith M. 1964. Plain Pigeon. Gosse Bird Club Broadsheet 2:19.

Johnston D.W. 1969. The thrushes of Grand Cayman Island, B.W.I. Condor 71:120–128.

Johnston R.F. & Selander R.K. 1964. House sparrows: rapid evolution of races in North America. Science N.Y. 144:548–550.

Kennedy P.G., Ruttledge R.F. & Scroope C.F. 1954. The Birds of Ireland. (Edinburgh.)

Kepler C.B. 1971. First Puerto Rican record of the Antillean Palm Swift. Wilson Bull. 83:309–310.

Kepler C.B. 1972. Notes on the ecology of Puerto Rican swifts, including the first record of the White-collared Swift *Streptoprocne zonaris*. Ibis 114:541–543.

Kepler C.B. & Parkes K.C. 1972. A new species of warbler (Parulidae) from Puerto Rico. Auk 89:1–18.

Kepler A. 1972. Ph.D. Thesis.

Klein D.R. 1968. The introduction, increase and crash of Reindeer on St. Matthews Island. J. Wildl. Mgmt. 32:350–367.

Lack D. 1946. Competition for food by birds of prey. J.Anim.Ecol. 15:123–129.

Lack D. 1947. Darwin's Finches. (Cambridge.)

Lack D. 1954. The Natural Regulation of Animal Numbers. (Oxford.)

Lack D. 1956. Swifts in a Tower. (London.)

Lack D. 1968a. The sequence in European bird-lists. (Letter) Ibis 110:107–113.

Lack D. 1968b. Ecological Adaptations for Breeding in Birds. (London.)

Lack D. 1969a. The numbers of bird species on islands. Bird Study 16:193–209.

Lack D. 1969b. Subspecies and sympatry in Darwin's finches. Evolution 23:252–263.

Lack D. 1970. The endemic ducks of remote islands. Wildfowl 21:5–10.

Lack D. 1971. Ecological Isolation in Birds. (Oxford.)

Lack D. 1973. The number of species of hummingbirds in the West Indies. Evolution 27:326–337.

Lack D., Lack E., Lack P. & Lack A. 1973. Birds on St. Vincent. Ibis 115:46–52.

Lack D. & Lack P. 1972. Wintering warblers in Jamaica. Living Bird 11:129–153.

Lack D. & Southern H.N. 1949. Birds on Tenerife. Ibis 91:607–626.

Land H.C. 1970. Birds of Guatemala. (Wynnewood, Pennsylvania.)

Lanyon W.E. 1967. Revision and probable evolution of the *Myiarchus* flycatchers of the West Indies. Bull.Am.Mus.nat.Hist. 136(6):329–370.

Lawrence G.N. 1878. Catalogue of the birds of St Vincent. Proc. U.S. natn. Mus. 185–198.

Lems K. 1960. Floristic botany of the Canary Islands. Sarracenia no. 5 (cited to me by S. Carlquist pers.comm.).

Lister C.E. 1880. Field-notes on the birds of St. Vincent, West Indies. Ibis (4)4:38–44.

MacArthur R.H. 1958. Population ecology of some warblers of northeastern coniferous forests. Ecology 39:599–619.

MacArthur R.H. 1965. Patterns of species diversity. Biol. Rev. 40:510–533.

MacArthur R.H. 1969. Patterns of communities in the tropics. Biol. J.Linn.Soc. 1:19–30.

MacArthur R.H. 1972. Geographical Ecology. (New York.)

MacArthur R. & Levins, R. 1967. The limiting similarity, convergence, and divergence of coexisting species. Am. Nat. 101:377–385.

MacArthur R.H., Recher H & Cody M. 1966. On the relation between habitat selection and species diversity. Am. Nat. 100:319–332.

MacArthur R.H. & Wilson E.O. 1963. An equilibrium theory of insular zoogeography. Evolution 17:373–387.

MacArthur R.H. & Wilson E.O. 1967. The Theory of Island Biogeography. (Princeton.)

March W.T. (& S.F. Baird) 1863. Notes on the birds of Jamaica. Proc. Acad. nat. Sci. Philad. 150–154, 283–304.

Marien D. & Koopman K.F. 1955. The relationships of the West Indian species of *Aratinga* (Aves, Psittacidae). Am. Mus. Novit. 1712.

Matthews, J.R. 1955. Origin and Distribution of the British Flora. (London.)

Mayr E. 1942. Systematics and the Origin of Species. (New York.)

Mayr E. 1944a. Timor and the colonization of Australia by birds. Emu 44:113–130.

Mayr E. 1944b. The birds of Timor and Sumba. Bull. Am. Mus. nat. Hist. 83(2):127–194.

Mayr E. 1946. History of the North American bird fauna. Wilson Bull. 58:3–41.

Mayr E. 1964. Inferences concerning the Tertiary American bird faunas. Proc. natn. Acad. Sci. N.Y. 51:280–288.

Mayr E. 1965a. The nature of colonizations in birds. pp. 29–43 *in* The Genetics of Colonizing Species. (New York.)

Mayr E. 1965b. What is a fauna? Zool. Jb., Syst. 92:473–486.

Mayr E. 1965c. Avifauna: turnover on islands. Science, N.Y. 150:1587–1588.

Mayr E. & Bond J. 1943. Notes on the generic classification of the swallows, Hirundinidae, Ibis 85:334–341.

Mayr E. & Phelps W.H. 1967. The origin of the bird fauna of the South Venezuelan highlands. Bull. Am. Mus. nat. Hist. 136(5):269–328.

Mayr E. & Short L.L. 1970. Species taxa of North American birds. A contribution to comparative systematics. Publ. Nuttall Orn. Club no. 9. (Cambridge, Mass.)

Meanley B. 1966. Some observations of habitats of the Swainson's Warbler. Living Bird 5:151–165.

Miles M.L. 1967. An addition to the avifauna of the United States: *Myiarchus stolidus sagrae*. Auk 84:279.

Monroe B.L. 1968. A distributional survey of the birds of Honduras. Ornithological Monographs no. 7 (American Ornithologists' Union.)

Moreau R.E. 1957. Variation in the western Zosteropidae (Aves). Bull. Br. Mus. nat. Hist. (Zool.) 4 (7):309–433.

Moreau R.E. 1961. In what order should birds be listed? Bird Notes 30:18–22.

Moreau R.E. 1966. The Bird Faunas of Africa and its Islands. (London.)

Morse D.H. 1967. Competitive relationships between Parula Warblers and other species during the breeding season. Auk. 84:490–502.

Morse D.H. 1968. A quantitative study of foraging of male and female spruce-wood warblers, Ecology 49:779–784.

Morse D.H. 1970. Ecological aspects of some mixed-species foraging flocks of birds. Ecol. Monog. 40:119–168.

Morse D.H. 1971. The foraging of warblers isolated on small islands. Ecology 52:216–228.

Newton I. 1967. The adaptive radiation and feeding ecology of some British finches. Ibis 109:33–98.

Oberholser H.C. 1899. A synopsis of the genus *Contopus* and its allies. Auk 16:330–337.

Orians G.H. 1969. The number of bird species in some tropical forests. Ecology 50:783–801.

Osburn W. 1859a. Notes on the birds of Jamaica. Zoologist:6368–73.

Osburn W. 1859b. Notes on the bats and birds of Jamaica. Zoologist:6587–94.

Osburn W. 1859–60. Notes on the mountain birds of Jamaica. Zoologist (1859): 6658–65, 6709–21, 6753–61; (1860): 6833–41, 6873–80, 6925–34.

Panton E.S. 1951. Further observations on the mockingbirds. Nat. Hist. Notes Jamaica 49:5–6.

Parnell J.F. 1969. Habitat relations of the Parulidae during spring migration. Auk 86:505–521.

Parslow J.L.F. 1967-8. Changes in status among breeding birds in Britain and Ireland. Br. Birds 60:2–47, 97–123, 177–202, 261–285, 396–404, 493–508; 61:49–64, 241–255.

Paterson A. 1972. Nesting of Chuck-will's-widow on Andros Island, Bahamas. Auk 89:676–677.

Peters J.L. 1931–62. Check-list of Birds of the World.(Cambridge, Mass.)

Phelps W.H. & W.H. 1958. Lista de las Aves de Venezuela con su Distrubución. pt. 1. Boln. Soc. Venez. Cienc. nat. 19 no. 90.

Praeger R.I. 1901. Irish topographical botany. Proc. R.Ir. Acad. 3rd. series. Vol. 7.

Praeger R.I. 1950. Natural History of Ireland. (London.)

Pulich W.M. 1968. The occurrence of the Crested Hummingbird, *Orthorhyncus cristatus exilis*, in the United States. Auk 85:322.

Pulliam H.R. 1969. The feeding ecology of Jamaican grassland finches. Gosse Bird Club Broadsheet 12:7–10.

Rebel H. 1940. Die Lepidopterenfauna des Azorischen Archipels. Commentat. Biol. viii(1).

Richards P.W. 1966. The Tropical Rain Forest. (Cambridge, reprinted from 1952.)

Ricklefs R.E. 1970. Stage of taxon cycle and distribution of birds on Jamaica, Greater Antilles. Evolution 24:475–477.

Ricklefs R.E. & Cox G.W. 1972. Taxon cycles in the West Indian avifauna. Am. Nat. 106:195–219.

Ridgway R. (continued by Friedmann H.) 1901–50. The Birds of North and Middle America. (Washington.)

Rothschild W. 1905. (Extinct parrots of the West Indies.) Bull. Br. Orn. Club 16:13–14.

Rothschild W. 1907. Extinct Birds. (London.)

Salmon L. 1966. Chestnut-bellied Cuckoo. Gosse Bird Club Broadsheet 6:19.

Salvadori T. 1891. Catalogue of the Psittaci, or Parrots, *in* the cat. of the Birds in the Brit. Mus. vol. 20, pp. 161–162. (London.)

Schoener T.W. 1965. The Evolution of bill size differences among sympatric congeneric species of birds. Evolution 19:189–213.

Schoener T.W. 1971. Large-billed insectivorous birds; a precipitous diversity gradient. Condor 73:154–161.

Schoener T.W. & Janzen D.H. 1968. Notes on environmental determinants of tropical versus temperate insect size patterns. Am. Nat. 102:207–224.

Schwartz A. & Klinikowski R.F. 1963. Observations on West Indian birds. Proc. Acad. nat. Sci. Philad. 115:53–77.

Schwartz P. 1964. The Northern Waterthrush in Venezuela. Living Bird 3:169–184.

Sclater P.L. 1858. On the general geographical distribution of the members of the class Aves. J. Proc. Linn. Soc. (Lond.) Zool. 2:130–145.

Sclater P.L. 1910. Revised list of the birds of Jamaica, *in* Handbook of Jamaica for 1910.

Scott M. 1836. Tom Cringle's Log. (Paris.)

Scott W.E.D. 1891–93. Observations on the birds of Jamaica, West Indies. Auk 8:249–256, 353–365; 9:9–15, 120–129, 273–277, 369–375; 10:177–181, 339–342.

Seaman G.A. 1959. Land snails as food of White-crowned Pigeon. Auk 76:232.

Selander R.K. & Giller D.R. 1959. Interspecific relations of woodpeckers in Texas. Wilson Bull. 71:107–124.

Selander R.K. & Giller D.R. 1963. Species limits in the woodpecker genus, *Centurus* (Aves). Bull. Am. Mus. nat. Hist. 124(6): 217–273.

Short L.L. 1965. Variation in West Indian Flickers (Aves, *Colaptes*). Bull. Fl. St. Mus. 10:1–42.

Simpson G.G. 1940. Mammals and land bridges. J. Wash. Acad. Sci. 30:137–163.

Sloane H. 1725. A Voyage to the Islands Madeira, Barbadoes, Nieves, S. Christophers and Jamaica, with the natural history of the last. Vol. 2, pp. 296 (London.)

Slud P. 1967. The Birds of Cocos Island (Costa Rica). Bull. Am. Mus. nat. Hist. 134(4) :261–296.

Smith R.W. 1971. Jamaican Owl. Gosse Bird Club Broadsheet 17 :29.

Smith W.J. 1966. Communication and relationships in the genus *Tyrannus*. Publ. Nuttall Orn. Club no. 6. (Cambridge, Mass.)

Snow B.K. & Snow D.W. 1971. The feeding ecology of tanagers and honeycreepers in Trinidad. Auk 88 :291–322.

Snow B.K. & Snow D.W. 1972. Feeding niches of hummingbirds in a Trinidad valley. J. Anim. Ecol. 41 :471–485.

Snow D.W. 1950. The birds of Sao Tomé and Principe in the Gulf of Guinea. Ibis 92 :579–595.

Snow D.W. 1971. Evolutionary aspects of fruit-eating by birds. Ibis 113 :194–202.

South R. 1906 (and later versions). The Butterflies of the British Isles. (London.)

Sprunt A. 1954. Florida Bird Life. (New York.)

Stewart D.B. 1969. An eighteenth century bird club. Gosse Bird Club Broadsheet 13 :8–10.

Taylor R.G. 1951. Some bird problems in Jamaica. Nat. Hist. Notes Jamaica 51 :51–52.

Turrill W.B. 1948. British Plant Life, pp. 56–57. (New Nat. London.)

Uyttenboogaart D.L. 1946. La peuplement des îles atlantides—Conclusions à tirer de la composition de la faune de Coléoptères. Mém. Soc. Biogéogr. 8 :135–152.

Van den Brink F.H. 1967. A Field Guide to the Mammals of Britain and Europe. (London.)

Vaurie C. 1959. The Birds of the Palearctic Fauna. Passeriformes. (London.)

Vaurie C. 1965. The Birds of the Palearctic Fauna. Non-Passeriformes. (London.)

Volsøe H. 1951. The breeding birds of the Canary Islands. I. Introduction and synopsis of the species. Vidensk. Meddr dansk naturh. Foren. 113 : 1–153.

Volsøe H. 1955. The breeding birds of the Canary Islands. II. Origin and history of the Canarian avifauna. Vidensk. Meddr dansk naturh. Foren. 117 :117–178.

Voous K.H. 1955. The birds of St Martin, Saba and St Eustatius. Studies on the Fauna of Curaçao and other Caribbean Islands. Vol. 6 :No. 25.

Voous K.H. 1957. The birds of Aruba, Curaçao and Bonaire. Studies on the Fauna of Curaçao and other Caribbean Islands. Vol 7 :No. 29.

Vuilleumier F. 1970. Insular biogeography in continental regions. I. The Northern Andes of South America. Am. Nat. 104 :373–388.

Wace N.M. & Dickson J.H. 1965. The terrestrial botany of the Tristan da Cunha islands. Phil. Trans. R. Soc. B. 249 :273–360.

Wetmore A. 1927. Scientific Survey of Porto Rico and the Virgin Islands. Vol. IX parts 3 and 4. (New York Acad. of Sciences.)

Wetmore A. 1957. The birds of Isla Coiba, Panama. Smithson misc. Collns. Vol. 134 no. 9.

Wetmore A. 1962. Nomenclature and commentary to article by G.B. Reynard "The rediscovery of the Puerto Rican Whip-poor-will." Living Bird 1 :54–55.

Wetmore A. 1968. The Birds of the Republic of Panama. Part 2. Smithson. misc. Collns. Vol. 150 part 2.

Wetmore A. & Swales B.H. 1931. The Birds of Haiti and the Dominican Republic. Bull. U.S. natn. Mus. 155.

White G. 1789. The Natural History of Selborne. Letter VII to Daines Barrington. Oct. 8, 1770.

Wiggins I. & Porter D.M. 1971. Flora of the Galapagos Islands. (Stanford.)

Williams E.E. 1969. The ecology of colonization as seen in the zoogeography of anoline lizards on small islands. Q. Rev. Biol. 44:345–389.

Williams G.R. 1953. The dispersal from New Zealand and Australia of some introduced European passerines. Ibis 95:676–692.

Wilson E.O. 1959. Adaptive shift and dispersal in a tropical ant fauna. Evolution 13:122–144.

Willughby F. 1678. The Ornithology of Francis Willughby. Ed. J. Ray. (London.)

Woodring W.P. 1954. Caribbean land and sea through the ages. Bull. Geol. Soc. Am. 65:719–732.

Yang S.Y. & Selander, R.K. 1968. Hybridization in the Grackle *Quiscalus quiscula* in Louisiana. Syst. Zool 17:107–143.

Zimmer J.T. 1941. Studies of Peruvian Birds no. XXXVI. The genera *Elaenia* and *Myiopagis*. Am. Mus. Novit. 1108 p. 20.

Zusi R.L. 1969. Ecology and adaptations of the Trembler on the Island of Dominica. Living Bird 8:137–164.

INDEX

The italic type refers to figures and the bold type refers to plates.